Human Rights

Human Rights

INDIA AND THE WEST

EDITED BY

Ashwani Peetush

AND

Jay Drydyk

OXFORD

UNIVERSITY PRESS

OXFORD
UNIVERSITY PRESS

Oxford University Press is a department of the University of Oxford.
It furthers the University's objective of excellence in research, scholarship,
and education by publishing worldwide. Oxford is a registered trademark of
Oxford University Press in the UK and in certain other countries.

Published in India by
Oxford University Press
YMCA Library Building, 1 Jai Singh Road, New Delhi 110 001, India

ISBN-13: 978-0-19-945352-8
ISBN-10: 0-19-945352-7

Typeset in Adobe Garamond Pro 11/13
by SPEX Infotech, Puducherry 605 005, India
Printed in India by Rakmo Press, New Delhi 110 020

To our families

Contents

Acknowledgements

We are grateful to the Social Science and Humanities Research Council of Canada for a grant that made possible the workshop in which these papers were initially presented. We express our appreciation to Carleton University for hosting the workshop, in particular, Dean John Osborne, for providing financial support through the Faculty of Arts and Social Sciences. We are also thankful to the Council for the Intellectual and Cultural Development of the Arts at Wilfrid Laurier University. In addition, we would like to thank Gordon Davis in the Department of Philosophy at Carleton for his encouragement and enthusiasm. We also thank both Joseph LaRose at McMaster University and Yasaman S. Munro at Wilfred Laurier University. We thank Peter Genzinger for his library research assistance at Laurier, John Barrett at Concordio University, Jane Osborne's administrative work at Laurier, along with Darlene Drecun and Peter Ferri for their assistance at Carleton. We express our deep gratitude to Angela Brown, our research assistant at Laurier, for her industry and attention to detail. We express our heartfelt gratitude to our families for their support and encouragement.

Note on Transliteration and Diacritical Marks

This book uses IAST transliteration for Sanskrit terms. There are two notable exceptions. Following Gandhi's own usage, Bindu Puri does not use any diacritical marks for Sanskrit terms. Ashwani Peetush's chapter contains two instances where he refers to 'ā' as 'ă' following an author's original usage, who employs Max Müller's transliteration schema for Sanskrit. In addition, please note that Niraja Gopal Jayal's chapter does not use any diacritical marks for the transliteration of Hindi or Urdu terms.

Introduction

Ashwani Peetush and Jay Drydyk

This volume is meant to contribute to an intercultural understanding of human rights in the context of India and its relationship to the West.[1] It is distinct in that it is multi-layered, addressing meta-ethical, normative, social, legal, and political issues in the theory, application, and implementation of human rights. Although there is extensive literature on human rights in the field of African, East-Asian, and Islamic studies, there is a comparative dearth of conceptual research relating to South Asia, and in particular, the sub-continent of India.[2] Moreover, most of the prior research that exists in this area is mainly of an empirical and sociological nature. The present approach is multi-layered and multi-disciplinary, with a special focus on conceptual issues in ethical, political, and legal discourse. Much of the previous literature on human rights and non-Western understandings has explored the manner in which human rights may be supported from within these frameworks, which is an important post-Eurocentric step to take. The essays in this volume pioneer an approach that takes a further step, asking what the West may learn about human rights from non-Western societies.

The legitimacy of the international legal order and state sovereignty is increasingly premised on the discourse and practice of human rights. Purported violations are seen to warrant and justify coercive intervention. The importance of human rights appears uncontroversial: such rights seek to specify the conditions under which human beings in society can live a minimally decent life; they are thought to apply universally and cross-culturally. The motivation for recognizing and realizing such rights arose in the aftermath of World War II. The *Universal Declaration of Human Rights* (UDHR) (1948) specifies an extensive list of basic and fundamental rights that all civilized nations must recognize as authoritative.

Given the purpose of the Declaration in specifying an extensive list of basic and universal rights and freedoms, one would assume that deliberation on such a critical matter would include the widest range of parties from as many diverse traditions as possible. After all, the Declaration is supposed to concern the 'human family', 'all peoples and nations', in 'the spirit of brotherhood' (UDHR 1948). Yet it is well known that the UDHR was drafted on the basis of little consultation with non-European peoples and nations. From its very inception, the Declaration has been criticized as parochial. Many non-Western peoples contend that this particular interpretation of the basic universal values underlying the Declaration, their definition and their prioritization, and indeed, their very articulation in terms of the language and philosophy of rights, is not cross-culturally shared. The Declaration strikes many as biased in favour of Euro-Western forms of social organization and governance, individualism, and liberalism. Such an objection usually further contends that demanding that non-Western nations comply with a document which they had no role in drafting perpetuates a Western imperialist colonial discourse that uncritically presumes that Western norms set the standard and non-European peoples must simply conform. Such a presumption hinders international intercultural dialogue on one of the most meaningful, necessary, and crucial issues of our times.

A common response from some Westerners is to interpret such a challenge as a wholesale rejection of human rights and the basic values and principles that underlie such rights. It is assumed that this challenge is a disingenuous mask for the arbitrary abuse of political power, a cover for nefarious self-interested intentions. While such a response may certainly be warranted in specific cases, it relies too heavily on over-generalization and ignores serious underlying concerns.

The charge of parochialism is often a demand for basic equality and a seat at the table: to have one's voice heard and to be recognized, to be an equal participant in drafting an agreement to which one is expected to conform. It is a demand for the power to define, interpret, balance, and prioritize the basic ethical values that underlie the UDHR within the contested and developing contexts, histories, power-struggles, philosophies, legal traditions, and social, economic, and political frameworks of one's self-understandings. If self-determination of formerly colonized peoples or *svarāj* in the Indian context (also a human right) does not enable them to achieve this freedom, then it has surely been a vacuous victory; this is a freedom that Western nations, on the other hand, arrogate for themselves as a natural birthright. That is, the salient point of the challenge is not a rejection of fundamental universal rights to basic freedoms and equality, or the project of attempting to converge on cross-cultural norms of decency, but rather an acknowledgement that such basic values are always articulated and justified, specified, prioritized, and implemented within the self-understandings of various communities. That is, they are, and must be, realized in the vernacular.

Values, norms, and legal practices that resonate with peoples' self-understandings and those which are justified from within various rich normative vernacular frameworks become rooted and have a better chance of success than those that are imposed. As such, it is reasonable and necessary that communities, nations, and peoples articulate, define, and justify universal values within their histories and moral, religious, and philosophical frameworks—as Jacques Maritain contended from the start, in 1948. What is critical in arriving at a global convergence on human rights in the context of diversity is agreement on basic ethical standards of freedom and equality, such as freedom from discrimination, civil and political freedom, equality before the law, and assurance of the basic necessities of life such as food, shelter, clothing, health, and education, without the requirement that these be justified from a Euro-Western metaphysical, philosophical, or legal framework. As Sarvepalli Radhakrishnan (1955), Hans-Georg Gadamer (Pantham 1997), and James Tully

(1995) contend: the purpose of such convergence is not uniformity in diversity, but rather, unity in diversity.

However, the attempt to specify universal ethical principles and norms within particular contexts gives rise to variances and divergences. Striving for global convergence on such norms requires deliberation on what is an acceptable spectrum of differences in understanding and implementation. As the essays in this volume highlight, divergences and disagreements range from attempts at greater specificity, to prioritization, to deep conceptual differences: for example, what freedom of speech requires, the prioritization of healthcare rights, educational rights, and economic rights to deeper issues involving grounding ethical principles on the 'dignity and worth of the human person' and members of the 'human family' as opposed to the value of life in general—such a position carries with it substantial epistemological and ontological assumptions that may not be shared. Some divergences challenge the very articulation of ethical values in terms of the language and discourse of individual rights. Such discourse places little emphasis on moral duty and obligation; rights discourse brings with it substantial philosophical and legal commitments that may not resonate with particular local self-understandings.

We should be careful to note that the issue here is not simply about where and how Indians can find internal sources within their own traditions to justify basic norms of moral decency. This is already to load the dice in favour of the Western self-congratulatory and etiolated spirit that too often characterizes the hegemonic discourse of human rights. Such a spirit hinders fruitful intercultural deliberation and excludes a priori, alternate Indian possibilities, insights, and understandings. On the contrary, differences that Indian articulations bring to light may be something from which Westerners can learn; these articulations may also provide a worthwhile and valuable contribution to the global deliberation on human rights.

Many variances regarding human rights norms occur within Western nations themselves. Of course we should expect as much, since cultures, traditions, and nations are multi-voiced and contested, enmeshed in internal struggles between the powerful and the disenfranchised. There is a gamut of disagreements concerning the nature of basic rights and their prioritization in Western countries: these include disagreements on the welfare state, health care, access to education, freedom of speech, capital punishment, the meaning of cruel and unusual punishment (for example, waterboarding), not to mention the place of non-human animals in our ethical considerations. Many neo-liberal Americans repeatedly reject economic rights, along with health rights, which are seen as private matters having nothing to do with social justice or public responsibility. These views differ substantially from the prevailing ideas in Canada and many other European countries. However, if Western nations may debate, deliberate, and even reject some portions of the UDHR in the name of their values, traditions, and self-understandings, without being charged or suspected of rejecting the basic enterprise of human rights and minimal ethical norms, then why are non-Western nations not afforded the same consideration?[3]

The essays in this volume are a multi-layered and multi-disciplinary contribution to ongoing global deliberation seeking to converge on human rights standards and norms. The book has three sections. The first part of the volume deals with meta-ethical and theoretical issues: Sonia Sikka begins by re-thinking the debate on relativism and universal values in the context of the UDHR; next, drawing on moral psychology, Nigel DeSouza finds the basis for people's mature appreciation of human rights in their pre-reflective moral formation. DeSouza argues for a John Rawls–Charles Taylor approach to convergence since it fits well with moral development in actual contexts. Jay Drydyk provides a critical examination of the 'overlapping consensus' proposed by Rawls and the 'unforced consensus' proposed by Taylor, asking whether these concepts capture the kind of mutual understanding that human rights require in a multi-cultural, pluralistic world. Sumi Madhok's chapter addresses the crucial issue of gender equality in India; examining the *Sathin* movement, she offers new insight into convergence of women's rights with the creation of vernacular rights cultures in India.

Unique strategies for justifying human rights can be found in Indian intellectual traditions. Contributors to the second part of this volume explore various normative sources for such justifications and show how these have the potential to broaden and enrich global deliberation of human rights. Shashi Motilal provides an analysis of the concept of dharma as a potential source for a duty-based understanding of human rights. In the following chapter, Gordon Davis analyses the specific Buddhist approach to human rights that was advanced by B.R. Ambedkar (father of the Indian Constitution); this is compared with other approaches both in Buddhist tradition and in contemporary Western political philosophy. Shyam Ranganathan explores an account of human rights grounded in Patañjali's theory of personhood. Finally, Ashwani Peetush argues that deliberation on basic human rights norms in a pluralistic global context needs to be based on a more robust concept of political toleration than is common in Western legal and political thought; he illustrates sources for such toleration within interrelated Indian conceptual and philosophical histories.

In the third section, we turn to lessons that may be learned about the realization of human rights from Indian social practices and applied contexts. To begin, Bindu Puri discusses Gandhi's interjection in the drafting of the UDHR; Puri argues that although Gandhi struggled for basic and fundamental rights for women and lower castes, he grounded such a struggle in the ideas of duty and *satyāgraha* or adherence to truth. Then Gopika Solanki focuses on *Dalit* communities and their social and legal battles for equality; she illustrates the varied meanings, uses, and success and failures of human rights within the modern Indian state and vernacular contexts. Amar Khoday focuses on freedom of religion and legal and the political controversies surrounding anti-conversion laws. In the context of displaced peoples and refugees in India, Niraja Jayal argues that human rights discourse can only be fruitful where citizenship rights are robustly effective.

Preview of Chapters

Meta-Ethical and Theoretical Issues

Sonia Sikka re-examines the debate between the purported universality of human rights and cultural relativism. She argues that cultural relativism, as it originates within anthropological literature, does not necessarily lead to moral relativism as philosophers have objected. Cultural relativism for most anthropologists is a methodological tool: a suspension of judgment to facilitate a more objective understanding of other cultures in order to combat potential Eurocentric bias; it is not the idea that all ethical values are arbitrary and subject to one's culture. At the same time, however, the view that divergent values and norms of a society be respected has shielded some societies from legitimate criticism and reform, which, for example, has had detrimental consequences for women. The reason is not that insufficient attention has been paid to the internal diversity of cultural values, but that another critical factor is neglected: *who* controls the means of production of cultural values. What may be offered as a cultural value may reflect nothing more than the interests of those who have the power in producing such value while disregarding the interests of the weaker. The caste system in India is a case in point, a stock example that is often used by Western anti-relativist discourse meant to amplify differences between 'us' and 'them'. However, it is odd to discuss the inequalities of caste, while neglecting the power relations that have produced this ideology of domination—not to mention the long history of internal resistance by the oppressed in India. Such neglect continues to inform superficial analyses of 'their values versus ours'. Furthermore, while Sikka agrees that there may certainly be a degree of commonality of shared human needs and interests, and corresponding tendencies to suffer from shared forms of deprivation, she argues that such universal principles allow for a good deal of variation in terms of their articulation. She thus argues for a pluralistic understanding of human rights where various societies may determine for themselves how to define, balance, and prioritize cross-cultural values.

In the following chapter, Nigel DeSouza explores the moral psychology of ethical judgments and human rights. He contends that James Griffin's recent account of human rights, which would require others to adopt Western substantive values of autonomy, liberty, and minimum provision, would fail to receive widespread justification. DeSouza points out that every human being is raised into an inter-related set of norms, values, and goods which make up the ethical fabric of their society. Each individual first acquires a pre-reflective and inner sense of the ethical, through the formation of their evaluative and motivational propensities, which manifests itself in the form of 'ethical know-how'. DeSouza argues that it is only on this basis that critical moral reflection is possible and that ethical/moral concepts make any sense at all—including the concept of human rights.

The ideas of overlapping consensus (Rawls) and unforced consensus (Taylor) recognize this fact and thus provide a better means for secur- ing meaningful justification of human rights, since they acknowl- edge that true justification of human rights for most people relates to the thick ethical languages of their communities. This opens the door to a broader model for conceiving the sources of justification of human rights that seeks to overcome the problem of being culturally ethnocentric.

Jay Drydyk then delves into the differences between Rawls's 'overlapping consensus' and Taylor's 'unforced consensus', focusing on the problem of how credible agreement on the value and importance of human rights can be reached in a world that is culturally and ethi- cally pluralistic. The consensus that Rawls had in mind is agreement on shared political values—not about what is valuable and important throughout life, but only about what is valuable and important in political life. 'Overlap' is achieved when people find further support for these values in their broader moral ideas. However, Rawls insisted that these broader moral ideas should not be put forward directly in political justification, for example, Christians should not advocate political arrangements such as human rights on purely Christian grounds, which they cannot expect their non-Christian fellow citizens to accept. Drydyk argues that to exclude people's actual moral values and paradigms from political justification in this way is ineffective, unnecessary, and excessive. He finds Charles Taylor's approach to be superior in that it calls for people to recognize that their different values and moral ideas are each in their own way worthwhile and may all converge in supporting human rights. The challenge posed by this approach is to show how and why such convergence might come about. After drawing out some possible solutions from Taylor's work, Drydyk aligns them with his own solution, 'responsible pluralism'.

Drawing on her ethnographic work with the sathins, a grassroots women's movement in rural Rajasthan, Sumi Madhok investigates the critical issue of gender equality and women's rights in India with the production of vernacular rights cultures. She contests the 'politics of origins' framework that dominates some human rights discourse and argues for a shift towards a 'politics of meanings'. Without losing sight of the historical power relationships and hegemonic motiva- tions that often accompany human rights discourse, she questions whether genealogical obsessions with the origin of human rights are justified. In contrast, her analysis focuses on the self-understandings, subjective and institutional articulations, of specific human rights struggles by women in India. Madhok illustrates how her conceptual framework, one of vernacular rights cultures, helps us to conceptually capture the dynamic politics of rights and entitlements in Southern Asia and overcome crude indigenisms and dangerous neo-nativisms that continue to disempower women. She suggests that, as a conceptual intervention, thinking in terms of 'vernacular rights cultures' will help us move beyond arguments of Eurocentrism, cultural relativism, or celebratory universalism that can no longer adequately capture the dynamism of the citizenship claims that are increasingly vocalized and struggled for. The experiences of making rights claims, that Madhok documents are like all gendered experiences and phenomena, and provide insights into a fascinating set of issues: the attachment of rights to privileged gendered bodies, contested and fought for by the marginalized, the precarious, and the powerless.

Normative Sources and Intellectual Traditions

Shashi Motilal argues that an unforced global consensus on human rights needs to revolve around the concept of moral obligation rather than individual rights. The discourse of rights is not a plausible candidate for global convergence since it carries with it substantial ontological, epistemological, and political presuppositions rooted in the Western liberal tradition that may not resonate well within the Indian context. Motilal contends that the concept of moral obligation is far more basic and has wider acceptance and appeal in diverse global contexts. Despite many differences that the major world ethical and religious traditions express in terms of their metaphysical, theological, and other commitments, a minimalistic notion of moral obligation in some form often exists. This can serve as the core element in justifying, defining, and determining an international code of conduct without undermining key elements of the diverse background traditions. Motilal explores particular aspects of the concept of dharma in Hindu traditions as providing a more suitable and hopeful contender for progressive convergence on basic ethical values and international norms in India. She illustrates how a re-interpretation of a dharma ethic would provide valuable insight and understanding not only about human well-being but also about the interrelatedness that such well-being has to the rest of nature.

Autonomy is seen as one of the underlying values of personhood that human rights seek to protect. Gordon Davis shows that there is a degree of convergence between the original justification of autonomy in Western Enlightenment thinking and justifications for autonomy in ancient Indian texts. Although there is little evidence of institutionalized human rights protection in either ancient Buddhist monastic traditions or ancient Indian society more generally (as is the case in ancient Western societies), the depth and scope of Buddhist ethical ideas provide resources for indirect justifications for valuing certain kinds of autonomy and for deriving rights related to individual autonomy. These justifications have become more explicit in the writings of modern Indian Buddhists such as B.R. Ambedkar. While a foundation for human rights can be developed out of ethical ideas in ancient Buddhist writings (including both the Pāli Canon and later Mahayana texts), this foundation would be distinctively teleological in its normative structure. Ambedkar's defences of human rights overlap with such an approach but add a concern with certain forms of justice that may be considered novel within Buddhist tradition. Davis discusses some recent normative theories of human rights, such as James Griffin's, which favour something along the lines of the ancient Buddhist approach more than an approach like Ambedkar's; but even a partial convergence of ancient and modern conceptions is an encouraging sign for those who wish to defend universalist claims about the foundations of human rights.

In his chapter on normative sources for human rights in Indian traditions, Shyam Ranganathan argues for an account drawn from Patañjali's theory of personhood. He contends that the question of human rights is ambiguous. On the one hand, it might seem to raise the question of the rights that humans have by virtue of being human; or, it may be a code for something else, that is, the rights of persons. Conflating human rights with the rights of persons is natural if one's perspective is tied to anthropocentrism. However, such a stance is certainly not culturally universal; historically, it is derivable from a cultural orientation that is Greek in origin. Such an orientation conflates thought with language (*logos*), and identifies humans as uniquely deserving of moral consideration, to the exclusion of non-human knowers. The thesis that thought is linguistic impedes insight and understanding of both Indian and Western contributions to political and moral thought. Along these lines, Ranganathan contends that the idea that we have rights by virtue of being human is problematic. In contrast, he argues for a broader account of the rights of persons derivable from Patañjali's philosophy. On this account, persons are understood more widely as non-natural abstractions with an interest in 'abstracting from content' (objects). Put another way, a person is a self-directed abstraction from content. Any organism that as a matter of self-direction has an interest in regulating its relationship to objects of interest is a person on this view. The rights necessary for the good of persons conceived of as such are those that detach from contextual factors; they are rights that transcend species, sex, caste, race, class, age, ability, and sexual orientation.

Given the plurality and diversity inherent in both domestic and global contexts, toleration and respect for differences is central to issues of justice and human rights. Indeed, in the context of uneven historical power relationships, toleration must frame the global deliberation on basic human rights norms. With this in mind, Ashwani Peetush explores the ideal of toleration in Indian traditions. He points out that, as an ideal, political toleration is commonly thought to be a product of European history and philosophical thought, originating in response to societal conflict and the Wars of Religion in the West, then exported to the rest of the world by colonialism or globalization. This ignores the rich indigenous sources for toleration that have existed in India for millennia. Peetush explores three central and predominant ideas in India as providing justification for distinctly Indian forms of legal and political toleration. He examines how toleration, and indeed more strongly, respect for difference and pluralism, emerge through three influential and related Indian self-understandings: the theory of *anekāntavāda* or non-absolutism in the context of multiplicity; in the context of multiplicity the concept of *ātman* or self; and the idea of *pratītyasamutpāda* or inter-connectedness. Peetush draws attention to the fact that in the Indian context, political toleration, recognition, and respect for various philosophical and religious doctrines and practices arise from principles internal to these vernacular traditions, not despite them. This difference from the European historical, legal, and conceptual background entails that one cannot simply graft Western articulations of toleration, secularism, and liberalism onto India, because they may lack relevant similarities. He concludes that perhaps it is the West that may have something to learn from Indian articulations of legal and political toleration and respect for diversity and differences.

Social Practices and Applied Contexts

Gandhi rejected the central idea of the 1948 Declaration that human rights belong to human beings simply in virtue of their humanity. This may appear odd, given Gandhi's central role in the historical struggle for basic equality and freedom for the oppressed and most vulnerable in society. Bindu Puri reconstructs Gandhi's position on human rights, his insistence on duty, non-violence or *ahimsa*, and local and concrete engagement with social, political, and economic injustice. It is evident, as Puri illustrates, that Gandhi's own specification of what justice requires was similar to the UDHR; Gandhi opposed human rights discourse only because he did not accept the presuppositions of the early liberal conception of human rights set forth in the UN Charter. Puri shows that Gandhi's position can be understood in light of two factors. First, the primary set of moral rules that constitute justice must be understood as involving unilateral duties and obligations towards others, not as individual entitlements. Such duties need to be understood as an extension of kinship relationships, where others are not seen as adversaries whose interests are different than our own, but rather, as kith and kin, towards whom we have foundational duties of love and respect. Getting one's due in terms of basic moral rights here emerges out of the process of giving others their due. This is a precondition of one's own sense of self-respect and consequently the source of legitimacy of one's claims to basic human rights. Second, justice as *satyagraha* or adherence to truth cannot be arrived at through third-party adjudication from international institutions, abstracted, and twice removed from the particular; justice requires non-violent resistance and local concrete engagement, where one has direct access to the situation and facts, unmediated or abstracted from the specificity of local contexts.

The possibilities and limitations for Dalits of availing human rights bodies, using strategic and ethical articulations of human rights as rhetorical and material tools to resist symbolic violence through law in Western India is the subject of Gopika Solanki's chapter. Tracing on-going cases filed under the Scheduled Castes (SCs) and the Scheduled Tribes (STs) (Prevention of Atrocities) Act (1989) that penalizes violence against Dalits and *Adivasis*, Solanki analyses the varied meanings of 'human rights' and 'social justice' that emerge from litigants, NGO workers, the police, judicial actors, and state and national human rights commissions during the course of investigation and trial. Viewing the process of adjudication as a productive encounter between a variety of state and societal actors, she discusses the institutionalization of ideas of human rights in the criminal justice system as a result of these interactions, and outlines the implications of their encoding in the everyday workings of criminal law in India. In addition, Solanki focuses on the political agency of dalit women and illustrates how dalit women's rights committees have, using the Atrocity Act, broadened the human rights approach from a legalistic approach to a development enterprise. They effected this change by establishing conceptual links between human rights and different conceptions of poverty and development and between law, social hierarchies, and social policies; in doing so, they have challenged the capture of the public distribution system and public policies by the elites and dominant castes, demanded accountability from state administrations, and offered different routes to challenge caste discrimination.

Religious conversions in India inextricably implicate human rights. Thus Amar Khoday explores the legal and political aspects of the controversies surrounding such conversions. Khoday argues that, in effect, anti-conversion laws in India are often a tool of upper castes in Hindu society to prevent lowercaste dalit communities from enacting forms of social and political resistance. In recent years, state governments in India have placed a number of limits on the ability of individuals to convert. These limits include having to provide prior notice to a government official of one's intent to convert and in effect demonstrate the genuineness of their new religious beliefs. Such legislation ostensibly seeks to protect vulnerable individuals from being forced to convert or being manipulated into converting through financial means, although its motive is far from clear given the historical power imbalance between upper and lower caste members. Khoday argues that such legislative manoeuvres are problematic for a number of reasons. They intrude into individual autonomy and the right to follow one's chosen religion and religious identity. Furthermore, these statutes portray those seeking to convert as helpless victims rather than agents making choices in their own best interests. Furthermore, these acts intervene to counteract socio-cultural resistance of Dalits, SCs, and indigenous groups against dominant caste communities seeking to preserve their power. Khoday argues that conversion is a form of social defection and is used to show disdain for the practices of those communities. It is a political tool and statement that seeks to emancipate the oppressed from social injustice and inequality.

Exploring Hannah Arendt's political thought, Niraja Gopal Jayal contends that human rights are rendered meaningless in many parts of India by lack of state presence and effective citizenship. Indeed, as Arendt argued, the horrors of the holocaust demonstrate that the idea of natural rights, in and of themselves, offers no protection whatsoever. The fact that millions were rendered homeless and stateless because of religious persecution, led Arendt to contend that human rights cannot be defined in isolation from the rights of citizenship. Similarly, the conditions of refugees in India illustrate that without juridical and political status a person is rendered in a condition of absolute rightlessness or 'abstract nakedness', a pre-political state of nature. Jayal's field research on Jodhpur and Jaisalmer migrants from Pakistan to India illustrates the classic sense in which such people search for recognition of their legal and juridical personhood, so that they may have access to substantive welfare rights and access to government education and other institutions, as citizens of India. However, as Jayal's study shows, juridical citizenship, although necessary for having rights, is far from sufficient for enjoying such rights. What is missing, Jayal argues, is the core element of Arendt's notion of belonging to a political community: civic agency in a robust sense, where belonging means being able to participate fully in the life of a community. This is something refugees lack. Jayal urges that while legally India has recognized an expanded set of socio-economic rights (the right to water, healthcare, housing, and the right to sleep) for which it must continue to ensure access, India also needs to nurture the conditions which make full civic agency possible: to construct a community and publicsphere where the voices of the dispossessed and displaced are seen as worthy of being heard.

Notes

1. We recognize that the dichotomy between the West and the non-West is used to characterize widely disparate and conflicting self-understandings, nations, and peoples; we use 'West' and 'non-West' to refer to the very real political distinctions that continue to inform social, economic, legal, and political imagination, and the power relationships that continue to exist between European nations and Western settler societies and their former colonies as a result of the history of European imperialism and colonization. The essays in the present volume illustrate that such a dichotomy is far too crude, general, and broad to capture diverse epistemological and ontological self-understandings, yet they affirm that the dichotomy is a concrete political reality that cannot be ignored without substantial cost to non-European peoples everywhere. The dismantling of such a dichotomy is often itself used by Western political theorists, not as a form of liberation for non-European peoples, but the opposite: to undermine the effort towards emancipation. This is often the case, for example, when Western theorists attack Aboriginal leaders for claiming substantive differences with Western nations in terms of their forms of social organization and other religious and philosophical commitments.
2. For example, regarding the East Asian values debate, see Joanne R. Bauer and Daniel A. Bell (1999), and Bhikhu Parekh (2000); with respect to Africa and Islam see Abdullahi Ahmed An-Na'im (2003) and (2001).
3. See especially Parekh, (1999), p.134 to 141.

References

An-Na'im, A.A. 2001. *Muslims and Global Justice*. Philadelphia: University of Philadelphia.

———. 2003. *Human Rights Under African Constitutions: Realizing the Promise for Ourselves*. Philadelphia: University of Philadelphia.

Bauer, J.R. and D.A. Bell (eds). 1999. *The East Asian Challenge for Human Rights*. New York: Cambridge University Press.

Pantham, T. 1992. 'Some Dimensions of the Universality of Philosophical Hermeneutics: A Conversation with Hans-Georg Gadamer', *Journal of Indian Council of Philosophical Research*, 9: 123–35.

Parekh, B. 1999. *Rethinking Multiculturalism: Cultural Diversity and Political Theory*. Cambridge, MA: Harvard University Press.

Radhakrishnan, S. 1955. *Recovery of Faith*. New York: Harper and Brothers Publishers.

Tully, J. 1995. *Strange Multiplicity: Constitutionalism in an Age of Diversity*. Cambridge: Cambridge University Press.

PART I

THEORETICAL ISSUES

1

Rights and Relativity

Sonia Sikka

In popular Western media representations, India is hardly seen as a paragon of human rights. Its moral, legal, and political flaws, moreover, are frequently interpreted as being products of its religion(s) and/or culture. A 1996 CNN report on 'bride-burning' is typical in stating that 'the practice is unlikely to end soon...as long as current Hindu attitudes about the place of women in a marriage prevail'. (Yasui 1996). Western media reactions to the brutal rape and subsequent death of a young woman on a Delhi bus in 2012 were likewise inclined to associate the problem of rape in India with deep-seated cultural attitudes. An editorial in the *Globe and Mail*, a leading Canadian national newspaper, insists that 'this hatred of women is a specific cultural development', a position the author defends against objections that rape is a problem all over the world (Saunders 2013). Western moral philosophers, too, have tended in their writings to associate Indian culture with morally condemnable practices such as *sati* and the caste system. A culture so profoundly in-egalitarian, one might naturally think, stands in sharp conflict with the commitment to human equality that is fundamental to the idea of human rights.

Jack Donnelly makes precisely this point. He rejects the view, put forward by some, that all cultures have some conception of human rights. 'It simply is not true' he contends, 'that all peoples at all times have had human rights ideas and practices, if by "human rights" we mean equal and inalienable paramount moral rights held by all members of the species.' (Donnelly 2003: 87). Rather, the idea of human rights is an invention of the modern West, because essential to this idea is the principle that 'each person has an inherent dignity and worth that arises simply from being human' and that, 'furthermore, human beings, in their worth and dignity, are radically distinguished from the rest of creation'. (Donnelly 2003: 83). For Donnelly, the clearest example of a hierarchical society that does not respect this principle is the caste system in India. He is therefore surprised to find a number of authors claiming that human rights ideas are present in traditional Hindu ideas and practice, a claim that strikes him as absurd. Since human rights 'derive from the inherent dignity of the human person' and 'the caste system…denies the equal worth of all human beings', it should be obvious that 'caste and human rights are clearly radically incompatible'. (Donnelly 2003: 83).

The view that the concept of human rights is based on a specifically Western constellation of ideas and values that might be alien to non-Western cultures has been advanced not only by defenders of this concept, but also by its critics. At times the argument has been disingenuous, functioning as an excuse on the part of governments and other political actors wanting to maintain certain hierarchical social arrangements, or simply to hold on to power. It has also been made sincerely, however, as it was by the American Anthropological Association (AAA) when it raised concerns during the United Nations' drafting of its now famous Declaration of Human Rights after the Second World War. The AAA's criticisms of the very idea of such a document were motivated by an opposition to Western ethnocentrism, and stressed the rights of non-Western nations to live according to their own values. This argument was rooted in a version of cultural relativism, formulated as a counter-position to the thesis that a set of transculturally valid moral principles can be derived from the purported commonality of human nature. While the discourse of human rights has greatly expanded in the past few decades, with the production of a growing volume of political documents premised on the acceptance of such rights, the thesis that there exists a table of universal human rights continues to be challenged in the name of cultural difference and within the context of debates about the cultural relativity of morals.

In this essay, I re-examine aspects of the history and present status of the debate on cultural relativism regarding morality, as deployed within anthropological and philosophical arguments, and with an orientation towards the question of the universality of human rights. I suggest, first, that due weight needs to be given to the concerns about the uses and abuses of 'culture' that motivated an earlier generation of American anthropologists to develop relativistic theses, and led to the AAA's challenge in 1947 to the UN's proposal for a Universal Declaration of Human Rights (UDHR). Second, I point out that the relation between cultural production and power, on the other hand, was neglected by Melville Herskovits, the primary author of the AAA's position, and has generally not been adequately taken into account within discussions of cultural relativism, both among anthropologists and philosophers. At the same time, I underline the concern that ethnocentrism is still alive and well, and that, within this context, anti-relativist discourses can be highly problematic, providing an excuse for not engaging with unfamiliar, and especially non-European, traditions, and for assuming the superiority of one's own culture in both subtle and not-so-subtle ways. In the end, I therefore argue in favour of a qualified relativism, contending that such relativism is not incompatible with universal human rights, provided that it is sufficiently sensitive to the issue of power inequalities and the distorting effects of ideology. I also argue for a more nuanced understanding of the term 'culture' in general, with particular attention to the role of power in determining the content of what come to be established as cultural traditions.

Cultural Relativism in Anthropology

With some notable exceptions, most moral philosophers see 'cultural relativism' as a position to be avoided, and philosophical accounts of cultural relativism in the domain of ethics tend to stress its incoherence, as well as its unacceptable consequences. A collection of articles published in a 2007 issue of *Anthropological Quarterly*, however, challenges this negative view of cultural relativism, addressing what the authors see as a serious disconnect between anthropological and philosophical discourses on the subject.[1] The collection originated from the dismay of one of its contributors, Thomas H. Johnson, over James Rachels's misunderstanding of the concept of relativism as used by anthropologists in his well-known introductory philosophy text-book on ethics (Johnson 2007: 791–802). Regarding the divergent uses of this concept by anthropologists and philosophers, Johnson writes that 'for anthropologists like Herskovits, cultural relativism is a practical means or method of discovery, not an ethical disaster. It leads 'not to moral relativism, but to an even stronger realization of moral and social problems and issues, inciting many anthropologists to take actions that would never have occurred to them (or to philosophers) if they had not studied another culture'. (Johnson, 2007: 796).

The other contributors to this discussion—David Perusek, Richard Feinberg, and Robert Ulin—also emphasize anthropology's commitment to methodological, as opposed to moral, relativism, while drawing attention to the context in which this commitment developed. Perusek, for instance, points out that the anthropological ideas about culture and cultural relativism which emerged in the early twentieth century were 'generated and articulated in response to what others at the time were saying and doing in the name of culture' (Perusek 2007: 821). Paramount among the concerns motivating these ideas was a common opposition to European claims of cultural superiority and to the way such claims were being deployed in the service of colonialism (Perusek 2007: 821). At the same time, all four authors question aspects of the concept of 'culture' as deployed within the history of anthropology (for example, Feinberg 2007: 786).

Perusek proposes that 'to the extent that cultural relativism has become a free floating signifier that can, and much of the time does, mean anything to anyone, an important means of preserving it as a useful tool may be to ground it as far as possible'. (Perusek 2007: 833). Doing so requires, among other things, that one examine the historical development of the idea, and Perusek's paper, along with Johnson's, makes some salient points about the conceptions of 'cultural relativism' that arose, and are still common currency, within the discipline of anthropology. Both authors want to point out that these conceptions are not equivalent to what philosophers commonly suppose 'cultural relativism' to be when they debate the position, usually in order to refute it. For anthropologists, they suggest, cultural relativism about morality does not entail strong moral relativism of the sort that holds that right and wrong are simply constituted by the prevailing norms of a given culture and cannot be legitimately judged from any other perspective. Rather, the anthropological conception of cultural relativism contains a number of superficially similar, but in fact quite different, theses. Above all, it names a methodological commitment, involving the attempt to suspend or bracket one's own culturally inherited assumptions, when studying the moral norms of another society. This methodological suspension of judgement is intended not only to facilitate the understanding of other cultures, but also, at least potentially, to give people some critical distance from their own.

The goal here is not everlasting neutrality, but a species of 'objectivity', understood in contrast with ethnocentric partiality. In the words of Melville Herskovits: 'With a means of probing deeply into all manner of differing cultural orientations, of reaching into the significance of the ways of living of different peoples, we can turn again to our own culture with fresh perspective, and an objectivity that can be achieved in no other manner.' (Herskovits 1972: 34). Ruth Benedict operated on a similar principle in *Patterns of Culture*, first published in 1934. A prime example is her argument that 'abnormality' is a socially constructed concept, an argument she employed against the view of homosexuality as a sexual perversion within her own society. 'Just as we are handicapped in dealing with ethical problems so long as we hold to an absolute definition of morality,' Benedict noted, 'so we are handicapped in dealing with human society so long as we identify our local normalities with the inevitable necessities of existence'. (Benedict 1959: 271).

It is worth adding that this methodological relativism has generally been accompanied by a belief that people should not be 'judged', in a certain sense, for following the moral norms of their societies, since that is what we all tend to do and cannot help but do. This is once more not equivalent to the claim that the rightness of an action is entirely constituted by its conformity with dominant cultural norms, let alone that people *ought* to follow those norms. But it does suggest that attributions of moral accountability, of blameworthiness, have to take social context into account. For example, one may judge human slavery to be objectively wrong, at all times in all places, while censuring ancient societies that engaged in this practice much less than more modern ones, on the grounds that the assumptions grounding slavery were at that time so widespread that it was difficult for anyone to question them, and very few people did. It does follow that moral praise and blame should be bestowed relative to the cultural horizons within which people's understanding of right and wrong take shape. We need, that is, to factor in the cultural context that shapes the values of individuals before we condemn them for holding and acting on those values, even if we want, finally, to criticize or reject the values themselves.

The elements of 'cultural relativism' so far described—methodological suspension of judgement and attention to historical context in assigning blame—do not define the species of cultural relativism that most commonly raises principled objections among philosophers, and others. And granted that within anthropology cultural relativism was, and still is, motivated by opposition to ethnocentrism, aiming to unsettle prejudice, there remains the question of anthropology's historical complicity in producing the more objectionable versions of this position. The assertions of some of the proponents of cultural relativism within anthropology have been ethically problematic, and not just at an abstract or theoretical level. Herskovits, for example, was the main author of the AAA's controversial 'Statement on Human Rights', submitted to the United Nations in the course of its preparation of the UDHR (AAA 1947). The statement argued that any such declaration 'must embrace and recognize the validity of many different ways of life', and that 'the rights of Man in the Twentieth Century cannot be circumscribed by the standards of any single culture, or be dictated by the aspirations of any single people'. (AAA 1947: 542–3). It refers to ascriptions of cultural inferiority used to exploit and subjugate non-Western peoples (AAA 1947: 540–1).

However noble its intentions, this idea that the divergent values and norms of different cultures should be respected has since then been used to shield some groups and societies from legitimate criticism and calls for reform. This has been detrimental to the well-being of many individuals within those societies, especially to women, upon whose bodies wars over 'culture' are so often fought. One might then reasonably ask whether these defensive culturalist discourses are based on the species of cultural relativism that form the subject of philosophical debates, and whether the assertions of anthropologists have helped to create these species. In other words, have anthropologists espousing cultural relativism sometimes implicitly endorsed either the ontological thesis that morality just is adherence to dominant cultural norms or the epistemological thesis that there is no position one could occupy that would allow one to pass cross-cultural moral judgements? The epistemological thesis is considerably weaker than the ontological one, at the theoretical level, as it would in principle allow for the existence of absolute principles. In practice, however, it offers no access to such principles, and therefore can be employed just as readily as a bulwark against unwanted criticism by cultural outsiders, or, for that matter, against insiders using an allegedly 'foreign' moral vocabulary. In fact, it is the more palatable candidate for defensive appeals to tradition and culture, as it does not undermine the fundamental nature of moral claims, and accords nicely with anti-colonialist sentiments that are widespread in the non-Western world.

There are good reasons to be concerned about the position on cultural relativism adopted by Herskovits, which does indeed help to lay the ground for justificatory appeals to culture that work against needed reforms. At the same time, a close examination of this position highlights a different problem than the one on which philosophers have generally focused in debates about the cultural relativity of morals.

Power and the Production of Culture

Herskovits's version of cultural relativism developed in reaction to a history in which, as he writes:

> Moral judgments have been drawn regarding the ethical principles that guide the behavior and mold the value systems of different peoples. Their economic and political structures and their religious beliefs have been ranked in order of complexity, efficiency, desirability. Their art, music, and literary forms have been weighed. (Herskovits 1972: 11).

Invariably, the 'they' that has been weighed and found wanting in the evaluative procedures to which Herskovits is alluding consists of peoples whose cultures are not descended from Europe, whereas the ones doing the weighing have been, and are, the representatives of the civilized 'West'. It is in relation to the pejorative generalizations drawn by the latter—particularly about allegedly 'primitive' peoples, and frequently buttressed by racial prejudice against, for instance, Africans—that Herskovits articulates his claim that 'the very core of cultural relativism is the social discipline that comes of respect for differences—of mutual respect'. (Herskovits 1972: 33). Thus, in judging Herskovits's claim that 'in the vast majority...objective indices of cultural inferiority and superiority cannot be established' (Herskovits, 1972: 36), one has to keep in mind who wanted to establish these indices, and how they were actually employed.

That said, when Herskovits goes on to speak of the 'validity of all ways of life for those who live in accordance with them' (Herskovits 1972: 48), his position (though not altogether clear from this phrasing) does raise difficulties of precisely the sort that critics of cultural relativism have often attacked. However, the central problem with Herskovits's analysis, I would maintain, has to do not with the concept of 'relativity', but with the concept of 'culture'. In his support for cultural relativism, Herskovits pays little attention to the issue of structural inequalities within a society, and the way in which these condition that society's 'culture': its values, norms, institutions, forms of social organization, and so on. He seems simply to suppose that the practices and values of a society reflect the perspectives and the common will of all or most of its members, a supposition that is false in the case of the majority of human societies over the course of history. Consider some further sentences from the 1947 Statement of Human Rights. Its formulation of cultural relativism runs: 'standards and values are relative to the culture from which they derive so that any attempt to formulate postulates that grow out of the beliefs or moral codes of one culture must to that extent detract from the applicability of any Declaration of Human Rights to mankind as a whole' (AAA 1947: 542). The Statement glosses this assertion by talking about the different ideas about right and wrong, good and evil, in different societies. (AAA 1947: 542) Near the end of the document, the conclusion is drawn that 'man is free only when he lives as his society defines freedom' so that the proposed Declaration needs to incorporate 'a statement of the right of men to live in terms of their own traditions' (AAA 1947: 543).

Feinberg argues that a basic shortcoming of the concept of culture is 'the old assumption that culture is homogeneous and neatly bounded' (Feinburg 2007: 786). Ulin, too, maintains that cultural relativism reproduces this assumption, supposing that 'the "other" has a set of identifiably, clearly distinct customs, beliefs and cultural practices that can be compared to our clearly identifiable and distinct customs' (Ulin 2007: 815). In truth, these authors suggest, cultures are internally varied, including a multiplicity of sometimes conflicting voices, and they are distinguished from one another only by highly porous borders. Thus, Perusek, in his discussion of women's rights in Iran, cites Maryam Namazie's objection that if Iranian society is Muslim, as cultural relativists say, why are there so many dissenting voices and actions within it, which the ruling regime adopts harsh measures to repress? (Perusek 2007: 831). Namazie's complaint here is that many people in Iran, and especially women, clearly do not agree with what cultural relativists might identify as the 'values' of this society. In adducing this example, Perusek, like Feinberg, is challenging the overly essentialist concept of culture upon which endorsements of cultural relativism within anthropology have been based.

In my criticism of Herskovits, however, I am drawing attention to a different issue: namely, the hierarchical social conditions under which 'culture', as an objectively existing body of traditions, institutions, and norms, is produced. In other words, I am focusing not on the internal diversity of 'culture', but on the question of who controls the *means* of cultural production and reproduction within a given society. The cultural values according to which a society is organized may, after all, reflect the interests of those who have had the power to participate in producing that culture, while minimizing, or disregarding altogether, the interests of those who have not had this power. Herskovits ignores this consideration, looking only at asymmetrical power relations between societies, and specifically between the West and its various others. While motivated by opposition to European ethnocentrism, the resulting relativist account is seriously flawed and ethically dangerous.

Another reason why it is important to be aware of systemic inequalities of power in the production of social conventions and values is that anti-relativist accounts which ignore this issue sometimes end up inadvertently reproducing ethnocentric assumptions. Take the two examples from Indian history that I mentioned at the start of this essay: the caste system and widow immolation, inappropriately termed 'sati'. These belong to the conventional stock of items produced in anti-relativist arguments as examples of cultural practices about which 'we' could not be relativists (female genital cutting is another well-known example of this type). It is, however, distinctly odd and misleading to talk about the inequalities of the caste system in India without discussing economic relations, or the ideologies that elites typically invent to justify their privileges, or the category of the abject into which particular groups of people are thrown by others. And it is utterly crucial to understand that the value-systems of hierarchically ordered societies are largely generated by those at the top of the hierarchy. When the social body is conceived as an organism, the image is produced by those who think they are the head, never by the poor labouring feet. In India, it is not garbage collectors, tanners and toilet cleaners who judge themselves to be polluted, and outside the social pale. While this point tends to be neglected in academic discussions of cultural relativism, especially by Western writers speaking of the cultural practices of others, it is emphasized often enough by the actual victims of these practices. B.R. Ambedkar, for instance, the most famous hero of the movement against untouchability and caste discrimination in India, once wrote:

> It must be recognized that the selfish interest of a person or of the class to which he belongs always acts as an internal limitation which regulates the direction of his intellect. The power and position which the Brahmins possess is entirely due to the Hindu Civilization which treats them as supermen and subjects the lower classes to all sorts of disabilities so that they may never rise and challenge or threaten the superiority of the Brahmins over them. As is natural, every Brahmin is interested in the maintenance of Brahmanic supremacy be he orthodox or unorthodox, be he a priest or a *grahastha* [householder], be he a scholar or not'. (Ambedkar 1990: 240).

For similar reasons, it is equally odd and misleading to talk about widow immolation without discussing property rights, family structure, and the material interests of in-laws. Uma Narayan makes this point in her analysis of the flaws in colonial and contemporary constructions of 'sati' as a central feature of Hindu 'culture'. (Narayan 1997: 41–80) She draws attention as well to the way in which the rhetoric used for dowry murders in Western discourses, including terms like 'bride-burning', implicitly conflates it with widow immolation. This reinforces the view that such harms to Indian women are rooted in their 'culture', whereas the 'cultural explanation' is not brought to bear on the victimization of Western women in the same way (Narayan 1997: 85). The conflation also leaves out contextual factors that would complicate the ideological binaries of East-West, modernity-tradition at play within such an interpretation, like the connection between dowry murders and ever-greater demands for lavish weddings and gifts in an increasingly materialistic society.[2] In cases like these—caste, widow immolation, dowry murder—appeals to 'culture' that ignore the role of power in cultural production move at the wrong level of analysis, create and reinforce false cultural stereotypes, and conceal important cross-cultural parallels.

In addition, talk about 'cultural relativism' in relation to such cases conceals questions about motivation that might affect our judgements about whether or not we are properly talking about 'morality' in a given case, assuming we are reasonably clear on how we understand this concept. If we judge that the gross inequalities of systems of class, caste, gender, and race across various societies are a function of the interests and neuroses of ruling elites, how do we want to describe the discourses—the value systems, the mythological narratives, the social prescriptions—that are employed by those elites? Are they 'moral' discourses? Or might one prefer to say that here we have selfishness and will to power masquerading as morality, an all too common phenomenon across the world? Does anyone, that is, wish to describe as 'moral' values inspired by material greed, by wanting to live off the work of others, by sexual desires and anxieties, by a lust for domination?[3]

It may be that discussions of cultural relativism have tended to neglect this issue out of a concern to avoid or oppose reductive accounts of morality. This is true, I believe, of Alasdair MacIntyre's well-known 1985 essay, 'Relativism, Power and Philosophy'. Originally a presidential address to the American Philosophical Association, this essay, in spite of its title, strikingly fails to address crucial dimensions of the relation between culture and power. With respect to that relation, MacIntyre argues that when there are no common standards to which opposing parties can appeal, 'human relationships are perforce relationships of will and power unmediated by rationality' (MacIntyre 1985: 11). He suggests that this is all we are left with by 'post-Nietzschean anti-Platonists' such as (supposedly) Foucault (MacIntyre 1985: 12). But the examples MacIntyre gives to illustrate his thesis—the relations between the Zuni and the Spanish and between the Irish and the English—should lead us to doubt that a lack of common standards for rational dialogue is really the central issue here. One has only to read the anguished protests of someone like Bartolomé de las Casas against the Spanish *conquistadores* to see that the latter at least did not generally act according to their own 'idiosyncratic conception of reasonableness' (MacIntyre 1985: 11) in imposing their will upon the native inhabitants of the Americas (Las Casas 1999). They were motivated by greed and a desire for status and power, unrestricted by the laws, and social conventions they would have encountered in their native country.[4] Their behaviour was actually inexcusable in terms of the Christian morality to which they claimed to ascribe, a point stressed by Las Casas, himself a Christian cleric and missionary. Far from providing an example of the dangers of relativism, their hypocritical self-justifications rested on the idea of a civilized European culture confronting primitive savages—exactly the kind of judgement that motivated Herskovits and other anthropologists to defend cultural relativism.

More significantly for my purposes, in his haste to dismiss what he interprets as 'theories which identify every form of rationality with some form of contending power' (MacIntyre 1985: 19), MacIntyre overlooks the critical force in analyses focusing on the productive role of power. Or perhaps it is the other way around, that MacIntyre generally underemphasizes the reality of power in shaping tradition, which results not only in a failure to appreciate the merits of accounts like that of Foucault, but also some serious shortcomings in his own position. As Frazer and Lacey note, MacIntyre's work simply lacks a theory of power, and therefore paints all traditional 'practices', with their associated 'virtues', as good. He therefore misses the point of critical work where 'the emphasis is on unequal power situations and on one group's interests being pursued and satisfied at the expense of another's' (Frazer and Lacey 1994: 273). MacIntyre's response to this criticism, which makes reference to 'the deformations and distortions to which practices may be subjected, and the consequent injustices to women and others' (MacIntyre 1994: 290) continues to miss the point, and illustrates very well the blind spot to which I am drawing attention. The cultural traditions that are supposed to express the ideals, practices, and virtues of a given society may be fundamentally unjust because they reflect the partial interests of a dominant group in that society. In that case, one cannot criticize them by appeal to 'deformations and distortions' of cultural traditions that are assumed to be good. One needs an analysis that could identify intrinsically 'evil' practices, as Frazer and Lacey suggest, and this requires looking at 'tradition' through the lens of power. As a facet of Indian culture, for instance, the social practice of untouchability cannot be properly analysed merely as a distortion of a tradition we should respect. It requires an analysis that raises suspicious questions about the unequal social relations at the origins of the practice and the class interests the practice serves. MacIntyre never asks such questions, nor do the majority of philosophical interventions in the debate about cultural relativism. Granted, we do not want to say that all moral discourse is only a mask for power, but that should not lead us to downplay the fact that inequalities of power, combined with self-interested motivations, shape the character of cultural norms in profoundly important ways.

Two Examples: Caste and Female Genital Cutting

Not all versions of moral relativism involve the claim that the validity of moral norms can be measured only in relation to social conventions, and some versions are sensitive to the kinds of concerns about power and ideology I have been raising. David Wong, for instance, argues for a 'pluralistic relativism' that allows for more than one 'true' morality but also places some constraints on what can count as an adequate morality. Drawing on the phenomenon of moral dilemmas involving 'internal' conflicts of value, Wong maintains that societies, like individuals, have to prioritize and make trade-offs between different values. These are typically not, he argues, radically incommensurable among different societies, but are values we can all come to recognize and respect. Those elements of varying moral codes that do not serve the functions of morality, however, can be ruled out. Thus, Wong is making a normative claim about adequate moralities, not describing an attitude people should adopt towards all existing moralities. He also asks for a shift in philosophical methodology, proposing that theoretical work on this subject 'needs to descend from highly abstract debates about relativism, universalism, and pluralism, as these are defined as general views, and get down to particular cases as to which ways of life might indeed fall in the range of justifiable or truly permissible ways' (Wong 2006: 99).

One of the constraints Wong places on inclusion within this range is 'that justification for following the norms and reasons of an adequate morality cannot crucially depend on falsehoods', stressing in particular justifications for social subordination (Wong 2006: 59). In this regard, he mentions the example of caste:

> Other kinds of justification for subordination may rest on metaphysical claims. The caste system in India, for example, rests on the claim that one's place in the social order is necessitated by *karma*, by one's deeds in a past life. This sort of justification averts the need to satisfactorily address the interests of the subordinated by making subordination a kind of metaphysical and moral necessity. (Wong 2006: 61)

I want to dwell on this example a little further, connecting Wong's falsehood constraint with the issue of power I have been highlighting. In doing so, I use the word 'caste' as shorthand for what is in truth only one dimension of caste in India, the designation of some people as belonging by birth to groups that are supposed to serve others or that are allegedly 'polluted'; in short, to the collection of groups that in India now most often refer to themselves as *Dalits*. We might note that the metaphysical justifications for this social division, to which Wong alludes, are almost never overtly defended in public anymore, at least within political contexts. In this respect, 'caste' in India has become rather like 'race' in America. Casteism in India certainly still exists as an extremely serious problem, as racism

does in America. In both cases, these forms of injustice are prevalent
in the form of discriminatory practices and attitudes, and also in
the form of communities being historically disadvantaged due to
enforced social subordination, where the disadvantages—poverty
and low levels of education, for example—are then handed down
from one generation to the next. But, at the same time, no politician
in America would publicly and overtly defend racial hierarchy now;
to do so is effectively to end one's public career, and the situation
regarding caste in India is similar.

Given how long the tradition of caste has persisted in India (using
'caste' in the shorthand stipulated above), the complete disappear-
ance of public justificatory discourse about it is striking. In large
measure, it is doubtless simply a function of democratic politics; political parties naturally do not want to alienate a large bank of potential
votes. Yet, it is also fair to say that the legitimating metaphysical
discourse about caste has been discredited through argumentation,
as legitimating discourse about racial hierarchy has been elsewhere.
And this discrediting has centrally used the strategy of exposing as an
ideological ruse the reasons traditionally given for this form of social
subordination being a 'metaphysical and moral necessity', in Wong's
words. The claim has been that indeed caste is part of the 'culture' of
India, but only because that culture has reflected the interests of the
upper castes who controlled its production. The accounts I have in
mind, such as those of Ambedkar and Periyar, are reductionist about
the status of the so-called 'moral code' of this 'culture', which has
included prescriptions for a hierarchical caste system, insisting that
in fact these prescriptions were a function of interest and power and
so were not actually moral at all. The analytic framework of Marxism
has understandably held a strong appeal for the formulation of such
arguments. But their approach also has some affinity with earlier,
indigenous criticisms of caste in India, which at times also questioned
motivations and/or pointed to hypocrisy. For instance, the criticisms
presented by the *carvaks*, an ancient Indian school of materialists,[5]
or by the medieval poet Kabir.[6] Basically, the reductionist argument
asserts that the justifications for caste rest on metaphysical claims for
which there is no evidence, and which are in fact motivated entirely
by the wish on the part of elite groups to maintain their domination
and be served by others. This assertion does not require any appeal

to universalist moral principles (although anti-caste arguments have often deployed these as well), since it criticizes the reasons given for subordination as being rooted in self-serving motivations that no group within the society would count as moral. It simultaneously draws attention to the fact that 'culture' is, to a large extent, a product of dominant elites.

Within the course of his analysis, Wong also discusses the practice of female genital cutting, though without explicitly relating it to his constraint regarding falsity. He obliquely alludes to concerns about power, insofar as he challenges a common interpretation of this practice as an exclusively patriarchal one, serving the interests of men at the cost of the interests of women. He does not reject the latter interpretation altogether; he argues only that the significations of female genital cutting are more multiple and complex than this interpretation suggests. He points out that many women defend and support the practice, and that, according to reported self-evaluations, some take it to be a test of courage in which they take pride, and a beautification of the female body (Wong 2006: 262–3). These are fair points, and worth making in a context where this practice is routinely presented as one of those about which 'we' could not be relativists, with the supporting values evoking condescending outrage (the West having no experience with patriarchy, it would seem, or with obsessions about female sexual purity).

Arguably, however, the multiple significations of female genital cutting for the women who practise and undergo it do not contradict its status as a patriarchal practice. It is admitted that the practice makes sexual intercourse more difficult, and often painful for women, and that it has health costs. The privilege of male interests is, moreover, visible in many of the justifications given: that the practice keeps women faithful (why is that so much more important than men being faithful?), that it helps to preserve families (even if true, why does that matter so much more than women's well-being?), and that it beautifies the body (for men's pleasure at the cost of women's health?)[7] These significations, which may indeed endow the practice with real value in the minds of many of the women involved, are still premised on the subordination of women's interests. One notices, for example, the absence of any value placed on women's sexual desire or satisfaction as opposed to that of men. Wong observes that in some of the communities where female genital cutting is practised, it is believed that women do not enjoy sex, but that may be a result of the procedure itself. It should be added here that one can appreciate and respect the virtues individuals display in living up to the moral norms of their societies, while not agreeing, in the end, with those norms themselves.

In light of my analysis, I would point out that, in the case of female genital cutting as in the case of caste, one has to take into consideration the social hierarchy within which the practice is produced and reproduced. This consideration goes beyond ascertaining 'consent'. Many women may consent to the practice—it is usually performed on children, but not always—and they may even take pride in it. And Wong is right to suggest it should not be viewed entirely through the prism of patriarchal oppression. But one should still ask how this practice came to be, and whether women have participated as fully as men in determining the values and norms of the society in which it is found.

In view of these two examples, caste and female genital cutting, and in relation to Wong's constraint on falsity in combination with my analysis of the relation between culture and power, I would highlight three points. First, we need to be aware that ideology is a widespread, not marginal, feature of the purported 'moral codes' of societies, so that its possibility needs always to be taken into account when discussing what are thought to be problematic elements of these codes. Second, we have to be equally aware that determining the truth or falsity of a reason given for subordination is often not a straightforward matter. I do not have proof that the theses about karma and reincarnation that have sometimes been presented in justification of caste hierarchy are false, or that they are the product of self-interest. And female genital cutting is based on views about women that subordinate their well-being in quite complex and subtle ways. This brings me to my third point, which is that the best, and perhaps the only, guarantee we can have that the moral principles and practices of a given society genuinely are moral—that is, that they are not ideologies—is if the competent members of that society are all given the opportunity to participate in the production of those principles and practices (with the non-competent members being represented by those who care for them). Consent is not enough, because we are all shaped by our culture and absorb its values whatever they are, but those values do change when previously subordinated groups are allowed a role in shaping them over a substantial period of time.

Ethnocentrism and Anti-Relativism

These considerations about the hierarchical power relations within which the dominant norms, values, and institutions of a society are produced neither affirm nor refute moral relativism. Rather, they problematize an aspect of the concept of culture as deployed within debates on this issue, by relativists and anti-relativists alike. My analysis does render untenable any form of relativism implicitly supposing that the traditional or existing moral conventions of a society—the conventions expressed in its 'culture'—reflect the views and interests of the whole society. But it also suggests reasons for being dissatisfied with the way in which cultural relativism about morality is represented by philosophical opponents of the position, and for not participating in refutations of cultural relativism so represented, especially since they often tacitly put aside legitimate concerns about ethnocentrism in the process. Clifford Geertz raised this concern many years ago in 'Anti Anti-Relativism', a paper first presented as a distinguished lecture to the American Anthropological Association and published in 1984, one year before MacIntyre's 'Relativism, Power, and Philosophy'. Geertz argued in this paper that 'whatever cultural relativism may be or originally have been (and there is not one of its critics in a hundred who has got that right), it serves these days largely as a specter to scare us away from certain ways of thinking and towards others' (Geertz 1984: 263). Geertz' essay may overstate its case, and it fails to address the genuinely problematic formulations and interventions of some anthropologists within the debate on cultural relativism. Nonetheless, one should still take seriously Geertz' statement that between the twin evils of a wholly non-judgmental 'anything goes' mentality on the one hand, and narrow-minded provincialism on the other, the latter is 'altogether the more real concern as far as what actually goes on in the world' (Geertz 1984: 265).[8] Eurocentric bigotry still exists, and is still strongly implicated in current universalist and anti-relativist discourse. This discourse may no longer rank civilizations overtly, but often still does so implicitly.

The problem, after all, is always 'their' practices and 'their' values, where 'they' are people belonging to non-Western civilizations. The purportedly universal moral principles against which these practices and values are measured, moreover, are always ones evolved within the European tradition. Thus, the *mission civilatrice*, with its contempt for other cultures and civilizations, is still at play. Even the old notions of savagery are still there, witnessed by the number of times refutations of relativism make reference to the practices of one 'tribe' or another. Philosophers are especially guilty here. If they can't find a suitably objectionable actual practice, they will just make one up ('Imagine a tribe in which...'), and they seem oblivious to the prejudices such moves evoke and reinforce, and the truly miserable history of oppression associated with them.

It is noteworthy that, while MacIntyre's analysis is directed against relativism, he does nonetheless share Geertz' worry about the Eurocentric bias in contemporary anti-relativism (MacIntyre 1985: 19–20). MacIntyre, however, sets the bar too high, and in the wrong place, when he asks 'that rationality requires a readiness on our part to accept, and indeed to welcome, a possible future defeat of the forms of theory and practice in which it has up till now been taken to be embodied within our own tradition, at the hands of some alien and perhaps even as yet largely unintelligible tradition of thought and practice' (MacIntyre 1985: 19–20). Most of the time, the Eurocentrism of anti-relativist accounts applies to matters of content that do not raise such radical difficulties for cross-cultural understanding.

As an illustration, let me return to the chapter on cultural relativism in Rachels's textbook, *The Elements of Moral Philosophy*, which occasioned the critical responses by Johnson and others cited earlier. The chapter does maintain that there is something to be learned from cultural relativism, that we should not suppose that the ethical norms of our own culture are in fact the true ones, and that studying other cultures can help us to understand this and to overcome our naive assumptions (Rachels 1999: 34). But how well are these lessons reflected in Rachels's own account? His discussion of cultural relativism is typical in setting up the issue as a matter of 'us' judging 'them'. Rachels offers the example of 'Eskimos' (sic) having practised infanticide (Rachels 1999: 23–4), along with the usual target of female excision practised in some African countries (Rachels 1999: 31).

He could have offered different examples. He could have pointed out that, among Europeans and descendant cultures, it has been almost universally assumed until recently that animals are entirely excluded from the realm of moral concern, an assumption that would seem odd and barbaric to people brought up in a Buddhist value-system, extending the principle of compassion to all sentient beings. He could have said that the complex of Western values involving freedom, individualism, and property rights might look bizarre to some traditional Native American perspectives, especially where a commitment to this complex generates massive material inequalities and operates to undermine the natural environment that sustains human life. Or he could have noted that the modern Western notion that parents have a firm moral as well as legal obligation to their young children, but that children have no reciprocal and equally binding obligation to their aged parents might seem peculiar and callous within the traditional value framework of some Asian societies. Along with the arguments he does make, Rachels then could have added that, if cultural relativism were true, if there were no cross-cultural criteria for moral judgement, people not brought up within a Western culture would have to judge such beliefs and practices to be 'right' for Euro-Americans, however primitive, irrational, or cruel they might seem to others.

But rarely (if ever) does one find within refutations of relativism examples where a Western cultural practice has been put into question by an engagement with the perspective of a non-Western society. This is telling, given that there is enough accessible information for Western authors to be capable of drawing such comparisons, if they wished to do so. The fact that they do not avail themselves of it is not a function of inevitable cultural bias. The relation between 'the West' and 'the Rest' on this point is profoundly asymmetrical. The Rest routinely compare their values with the West without assuming that the latter have nothing good to offer them, but the reverse is not true. The problem is that very straightforward forms of Eurocentric ignorance are decidedly alive and well, however much people might like to congratulate themselves on either their 'cosmopolitanism' or their 'multiculturalism'. It is sad that among philosophers especially, attention to non-Western values continues to revolve mainly around bad practices, adduced as instances of the limits of tolerance, or the flaws of cultural relativism. The importance of cross-cultural understanding for exposing the idols of *our* tribe—a central concern for anthropologists like Benedict—thereby disappears from view. Re-contextualizing the debate on cultural relativism, with a greater critical focus on the concept of culture, can help to avoid re-inscribing such ethnocentrism, without sacrificing the entirely legitimate intuition that a practice's correspondence with the dominant cultural norms of a given society does not suffice to make that practice morally right.

In this context, focusing on the role of power in the production of cultural norms is helpful for pragmatic reasons as well as purely theoretical ones. At a theoretical level, it allows us to get clearer on what we are talking about when we debate 'cultural relativism'. At a pragmatic level, it is important that the terms of these debates, and our views of morality in general, do not end up re-inscribing the Euro-American ethnocentrism that cultural relativism originally sought to challenge, thereby provoking predictably—and understandably—hostile reactions among the peoples whose cultures are being denigrated. For instance, it is both false and dangerous to set up an opposition between 'universal values' and 'cultural norms' which in fact identifies the universal values with the liberal West and the cultural norms with the Rest. Within philosophical discussions, the topic of cultural relativism is usually formulated in neutral terms, as if it were referring to the possibility of universal ethical principles in general, without anyone having decided whose culture actually embodies these. This is true also of debates on multiculturalism that address tensions and potential conflicts between universal values and cultural norms, sometimes conceived as conflicts between the rights of individuals and the rights of cultural communities. But, as I have suggested, the examples routinely presented almost always advance the problem of culture as a problem about others. As Anne Phillips notes, 'culture, it seems, has been redefined as something that characterizes non-Western or minority groups' (Phillips 2007: 29). To make matters worse, the values of the West are generally defined in terms of the very best imaginable version of stated ideals, whereas the values of the Rest are defined in terms of the worst acts people in fact commit. On this point, Phillips cites Anne Norton, reviewing Susan Okin: 'When men in the United States beat their wives, it is an aberration, counter to the liberal principles that govern here. When Muslim men beat their wives, it is an act representative of the principles of Islam—whatever Koran or hadith may say' (Phillips, 2007: 28). This characterization of the two 'cultures' ignores the fact that at one time liberal principles were themselves invoked in defence of men's rights to do what they wished within the domestic sphere, which was positioned as private. But liberalism has a remarkable capacity to reinvent itself in the light of criticisms, while claiming that this reinvented version of itself is what its principles really entailed all along. Unfortunately, it rarely grants to other traditions a similar capacity for internal self-criticism and reform.

My central point, though, is that maybe the men who beat their wives do so for roughly similar reasons in many different societies, and maybe it is to be expected that they will come up with excuses for why they should be allowed to do this, which they baptize as moral or religious prescriptions. In such a context, we should be talking about patriarchy, or hypocrisy, or viciousness, or cruelty—but not 'culture', except suspiciously, with an eye to the problem of power. Speaking unsuspiciously of culture in contexts like this risks handing to powerful exploitative groups tools they can use in maintaining forms of oppression that serve their own interests—power over women, for instance—and can help them to gain the cooperation, and sometimes even active support, of the very groups one should want to empower. Many women will not want to endorse moral discourses that they feel embody contempt, in one way or another, for their race, culture, or nation, or they may be put in a position where their opposition to a form of mistreatment is framed as cultural betrayal.[9] Setting up a conflict between 'individual' and 'group' rights exacerbates this danger, as Western individualism is often represented as socially and spiritually harmful, and at the same time as alien to the less self-centred values of other civilizations. Asking about motivation and power, on the other hand, can provide a means of criticism that is, in a sense, 'internal'. Since the overt justification for social practices held to be morally right is never that they serve the self-interest of some at the cost of others, arguing that they in fact do is a way of exposing them as immoral, without recourse to principles that might be judged as alien to the society in question.

* * *

The belief in a common human nature that could serve as a basis for human rights is by no means invalidated by the fact of cultural difference. As Terence Turner points out, 'that cultures differ in specific ways…does not in itself contravene, but rather logically presupposes, the possibility that universal properties or principles of culture might exist at a more general level' (Turner 1997: 278). These universal properties would be due to some degree of commonality among the species, some shared human needs and aspirations, with corresponding tendencies to suffer from shared forms of distress and deprivation. Supposing that there is such commonality, which it would be hard to deny, Rawls's claim that it is possible to identify some goods people will want no matter what else they want is highly plausible. And the thesis that some rights should be regarded as universal human rights is equally plausible, when stated in broad terms, and applied to stark issues about respecting personal security and freedom, as well as meeting basic needs (although this latter aspect is the one that in practice has met with the greatest resistance from governments).

However, as Galeotti notes, 'universal principles and values cannot provide clear-cut, straightforward answers to practical issues and hard cases by means of simple deduction' (Galeotti 2007: 105). Such principles allow for a good deal of variation. It is far from clear, for instance, what it means in practice to respect 'religious freedom', as is revealed by the fraught legal and political contestations surrounding this commonly-asserted right, at national and international levels. Furthermore, as suggested by several contributors to this volume, the obligation to respect certain core prescriptions can be justified in the context of quite different moral discourses and world-views. These world-views may not endorse the concept of the human person in its absolute distinction from 'the rest of creation' that Donnelly, for one, sees as essential to human rights, for principles like *ahimsa* and *dharma* within Indian traditions carve out a different conceptual space. But that space might still provide a sufficient basis for reaching an overlapping consensus on human rights.

Furthermore, if one should worry about crude relativism, one should also worry about ruling out possibilities for social and political organization, as well as for the definition and prioritization of goods and values, that may be not only 'minimally decent', to use Rawls's formulation, but even excellent in promoting human flourishing.

It is not merely that principles drawn from Indian traditions, for instance, can agree with ethical and political conclusions rooted in Western views of the person. They may point to some different conclusions that enrich the global conversation: the need to extend compassion to non-human creatures, for example, or to focus on duties rather than exclusively on rights. These alternative possibilities can easily be lost under the force of hegemonic discourses that claim universality but are in fact highly limited and particular. That all moral discourses are in fact limited and particular comes into view as soon as one begins to spell out comprehensively and in detail what the common nature of humanity is, what inclinations and desires we all have, what we all suffer from, how society should be organized in order to best reflect and serve our interests.[10] In fact, even this description is slanted towards a picture of human beings as utilitarian agents distinct from nature and seeking to maximize their needs, which perhaps not every society would want to accept. At a global level, we need formulae allowing societies to determine such matters for themselves, while drawing critically on whatever sources are useful to them—their 'own' traditions, 'other' traditions, the resources of 'modernity'—without insisting that the results conform to a single anticipated shape, which would inevitably be the product of a specific globally dominant culture, as Herskovits worried.

These formulae must, however, also take into account the power inequalities within societies, and the ways in which these shape the production of a society's 'culture', including its social values and moral prescriptions. This is an issue Herskovits ignored, and the central problem with 'cultural relativism', I am suggesting, lies here, in the fact that cultural values and prescriptions are bound to reflect the interests and partial perspectives of the elites who create and sustain them. Recognizing this reality helps us to differentiate between respectable moral differences of the sort that Wong rightly highlights, and practices that are indeed traditional or widespread elements of a 'culture' but are oppressive. It also opens space for a mode of critical discourse that does not rely on principles formulated within a specific tradition. And acknowledging the relation between culture and power can ground a commitment to democracy, understood as the right of all members of a society to participate in shaping the values according to which they will live[11]—not because that is required by universally valid moral code, but because only then can we be assured that any 'code' according to which a morality is said to be 'relative' is not merely an ideology, expressing the self-serving interests of a dominant group: men, upper castes, landowners, etc. This genre of argument for democracy can include broad and renegotiable principles of human rights based on our shared species-being, because it does not rely on a specific set of values asserted as universal;[12] however, it goes some distance towards addressing Herskovits's original worries about the UN Declaration of Human Rights, and on-going concerns about the culturally bigoted and racialist judgements implicated in Western discourses supporting a universal morality. Steven Lukes, who rejects moral relativism, nonetheless acknowledges that 'the surviving appeal of moral relativism is indeed that it recognizes the idea that there is no single best way for human beings to live; or, to express the same idea in another way, that there are many such best ways, where what is best is internal to a range of alternative conceptions of the good' (Lukes 2008: 158). I maintain that this relativistic—or, if you prefer, pluralistic—idea is a benign one, and that the danger of the position usually defined as moral relativism has to do not with relativity but with power. In other words, one *can* be a 'moral relativist', granting that there is more than one true morality and more than one good political system, and that it is up to a given society to determine these for itself in accordance with its own culture and traditions—provided that 'society' does not name only one or more privileged groups, and 'culture' does not name only what serves the interests of those groups.

Notes

1. For the remainder of this essay, my use of the term 'cultural relativism' will be limited to the area of ethics. I do not broach the separate issue of epistemic or cognitive relativism.
2. This factor is stressed in some Western media reports, it should be said: for instance by Priya Virmani, 'Dowry deaths are the hidden curse of the big fat Indian wedding' (Virmani 2012) and Rahul Bedi, 'Indian dowry deaths on the rise' (Bedi 2012)—though one also cannot help but notice that both of these authors are of Indian origin.
3. I explore this issue at greater length in 'Moral Relativism and the Concept of Culture' (Sikka 2012).

4. Cf. William Talbot: 'For many of the false claims made about the American natives by Columbus and his countrymen—for example, the claims that the natives had no religion and no culture…it is hard to tell which ones were conscious lies, aimed at providing others with reasons for believing that the mistreatment of the natives was justified, and which were the result of unconscious bias due to their all-consuming desire for wealth. What seems almost certain is that they were not simply honest mistakes' (Talbott 2005: 69).

5. For instance, in the following statements attributed to the *carvak* school:

> This also has been said by Brhaspati:
> There is no heaven, no final liberation,
> nor any soul in another world,
> Nor do the actions of the four castes,
> orders, or priesthoods produce any real effect.
> The Agnihotra, the three Vedas, the ascetic's three staves,
> and smearing oneself with ashes—
> Were made by Nature as the livelihood of those destitute of knowledge
>   and manliness
>   …
> If he who departs from the body goes to another world,
> How is it that he comes not back again, restless for love of his kindred?
> Hence it is only as a means of livelihood that Brahmans have established
>   here
> all these ceremonies for the dead—there is no other fruit anywhere'.
>   (Acharya 1914: 10).

6. Kabir's criticisms of caste do not directly expose it as ideology, but he does often point to the less-than-spiritual motivations of those who claim to stand at the top of the caste hierarchy:

> 'Says Kabir,
> The pundit learned in scriptures
>   Can deliver talks of advice
> The words do never touch his heart
>   For others he does it for a price'. (Kabir 1991: 71).

> 'Had the idol been alive,
> It would have
> Lashed out at the sculptor.
> It would have seen through the priest

> Who grabs all the food
> The faithful bring,
> Leaving the scraps to the idol'. (Kabir 2011: 31).

7. Compare Kopelman:

> 'According to four independent series of studies conducted by investigators from countries where female circumcision is widely practiced... the primary reasons given for performing this ritual surgery are that it (1) meets a religious requirement, (2) preserves group identity, (3) helps to maintain cleanliness and health, (4) preserves virginity and family honour and prevents immorality, and (5) furthers marriage goals including greater sexual pleasure for men'. (Kopelman 2001: 314). I would argue that all of the reasons listed here can be plausibly construed as privileging—in subtle and more overt ways—the interests of the men who are their primary authors.

8. Thus, as Susan Sherwin notes: 'Many social scientists have endorsed versions of relativism precisely out of their sense that the alternative promotes cultural dominance. They may be making a philosophical error in drawing that conclusion, but I do not think they are making an empirical one' (Kopelman 2001: 320).

9. Cf. Radhika Coomaraswamy, commenting on violations of human rights in relation to cultural practices involving violence against women:

> 'The situation is made more complex by the fact that women also identify with their culture and are offended by the arrogant gaze of outsiders who criticize their way of doing things.... Some women have told the Special Rapporteur that they do not mind wearing the veil because they see the veil as subversive against imperialism. Cultural markers and discrimination of a more powerful ethnic or political majority often entail restrictions on the rights of women'. (Coomaraswamy 2008: 565)

> Steiner, Alston, and Goodman's *International Human Rights in Context* (2008) also contains a representative selection of other texts relevant to this issue. See Chapter 7, 'Conflict in Culture, Tradition and Practices: Challenges to Universalism' (517–668).

10. I do not accept the strong form of the liberal claim that society should and can be organized so that 'individuals' can decide all of these matters for themselves, for reasons that cannot be presented within the scope of this chapter.

11. I am here appropriating John Dewey's understanding of democracy as a 'way of life' involving 'the necessity for the participation of every mature human being in formation of the values that regulate the living of men together' (Dewey 2008: 217).

12. My argument does rest on a universal intuition about what morality is, however, or at least what it is not: namely, that it is by definition

not a function of self-interest. But I would maintain that a normative code which does not fit this criterion cannot be recognized as moral at all. As Philippa Foot once pointed out, there has to be some common meaning to the term 'moral' or we cannot even talk sensibly about differing moral codes (Foot 1958: 511–12).

References

Acharya, M. (trans. by E.B. Cowell and A.E. Gough). 1914. *Sarva Darsana-Samgraha* (14th Century). London: Kegan Paul, Trench, and Trubner.

Ambedkar, B.R. 1990. *Writings and Speeches, Vol. 7*. Bombay: Education Department, Government of Maharashtra.

American Anthropological Association (AAA). 1947. 'Statement on Human Rights', *American Anthropologist*, 49(4): 539–43.

Baghramian, M. 2004. *Relativism*. New York: Routledge.

Bedi, R. 2012. 'Indian dowry deaths on the rise', *The Telegraph*, 27 February 2012. www.telegraph.co.uk/news/worldnews/asia/india/9108642/Indian-dowry-deaths-on-the-rise.html (accessed 7 June 2013).

Benedict, R. 1959. *Patterns of Culture*. Boston: Houghton Mifflin Company.

Benhabib, S. 2002. *The Claims of Culture: Equality and Diversity in the Global Era*. Princeton, NJ: Princeton University Press.

Coomaraswamy, R. 2008. 'Report on Cultural Practices in the Family that are Violent Towards Women: Commission on Human Rights, E/CN.4/2002/83, 2002', in H. Steiner, P. Alston, and R. Goodman (eds), *International Human Rights in Context: Law, Politics, Morals: Text and Materials*, pp. 565–8. New York: Oxford University Press.

Dewey, J. 2008. 'Democracy and Educational Administration', in J.A. Boydston (ed.), *John Dewey: The Later Works, Vol. 2*, pp. 217–37. Carbondale: Southern Illinois University Press.

Donnelly, J. 2003. *Universal Human Rights in Theory and Practice* (2nd edition). Ithaca: Cornell University Press.

Feinberg, R. 2007. 'Dialectics of Culture: Relativism in Popular Anthropological Discourse', *Anthropological Quarterly*, 80: 777–90.

Foot, P. 1958. 'Moral Arguments', *Mind*, 67: 502–13.

Frazer, E. and N. Lacey. 1994. 'MacIntyre, Feminism and the Concept of Practice', in J. Horton and S. Mendus, *After MacIntyre*, pp. 265–82. Notre Dame: University of Notre Dame Press.

Galeotti, A.E. 2007. 'Relativism, Universalism, and Applied Ethics: The Case of Female Circumcision.' *Constellations*, 14(1): 91–111.

Geertz, C. 1984. 'Anti Anti-Relativism.' *American Anthropologist, New Series* 86: 263–78.

Harman, G. and J.J. Thomson. 1996. *Moral Relativism and Moral Objectivity*. Cambridge MA: Blackwell.

Hatch, E. 1983. *Culture and Morality: The Relativity of Values in Anthropology*. New York: Columbia University Press.

Herskovits, M.J. 1972. *Cultural Relativism: Perspectives in Cultural Pluralism*. New York: Random House.

Horton, J. and S. Mendus (eds). 1994. *After MacIntyre*. Notre Dame: University of Notre Dame Press.

Johnson, T.H. 2007. 'Cultural Relativism: Interpretations of a Concept.' *Anthropological Quarterly*, 80: 791–802.

Kabir. (ed. and trans. by G.N. Das). 1991. *Couplets from Kabir*. Delhi: Motilal Banarsidass.

———. (trans. by A.K. Mehrotra). 2011. *Songs of Kabir*. New York: New York Review Books.

Kopelman, L.M. 2001. 'Female Circumcision/Genital Mutilation and Ethical Relativism', in P.K. Moser and Thomas L. Carson, *Moral Relativism: A Reader*, pp. 307–26. New York: Oxford University Press.

Las Casas, B. de. (trans. by N. Griffin). 1999. *Short Account of the Destruction of the Indies*. London: Penguin.

Lukes, S. 2008. *Moral Relativism*. New York: Picador.

MacIntyre, A. 1985. 'Relativism, Power and Philosophy', *Proceedings and Addresses of the American Philosophical Association*, 59: 5–22.

———. 1994. 'A Partial Response to My Critics', in J. Horton and S. Mendus (eds), *After MacIntyre*, pp. 283–304. Notre Dame: University of Notre Dame Press.

Narayan, U. 1997. *Dislocating Cultures*. New York: Routledge.

Perusek, D. 2007. 'Grounding Cultural Relativism', *Anthropological Quarterly*, 80: 821–36.

Phillips, A. 2007. *Multiculturalism without Culture*. Princeton and Oxford: Princeton University Press.

Rachels, J. 1999. *The Elements of Moral Philosophy* (2nd edition). New York: McGraw-Hill.

Rescher, N. 2008. 'Moral Objectivity', *Social Philosophy and Policy*, 25(1): 393–409.

Rasmussen, D.B. 2008. 'The Importance of Metaphysical Realism for Ethical Knowledge', *Social Philosophy and Policy*, 25(1): 56–99.

Saunders, D. 2013. 'Rape is a crime everywhere, but India's crisis is unique', *Globe and Mail*, 5 January 2013. www.theglobeandmail.com/commentary/rape-is-a-crime-everywhere-but-indias-crisis-is-unique/article6931835 (accessed 6 June 2013).

Sikka, S. 2012. 'Moral Relativism and the Concept of Culture', *Thoeria*, 59(133): 50–69.

Steiner, H., P. Alston, and R. Goodman. 2008. *International Human Rights in Context: Law, Politics, Morals: Text and Materials*. New York: Oxford University Press.

Talbott, W.J. 2005. *Which Rights Should Be Universal?* Oxford University Press.

Turner, T. 1997. 'Human Rights, Human Difference: Anthropology's Contribution to an Emancipatory Cultural Politics', *Journal of Anthropological Research*, 53: 273–91.

Ulin, R.C. 2007. 'Revisiting Cultural Relativism: Old Prospects for a New Cultural Critique', *Anthropological Quarterly*, 80: 803–20.

Virmani, P. 'Dowry deaths are the hidden curse of the big fat Indian wedding', *The Guardian*, 23 May 2012. www.guardian.co.uk/commentisfree/2012/may/23/dowry-deaths-big-fat-indian-wedding (accessed 7 June 2013).

Williams, B 1982. 'An Inconsistent Form of Relativism', in J.W. Weland and M. Krausz (eds), *Relativism: Cognitive and Moral*, pp. 171–4. Notre Dame: University of Notre Dame Press.

Wong, D.B. 2006. *Natural Moralities: A Defense of Pluralistic Relativism*. Oxford: Oxford University Press.

Yasui, B. 1996. 'Bride-burning claims hundreds in India', *CNN World News*, 18 August 1996. www.cnn.com/WORLD/9608/18/bride.burn/ (accessed 7 June 2013).

2

Ethical Naturalism and Human Rights

Nigel DeSouza

The question of the foundations of human rights is one that has become an increasingly pressing issue over the last few decades. One of the most compelling recent attempts to provide an answer is James Griffin's *On Human Rights*. What is novel about Griffin's account is his conviction that we need a 'substantive' account of human rights in order to render more determinate just what we actually mean by 'human right'. To this end, Griffin develops and draws on a conception of ethical naturalism which I lay out in the first section of this paper. I then contrast it with an alternative, 'second-nature' conception of ethical naturalism that I present in the second section, drawing on the work of John McDowell and David Wiggins. My objective in doing so is to show in the third and final section that while Griffin's account may succeed at the theoretical level in providing substantive criteria for deciding what qualifies as a human right, it fails as a candidate for widespread justification of human rights. The alternative conception of ethical naturalism makes the reasons for this clear and shows why an overlapping consensus on human rights is the right model of justification.

Griffin's Ethical Naturalism

James Griffin's approach to grounding human rights centres on working towards a more determinate conception of what we mean, or should mean, by the term 'human right'. But human rights are not to be understood as rights we have simply in virtue of being human, because this is true of moral claims in general (Griffin 2008: 17). Rather, there must be something special about the kinds of claims human rights represent, which warrant their enunciation in this particular form. This specialness is captured in the characterization of human rights as 'protections of normative agency' (Griffin 2008: 2). Already with this claim, the nature of Griffin's approach is evident: he firmly believes that only a substantive account of human rights will suffice (Griffin 2008: 22). One of the virtues of such an account, which will provide criteria for deciding what qualifies as a human right and why, is that it will help stop the runaway growth of the extension of the term in recent times and preserve its integrity and credibility (Griffin 2008: 17). As we will see, Griffin will ground his substantive account in ethical naturalism. A key part of his approach to grounding human rights, however, are the historical connections he draws between it and what he calls the Enlightenment project of human rights. I thus turn to his consideration of history first.

In *On Human Rights*, Griffin begins with a brief historical account of the history and origins of human rights discourse. The whirlwind tour we get of the likes of Aquinas, Suarez, Grotius, Pufendorf, and Locke is unified by the clear tendency in their accounts of natural law and natural rights *qua* precursor to our modern conception of human rights: human beings are able to work out and understand for themselves the natural laws, precepts, or moral principles needed in order to live together in stable societies (Griffin 2008: 9ff). In fact, in the case of Aquinas, we already see a model for Griffin's own ethical naturalism:

> In the universe, as conceived by Aquinas, everything has its divinely assigned end. One could therefore see human ends as part of, and readable off, nature. This view, developed in a certain way, can support a strong form of natural law. It can support, for instance, a form of moral realism—that is, the view that human goods and perhaps

even moral principles are not human constructs, but part of a reality that is independent of human thought and attitude. And this sort of moral realism can, in turn, support the epistemic view that judgements about human good and moral principles are capable of truth and falsity in the strong sense that more familiar kinds of report about nature are. (Griffin 2008: 11–12)

Despite its obvious religious/theological foundations, Aquinas's theory succeeds in pointing to nature as a source for grounding human rights, a source independent, to use our terms, of cultural variation. In the course of the seventeenth and eighteenth centuries, however, there is a steady falling away of the religious and theological underpinnings of natural law and a move towards secularization to the point that the idea of natural law comes to mean nothing more than 'the claim that there are moral principles independent of positive law and social convention' (Griffin 2008: 12). The final outcome of this process is the Enlightenment notion of human rights that emerges at the end of the century, as contained in documents such as the French *Declaration of the Rights of Man and of the Citizen* (1789) and the United States *Bill of Rights* (1791). This is the notion of human rights, Griffin claims, that we still have today, there having been 'no theoretical development of the idea itself since then'. (Griffin 2008: 13). It is this notion, however, which remains woefully indeterminate; for saying a human right is one we have simply in virtue of being human, without any further specification of what 'human' means, is insufficient for determination of what properly can count as a human right. Nevertheless, the historical discourse on natural law and natural rights and the Enlightenment notion do provide us with a clue: '[n]atural law began as a part of a teleological metaphysics capable of supporting strong interpretations of how morality is rooted in nature' (Griffin 2008: 14). But, Griffin asks, once that foundational metaphysics is abandoned, what do we have left to go by, and is it enough? (Griffin 2008: 14). This is where the account Griffin is going to provide comes in. His proposal for grounding human rights in ethical naturalism is clearly intended to be understood as emerging out of, and as completing, the Enlightenment project of human rights. His substantive account fills the gap that has been left since the end of the eighteenth century.

Griffin provides an overview of his substantive account in the second chapter of *On Human Rights*. Human rights, at their most basic, are protections of our human standing or personhood. If personhood is broken down by analysing the notion of agency, three values emerge from three features of agency which are constitutive of it. These are: (i) autonomy ('one must (first) choose one's path through life'); (ii) minimum provision (in order for 'one's choice [to] be real...one must have at least a certain minimum education and information [and] one must have at least the minimum provision of resources and capabilities it takes' to be able to act); and (iii) liberty ('others must also not forcibly stop one from pursuing what one sees as a worthwhile life') (Griffin 2008: 33). These are the three values which Griffin will use to derive the 'highest-level human rights' and subsequently to develop that account in Part II of his book, before turning to various applications in the Part III. Before that, however, Griffin owes us a fuller explanation, justification, and grounding of his substantive account and it is here that he turns to ethical naturalism.

Human rights are grounded directly in the central substantive values of personhood: autonomy, liberty, and minimum provision. These values and their associated rights, however, are not derived from any abstract moral theory, via a formal principle such as Kant's Universal Principle of Right or Mill's Principle of Utility (Griffin 2008: pp. 2ff). Rather, they are grounded in merely what is needed for a human being to be a human being, for human status. Among other things, personhood on its own generates the right to life and security of person (since personhood would be impossible without it), political voice, free expression, assembly, and press (all generated from autonomy), and rights to education and minimum provision (Griffin 2008: 33). While it must be acknowledged that a number of the generated rights depend on the nature of the society in question—there must be a press for there to be a right to freedom of press—Griffin later associates these with the 'practicalities' that need to be considered in determining specific rights (Griffin 2008: 37ff)—the underlying values are basic to being a human being. But what are the grounds for this claim? As Griffin himself puts it, '[s]tatements about human nature could most easily lay claim to cross-cultural standards of correctness if they could be seen, as some classical natural laws theorists saw them, as observations of the constitution and workings of part of the natural world' (Griffin 2008: 35). But he is quick to anticipate the response to this: 'this looks like trying to derive values (human rights) from facts (human nature), which generations of philosophers have been taught cannot be done' (Griffin 2008: 35).

Griffin, however, thinks that we have a new way of grounding such claims which can replace the religious or metaphysical under-pinnings deemed necessary by the likes of Aquinas, but which are no longer accessible to us today. The criticism that we are deriving a value from a fact only stands in this case if we buy into 'a certain conception of nature: namely, the conception that sees nature as what the natural sciences, especially the physical sciences, describe' (Griffin 2008: 35). Griffin, in contrast, proposes that we adopt a different understanding of what is 'natural' which accommodates his understanding of what is 'human'. His argument is essentially that it is simply inadequate to define the 'human' in natural scientific terms alone, for any resulting definition will be missing crucial aspects of what it is to be human which cannot be captured in such terms. Most important, according to Griffin, are basic human 'interests' which ground notions like autonomy and liberty, which are, in turn, central to functioning human agents. These basic interests are fundamental to our understanding of human nature and clearly transcend the narrow terms of natural science. Griffin unabashedly claims that his 'notions of "human nature" and "human agent" are [thus] already well within the normative circle, and [that] there is no obvious fal-lacy involved in deriving rights from notions as evaluatively rich as they are' (Griffin 2008: 35). The reason for this is clear: 'it is...much too quick to think that what is evaluative cannot also be objective... that it cannot also be natural' (Griffin 2008: 35). We must instead see basic human interests as features of the natural world, as basic to human nature. As Griffin puts it, he is calling for an 'expansive natu-ralism' which 'gives hope of restoring a form of that central feature of the human rights tradition: namely, that these rights are grounded in natural facts about human beings' (Griffin 2008: 36). The link with Aquinas is only too clear.

Griffin's ethical naturalism does not end with his defence of universal human interests as the proper ground of human rights, for it could plausibly be argued that the 'naturalness' of these interests seems to be grounded in nothing more than his mere claim that they have this status. In chapter six of *On Human Rights*, entitled 'The Metaphysics of Human Rights', Griffin goes a step further and provides an account of the interests themselves and their origins. In contrast to what he calls 'the taste model', which he associates with Hume and according to which values are seen as entirely reducible to subjective preference, Griffin maintains that some basic human interests must be seen as having an objective status (Griffin 2008: 111–12). His argument here draws on Wittgenstein's notion of a 'form of life' (and Donald Davidson's ideas regarding what is necessary for us to be able to interpret the language of others) (Griffin 2008: 113ff). Griffin focuses on Wittgenstein's insight that a language is only possible because the rules for the use of words are not akin to a mental template but rather can only be understood as part of the shared practices of a community, which, in turn, 'are possible only because of the human beliefs, interests, dispositions, sense of importance, and so on that go to make up what [Wittgenstein] called a "form of life"' (Griffin 2008: 113). What this points to is the fact that there are all sorts of ways in which we see and understand each other that are fundamental to the possibility of us being able to share a language. '[A] form of life seems to consist in part in a shared set of beliefs and values' (Griffin 2008: 113). It is this shared form of life that is the repository of certain basic human interests and values which, in turn, are part of the necessary conditions for language in the first place. Griffin believes that these 'will be confined to a few of the most basic human interests…that we want to avoid pain and anxiety, that we have goals and attach importance to their being fulfilled (and perhaps also a few moral norms closely connected with these interests, such as that cruelty is wrong)' (Griffin 2008: 114). What is also true about sharing a form of life is that one's standards for evaluating one's life can no longer be seen as entirely subjectively generated. Griffin gives the example of 'accomplishment' and notes that standards by which I can claim to have achieved something of significance in my life are not chosen by me, such that (using Rawls's example) I could not claim counting all the blades of grass on various lawns as a genuine example of 'accomplishment' (Griffin, 2008: 114). All this Griffin associates with what he calls 'the perception model' and according to which '[f]or me to see anything as enhancing my life, I must see it as enhancing life in a generally intelligible way, in a way that pertains to *human* life and not just to my particular life' (Griffin 2008: 114).

On this basis, Griffin makes his central claims about the naturalness of certain human interests. There are certain biologically-based human interests such as nourishment and nurturing necessary to avoid ailment, pain, and malfunction (including psychological) which he terms 'disvalues' and which are, he claims, 'part of the framework necessary for the intelligibility of language' (Griffin 2008: 116). But as reflective, rational creatures, we also have certain 'non-biological interests' such as accomplishment, which Griffin claims are 'as deeply embedded in human nature as biological ones'. The list Griffin provides is: 'accomplishment, enjoyment, deep personal relations, certain kinds of understanding, and…the components of personhood' (Griffin 2008: 116). In a word, 'biological interests are embedded in our animal nature, and non-biological ones in our rational nature' (Griffin 2008: 117). All of these basic human interests are available or accessible to us in virtue of our participation in a form of life and our knowledge of its associated language. Griffin invokes the idea of a certain kind of sensitivity that, under the right conditions, a human being will have to these interests, which Griffin associates with 'prudential values', such that she will both recognize and have the appropriate reaction to them (Griffin 2008: 117ff). The analogy here is to visual perception. Just as there are conditions we can point to that are necessary for successful seeing—good light, good eyes, good position—we can also work out 'the conditions for the successful workings of our sensitivity to prudential values' (Griffin 2008: 119). Griffin acknowledges that the conditions for the operation of sensitivity to prudential values is far more complex than those necessary for successful visual perception. 'One needs, first of all, a lot of knowledge of the familiar, undisputed factual sort about the world. One has also to have sufficient human capacities to know how enjoyment, say, figures in human life.' (Griffin 2008: 118–19). Correspondingly, a failure in sensitivity would have various causes: lacking the concept, information, certain human capacities (Griffin 2008: 119). The point here seems to be that since these biological and non-biological basic interests, now characterized as prudential values, are deeply embedded in human nature, as long as we are functioning as normal human agents (as complex as the conditions for that are), we will all naturally be sensitive to these interests/values. As Griffin puts it, '[a] full account of deliberating about human interests suggests that in the right conditions we are sensitive to certain things' making life go better' (Griffin 2008: 119).

Crucial to Griffin's argument is that these interests be seen as part of human nature, and not as relative to a particular society or culture. In order to make this clear, he draws an analogy between an ointment being 'soothing' and an accomplishment being 'life-fulfilling'. Because both these concepts are deeply embedded in the human perspective, our recognition of their occurrence brings with it a reaction, an appropriate reaction, when our sensitivity is functioning properly (Griffin 2008: 122). It is no argument against the objective validity of these concepts to say that, because they are embedded in a human point of view, they are not truly objective. The question is whether they are inescapable components of our best account of what happens in the natural world, of which human beings are a part (Griffin 2008: 122). And Griffin believes that their fundamental relation to basic human interests gives them this status. Our natural sensitivity to these interests is proof of this. In the case of pain, one cannot separate recognition and reaction—our reaction to pain is in part constitutive of our recognition of it as pain:

> [I]t is not that, as a matter of fact, we just find ourselves desiring to avoid pain or to have it alleviated. What is going on is more complex: we have these desires *because* we find pain undesirable. We have an attitude towards it; we find it bad, and for obvious reasons. Some basic values are part of the framework necessary for language, and the disvalue of pain must be one of them. The distinction between fact and value...becomes difficult to sustain at this point. (Griffin 2008: 123)

And the same logic holds for basic human interests in general, interests embedded in our nature as human beings:

> Cases of interests' being met and unmet, I think, earn their way into the world of facts. We can place them in our everyday natural world, and do not need to resort to anything remotely like a

detached 'value realm'. That conclusion brings out what seems to me immensely plausible about ethical naturalism. In talking about human interests we are not talking about entities in such an other-worldly realm…but, rather, about certain things that happen in the only realm that values need: mainly, what goes on in human lives, that *this* or *that* meets an interest, and so makes a life go better. (Griffin 2008: 123)

Griffin sees this 'ethical naturalism' as part of that wider 'expansive naturalism' we encountered above, according to which what we mean by 'natural' or 'factual' now comes to include human interests (Griffin 2008: 124). At base, it is from these human interests and their associated prudential values that human rights are derived and properly grounded. The values of autonomy, liberty, and minimum provision underlie, and are the criteria for, the human rights derived from them that serve to protect normative agency.

Second-Nature Ethical Naturalism

Griffin's ethical naturalism starts from a first-person perspective on the world in which, if all goes well and I become a normal, func-tioning human agent, I am sensitive to various interests and related values which 'make my life go well or better'. I recognize and react appropriately to things as different as pain, on the one hand, and accomplishment, enjoyment, deep relations with others on the other. These interests and values correspond to basic features of a recogniz-ably human life. We are not just biological organisms, we are also rational, reflective organisms, and the interests and values associ-ated with being such are just as natural to us. For example, because I am capable of leading a life, choosing it for myself, the value of autonomy is natural to my being, to any human being. Because I am capable of feeling fulfilment, the value of accomplishment is natural to my being. Griffin's ethical naturalism thus begins from natural features and capacities of human agency—which the over-arching adjective 'normative' is meant to capture—and shows how the interests and values associated with them are ones to which we are normally sensitive because they are embedded in our language and its connected form of life. The move from the prudential to the moral comes when I see others as capable of the same things, as having the same interests and values—at the most basic, I recognize and react to your pain as I would to my own (Griffin 2008: 124ff; Griffin 1996: 71ff).[1] 'For me to see you as human is to see you as having certain physical and psychological states that you want to avoid or to have alleviated, as having goals that can be achieved or frustrated, [etc.]' (Griffin 1996: 69). In a word, I start from my own perspective and understand you by projecting that perspective onto you and respecting those same values at stake in your life (Griffin 1996: 69). Another source of my moral relationship to others is the fact that my realization of my own interests deeply involves them. As Griffin puts it, the explanation of prudential values must involve according a large place to 'the value represented by other persons' (Griffin 1996: 69). For example, I cannot achieve accomplishment without others, deep personal relations by definition involve other human beings, etc. (Griffin 1996: 69–71). What is striking about the underlying structure of Griffin's argument here and his ethical naturalism in general is the distinct resemblance it bears to early modern and Enlightenment theories of human nature and society, often termed Epicurean, which were premised on self-preservation as the most basic motive of human nature. Naturally, Griffin's account is much more nuanced, but the starting point is nonetheless human interests and prudential values. The moral level can be understood as having to do with the issue of the social coordination of self-interested agents, and moral norms as involving a large element of 'policy' that emerges over time in societies (Griffin1996: 93ff; Griffin 2008: 127ff).

Now there is a different way of understanding 'ethical naturalism' whereby 'naturalism' consists not in giving a substantive account of the interests and prudential values that are 'deeply embedded in human nature', but rather in providing an account of how human beings become ethical agents in the first place. The idea of a 'form of life' as basic is present here too, but a key difference is that the values belong to their own kind of language and are not only part of one's spoken language or part of something more basic which renders language possible in the first place. One is instead initiated into an ethical language shared by the members of a society and the values of this ethical language are both intrinsically self and other-regarding. That is, one does not start from purely prudential values alone, but rather from values that relate to others too, such as honesty, generosity, etc. Likewise, the ethical sensitivity to these values is different from Griffin's conception of sensitivity, for it is something one originally acquires from others and develops. But this ethical sensitivity, and the very capacity to acquire it and to act according to a web of values, is seen as a natural feature of the human form of life. So, despite the already apparent differences, this understanding of ethical naturalism is in complete agreement with Griffin that our understanding of 'naturalism' must be broadened to include features of human agency that cannot be captured within the terms of natural science. Let me now try to flesh out this alternative conception of ethical naturalism whose focus, in contrast to Griffin, is on how human beings become ethical agents.[2] I turn first to the insights of John McDowell and David Wiggins.

A good place to start is with the notion of values. Both McDowell and Wiggins defend an approach to values that construes our perception of them as analogous to our perception of colours (McDowell 1998: 132ff; Wiggins 1987: 189ff). But, as we will see, their 'perception theory' of values is rather different from that of Griffin's. To start with visual perception, if we were to say that our experience of seeing the colour 'red' should really be explained in terms of the primary qualities of the object we are looking at, its microscopic structure, say, then we are, quite simply, no longer explaining the experience itself, as it is subjectively experienced. Secondary qualities such as colours, therefore, do have objective reality. While they depend on beings like us to be seen, as long as we exist, they exist for us and independently of us. We, as it were, each subjectively experience them objectively, under favourable circumstances (the right lighting, etc.). McDowell and Wiggins construe values as having an analogous reality. Values are not arbitrarily subjective, in the manner of the 'taste theory' Griffin rejects. When I feel a sense of nausea, whatever object it is that causes my nausea is, for me, nauseous. That I find vanilla ice cream more 'delicious' than chocolate is likewise a simple subjective preference. But when it comes to values, my ascription of a value-property to an action or person, while depending on my subjective experience and judgement, can also be criticized and the question as to whether the action or person merits the value-property-ascription can be asked. While values are subjectively experienced, they also have an objectivity to them in so far as we can ask whether someone really is honest or whether that action really was generous. More basically, their objectivity derives from the fact that human beings in a society can perceive the properties of actions or characters in a manner analogous to how they perceive colours. While our sharing the same basic visual perceptual apparatus is the condition of our shared colour perception, an analogous case can be made for the genesis of our shared capacity for value-perception. McDowell and Wiggins provide accounts of this genesis which are similar in important respects. Both of them, for example, argue for a naturalistic understanding of this account of the phenomenology of value experience that resists the reductivist terms of a natural science.

Wiggins develops his account of our shared capacity for value-perception in 'A Sensible Subjectivism' and 'Moral Cognitivism, Moral Relativism, and Motivating Moral Beliefs'. He shows how a historical social process can lead to the establishment of shared moral responses to inter-subjectively discernible features that engage our sentiments or feelings. This process 'creates a form of life that invests certain features of people, acts and situations with the status of values' (Wiggins 1990: 79). In growing up within such a form of life, Wiggins says, our original participation in a general way of feeling and of being motivated leads to us 'finding' or 'discovering' that X deserves such and such a response, or has such and such a value. Wiggins also defends this moral phenomenology by arguing for its naturalist credentials along Humean but avowedly cognitivist lines—he claims Hume has never deserved the hostility of moral cognitivists. Wiggins argues, like Griffin, that if value properties are not replaceable by physicalistic/scientific explanations, then they are making a difference. But the values Wiggins (and McDowell) are talking about are, of course, rather different from the prudential values embedded in human nature of which Griffin speaks. They are not all prudential, and they are not embedded in human nature. Wiggins goes on to claim that value properties reveal how human beings respond not only to natural features of the world, but 'to features that mind itself, as it has taken on a life of its own, has marked out there. Value properties are properties that mind critically delimits and demarcates in the world' (Wiggins 1990: 84). If these properties are indispensable and irreducible, Wiggins concludes that 'this is surely what it is for consciousness not merely to arrive in the natural world, but for it to make itself at home there. By critically determining the presence there of valuational properties, we colonize that natural world' (Wiggins 1990: 84). This grounding of moral phenomenology in human nature and historical social processes is Wiggins's own version of ethical naturalism that rejects any reductivist scientific view of nature—something Wiggins explicitly does on several occasions—in favour of a Humean naturalistic view which 'treats human morality as a certain sort of natural phenomenon, a phenomenon of feeling' (Wiggins 1990: 68). Wiggins thus not only gives an account of how we encounter values in our world; he goes further and tries to provide a genetic, naturalist account of it on the basis of a broader understanding of 'naturalism'.

While Wiggins provides us with a way to understand how an ethical language or web of values in a form of life might have come about, John McDowell provides us with a more detailed account of how human beings become ethical agents. His conception of 'second nature' is central to this account. Drawing on Aristotle's *Nicomachean Ethics*, McDowell paints a picture of how human beings acquire an ethical character through their upbringing. The process involves the moulding of motivational and evaluative propensities which results in the formation of the practical intellect and the concomitant acquisition of practical wisdom or *logos* (*phronēsis*). The virtuous character that is acquired does not consist merely of habitual inclinations, but of a sensitivity to certain kinds of reasons for acting. Both motivational and evaluative propensities are shaped:

> In acquiring one's second nature—that is, in acquiring *logos*—one learned to take a distinctive pleasure in acting in certain ways, and one acquired conceptual equipment suited to characterize a distinctive worthwhileness one learned to see in such actions, that is, a distinctive range of reasons one learned to see for acting in those ways. (McDowell 1998: 188)

Beyond the affective and cognitive shaping that comes with an ethical upbringing, McDowell is here pointing to another fundamental feature of an ethical outlook: its autonomous nature. The reasons to which we become sensitive are interrelated and mutually supporting—they constitute their own form of *logos*. McDowell's analysis is of a second nature of virtue, which he recognizes as one possibility among many (McDowell 1998: 188–9, 194). Now on the Aristotelian conception, virtue is unified. One is not sensitive to virtues one by one; rather, only someone who possesses them all can possess any one of them fully. As McDowell emphasizes in 'Virtue and Reason', this particular ethical outlook involves the instilling of 'a single complex sensitivity' (McDowell 1998: 53). This sensitivity ultimately amounts to a conception of the kind of life a human being should lead, of how a human being should live. The upshot is that this ethical outlook is not codifiable (McDowell 1998: 57–8). One cannot derive universal principles of action from it which could be rationally justified from an external point of view, for example, as producing the greatest good or as being the most conducive to human flourishing. The rationality of virtue is internal to its associated ethical outlook (McDowell 1998: 71). The example of courage can serve to illustrate this. A courageous action in the face of danger, for example, can also be motivated by benevolence and justice. In addition, as McDowell also emphasizes, 'courageousness is primarily a matter of being a certain kind of person' and this entails not being the kind of person who is 'ready to rethink the rational credentials of the motivations characteristic of being that kind of person, on occasions when acting on those motivations is in some way unattractive' (McDowell 1998: 192). There is, of course, a connection between courage and human interests. As McDowell formulates it, 'human beings need courage if they are to stick to their worthwhile projects, in the face of the motivational obstacle posed by danger'. (McDowell 1998: 191). But this is part of the 'reflective background' of one's second nature and is not directly in play when one acts courageously. One precisely does not engage in a rational weighing of considerations; rather, 'what directly influences the will is the valuations of actions that have come to be second nature'. (McDowell 1998: 191).

Practices, dispositions, virtues all belong to the second nature that we as human beings acquire in our upbringing and this second nature opens us up to a space of reasons which has its own inner rationality or *logos*.[3] McDowell seeks to secure the autonomy of the 'space of reasons'[4] from the space of nature *qua* natural scientific intelligibility (McDowell 1994; McDowell 1996: 236). At the same time, however,

McDowell insists on seeing the ethical as intrinsically bound up with the natural—it does not inhabit some realm of pure practical rationality utterly disconnected from human beings as natural organisms. As McDowell puts it, his proposal is for a 'naturalized' Platonism, not a 'rampant' one (McDowell 1994: 83–4, 91–5). What is key, however, is to carve out a conception of naturalism which is not defined in exclusively natural scientific terms and which preserves the intelligibility and integrity of the space of reasons particular to the ethical. Hence his call for an expansion of our conception of what is natural, just like Griffin, is to include more than what is intelligible in exclusively natural scientific terms. The concept of 'second nature' is his candidate for showing how the space of reasons and the space of nature can be joined. Human beings' capacity to be responsive to reasons is not something supernatural, it is part of their mode of living, and this mode of living corresponds to the specifically human way of actualizing themselves as animals (McDowell 1994: 78). It is through human beings' acquisition of a second nature, which cannot 'float free of potentialities that belong to a normal human organism', that they acquire a capacity to be responsive to reasons (McDowell 1994: 84).

McDowell's discussion of the concept of second nature is avowedly focussed on a second nature of virtue, but he clarifies that '[a]ny actual second nature is a cultural product' and that 'some outlooks are informed—as Aristotle's is not—by a lively sense of alternative possibilities for human life, lived out in cultures other than one's own'. (McDowell 1998: 194). What remains common, however, to these cultural products is the basic structure of a second nature. While one could plausibly speak of cultures as inculcating a 'cultural second nature' in its members (allowing naturally for degrees of heterogeneity and pluralism), one can speak of a more specific 'ethical second nature'. Every human being acquires an ethical second nature during childhood and adolescence that comprises the interrelated, and possibly conflicting, values, virtues, goods, rights, behaviours, attitudes, etc. which make up the ethical fabric of that culture. In this respect, one could not have an ethical second nature of virtue alone, for the ethical fabric of a culture cannot possibly consist only of virtues—it must be broader and deeper than this. Similarly, and more obviously, one's upbringing does not impart a stand-alone sense of what is

morally 'right and wrong' or a narrow conception of 'the moral'. Just
as an ethical fabric never in fact consists of a sense of right and wrong
alone, so too is an individual's ethical second nature never reducible
to this. Rather, the sense of right and wrong only makes sense in the
context of the ethical fabric, and one's corresponding ethical second
nature, as a whole. A related crucial feature of an ethical second nature
is the fact that in opening us up to an ethical space of reasons, it is in
fact constitutive of one's sense of the ethical, including the narrowly
moral sense of right and wrong or 'right action'. The very moulding of our motivational and evaluative propensities is what opens up
the ethical for us. Normativity is rooted in the ethical fabric we are
enveloped in as youngsters and the ethical second natures we develop
as a result. Our sense of what is courageous or generous or noble,
for example, is not based on any kind of external and reflective reason
by which we make an evaluation. Rather, our sense will be inner and
unreflective. Naturally, depending on the kind of ethical upbringing
and the individual's own nature, this ethical sensitivity will vary; but
the underlying point is unaffected by this, for no average human
being is without an ethical second nature.

Bernard Williams's discussion of generosity highlights the fact that
a genuinely generous action cannot stem from an external consideration such as feeling one ought to be generous (Williams 1981: 48).
I would like to claim that, in fact, this point applies to the way we
primordially evaluate all ethical actions. Our primordial ability to
recognize and perform actions that are generous, honest, courageous
is from an inner sense of these virtues. The ethical space of reasons
can only be opened up by this kind of inner sense of the ethical. We
perform and have a sense of ethical actions first in a pre-reflective
manner, only later developing a way of understanding and justifying them in a reflective and possibly rule-oriented manner. And it is
that seamless integration of the motivational and evaluative which
endows us with this inner sense of the ethical. Our sense of the normative could thus never be derived from a theory we learn as an
adolescent or adult. As McDowell puts it, reason is not what orders
human beings to join duty's army; rather, 'they were not in a position
to hear its orders until they were already enrolled'. Nevertheless, it is
true that 'their continuing service…is obedience to reason's categorical demands'. (McDowell 1998: 197). It is also the case that reason

and reflection, once acquired, allow us to work on the ethical fabric of our culture, but this important process of criticism and reform is always like Neurath's boat which, while at sea, can only be replaced plank by plank at best (McDowell 1998: 189).

Ethical Naturalism and the Justification of Human Rights

It is the ramifications that these two different conceptions of ethical naturalism have for how we think about the grounds and the grounding of human rights that I will turn to in this final section. I make this perhaps dubious distinction between 'grounds' and 'grounding' for a reason. One possibility to consider is that Griffin's conception of ethical naturalism provides 'grounds' at a theoretical level for working out which human rights really should count as human rights, while the alternative, second-nature conception is better for understanding what is practically needed for a 'grounding' of human rights that is meaningful for peoples and cultures around the world.

In *On Human Rights*, Griffin discusses the two candidates he believes are the only viable ones for bringing about a greater convergence on the justification of human rights. The whole point of his book is to argue that we need a substantive account of human rights, so for this reason early on he casts aside the various other non-substantive accounts of human rights such as John Rawls's 'contractualist account', Charles Beitz's 'legal-functional account', and the 'structural accounts' of Joel Feinberg, Ronald Dworkin, and Robert Nozick (Griffin 2008: 20–8). He characterizes his two favoured accounts as the 'more ethnocentric approach' and the 'less ethnocentric approach'. The first consists in 'the continued spread of the largely Western-inspired discourse of human rights' of which Griffin's account is meant to be seen as the latest and fullest articulation. The second is the now well-known model articulated by John Rawls and Charles Taylor of an 'overlapping consensus' on human rights. What qualifies these two candidates for consideration is their acknowledgement of the need for substantive foundations for human rights: 'they involve an agreement directly on values—not on a comprehensive moral view, it is true, but on a particularly deep conception of agency that figures, or can without daunting difficulty come to figure, in all of them. Human rights can, therefore, be directly grounded in values without becoming culturally limited'. (Griffin, 2008: 27).

Griffin believes that his 'more ethnocentric approach' is in fact the better choice for a justification of human rights. But while Griffin clearly acknowledges that it is 'largely Western-inspired'—hence his admission of its greater ethnocentricity than an overlapping consensus model—he believes that it is much less culturally specific than a top-down moral theoretical justification that would rely on a principle like Kant's Universal Principle of Right or Mill's Principle of Utility. This is one of the consequences of grounding human rights in a certain conception of ethical naturalism. The interests and values Griffin has outlined which are embedded in human nature—autonomy, liberty, minimum provision—provide a naturalistic foundation for human rights that can truly claim objectivity. They are the conditions of possibility not of 'human flourishing', for that is beyond the proper moral scope of human rights, but only of 'human status'. (Griffin 2008: 34) As foundational criteria, they allow us to determine what should really be on the list of human rights and they provide guidance in working out practical applications, such as when human rights conflict with other rights and goods, topics Griffin addresses in detail in his book. Nevertheless, Griffin sees his account as Western-inspired and, despite this, as the best option for securing widespread justification. He adduces many practical considerations in support of his position and against the idea that human rights discourse's being Western-inspired should pose a serious obstacle to its international acceptance: Westerners have overcome the alien in order to adopt Eastern religions, so why can't Easterners 'in the case of much more accessible Western human rights?'; the oft-repeated belief of Rawls that 'a radical inter-society pluralism of conceptions of justice and the good' is 'a pervasive and ineradicable feature of international life' is exaggerated; human rights are not absolute, for there is much 'flexibility and qualification' where other conditions can 'outweigh or qualify human rights'. (Griffin 2008: 137–8). Griffin also raises a key objection to the less ethnocentric approach of the overlapping consensus model. He characterizes this model in the following way:

> The less ethnocentric approach…would come down to finding local values similar to the Enlightenment values of autonomy, liberty,

justice, fairness, and so on. It would look for local counterparts of whatever Western values back human rights. It would then have to rely on the indigenous population's seeing how valuable these values or close counterparts of them are, and how they can serve as the ground of human rights. (Griffin, 2008: 139).

* * *

Griffin maintains that while this might lead to agreement on basically the same list of rights, the underlying values might in fact diverge, and this is precisely what his account has sought to render determinate. For 'a useful human rights discourse is not made possible just by agreeing on the *names* of the various rights.… We need also to be able to determine a fair amount of their content to know how to settle some of the conflicts between them'. (Griffin 2008: 140). This is why the more ethnocentric approach is to be preferred. In specifying the foundational values of autonomy, liberty, and minimum provision, it provides the required content.

Now on the alternative conception of ethical naturalism that was developed in the second section of this paper, the clear preference would be for the overlapping consensus model. While Griffin's model might be seen to provide a convincing account of the basic human interests that are at stake in human rights, and of the associated values of autonomy, liberty, and minimum provision, locating these as 'deeply embedded in human nature', as part of a complete, naturalistic account of what is required for human status is not enough to render it truly amenable to widespread justification. The main reason for this is that Griffin is still asking people to assume an objectively rational stance and develop an understanding of a theoretical account of human nature, or rather, 'normative agency', and therein find the justification for their belief in, and commitment to, human rights. But as the second-nature conception of ethical naturalism shows, the values that Griffin believes people have a natural sensitivity to are in fact accessed via a process of ethical formation in upbringing whereby they are initiated into the ethical fabric of their community. The closest that Griffin comes to showing an awareness of the primordially inter-subjectively shared and constituted nature of these values is in his discussion of the 'convergence of belief'. But this convergence is based on the erroneous prior idea that sensitivity to values is an individual matter: '[c]ertainly, if the explanation I suggested in the one-person case is plausible, it will be a likely candidate in the many-person case'. (Griffin 1996: 64). Rather, by being initiated into the shared and pre-existing ethical fabric of their community, individuals develop a pre-reflective understanding of the values of autonomy and liberty and this understanding depends on their pre-reflectively grasping a whole host of other values that provide the context without which they would not make sense. These values, in turn, are broader than the prudential values Griffin speaks of, extending to ethical values that are other-regarding. Whereas Griffin must account for the move from the self-interested to the other-regarding, from the prudential to the moral, the second-nature conception sees both kinds of values as interconnected from the very beginning in the web of values constituting the ethical fabric of a community. The underlying point is that it is the shaping of evaluative and motivational propensities that opens one up to the very space of the ethical in the first place. For most people around the planet, the kind of justification favoured by Griffin is simply unfeasible. Although it certainly seems more objective in trying to ground human rights in a naturalistic understanding of basic human interests and values, Griffin is wrong to conclude that it is on the basis of a sensitivity to these prudential values that human beings' ethical nature and agency is founded. Rather, all human beings' sense of normativity or ethical sensitivity is based on the ethical second nature they acquire in childhood and the web of values which they develop in a pre-reflective sense. This is the true basis of any ability they will have to make sense of human rights. The more narrowly moral sense of 'right and wrong' which human rights reflect is one they will have acquired from within their own ethical context, and it will also make sense to them as it relates to the wide range of other broadly ethical values of which they have an understanding. This is also why Griffin's objection that an overlapping consensus will merely amount to a search for 'counterpart individual values' to the values of autonomy, liberty, and minimum provision gets the whole picture wrong. For it is rather a question of seeing how human rights and their moral content can be made to fit into or be contextualized within a pre-existing ethical framework and outlook.

An overlapping consensus model of the justification of human rights thus has better prospects of securing meaningful and widespread justification of human rights. On a practical level, it is the only model that truly reflects and does justice to the way most people acquire, and possess through most of their lives, their ethical sensitivity. While Griffin's account may prove effective at the theoretical level in providing foundational criteria for what does and does not count as a human right, thus rendering the concept more determinate, what the overlapping consensus model recognizes is that true justification of human rights for most people must relate these rights to the thick ethical languages of their communities. This is the insight that underlies the overlapping consensus model. And it is the second-nature conception of ethical naturalism which shows why it is right.

Notes

1. Griffin discusses the move from prudence to morality in section 6.4 of *On Human Rights*. He provides a more extensive discussion in his earlier book, *Value Judgements: Improving Our Ethical Beliefs*.
2. The following draws on DeSouza, 'Pre-Reflective Ethical Know-How' (2013) and DeSouza, 'Charles Taylor and Ethical Naturalism'.
3. This of course does not mean that second nature is not fundamentally related to first nature, for it of course is. As McDowell makes clear: 'the innate endowment of human beings must put limits on the shapings of second nature that are possible for them', in part because second nature works on the motivational tendencies of first nature, but also because, if second nature is subjected to reflective scrutiny, first nature is one of the sources that limits what can intelligibly be a part of it'. (McDowell 1998: 190–1). An important line of inquiry would also seek to understand just how a constructed second nature meshes with an innate first nature, for example, how much what we come to value owes to how impulses are shaped and how much to the nature of those impulses themselves.
4. McDowell draws on the ideas of Wilfrid Sellars here in distinguishing the space of reasons from the space of nature (Sellars 1963).

References

DeSouza, N. 2013. 'Pre-Reflective Ethical Know-How', *Ethical Theory and Moral Practice*, 16(2): 279–94.

DeSouza, N. 'Charles Taylor and Ethical Naturalism', in J.T. Levy and D. Weinstock (eds), *Charles Taylor at 80* (volume in preparation). Montreal, Quebec: McGill-Queen's University Press.

Griffin, J. 1996. *Value Judgement: Improving Our Ethical Beliefs*. Oxford: Clarendon Press.

———. 2008. *On Human Rights*. Oxford: Oxford University Press.

McDowell, J. 1994. *Mind and World*. Cambridge, MA: Harvard University Press.

———. 1996. 'Précis of Mind and World', *Philosophical Issues*, 7: 231–9.

———. 1998. *Mind, Value, Reality*. Cambridge, MA: Harvard University Press.

Sellars, W. 1963. 'Empiricism and the Philosophy of Mind', in *Science, Perception, and Reality*, pp. 127–96. Atascadero, CA: Ridgeview.

Wiggins, D. 1987. *Needs, Values, Truth*. Oxford: Clarendon Press.

———. 1990. 'Moral Cognitivism, Moral Relativism, and Motivating Moral Beliefs', *Proceedings of the Aristotelian Society*, 91: 61–85.

Williams, B. 1981. 'Utilitarianism and Moral Self-Indulgence', in *Moral Luck*, pp. 40–53. Cambridge: Cambridge University Press.

3

Two Concepts of Overlapping Consensus

Jay Drydyk

For the pre-eminent thinkers of Indian modernity, Ananya Vajpeyi has observed, the *swa* (self) and *raj* (rule) of the *swarāj* (independence) movement had come apart. 'They understood, each in his own way...that raj would have to be found in the future, that swa would be discovered in the past, and that the effort made in the present was itself the necessary but forever ambiguous ligature between past and future, between swa and raj, between self and sovereignty.'[1] The task of tying the two together was made even more difficult by two tendencies. One was a tendency to source philosophical foundations for an independent India from ideas of Western liberalism, a tendency reinforced by the fact that 'Indian youth from elite families were taught to think like Englishmen...estranged from Indian traditions by both force of habit and free choice'. (Vajpeyi 2012: xvi) It was equally problematic that 'the traditions that had formed the selfhood of Indians in the centuries leading up to colonial rule were themselves in a severe state of crisis...atrophied from internal decay'.

(Vajpeyi 2012: xiv). The greats of Indian modernity responded to this conundrum by re-appropriating and reinterpreting Indian traditions of moral and political thought with astounding creativity.

Why? Why bother with traditions? Vajpeyi provides convincing answers: 'All five of the founders were acutely aware of the limits of European liberalism in an Indian context, as well as the residual normative appeal of Indian traditions to the people of India'. (Vajpeyi 2012: xviii). Those traditions, 'weakened as they were, were still seen as the repositories of a number of political norms, moral values, and aesthetic resources that, with some effort at revitalization and recalibration, would make sense to, and work for, ordinary Indians because they belonged within India's pre-colonial history and emerged from it into the colonial moment' (Vajpeyi 2012: xviii).

More recently this choice, whether to invoke moral traditions in order to understand and motivate justice, has figured in some important debates within Western political philosophy. These debates centre on some of John Rawls's contentions concerning public reason, the process of rational deliberation on how justice is to be realized within a society. Rawls contended that this deliberation should be based entirely on 'purely political' ideas and that comprehensive moral doctrines should be kept more or less in the background. This provoked a storm of objections, largely from religious thinkers, claiming that their voices would be unfairly disadvantaged if public reason followed the Rawlsian model.[2]

Tensions between the universality of human rights and the diversity of human traditions have long been seen to pose practical problems. However, there is also an underlying epistemological problem. As I will argue and illustrate in the first section of this chapter, having justifications is crucial to human rights. But how will these justifications be made, or, in other words, how can we know what our human rights are? Standardly, knowing something is taken to mean not just believing something that is true, but doing so for the right reasons. Must human rights, then, be justified to everyone for the same reasons? But not everyone will have the same reasons, if they follow their own values and moral paradigms.[3] This generates what I will present, in the first section, as the 'dilemma of pluralism'. My goal in this chapter is to examine two concepts of overlapping consensus with a view to assessing how well they can resolve this dilemma.

These two concepts of 'overlapping consensus' have been given to us by John Rawls and Charles Taylor. Rawls proposed that we must start with agreement on 'purely political' premises that do not invoke divisive moral, metaphysical, or religious ideas. The Taylor model seems more open to diversity of opinion on this level and instead seeks agreement on broad understandings of how we all need to be protected (even though these understandings may be realized somewhat differently in different places). The Taylor model is superior in one way: it provides greater recognition to people for their distinctive moral perspectives. Less clear is how it promotes agreement at all. I will argue that scope for disagreement can be reduced if the parties form a further consensus on harm, agreeing to constrain and shape their high-level moral ideas so as to avoid consequences that would cause unequal and avoidable harm and neglect. This alternative, which I call 'responsible pluralism', promises to resolve the dilemma of pluralism in a way that the two conceptions of overlapping consensus cannot.

Justifiability and the Dilemma of Pluralism

Justifiability is especially important for human rights. In fact, in a certain sense, justification is intrinsic to their existence. Before they are realized in law, human rights come to life as bare 'moral guarantees' (Nickel 2007; Nickel 1992). Such guarantees are typically advocated for some time before they are formally recognized and enforced, and during this period of advocacy they can be said to exist in no sense other than that they are justified. Similarly, in cases where human rights break down (for example, genocide, failed states, repression), it remains the case that human rights are violated, though they are no longer in force. Both before and after human rights are in force, they have a precarious and immaterial existence that consists of nothing more than their justifiability. For human rights, to be is to be justified.

The justification relation also has a precarious structure. Human rights are universal. Hence they need to be justified by diverse communities with a great many different moral perspectives. Are human rights to be grounded on these values and ideas—the ones that people actually believe and use? If so, is it reasonable to expect the same conclusions to result from these very diverse moral premises?

Alternatively, suppose we allow that human rights can have some justifications that do not rest on people's most familiar and trusted moral values and paradigms. Then we face another question: is it reasonable to expect people to uphold human rights if their public justification has little to do with their own moral outlooks? Let us consider this dilemma more closely.

When we recognize a society as morally pluralistic, what kinds of differences do we see? There would likely not as often be differences in the moral rules being followed, as much as in the broader conceptions that people use to discuss, explain, and interpret those rules. There is little disagreement on the idea that killing human beings is wrong, but differences emerge on the question of why this is wrong. Some would say it is because our lifespan should depend on God's will, not the will of other human beings (Locke 1980: 6). Others would say that a world in which anyone is permitted to kill anyone else is not a world anyone could accept, or wish upon anyone else. Still others might derive it from the thought that doing harm to any living being is wrong.

Moreover, our moral paradigms are also different 'in kind'. Some rely on distinctive ideas or procedures (for example, golden rule, compassion), others are informed by their traditions (for example, Judaic, Cree, Akan, Jain), while others are inspired by exemplary leaders (for example, Jesus, Buddha) or thinkers (for example, Aristotle, Kant). Each of us finds some of these ways of moral thinking more familiar and plausible than others. Those who bother to find out about other moral paradigms, beyond those that are most familiar to them, would probably find them surprisingly reliable at avoiding erroneous conclusions, so that these various ways of moral thinking turn out, after all, to support a surprisingly large common morality. Nevertheless, some people also find their distinctive moral paradigm to be an important marker of their personal or group identities.

Now consider how human rights might be justified in a world that is pluralistic in the way I have described. One question we face is whether human rights should be justified pluralistically, based on all the various moral perspectives that people actually use and trust. From either answer to this question—yes or no—worrisome consequences seem to follow.

Suppose we say yes, human rights must be supported by all reliable moral outlooks. From a logical point of view, it might seem a rather unlikely outcome that many different sets of premises should all converge[4] on the same conclusions. For all we know, some moral perspectives, though reliable on other questions, might be hostile to human rights, or they might argue for achieving the goals of human rights by different means. Ambiguities are also possible, so that any one moral outlook might contain both anti-human-rights and pro-human-rights tendencies. In that case we might get dissenting overlaps instead of overlapping consensus; we have dissenting overlaps, when, for instance, some liberals and some Christians might jointly support social, economic, and cultural rights, while other liberals and Christians might jointly oppose them.

The other horn of the dilemma is also worrisome. Suppose we answer no, human rights do not need to be supported by every reliable way of moral thinking. That would mean building support for human rights on some consensus, a single set of reasons that everyone affirms. The worry is, how strongly will everyone believe this justification and the consensus on which it rests, especially if it includes moral ideas that are foreign to some moral outlooks? If belief is weak, so will motivation be weak, and as a result we may find that while human rights are affirmed, they are only weakly upheld. Worse, they may be perceived as foreign impositions that are lacking in cultural legitimacy (An-Na'im 1992: 20; An-Na'im 1990). As I noted above, identities can be bound up with shared values and paradigms; shared ways of moral thinking become ingredients in shared ideas of what it is to be a good person, which in turn can shape our shared ideas of who we are as a group. If, for a group, there is no strong connection between upholding human rights and being who they are, and want to be, then they might not be as strongly motivated to uphold and promote human rights (Barnhart 2004: 2). Arguably the freedom to be who we are and want to be is as a kind of cultural liberty (UNDP 2004), essential to human rights thinking, and in that case the problem is compounded.

Thus we face a dilemma. Either pluralistic justification based on all moral outlooks is required for human rights, or it is not. If it is required, is it reasonable to expect convergence? If it is not required, how can the resulting problems of cultural liberty, identity, and motivation be resolved?

Rawls

Although the phrase 'overlapping consensus' appeared initially in *A Theory of Justice* (Rawls 1971: 387–8), it was some fifteen years later that Rawls developed the idea more fully. In 1999, Charles Taylor introduced a quite different idea of 'unforced consensus' on human rights. Despite Taylor's claim that the two ideas are similar, there are actually some very important differences between them, and these differences are especially apparent in the context of the pluralistic dilemma, for which the two ideas support two quite different solutions. Taylor's idea supports a strategy of convergence[5] on human rights from the values and moral paradigms that people actually hold and use, while Rawls calls for a strategy of consensus based on purely political values, relegating people's non-political values and moral thinking to the background, where he hoped the needs of motivation, identity, and cultural liberty might still be met.

Rawls's strategy was one of several innovations he introduced in the 1980s as he adopted a new conception of political philosophy, captured by the slogan 'political, not metaphysical'. The goal of political philosophy, he thought, should not be asserting the 'truth' of a conception of just and right social organization (Rawls 1985: 230). That, he thought, should be left for citizens to consider, guided by their own moral outlooks, which will be informed by diverse moral, religious, and philosophical doctrines (Rawls 1987: 12). Instead, political philosophy should seek ideas of social cooperation, to be underwritten by state power that can enjoy widespread moral allegiance on the part of citizens (Rawls 1987: 2, 21). 'Moral' allegiance means having not merely prudential motives but moral reasons for supporting and willingly following the norms of state and society (Rawls 1985: 230, 235), rather than rejecting or resisting them.

Thus a central question of political philosophy is: what kinds of ideas can elicit this kind of allegiance? Rawls proposed that these are normative ideas pertaining only to state-enforced social arrangements (Rawls 1989: 241). In any society with a history of democratic rule, one can expect to find 'not only some public understanding of, but also some allegiance to, democratic ideals and values as realized in existing political institutions'. (Rawls 1987: 2). By 'values' let us mean beliefs about what is valuable and important in a certain range of life activities. (While such an understanding of 'values' is not endorsed explicitly by Rawls, neither does he contradict it.) Thus, democratic values are beliefs about what is valuable and important to have and to do, with regard to living in a democracy. Political values are beliefs about what is valuable and important to have and to do in that portion of social life that is regulated by the state; the belief that it is valuable and important for the state to protect and regulate freedom of speech in social life is a political value in this sense, the value of free speech. In addition to such values, political ideas would also include norms (such as ideals and rules or principles) for this sphere of life.

This class of political ideas stands in contrast with the class of non-political moral ideas. Some of these will be action-guiding throughout life, not merely in one sphere or another, and Rawls has called these 'comprehensive'. For instance, the Kantian ideal of autonomy is held to be valuable and important throughout life, as is John Stuart Mill's conception of individuality. These are not limited political values, but unrestricted or comprehensive values. Similarly, the categorical imperative and the utility principle are not merely political; they are unrestricted or comprehensive principles. Likewise, if one follows Jesus or Buddha as a model of moral virtue, one is not likely to do so in just one sphere of life (for example, politics, or the family, or business), but rather throughout life, and so moral ideals like these are also unrestricted or comprehensive.

Rawls argues that it is only the former, political ideas, restricted in scope to the political domain, which can justify the kind of moral allegiance to state and society that political philosophy seeks. This is the case not because the comprehensive ideas are unrestricted in scope but because of their specificity and diversity—in short, because there are so many of them. To illustrate: the value of Kantian autonomy will appeal mainly to Kantians, Millian individuality mainly to liberal individualists, Buddhist compassion mainly to Buddhists, and Christian love mainly to Christians. None of these values will, on its own, appeal to every citizen, or even to an overwhelming majority, as long as citizens are free to choose among them. On the other hand, denying free choice among them by punishing and deterring interest in all but one 'could be maintained only by the oppressive use of state power' (Rawls 1987: 4), which is ultimately unsustainable, as modern political history shows. Therefore, it is only political values and norms that can give reason for widespread allegiance to a state and social structure.

This line of thinking leaves only one option for resolving the pluralistic dilemma. It is not possible for human rights to be justified entirely within the reliable unrestricted or comprehensive moral thinking that people actually use. Instead, justification must be based on widespread consensus about political values and norms providing moral reasons for widespread allegiance to specific political and social arrangements. Justification for human rights (among other social arrangements) must be based fundamentally on this consensus rather than pluralistic convergence.

Nevertheless, Rawls recognized that diversity of moral thinking is not a temporary phenomenon; rather, this 'fact of pluralism' is 'a permanent feature of the public culture in democratic societies' (Rawls 1987: 4). It is not reasonable to suppose that people would simply stop thinking in these ways about state and society. How would their unrestricted moral thinking cohere with their political thinking? Moral and political values might conflict insofar as people's morality tells them that their allegiance to state and society is somehow immoral (as pacifists feel when their taxes support wars, or as fundamentalists feel in a secular state). Incoherence between people's moral thinking and their specifically political values and norms would likely weaken their allegiance to state and society, since while their political values may continue to give some reason for continued support and compliance, their moral thinking gives reason for opposition or resistance. It is a fair interpretation of Rawls, then, to say that his longstanding concerns about 'stability' are primarily concerns about the stability of citizens' moral allegiance[6] to their state and social structure.

Promoting such stability is the role which Rawls assigns to overlapping consensus.[7] The consensus precedes the overlaps: what Rawls had in mind is that, before applying their more comprehensive moral thinking, people already accept at least the main lines of a political and social structure on the basis of shared political values and norms. The overlaps occur in so far as people call upon their more comprehensive but unshared patterns of moral thinking to derive further support for these political values and norms, and the broad conception of justice that they support. 'An overlapping consensus exists in a society when the political conception of justice that regulates its basic institutions is endorsed by each of the main religious, philosophical, and moral doctrines likely to endure in that society from one generation to the next.' (Rawls 1989: 233 n. 1)

The pluralistic dilemma is to be resolved fundamentally by consensus, but with the support of convergence from distinct moral outlooks. Consensus is fundamental in a number of ways. One is that consensus on political values and norms should provide a form of political and social structure with its primary ground independent of unrestricted moral thinking. Convergence is limited to providing further support and reducing strains on allegiance. But consensus is also fundamental insofar as it motivates the search for convergence. Rawls's thought was that moral doctrines are open to interpretation, and if one has strong independent political reasons for allegiance to a type of state and social structure, then one might wish (for the sake of consistency) to seek interpretations of those doctrines that support, or at least permit, this structure (Rawls 1987: 19).

Consensus is also fundamental in a third way, which is expressed in the principle that Rawls referred to as 'the proviso'. It is that 'reasonable comprehensive doctrines, religious or nonreligious, may be introduced in public political discussion at any time, provided that in due course proper political reasons—and not reasons given solely by comprehensive doctrines—are presented that are sufficient to support whatever the comprehensive doctrines introduced are said to support'. (Rawls 1997: 783–4). The meaning of this, one suspects, is that comprehensive doctrines can be introduced as long as they are redundant. There is some truth to this suspicion: though admitted into political discussion, comprehensive doctrines are still to be excluded from political justification. 'It is important also to observe that the introduction into public political culture of religious and secular doctrines, provided the proviso is met, does not change the nature and content of justification…[which] is still given in terms of a family of reasonable political conceptions of justice'. (Rawls 1997: 784).

Engagement or Exclusion?

In the context of pluralism, approaches to human rights justification that give priority to consensus face three risks. First, if justification is not based primarily on people's actual moral outlooks, they may not be as well motivated to realize or even respect human rights. Second, if a moral outlook is perceived as an element of a group's identity, they may perceive the human rights enterprise not as their work but as the work of outsiders. Third, if they are not permitted to use their moral outlooks when they do participate in the human rights enterprise, their cultural freedom—freedom to be who they are and who they wish to be—is diminished. How well does the Rawlsian approach manage these risks?

One might say that the Rawlsian approach attempts to solve the problem of identity by means of hyphenation. I have stressed, perhaps more than other commentators have done, that overlapping consensus begins with a consensus. Citizens may indeed carry out their moral thinking in diverse ways, but this does not prevent them from having shared values and norms concerning what is valuable and right in one sphere of life, namely those parts of social life that are important enough to be regulated by the state. These values and norms shape their shared conception of how that sphere of life ought to be ordered, and they justify people's allegiance to a society that is ordered in that way. Since people already share political values, justification does not need to rely in the first instance on their wider moral thinking. The latter provides, at most, further support for already shared political thinking.

Of course, it is possible that the wider moral thinking of some will contradict the shared political thinking. However, Rawls argued that shared democratic values and ideas are held strongly enough to motivate people to reinterpret their wider moral thinking, if necessary, to harmonize with the requirements of democratic societies.

Further motivation for such harmonization may also be provided by certain benefits that democratic societies provide. (i) Realizing a liberal conception of justice establishes equal basic liberties and gives priority to them; as a result, citizens enjoy mutual respect. (ii) Mutual respect is also enjoyed in so far as the realization of justice is guided by public reason, in which public policies are chosen that are seen to be supported by the best reasons, based only on shared values and common knowledge, including non-controversial results of science. Mutual respect is ensured insofar the political conclusions are drawn from premises and procedures that anyone could accept; premises and procedures that could not be accepted by all are excluded. 'Arguments supporting political judgments should, if possible, not only be sound but such that they can be publicly seen to be sound.' (Rawls 1987: 22). Public reason, as Rawls conceived it, prevents particular, unshared thinking from becoming privileged by the simple, if draconian, tactic of excluding it from justification. (iii) Public reason should also promote certain 'cooperative virtues' in political life: 'reasonableness and a sense of fairness, a spirit of compromise and a readiness to meet others halfway, all of which are connected with the willingness if not the desire to cooperate with others on political terms that everyone can publicly accept consistent with mutual respect.' (Rawls 1987: 17). A political culture possessing these virtues can be seen as advantageous by anyone, Rawls thought, no matter what their particular values and moral paradigms might be. (iv) Notice, also, that all three outcomes facilitate people's development and use of their 'two moral powers': a capacity for seeking reciprocal agreements (sometimes called a 'sense of justice') and a capacity to set one's own goals, to reduce tensions among them, and to find effective means of achieving them ('rationality'). Rawls held that 'citizens are thought to have and to want to exercise these powers whatever their more comprehensive religious, philosophical, or moral doctrine may be'. (Rawls 1989: 23).

All of this goes some distance towards managing the risks that are attendant on a consensus strategy for solving the pluralistic dilemma. The first risk is motivation: if human rights are not to be justified on the basis of people's own values and moral paradigms, then they will be less well motivated to support human rights, especially when tensions arise between rights and morality. But the hyphenated Rawlsian citizens not only have purely political values that provide strong independent support for human rights, they also have reasons for interpreting their values and moral paradigms in ways that harmonize with human rights; in return, Rawlsian citizens are accorded mutual respect as citizens.

The identity problem may also be resolvable by the strategy of hyphenation. Democracy will not appear to be an alien imposition on utilitarians, for example, if they think of themselves as utilitarian-democrats—and likewise for other groups that identify themselves by specific values and moral paradigms.

The third risk, I suggested, is one of exclusion, as a restriction on cultural freedom, which I characterized loosely as people's freedom to be who they are and who they want to be. In so far as a public's shared values include freedom of conscience and freedom of expression, and overlapping consensus harmonizes these values with the various moralities within a society, people's freedom to express and live those moralities is protected, and this is a fundamental protection of their cultural freedom. On the other hand, the price that people pay for this protection is a form of political exclusion. It is not the citizens who are excluded, but rather their broader values and moral paradigms. Though these are not excluded from political 'discussion', they are excluded from justification. Of course, not every type of exclusion is wrong, and not every type of cultural freedom ought to be protected. One can easily imagine expressions of cultural freedom that are antisocial. The critical question is whether this exclusion, the exclusion of broader values and moral paradigms from political justification, is warranted.

Far from being warranted, this exclusion, I find, is ineffective, excessive, and unnecessary. It is ineffective because it does not remove all of the threats to moral allegiance that it purports to remove. It is excessive because it would exclude even points on which all moral values and paradigms agree. It is unnecessary because Rawls's arguments that it is necessary are fundamentally unsound. I will discuss each of these failings in turn.

Ineffective

The goal of the consensus Rawls seeks is to give all citizens moral reasons for allegiance to a society and state and to the standards of justice which they are to achieve. Only political values and norms can achieve this, since people are divided by their broader values and moral paradigms—for instance, Kantians will not accept utilitarian reasons for allegiance, Buddhists will not accept a Christian rationale, and so on. However, limiting this political discourse to political values and norms does not screen out all threats to allegiance. We can imagine a person who met all of Rawls's criteria for reasonableness yet held anti-secular political values. This person might believe that states and societies ought to be held accountable to spiritual standards. This person might also modestly acknowledge that there is a plurality of views about what those standards are, some people conceiving them as enlightenment, others as the will of God. But this person's view is simply that aspiring to meet spiritual standards, whatever they might be, is valuable and important in political life. Hence a purely secular state will not win this person's moral allegiance. And yet, the values underlying this are limited to the political sphere. No comprehensive doctrines are involved. Limiting discussion to values and norms that are purely political in scope does not eliminate conflicts in allegiance, in this case because secular democratic ideas will not appeal to people with anti-secular spiritual values, nor will ideas of spiritually guided politics appeal to people with secular democratic values. Stalemates such as this can continue even when unrestricted moral values and paradigms are excluded from discussion. Hence this exclusion is not as effective as Rawls thought at promoting moral allegiance.

Excessive

Restricting discussion to ideas that are purely political in scope excludes some ideas that are not comprehensive doctrines. Peter Singer famously introduced the idea that if we can prevent bad from happening, without sacrificing anything of comparable moral importance, we ought morally to do so. Suppose we allow that 'bad' and 'comparable moral significance' should be open to the various interpretations they would receive within various moral outlooks— as Singer himself has proposed (Singer 1993: 230–1). In that case Singer's harm principle does not presuppose any specific comprehensive doctrines, and so it would not be divisive. Yet it is not limited in scope to matters political: it applies as much to individuals as to states. For that reason it would be excluded from political discourse. But if the purpose of these exclusions is to reduce conflicts of allegiance based on opposing comprehensive doctrines, the exclusion in this case is excessive.

Unnecessary

Moreover, the premise that comprehensive doctrines are divisive should be given second thought. Among some of Rawls's formulations of this claim there is an equivocation. He sometimes claims that a single comprehensive doctrine cannot be supported as the single rationale for a conception of justice: 'A public and workable agreement on a single general and comprehensive conception could be maintained only by the oppressive use of state power' (Rawls 1987: 5). But elsewhere he asserts, less plausibly, that no such idea can provide any basis for a conception of justice: 'as a practical political matter no general moral conception can provide a publicly recognized basis for a conception of justice in a modern democratic state'. (Rawls 1987: 5). Rawls overlooked the possibility that a comprehensive doctrine can provide 'a' basis without providing 'the' basis for a model of justice. This obtains when a doctrine is only one among several bases for a model of justice. Suppose it is apparent that a plurality of moral outlooks all support particular standards of justice; as long as everyone can see that their outlook is included, everyone has some reason for allegiance that is part of the public justification. In other words, the full public justification in this case is a composite of, say, Kantian, utilitarian, and religious justifications. Because members of each group are aware that their justification is included, the composite public justification gives everyone reason for allegiance to the standards of justice. In this way, the claim that 'as a practical political matter no general moral conception can provide a publicly recognized basis for a conception of justice in a modern democratic state' (Rawls 1987: 5) is simply false. Promoting allegiance to standards of justice does not require excluding the plurality of moral outlooks from the public justification of that model. The exclusion is unnecessary.

One response that comes readily to mind is Rawls's often repeated admonition that in order to reach agreement one must start from agreement (Rawls 1971: 580ff). Strictly speaking, this is not true. A group can have different reasons for wanting to adopt a common course of action, and it is not required that each member must agree with each reason. Analytically, we might say that they all believe that either one reason or some of others are true; what they share is belief in a disjunction. If each gives reason for the same conclusion, then from this and the disjunction, the conclusion follows. This takes the common argument form of disjunctive syllogism, for example, p or q, if p then r, if q then r, therefore r.

It could be objected that such a disjunction commits each member of the group to accepting some other reason, from the disjunction, if it is shown that this person's preferred reason is not true. This might be a stronger commitment than members of this group might actually be willing to make. For instance, Kantians and utilitarians may agree, for their own reasons, that murder should be a crime. Both can accept that either Kantianism or utilitarianism is true, from which it follows that they agree on criminalizing murder. But can they really accept the disjunction? This would imply that if it turns out that Kantianism is mistaken, then Kantians would accept utilitarianism. But this could be too much to expect.

The picture changes favourably if we concern ourselves not with truth but reliability. We find a moral outlook reliable if we find that it is very likely to lead people to true or correct moral judgments. Since Kantianism and utilitarianism agree far more often than they disagree about which courses of action are right and which are wrong, it would be unreasonable for either one to deny that the other is reliable. If the adherents of any specific moral outlook lose confidence in it, or if they find it difficult to justify a particular course of action from it, they may still accept that course of action by recognizing that it is supported by many other outlooks that are reliable. Accepting that another outlook is reliable does not mean giving up on one's own, nor does it mean failing to think for oneself. Actually, the assessment of reliability must involve thinking for oneself; one must determine how likely it is that the other outlook will generate judgments that, by one's own reckoning, are true. Thus reliable moral outlooks can be invoked in public justification without threatening anyone's autonomy and without weakening anyone's moral allegiance to a model of justice that is justified in this way.

This alternative would seem to offer a solution to the pluralistic dilemma that is in several respects superior to Rawlsian public reason and overlapping consensus. Rawlsian public reason offers citizens mutual respect of a rather restricted kind: each is respected with an assurance that political action and governance will not be guided by beliefs, values, and norms that they do not share. In the alternative that I have just sketched, this very thin mutual respect is replaced by mutual understanding, which includes both mutual recognition and mutual appreciation.

Mutual recognition comes with including the plurality of moral outlooks as bases for justifying judgments[8] about social arrangements. In response, it could be argued that this offers no real advantage over Rawlsian public reason, which accords recognition in its own way, under 'the proviso'.

However, what mutual understanding adds to recognition is an appreciation that the moral outlooks which are included in public justification are not merely reasonable, but reliable. Rawls is clear that there must be an explanation of moral disagreements that does not impugn the competency of their adherents to participate in public reason or in the prior discussion of fair terms of social and political cooperation (Rawls 1989: 236). Still, acknowledging that others are not incompetent falls considerably short of appreciating that their outlooks are reliable.

Thus where Rawlsian public reason offers mutual respect, the alternative offers moral recognition, and where the Rawlsian view calls upon citizens to recognize that fellow citizens with different moral outlooks are not incompetent as discussion partners seeking fair terms of cooperation, the alternative invites them to consider how reliable those other outlooks may be. In the alternative, a public can be seen by its members as a plural subject, a 'we' who have different reasons for reaching some of the same judgments about how their social relations should be organized. Each can say, for instance: 'We oppose slavery, for different reasons. Some of them I agree with, others I do not. Nevertheless, all of them are supported by moral outlooks that are reliable'.

This alternative also brings to light some further weaknesses in the Rawlsian solution to the pluralistic dilemma. With respect to cultural freedom, the Rawlsian approach excludes the use of particular moral outlooks from public justification of standards of justice and means of meeting them. In discussing these justifications, adherents of those outlooks cannot be who they are and who they want to be, as moral thinkers, unless, like Rawlsians, they have reason to endorse this exclusion. On the alternative approach, not only is there no exclusion, but the plurality of outlooks can be appreciated as reliable.

Taylor and Beyond

The alternative approach that I have just presented is similar to that of Charles Taylor. One difference, however, is that Taylor did not distinguish his view explicitly as an alternative to that of Rawls as, I think, he should have done. Indeed, Taylor seems to have overlooked a fundamental difference between the two: whereas Rawls insists that a public must begin from a consensus on shared political values and norms to reach consensus on standards of justice, Taylor expects that consensus will form not at the beginning but only at the end, over normative standards, such as human rights standards. The ways in which these standards are realized in different societies may diverge again (Taylor 1999: 143). So Taylor's strategy for resolving the pluralistic dilemma is one of convergence from divergent moral outlooks, not one that starts from consensus over shared values, and in that respect his repeated suggestions of similarity with Rawls are quite misleading (Taylor 1999: 124, 133, 143).

Taylor's most important contribution to this debate may be his advocacy of mutual understanding. His argument has two parts. First, it is unrealistic to expect any consensus to be permanent: any consensus that is achieved concerning standards for justice will need to be reinterpreted from time to time as new circumstances and problems arise to which it must apply. If the adherents of different moral outlooks have little confidence in each other's capacity for arriving at the right moral judgements, they will have equally little enthusiasm for engaging in such discussions with them. 'If the sense is strong on each side that the spiritual basis of the other is ridiculous, false, inferior, unworthy, these attitudes cannot but sap the will to agree.' (Taylor 1999: 138). Rawlsian public reason does go some distance towards avoiding this extreme case insofar as citizens accept pluralism as reasonable—the result of people being reasonable and rational in different historical circumstances. But it does not go so far as assessing and appreciating others' moral outlooks as reliable, and so it allows for considerable lack of confidence that their adherents—Kantians, Buddhist, Muslims, etc.—will be reliable partners in working out new interpretations of the consensus as they are needed. Without confidence in their reliability, one could not expect successful reformulation except on the basis of considerable luck. The Rawlsian response is that one need not rely entirely on luck, because the parties are after all rational and reasonable, and, being reasonable, they are seeking terms of cooperation that would be acceptable to each if carried out by all. On the other hand, seeking and finding are not the same: people can be disposed to seek many things—wealth, fame, and love among them—without being very good at finding them. Whether they are very good at finding the right moral judgments is our concern here, and the ones whose moral thinking is reliable are the ones who are good at this. So it is not just a desire for justice or right social arrangements that matters, but reliability in judging what they are. Confidence in the process of renewing and reinterpreting agreement about what is just and right, therefore, requires confidence that the moral thinking of others is reliable, which is provided by mutual understanding. In this way, mutual understanding is required in order to sustain and renew any consensus that has been achieved over normative social standards, including human rights.

Taylor also argues that there may be some cases in which mutual understanding is needed not only to renew consensus but in order to achieve it. To illustrate this problem, he cites the tensions that can arise between the sorts of gender equality that are required by human rights and the sorts of gender difference that are required by some traditional cultures. Reaching an unforced consensus on the equality rights of women will require considerable reinterpretation of the traditional cultures. However, resistance rather than acceptance will likely result if a tradition as a whole is perceived to be under attack. In cases, like these, mutual understanding is needed if a tradition is to be brought into a consensus (Taylor 1999: 140). Outsiders must convey that the tradition is worth being reinterpreted, and that requires recognizing its broader reliability.

So, in order to renew and extend support for human rights in some cases, and to generate initial support in others, Taylor concludes that mutual understanding of people's moral outlooks is one of the conditions for an unforced consensus on human rights standards.

As a strategy for resolving the dilemma of pluralism, Taylor's approach, which is, properly speaking, one of convergence rather than consensus, does not encounter the problems faced by consensus approaches like that of Rawls. Because the values that people actually hold and the moral paradigms that they actually use are not excluded from the public justification of human rights, the problems of motivation, identity, and cultural freedom do not arise. As I argued previously, this justification will include many arguments that you or I might not accept; nevertheless we, as an inclusive plural subject, can regard all of them to be ours, as a public.

Still, Taylor's approach is not problem-free. The central issue is why different values and moral outlooks can be expected to converge. Is it sheer luck that this occurs? Or are there some underlying facts and circumstances that make convergence, especially on human rights, likely to occur? Not only is the prospect of too little agreement a concern, but, in a different way, so is the prospect of too much agreement a concern. What is to prevent dissenting overlaps in which some adherents of two moral outlooks support a particular right while other adherents of the same outlooks oppose it? For instance, some Christians and Muslims might agree that the right to life forbids capital punishment; others might disagree.

In 'Towards an Unforced Consensus', Taylor suggests that convergence might be promoted by a growing aversion to suffering and pain. 'We are much more concerned about pain and suffering than our forebears,… we see pain and suffering and gratuitously inflicted death in a new light because of the immense cultural revolution that has been taking place in modernity, which I called elsewhere "the affirmation of ordinary life."' (Taylor 1999: 141). Elsewhere he makes clear that this growing concern is not narrowly focused on pain and suffering but extends to 'respect for the life, integrity, and well-being, even flourishing, of others', which, he claims, has become 'perhaps the most urgent and powerful cluster of demands that we recognize as moral concern' (Taylor 1989: 4). Along with this concern for people's well-being, this complex attitude of respect is concerned with their autonomy, whether it is in conceiving of their own good, in finding ways to achieve it, or in exercising their rights. Finally, priority is given to 'ordinary' life (Taylor 1989: 13), to the activities of making a living, taking care of oneself and others, enjoying the company of others, including whatever free-time activities may be feasible, or, in Taylor's somewhat too-succinct phrase, 'production and reproduction'. (Taylor 1989: 23). What makes this a distinctively modern attitude, according to Taylor, is that it displaces any vaunted 'superior' forms of life—often accessible only to elites, as for instance

Aristotle's life of virtue requires sufficient time for contemplation and sufficient money to cultivate and exercise the virtue of 'magnanimity' (comparable in contemporary terms to grand philanthropy). This 'sense of the importance of the everyday in human life…along with the central place given to autonomy…is peculiar to our civilization, the modern West' (Taylor 1989: 14).

Could this complex sense of respect for human beings contribute towards convergence from diverse moral perspectives towards agreement on human rights protections? Several issues could arise. First, aversion to pain, suffering, and other harms is not uniquely modern. There are numerous ancient examples, such as Emperor Ashoka's conversion to Buddhism after witnessing the brutal slaughter he had carried out in the Kalinga war; some of the famous edicts that he subsequently decreed concern protections that we now associate with human rights. Second, Taylor's suggestion is Eurocentric, and unnecessarily so. Steven Pinker has suggested that a decline in violence over the past five hundred years has its roots in more universal features of human psychology (Pinker 2011: Chapter 9).

Third, this complex respect for human beings does not exhaust all of morality, and we must know what kinds of relationships it should have to our other moral ideas, to be confident that it can steer us towards convergence. Taylor himself distinguishes two further dimensions of moral life. (i) Though our respect for others may focus on their ordinary lives, the question of what constitutes a truly good and full life remains open. While some people may frame their idea of a good life specifically as a good ordinary life, others may have higher aspirations. Whereas a tradition may draw attention to some common frame for a good and full life, modernity dissolves these so that our aspirational space is more open. (ii) A third 'axis' of moral life concerns dignity, which might comprise any characteristics people have, which they believe to command the respect and esteem of others.[9] In relation to these two further dimensions of morality, it is not clear how respect for well-being, autonomy, and ordinary life will steer us towards convergence on human rights protections. Much traditional Indian political philosophy was devoted to the principle that living a good and full life meant living according to the duties of one's caste, including the duty of preserving caste relations. The Catholic Church still maintains that a good and full life is properly a heterosexual life. Insofar as these views shape people's views of well-being, legitimate autonomy, and ordinary life, there will be little steering towards convergence on protection against heterosexist or caste repression, because respect for well-being, autonomy, and ordinary life will have been blinded to such repression.

So we are left wondering how Taylor's three axes of moral life must interact, in order to provide a basis for an unforced consensus on human rights.

I would propose a two-part answer. The first part is that respect for well-being and autonomy in ordinary life should be recognized as the trump suit, overriding when necessary ideas of dignity and of a full and good life. The second is that our experience of well-being and autonomy in ordinary life should be robustly independent from moral stipulations: we must be able to learn from our experience of taking care of ourselves and others with our eyes open, not blinkered by moral preconceptions of what it means to live well.

* * *

This would yield more or less what I have called 'responsible pluralism' (Drydyk 2011). This is an approach to public reason in which we commit ourselves to doing two things. The first is to recognize that there are other moral discourses, which, while you or I may not agree with them, nevertheless reliably lead their adherents to moral and normative political judgments that seem correct. Thus humanists and theists (as well as Kantians and utilitarians) who took this approach would commit to recognizing that, while they disagree on some issues, the other party does very often reach the right moral or political conclusions. This is the commitment to pluralism. The second commitment is for each of us to screen out conclusions from our preferred moral discourse that lead to avoidably unequal harm or neglect—based on our experience of taking care of ourselves and each other. Doing this kind of screening is exercising a kind of good judgment. It is a commitment to this kind of good judgement that renders our pluralism responsible.

Unlike the Rawlsian approach, responsible pluralism does not require that standards of human rights and justice be justified by a consensus on purely political values and norms; nor does it exclude moral outlooks from public reason. Hence it does not raise tensions of motivation, identity, or cultural freedom. On the other hand, the commitment to screen out implications of those outlooks that condone or demand avoidable and unequal harm or neglect should reduce the potential for stalemates and dissenting overlaps. Hence these weaknesses of Taylor's approach too may be avoided, or at least mitigated.

Achieving public recognition of harm sometimes requires considerable effort and perseverance. Of the great thinkers of Indian modernity, one was especially aware of the harm suffered under caste, and that was, of course, Ambedkar, who experienced it directly as a Dalit. Nevertheless, along with Gandhi, Rabindranath Tagore, and Jawaharlal Nehru, he displayed formidable perseverance not only in keeping the eyes of India open to the inequalities and ills of caste, not only in screening out implications favourable to caste, but in drawing upon Indian values to forge new ways of moral thinking that demanded removing those inequalities and ills. Their achievements testify to the promise of responsible pluralism.

Notes

1. Vajpeyi is referring to Rabindranath Tagore, M.K. Gandhi, Abanindranath Tagore, Jawaharlal Nehru, and B.R. Ambedkar (Vajpeyi 2012: xiv).
2. For an incisive review and intervention into this debate, see Eberle 2002.
3. By 'values' I mean beliefs about what is valuable and important in life. By 'moral paradigm' I mean something that people can follow in working out what is right and what is wrong. For instance, they might follow a theory, or an exemplary person, or custom, or even myth. By 'moral perspective' or 'moral outlook' I mean a combination of values with a moral paradigm.
4. A strategy of 'convergence' allows a conclusion to be derived from premises that not everyone shares, whereas a strategy of 'consensus' requires the conclusion to be derived from premises that are shared.
5. On the distinction between strategies of consensus and convergence, see note 3, above.
6. I mean 'moral allegiance' in the broadest sense: allegiance based both on specifically political values and norms and on unrestricted or comprehensive moral values and norms.

7. '...the idea of an overlapping consensus is introduced to explain how, given the plurality of conflicting comprehensive religious, philosophical, and moral doctrines always found in a democratic society—the kind of society that justice as fairness itself enjoins—free institutions may gain the allegiance needed to endure over time'. (Rawls 1989: 234).
8. Note I am no longer assuming that justification is sought merely for models or conceptions of justice. These are characteristic of a transcendental institutional approach to justice, rather than a comparative realization-oriented approach as advocated by Amartya Sen. Justification may also be required for more specific judgments about which social changes would render a society 'more just'.
9. Here Taylor stipulates that 'respect' does not mean concern for well-being, autonomy, and ordinary life, as it does in the first 'axis' of moral life. Here, in the third, it refers to attitudinal respect, that is, 'looking up to' someone.

References

An-Na'im, A.A. 1990. 'Problems of Universal Cultural Legitimacy for Human Rights', in A.A. An-Na'im and F.M. Deng (eds), *Human Rights in Africa: Cross-cultural Perspectives*, pp. 331–67. Washington, D.C.: The Brookings Institution.

———. 1992. 'Toward a Cross-Cultural Approach to Defining International Standards of Human Rights: The Meaning of Cruel, Inhuman, or Degrading Treatment or Punishment', in A.A. An-Na'im (ed.), *Human Rights in Cross-Cultural Perspectives: A Quest for Consensus*, pp. 19–43. Philadelphia: University of Pennsylvania Press.

Barnhart, M. 2004. 'An Overlapping Consensus: A Critique of Two Approaches', *The Review of Politics*, 66(2): 257–83.

Drydyk, J. 2011. 'Responsible Pluralism, Capabilities, and Human Rights', *Journal of Human Development and Capabilities*, 12(1): 39–61.

Eberle, C. 2002. *Religious Conviction in Liberal Politics*. Cambridge: Cambridge University Press.

Locke, J. 1980. *Second Treatise on Government*. C.B. Macpherson (ed.). Indianapolis, IN: Hackett Publishing Co.

Nickel, J. 1992. 'Human Rights', in L.C. Becker and C.B. Becker (eds), *Encyclopaedia of Ethics*, pp. 561–5. New York: Garland.

———. 2007. *Making Sense of Human Rights*, 2nd edition. Malden, MA and Oxford: Blackwell.

Pinker, S. 2011. *The Better Angels of our Nature: The Decline of Violence in History and its Causes*. London: Allen Lane.

Rawls, J. 1971. *A Theory of Justice*. Cambridge, Mass.: Harvard University Press.

———. 1985. 'Justice as Fairness: Political not Metaphysical', *Philosophy and Public Affairs*, 14(3): 223–51.

———. 1987. 'The Idea of an Overlapping Consensus', *Oxford Journal of Legal Studies*, 7(1): 1–25.

———. 1989. 'The Domain of the Political and Overlapping Consensus', *New York University Law Review*, 64(2): 233–55.

———. 1997. 'The Idea of Public Reason Revisited', *University of Chicago Law Review*, 64(3): 765–807.

Singer, P. 1993. *Practical Ethics*, 2nd edition. Cambridge and New York: Cambridge University Press.

Taylor, C. 1989. *Sources of the Self: The Making of the Modern Identity*. Cambridge, MA: Harvard University Press.

———. 1999. 'Conditions of an Unforced Consensus on Human Rights', in J. Bauer and D. Bell (eds), *The East Asian Challenge for Human Rights*, pp. 124–44. Cambridge: Cambridge University Press.

United Nations Development Programme (UNDP). 2004. *Human Development Report 2004: Cultural Liberty in Today's Diverse World*. New York: Oxford University Press.

Vajpeyi, A. 2012. *Righteous Republic: The Political Foundations of Modern India*. Cambridge, MA: Harvard University Press.

4

Developmentalism, Human Rights, and Gender Politics

From a Politics of Origins to a Politics of Meanings

Sumi Madhok

I write this in the aftermath of huge public protests that erupted in mainly urban India in the wake of the brutal gang rape of a twenty-three year old woman; the protests were remarkable not only in terms of their numbers despite the state brutality and repression unleashed to suppress them, but also because of unapologetic language of freedom and autonomy that were voiced in these protests. To be sure, some of these demands were couched in the patriarchal language of 'revenge', 'protection', and of 'saving' but these jostled uneasily alongside unequivocal ones for women's right to autonomy, equality, and freedom; freedom to use public spaces, to wear what they wish, and to exercise their rights as citizens without fear, violence, or coercion. Now protests against rape or sexual violence are hardly a new phenomenon. The feminist movement in India has been at the forefront of highlighting the institutional and legal shortfalls in meting out justice to victims of sexual assaults, organizing the first major public demonstrations and protests in 1979–80 against the gender prejudicial interpretation and workings of legal and institutional bodies in the aftermath of the acquittal in the Supreme Court of the policemen involved in the custodial rape of two women, Rameeza Bee and Mathura (John 2002; Ram 2000), both occupying marginal subject positionings—one belonging to a 'tribal' community and the other a poor Muslim—which led to a decade long campaign for legal reforms culminating in the drafting of new legislation intended at 'protecting' women from violence (Agnes 1997). But the December 2012 protests were striking not only because of the language of the demands but also because the thousands of men and women demanding rights and freedom from violence managed to escape— at least to a large extent—the delegitimizing 'Western' tag that had plagued feminist inspired mobilizations of the past. In other words, the rights/human rights they were demanding were not disqualified or disregarded as representing 'Western feminist' ideas of women's rights.

In my view, these December mobilizations present us with yet another occasion through which to consider carefully the framework within which we talk about human rights/rights in 'India and the West'. More specifically, to ask whether these mobilizations in any way displace the framework of a 'politics of origins' that almost always structures discussions of human rights in the 'Non-West'. I suggest that they do. Instead of this near pervasive stranglehold of the 'politics of origins' discourse on rights talk, I propose we focus on a 'politics of meanings'—one that has at its core, a focus on the meanings, subjectivities, ideational and political energies, and cultures that come into being as a result of rights. But of course, such an exercise is not without its risks; in particular, it is vulnerable to orientalist representations, to crude indigenisms, even dangerous neo-nativisms, all of which, pay inadequate attention to the multiple sources and contestations which feed conceptual histories and by failing to attend to the exclusions and 'othering' that occur both within and through the discourse and practice of rights. However, once we have acknowledged and steered clear of these risks, efforts to refuse the originary discourse of human rights opens up new avenues for thinking about human rights politics in different parts of the world.

In this chapter, I attend to some elements of the 'politics of meanings', namely the formation of subjectivities, rights claims, entitlements and participation, subjection, coercion but also new modes of agency that result from a practical and moral encounter with the language of rights. In deploying the phrase 'encounter with rights' I mean to emphasize quite simply that the contact with rights is a deliberate one, and in this chapter, I focus on the encounter with developmentalism, a developmentalism that is embraced by both state and non-state actors including feminist groups. The political and discursive context I write about here is one of an explicitly 'rights based' developmentalism, in particular, the strand of developmentalism explicitly concerned with developing poor women as 'subjects' of development. In this rights encounter, I focus, in particular, on the deployment of specific literal and conceptual languages of rights—both the literal term for a right, which is *haq*, an Urdu/Arabic literal term, used in large parts of Southern Asia, to invoke a right as well as its justificatory premises. But of course, 'haq' is hardly a discrete conceptual term and comes enmeshed in a cluster of conceptual ideas. It is, however, not enough to only speak of literal and conceptual terms alone; one also needs to actively investigate the specific linguistic, sociological, and political histories and practices that underpin and make possible the life worlds of these words, and examine the forms of political cultures, subjectivities, administering practices, and forms of subjection produced by these rights cultures. The empirical and conceptual material in this chapter draws attention to the production of 'vernacular rights cultures' and new gendered subjectivities and forms of subjection that come into being as a result thereof. These rights cultures are co-produced and are a result of various forms of discursive and policy interventions including metropolitan feminist activism, statism, legal constitutionalism, developmentalism, transnational human rights discourses, groups and institutions, and grassroots citizen and feminist organizing. In particular, it draws on ethnographic work conducted since 1998 at two sites in Rajasthan, North-West India: the first, an institutional setting established by a state sponsored programme for women's development and empowerment known as the Women's Development Programme (WDP), Rajasthan, but financed in its initial years by UNICEF;[1] and the second documents rights-based citizen activism and mobilizations to push for expanding constitutional rights guarantees to include rights to food, information, and employment. While the latter has been successful in mounting both a legal and policy challenge to the Indian state—there now exist laws that guarantee rights to information, employment, and also to food—for the purposes of this paper, both sites offer concrete descriptions and images of complex articulations of rights cultures and the subjectivities these engender within specific historical relations of dominance, subjection, materiality, statism, and politics.

On Conceptual Categories, 'Feminist Movement', 'Developmentalism', and 'The West'

Theoretical and empirical discussions of human rights/rights take place in conceptually saturated and 'over-determined' discourse of a 'politics of origins', one which can be entered into only through a clearing exercise or even a refusal; a refusal that ironically only reproduces this originary discourse on human rights all over again. Keeping this risk in my mind, I outline what I mean by a framework of a 'politics of origins'. By it, I simply mean that the guiding assumptions framing rights debates and questions invariably begin with an orientalist assumption common to both the celebrators and detractors of human rights, mainly that the conceptual, philosophical, and empirical experience of rights across the globe owe their formulation to the three revolutions of the modern West: the Glorious Revolution (1688), the American Revolution (1776), and the French Revolution (1789). Not only are rights politics viewed as Western derived, but they are also regarded as symbolic of this continuing Western tradition of human rights. Of course, the documentation of this global proliferation of human rights (or indeed its refusal) is hardly a descriptive project; it is, if anything, a normative one. Human rights represent civilizational progress to which 'other' nations and peoples must aspire, even if it means justifying the spread or the protection of human rights through imperialist military invasions and 'humanitarian' interventions. On the other hand, there are powerful detractors of human rights who similarly place rights on a continuum of modernity, progress, and linear historical time, but prioritize economic development as a necessary precondition in the progress towards political and civil freedoms. Both these positions involve significant historical and intellectual inattentiveness. Not only are universal human rights a recent intellectual and political project within the global North, and one that has been mired in social conflict and continues to be bitterly fought for, but discourses of rights and entitlements are powerfully invoked in the global South too. But the challenge of resisting originary discourses on human rights nevertheless remains. So how do we resist the nomenclatural politics and also think of the movements/rights claims and politics that take place outside the non-European world without losing either their historical and political specificity or their geo-political location and hierarchical relationship with hegemonic human rights discourses? In other words, how do we go about 'worlding' human rights without losing sight of their historical, linguistic, and political specificities including the very specific ways in which these are mobilized and the rights politics that are engendered as a result of their mobilization? Recent years, however, have seen a rise in sophisticated arguments pointing to the often contradictory, alienating, exclusionary, and politically conservative effects of a universalizing and homogenizing (Kiss 1997), human rights politics (Brown 1995, 2000; Menon 2004; Crenshaw 2000), implicated and invested in upholding existing global power relations and hierarchies of representation (in both senses); of being yet another form of 'transnational governmentality' (Grewal 2005) and of constituting a 'central' element of US led globalization, capitalism, and world trade (Asad 2000; Mignolo 2000). In recent years, anthropological scholarship has made a significant intervention in thinking about questions of rights (Abu-Lughod 2010; Comaroff and Comaroff 2012; Goodale 2006; Goodale and Merry 2007; Mamdani 2000; Merry 2009; Povinelli 2011; Wilson 1997) and about the nature and limits of modernity within transnational and cross cultural frames. But the question of categories and nomenclature remains.

Discussions of women's rights in India are hardly a stranger to the 'politics of origins' mode of discourse. My caution in using the category of the 'West' and 'non-West' in binary terms owes in some part to the hostile criticisms and reception, designed to undermine and disqualify claims for gender equality directed at the feminist movement in India, which, in effect, continues to be haunted by two characterizations. The first antagonism that is often heaped in its direction by its detractors is that it is elite, upper class and caste, and seeks to assume the voice and mantle of leadership, thereby illegitimately 'speaking for' (Alcoff 1995) all Indian women, and the second questions the 'authenticity' and cultural propriety of feminist politics as those of 'Western' import and therefore foreign and also illegitimate. While both these characterizations can be traced to the identity crafting that occurred during the Indian nationalist anti-colonial struggles, these have continued to find a resonance in post-colonial politics in India (Mani 1989; Rai 2002), ensuring that even where women's rights have been explicitly under discussion, these have to be seen to be in alignment with emerging definitions of authentic culture/scriptural tradition as also a 'modern Indian' identity.[2] Consequently, the debate on citizenship in post-colonial India has been circumscribed by a careful balance between women's citizenship rights, that is, their public identities and their religious and cultural roles or their private identities (Kapur and Crossman 1996). Two things must be said here: while it is entirely legitimate to raise questions about location, voice, representation, and leadership within the Indian feminist movement, it is also important to note that the women's movement, despite difficulties in relation to these, has displayed reflexivity and sensitivity to questions of poverty, power, social hierarchy, and institutional elitism both in its campaigns and in the readings of its historical archives (John 1996, 1998a, 1998b, 2002; Rajan 2003; Ram 2000). And as I have noted elsewhere (Madhok 2010), the idea that advocating women's rights and feminist politics constitutes inauthentic politics and an inauthentic social mobilization because feminism happens to have 'originary' moment in the 'West' is weak not least because women's rights were mooted during the anti-colonial nationalist movement itself (Ram 2000; John 1998a), but also because the difficulties with rights in India are less to do with their being 'misfits' or 'out of place' with Indian culture/tradition and more to do with the fact that they arise out of the experiential failure of rights (Rajan 2003) and from the absence of accountability and non-individuation of citizen identities (Ram 2000).

In my view, therefore, it is more productive to think of human rights as not wholly derivative from the three major revolutions in the West—the American, the French, and the English—or entirely oppositional to Western notions and conventions of human rights, or indeed, entirely discrete in form, in that one would be hard pressed to find hermetically sealed or 'pure' indigenous rights traditions, but they are, instead, interlocked into relations that are historically, productively, intimately, and coercively produced and experienced, attending to the particular forms of encounters with rights such as colonial encounters, those with anti-colonial nationalism, the constitutionalism spearheading the post-colonial state and its distinct forms of developmentalism and bureaucratization, and, more recently, through the impact of the increased 'destatization' and the proliferation of the non-state organizations advocating 'human rights'.

But of course, to say that we must be cautious/reflexive towards categories such as the 'West' when speaking of human rights and of human rights discourse is not to suggest that we ignore the geopolitical power relations upheld and signified by the 'West', nor that we lose historical specificity and the historically specific ways that human rights discourses and politics have emerged, evolved, travelled, are translated, and debated. It simply means that we must think carefully about the implications that accompany the binary categories such as the 'West' and 'non-West'—reproducing as they do the very representations and power relations we wish to refuse, their deployment both rearticulating while also leaving unchallenged the justificatory premises that underpin and govern the terms of human rights talk not least, privileging and disqualifying particular modes of lived experience. In my view, it is much more productive to think of human rights both in a transnational mode, recognizing the modes of nodes, circuits, and circulation of power, and also in terms of specific conceptual categories, languages (both literal and conceptual), anxieties, displacements, and movements as well as the more settled politics and claims for rights and entitlements. In order to conceptually and empirically illustrate the shift to a 'politics of meanings', I adopt the framework of 'vernacular rights cultures' which I shall discuss in greater detail towards the end of the paper.

But, you might ask, what would these moral encounters in very marginal contexts with developmentalism and rights bring to how we think of the difficult questions around global human rights discourse? In my view, these negotiations shine a light on at least three things. First, they question whether our genealogical investigation of rights and our obsession with the 'politics of origins' of human rights is actually justified empirically and practically. Second, they highlight the gendered nature of rights, of how the exercise of rights invariably throws up deep seated questions of gender relations, and finally, they highlight the transnational circuits of rights, and of the different routes through which rights travel, get picked up, are transformed, and are 'vernacularized' (Levitt and Merry 2009).

Developmentalism, Gendered Subjectivities, and the 'Doing' of Rights

Although a prominent part of this rights-based developmentalism I focus on here is in a significant way concerned with disseminating and enforcing accountability of state developmentalism and discernibly less about encouraging individual rights and personal liberties, it is hard to separate these except in analytic terms; however, in this chapter, I shall be focusing to a larger degree on the former. Before all else, however, let me offer a few clarifications. The language of developmentalism is not only beamed/spoken by the state alone, even though sometimes, the success of the state is viewed through how well it has been able to reach 'development' to what Partha Chatterjee refers to as 'dark zones' (Chatterjee 2004.). This exclusive focus on the penetrative capacity of the state, however, risks sliding into 'statism' and 'ignores development's vast hinterland, installed, regulated and reproduced through intricate networks of governmental technologies of power and engaged in manufacturing consent and mobilising legitimacy for developmentalism. One only has to cast one's eye at the list of thousands of 'NGOs' enlisting themselves as primarily involved in development to witness the extraordinary desire for development. By developmentalism, a term I prefer to 'development, I refer to not only a set of institutions, discourses and practices but also to a 'condition' or a way of being'. (Madhok 2013a). This developmentalism, as I conceive it, is normative in its aims; it speaks the language of self-empowerment and individual rights and has the transformation of subjectivities as its explicit aim. This normative basis for developmentalism accompanies both the state and non-state actors engaged in 'development', even though the normative ethic that they might be pursuing might be quite different. Feminist politics in India has been keenly invested in developmentalism, and since the 1970s, it has been a vocal critic of the exclusionary politics, institutions, 'initiatives', and policies of the developmental state. The social unrest of the 1960s also gave rise to demands for more specific and group focused development interventions, including a focus on women as a 'group' within state-led developmentalism. While the increasingly vibrant and visible women's movement, instrumental in making sure that it would no longer be acceptable for policy makers to be indifferent to gender relations and to the exclusion of women from state developmentalism—here it was both in step with the emerging critique of the dominant representations of women in international 'development apparatus' (Escobar 1995) and in tandem with the burgeoning academic scholarship on women's roles within development—the actual policy shift in this regard only came much later, more specifically with the insertion of a chapter on women and development in the sixth Five-Year Plan, and subsequently into state plans at the provincial level. The WDP launched by the Government of Rajasthan in April 1984 was a direct result of this attention to women within development policy thinking in India, and in turn, facilitated in particular, the rights encounter of the sathins whose rights encounter constitutes a significant part of this chapter.[3]

The feminist movement has raised questions of women's rights and gender relations looming against the background of discourses of constitutionalism, developmentalism, and empowerment. These are not ordered in terms of hierarchical progression, but instead are influenced in large part by the prevailing political imperatives. The 'autonomous' feminist movement is seen to have emerged as a separate movement in its own right amidst the social unrest and the looming political crises of the 1960s, which came to a head with the imposition of emergency measures by the federal government (1975–7) and suspension of constitutional liberties. It is important to note that the phrase 'Indian feminist movement' in singular terms does little to capture the internal variety or dissent within it. Different strains within the movement have championed a diverse range of issues related to the environment, sexuality, representation, health, and civil rights (Kumar 1999); in fact, the movement is often said to have experienced three discernible 'waves' (Gandhi and Shah 1992;

Menon 1999): its anti-colonial/nationalist phase, its autonomous/ large classed mobilization phase, and the 1980s onwards which is witnessing the 'third wave' of the women's movement in India (Menon 1999). It was only in 1997 that a resolution was passed by the Indian women's movements congress, recognizing rights of non-heterosexual groups (Menon cited in Phadke 2003). Currently, the women's movement has found itself at the forefront of debates on sexualities, intersectional oppressions, identities, and renewed emphasis on institutional and legal reform and citizenship—with sexual rights, parliamentary quotas, and guaranteed citizenship entitlements becoming increasingly important.

On Encountering Rights and Developmentalism

The moral, ethical, and practical encounter with the rights language that I describe here takes place in the context of developmentalism subscribed to by both non-state and state actors, although there is a discernible difference between the forms that are practised by the two. For instance, while both the state sponsored developmentalism and non-state practitioners are state focused, by which I mean, they are both attached to the state in different ways, there are important differences. The main plank of developmentalism, pursued by the non-state actors, is very much aimed at enforcing state accountability over formal rights already committed to whilst also demanding an extension of the list of citizenship entitlements (but these are seldom raised in terms of individual rights), whereas the state sponsored developmentalism that is released is explicitly concerned with raising awareness of state development schemes and of widening the net of 'beneficiaries'. However, it would be a mistake to think of these two strands in binary terms; I will go on to show how they overlap and even intersect. The main point that I wish to highlight in this section is the deployment of the literal term for right, which, as I pointed out earlier, is haq, and a few of its conceptual and philosophical underpinnings.

In the case of the sathins, for instance, who are after all development 'workers'[4] of the state, engaging with the statist discourse of rights and developmentalism in very interesting and creative ways, it is important to note that the state provides a very real sense of support/legitimation of their rights work while also drawing attention to them as targets of serious conflict. In the initial years of their participation within the programme, the sathins would, for example, use a very statist language of rights in order to make the case for rights. For example, consider the following excerpted narrative:

> At the (WDP) 'training', I was taught that women had rights too, and that practising untouchability was wrong. I had learnt that no one was an untouchable and that everyone had equal rights. And when I went back to the village, I went to draw water along with four *Kumhars*. A man belonging to the *Meena* caste came there and shouted at me saying, 'How dare you come and draw water from here?' I replied, 'Is it your father's tube well that we can't use it? The *sarkar* has installed it and we all have an equal access to it'. Our *sarpanch* came and said that I was right and now everyone draws water from the tube well.[5]

But as I have documented elsewhere, this fairly straightforward defence of rights becomes more complex as the relationship with the state becomes more fraught or enters what I call a 'crisis of reflection'. The process through which this 'crisis of reflection' occurs is both moral as well as practical. The moral process comprises a dynamic ethical reflection consisting of attempts to not only rethink many of the moral rules informing their own moral frameworks, but also of selectively absorbing many of these 'new' ideas and language in creative and somewhat less unhesitant ways. In an important way, this moral regression of the state among the sathins is brought about through its failure to come through on its promise of protecting women's rights, forcing the sathins to weave an independent mainstay for rights, separate from the state. These new ideas of rights, in the first instance, may appear to be closely associated with the state, but as a result of a gradual process of moral regression of the state in their popular perception—from primarily a principled entity backed by an 'irresistible power', deploying its power to establish the good in society to being viewed as aligned to special class/caste interests—the sathins realize that the state can be no longer provide the philosophical mainstay for rights. And thus, with this changed view of the state from one comprising not just a 'pack of principles' but also a 'structure of practices', the sathins find themselves left with an intellectual need to justify the principles that they had hitherto attributed to the state. However, in proposing an alternative philosophical justification, the sathins also need to justify this new normative basis for rights in a language that is acceptable, comprehensible, and morally significant. In order to justify principles of rights upon an alternative premise, the sathins turn to a conceptual term of high moral value within the vernacular to legitimize this non-statist justification for rights. They begin to legitimize their use of haq by invoking it in synonymy with Truth. In their case, it is not so much a creation of new literal terms or neologisms to accommodate the new language of individual rights but of manufacturing a new moral legitimacy for this new conceptual thinking. Consider, for example, the following:

> We sathins exist so that we can assist the depressed and deprived women and become their voice. 'Sathin ko karyakarm bohut tej khopri che' [the sathin programme is a very clever one]. If there is any injustice happening, say for example on a bus, the educated women just sit straight in their seats, they don't utter a word. They have money, they are privileged, why should they get their hands dirty and speak up? We speak the Truth and walk the path of Truth. The *Sarpanch*, the *Patwari* can go whichever way they want, but I will always walk the way of Truth. There is only twenty five per cent Truth in politics. The *Sarpanch* and *Patwari* are partners in corruption— why should they speak the Truth? They benefit by not walking the path of Truth. Whereas the *sathin* always speaks the Truth as she is not in with them and their corrupt schemes.[6]

Before we discuss these narratives further, I must also point out here that the developmentalism that is beamed at the women develop-ment workers is quite explicitly engaged in producing a particular 'development subject' and in facilitating the emergence of certain forms of subjectivities amenable to 'development'. This moral encoun-ter of the sathins with rights and developmentalism, as I have shown elsewhere, is creative, injurious, risk-laden and deeply destabiliz-ing, leading to the sathins fashioning not only new ways of view-ing their social and moral worlds, but also of crafting a new lens through which to both view themselves and their subject/gender positionings (Madhok 2013a, 2013b).[7] For state developmentalism, women selected as sathins undergo a 'training' (also referred to in the narrative above) so as to align themselves with the normative impulse of this new (and dynamically unstable) discourse of developmentalism. Becoming a sathin, therefore, requires a certain re-orienting and re-crafting of the self so as to meet the expectations of personal transformation in matters not only ethical and moral, but also of comportment, speech, and sartorial. These exercises in the refashioning of subjectivities and the constituting of one's self as a development 'subject'—as articulated in the speech practices of the sathins—must not be seen as either autonomous practices deployed by retreating into an hermetically sealed inner-self, nor should these be seen as any way freely chosen. On the contrary, the self-conscious operations or 'technologies of the self' (Foucault 1994: 225) that the sathins perform upon themselves in order to develop a desirable subjectivity that helps focus attention on the 'technologies of power' (Foucault 1994: 225) that accompany developmentalism as a form of governmentality (Murray 2007) oriented towards 'shaping' particular modes of being and kinds of subjectivities (Burchill 1996).

In contrast to the statist developmentalism encountered by the sathins, the version of 'development' that the participants of various non-state citizen mobilizations, which I have been ethnographically documenting since 2004 encounter, are engaged in the production of a particular kind of activist citizen subject. By this, I do not mean to imply that the sathin is not an activist subject, but only that her activism is of a slightly different kind. The activist citizen subjects mostly tend to direct their activism at the shortcomings of the developmental state, exercising a constitutionally sanctioned language of citizenship rights and claims in order to press for fulfilment of existing entitlements or for a more expansive interpretation of these. But this separation between the two kinds of citizen activism, between the non-state and the statist is, in effect, an analytical separation really, and cannot be sustained after a particular point. And let me illustrate here what I mean by this through examining two narratives from my documentation of rights, citizenship, and entitlements within citizen mobilizations.

Consider for instance, Prem Bairwa's deployment of the rights language. Prem Bairwa is a Dalit woman who at the time of this interview was a member of the village council in her village of Kotkhawada, Jaipur district. In addition to her role as a member of the local village council, Prem Bairwa is affiliated to a large and internationally funded NGO,[8] and is also closely associated with the National Campaign for Dalit Human Rights (NCDHR), a national level advocacy organization in India.

According to her:

> As a council member, I have a haq in the panchayat (village council) to get development done in the village. Do only men have the right to speak and conduct political business; are not women to enjoy these rights equally? It is a fight for my haq and a fight I have to fight myself. The government has given these rights to women; Indira Gandhi has started the *mahila raj* of women. Before her, there were no women's rights. In case governments change 'our' rights then we have to fight the government. After all, it is 'us' who make the government.'[9]

Another version of this 'activist citizen subject' is also evoked in my fieldwork among the political and field workers of the Mazdoor Kisan Shakti Sangathan (MKSS). This active view of citizenship rights contains fluent expressions of an activist oriented view of citizenship, replete with notions of self-governance, accountability, and responsibility that define 'active' citizenship. The MKSS or the 'Association for Workers and Farmers' have been involved in a long drawn struggle for the right of ordinary people to gain access to state financial records and state audits of development projects, and has spearheaded a social movement espousing the right of public information and the people's right to know about the government's economic functioning. The right to information (RTI) movement began in the early 1990s to highlight the gross failures of the state to uphold minimum wage legislation, particularly within drought relief programmes set up in order to provide stipulated employment to people in drought affected districts and to focus on the flagrant inefficiencies and corrupt practices within the state public distribution system (PDS). However, the activities of the MKSS have not been limited to exposing the everyday forms of official corruption and focusing on procedures of governmental accountability but have also come to expose the 'multifaceted nature of corruption' within the legal and political system (Jenkins and Goetz 1999). In their decade long movement, the MKSS have championed innovative social techniques of mobilization and public appraisal. Perhaps, the most innovative feature of MKSS's campaign for RTI has been the introduction of participatory social audits of public expenditure or *jan sunwais*. Typically, a 'jan sunwai' consists of the submission of individual and collective testimonies about corrupt official practices, for instance, of fake muster rolls and corrupt state officials, including state affiliates such as ration shop owners and elected local government representatives, at a pre-designated public space to which the concerned state officials/political representatives are invited to present their defence or give an account of their practices.

The interview below is excerpted from a lengthy conversation with two prominent members of the MKSS. According to them:

> The road is built with our money. It is "our" money because we pay income tax and we pay also tax on whatever we buy such as rice, *dal* and cooking oil. That is how the *sarkar* (the state/government) builds hospitals and schools. It builds these with "our" money. The money that people used to think was *sarkari* or the building that was deemed to be sarkari, we tell the people it is not sarkari but it is "our" building and it is "our" money. 'Our' democracy must be safeguarded for that will make our rights safe. "Our" effort should be that the constitution continues to guarantee the rights of citizens. (Interview with Tej Singh and Narayan, Rajsamand, 2004)

Even though we can discern a clear deployment of haq running through each of these narratives, each one of these must be considered in their distinct discursive, institutional, and political context. These activist subjects must not be confused with embodying either ideas of civic republicanism—self-governance, rights, and public service—nor as whole heartedly endorsing liberal citizenship (subjects of rights and entitlements). Both liberal citizenship and civic republicanism in so far as they are premised upon a contractual arrangement between the individual and the state, affirming negative liberty and autonomy for individuals on the one hand with civic participation on the other, presume the presence of homogenous political communities. Neither liberal rights and selfhood nor homogenous political communities inform the justificatory premise of haq as citizenship; and even when citizenship is considered explicitly based on a common identity, the practice of rights has brought this homogeneity under considerable strain. Moreover, when we consider all four narratives together, we find a peculiar but a discernible pattern emerging from these. Many of these narratives, whether they rest their justificatory premise of rights on law or the state or on the constitutional rights and obligations of citizens, retain with the people in the final instance, the right to change both the law/government or the constitution if it fails to uphold the rights of citizens. In other words, although the justificatory premise of rights in both is placed in law/constitution and in citizen prerogatives, in both cases, there is a clear enunciation that somehow although law/constitution is required to justify these rights, haq has an independent justificatory premise separate from the prevailing legal regime. Haq thus can be said to lie in a 'zone of non-coincidence between individuals and the positive legal order of the state' (Brett 2003: 98). Therefore, whereas the law regulates rights and upholds these, it cannot extirpate these. The reference to haq is to an entity, which exists independent of the law and possibly has a moral authority of its own. But this does lead us to think about haq and its meanings and it is to this that I shall now turn to.

The Routes, Meanings, and the Politics of Doing *haq*

At this point, you might ask: what of haq and how does it relate to human rights/rights? The literal term 'haq' is remarkably cosmopolitan and has an interesting intellectual history. As the principal Arabic word used to denote a 'right', it enjoys an intellectual recognition across Arabic-speaking peoples across the Middle-East and North Africa and among several communities in South Asia. In Southern Asia, the literal term 'haq', a pre-Islamic Arabic word also available in classical Hebrew, Persian, and in some of the older Semitic languages such as Aramaic and Phoenician, transcends geographical and religious boundaries and is used to invoke a 'right' by different religious and linguistic communities in northern India as well as in Pakistan. I have written about the etymological history of the word 'haq' and of some elements of its conceptual history elsewhere (Madhok 2009), but here I will simply like to point out that it is, in fact, the word that was deployed by my fieldwork respondents both in India and in Pakistan. The presence of this word begs several questions for me, not all of which can be addressed in this paper but let me iterate some of these, nevertheless. If the word 'haq' was already present in the social vocabulary then why did the language of rights appear so novel, alien, exclusionary, and unavailable? What sorts of intellectual, conceptual, and philosophical cultures was haq embedded in; what particular traditions of orality and textuality supported haq as a claim; what kinds of political cultures of rights were these rights movements drawing upon and creating in turn? What were its spheres of influence and implementation? Did it belong to those who already had rights? And what sorts of rights meanings were being advanced, and how did these, in turn, impact mainstream Western-derived thinking on rights? What sorts of narratives or forms of belonging did the word 'haq' invoke? Intrigued by the presence and the deployment of the term, I focused on trying to think about the function of rights, or of haq, its meanings, and the justificatory premises that underpinned its life world in the subcontinent and the work that it did or was made to do. I have now documented five different justificatory premises of haq; three of which I have provided snapshots of in this paper, namely rights as a statist doctrine, as one that inaugurates an 'activist citizen subject', and right as signifying 'truth'. The two that do not find their exposition here are: haq as a cosmological idea and as an Islamic doctrine. I have examined each of these in detail elsewhere (Madhok 2009) and here I shall simply go on to talk about the experiential and ethical interventions of rights in the life worlds of my field subjects.

Throughout my fieldwork amongst the sathins, for instance, I found them to express a cautious enthusiasm for political rights; an important reason for supporting political rights, according to the sathins, was the promise of meaningful political citizenship and 'recognition respect' (Darwall 1977) they held out. The language of rights makes available—and for many sathins, for the first time ever—a discursive terrain whereby they find themselves becoming 'available' to themselves and to others through a shared political subjectivity: that of a citizen. The language of political rights then opens up the arena of citizenship, or at least its possibility, albeit, however, fragile, and one to which the sathins aspire. What was undeniable in their narratives, however, was the ideational energy that rights brought to developmentalism. This ideational energy of rights, particularly around political rights, produced in its wake distinct subjectivities and self-representations among the sathins, namely those of a rights-bearing subject, a relational-political subjectivity and political literate subjectivities (Madhok 2013a). Their high level of political literacy, however, only made the sathins very cautious on rights; rights were both a route to gaining a citizen subjectivity—and one which had been hitherto denied to them—whilst also a great magnet for conflict, so while it is the case that rights made available the grammar of recognition respect, the actual claiming of this recognition respect was a different matter altogether, and one that was not without conflict, struggle, violence risk, and injury. Another aspect of rights reflected in their narratives was that of their indivisibility and intersectional nature; rights were neither clearly divisible nor discrete while also co-existing with patriarchies and oppressive gendered practices. Consider, for example, the case of Manohari Bai, a member of 'Marudhar Ganga Society', a local NGO working for Dalit rights based in Jodhpur district, who stood up during the *gram sabha* and demanded the right to know what was happening to the proposal to build a school for girls in her ward. She was mercilessly beaten by the *Sarpanch* (a Choudhury by caste and his supporters) and her clothes torn off. Manohari Bai describes the incident in the following interview:

> In 2002, sometime in August–September, I went to the *gram sabha* meeting where I stood up and asked about what had happened to the proposal for the girls school which had been approved in our ward (no. 14). The Sarpanch said, *"chup ho ja, tu kaun hain bolne wali"* [you must shut up, who do you think you are to pose these questions?]. Then all violence broke loose. There were 500 men who shouted obscenities at me and I was beaten up, my *dupatta* and other clothes were torn off me whilst all the time the people kept shouting *"randi baith ja"* [sit down you whore]. My attackers were mainly Rajputs and Jats but there was also one Mali and even a *sarkari karamchari*, I mean he was a *Patwari*...I went to Osian, and then after a month and a half the police registered a case against them. The police only registered my case after I pleaded my case with the Chief Minister and he ordered a case to be registered. The police did register a case after pressure from the Chief Minister's office, but they put a FR (False Report) against it. In the courts, the magistrate was pressured by the police and the Sarpanch, and he dismissed the case. I didn't give up though, and I took the case up to the high court in Jodhpur. I am now waiting for a date for a hearing to be announced.'[10]

Apart from the graphic account of the violence that Manohari Bai recounts, her narrative also points to the intersecting nature of rights. For instance, demanding the 'right to information' from elected representatives or public officials about public work programmes of health, education, or work programmes can, in many cases, involve a simultaneous claim for gender and caste equality whilst in the same breath drawing attention to corruption within the local and state bureaucracies, the judicial system, and to the flouting of procedural norms within the administrative, executive, and legislative system itself. Perhaps, it is the indivisible nature of rights (and the futility of analytically trying to isolate them into categories)—of political and civic entitlements intersecting and interwoven with personal/individual rights—that makes rights politics so conflicted.

And finally, the third reflection on rights that emerges from an examination of the sathin narratives is one not dissimilar to what feminist scholars have long pointed out, namely, the paradox of liberal rights—the formal promise of equal rights and citizenship for the free-standing, abstract, and unencumbered individual becoming hollowed out and rendered unrealizable for the concrete and socially located one—which found a clear articulation in the speech practices of the sathins. In short, while it is certainly the case that the sathins employ the language of constitutionally guaranteed rights, this use is never unqualified or unaccompanied by disappointment, frustration, and despair at the elusive and near unrealizablility of rights (Madhok 2013b).

A Few Reflections on Vernacular Rights Talk and Feminist Politics of Rights

My aim through presenting brief ethnographic glimpses of the encounter with rights has been to present elements of an analysis constituting a 'politics of meanings', which I have argued will help us think more closely about how the contact with rights occurs, how rights travel, and how they impact everyday ways of living and doing politics; in other words, it is a plea towards putting in place an analysis of political cultures created in the wake of rights. I have also referred to these rights cultures as vernacular rights cultures here, and elsewhere (Madhok 2009). In speaking of 'politics of meanings'

and vernacular rights cultures, and for the need to abandon 'originary rights talk', I am neither suggesting that we divorce rights talk
from how rights operate globally, as that would not only be to feign
ignorance—or even worse, wilful blindness of how circuits of power-
histories, discourses, and institutional politics within which all rights
talk operates—nor am I advocating a 'global/local' framework of
rights talk, which I find on the whole quite unhelpful. By speaking
of vernacular rights cultures, I am, however, setting up a normative
hierarchical power relation—that between hegemonic universal
discourses of human rights and those which are not simply 'vernacularized' (Merry 2009), but have their own histories and politics; I
am highlighting certain forms of meaning including 'strategies' of
utilization of rights linked not only to the historical and cultural
identity of the group making a rights claim, but also to the particular kinds of politics and institutional settings that they inhabit
and strive towards; and finally, I am also suggesting that these rights
cultures exist in a relation of marginality and subalternity in respect
of majoritarian rights discourses associated with the nation state,
legal constitutionalism, and developmentalism.

As a feminist scholar studying vernacular rights cultures, I am
only too aware of the dangers, injuries, asymmetrical power relations,
violence, and precarities surrounding the doing of rights. Feminist
scholarship has demystified the gendering/exclusionary/culture-
reifying/civilizational discourses that human rights lend themselves
to. In particular, they have shown how a certain form of imperial
politics plays out when human rights are deployed as championing
women's rights—one where the discourse of 'saving' the natives from
themselves, or indeed Spivak's formulation of 'white men saving
brown women from brown men', comes in only too handy (Abu-
Lughod 2002, 2010; Brown 1995, 2000; Crenshaw 2000; Grewal
2005; Menon 2004; Spivak 1999). In my view, feminist intellectual
work on the institutional articulation and workings of rights must
be accompanied by an attention to the ways in which rights languages are picked up and put to use in different political contexts by
disparate and especially marginal groups so that we might produce
accounts of how this manifold use complicates and expands current
rights thinking. Rights are inherently political and must be seen
as operating within fields of power, and therefore, the task is not

only one of examining the discursive formulations and the political use that rights are put to, but also one of investigating the political cultures that rights create (Brown 1995) and the new forms of subjectivity and subjection these produce. However, a dilemma for our present is the following: how to reconcile the often paradoxical and unintended conservatism of rights thinking about the ever present dangers of imperial politics with the increasing articulation and rights based social mobilizations in different parts of the world. As Pheng Cheah has evocatively pointed out, rights remain the 'only way for the disenfranchized to mobilize' (Cheah 2006: 172). Given the marginal socialities within which vernacular rights cultures operate, the work of documenting rights talk and thinking in marginal contexts involves at least three things: it means not only undertaking detailed ethnographic work that documents both the nature of the contact with hegemonic rights discourses, but also the precise nature and consequences of these 'modernizing' interventions; it involves documenting the creative languages and conceptual ideas that are produced in the wake of this encounter and the ways in which the poor and the marginal stake their wager as 'active claimants of modernity' (Ram 2008: 16); and finally, in addition to the work of tracking and documenting rights languages, we also need to put in place analytical frameworks that enable us to track, document, and also conceptually capture the kinds of political, linguistic, and normative strategies released by these rights encounters, released to stretch and dislodge the existing normative boundaries of the universal (Butler 1997), expand the language of entitlements, and consequently impact and transform public policy.

Notes

1. For details on the programme, see *Rethinking Agency: Developmentalism, Gender, and Rights* (Madhok 2013a).
2. The unease with 'feminism' as a western import, although not confined to the non-feminist camps alone (John 1998b), found a renewed chorus with the dominance of religious identity politics in the 1980s and 1990s (John 1998a).
3. The *Women's Development Project Rajasthan*, DRDPR, Government of Rajasthan, 1984.

4. For disputes over their status as 'workers' of the state, see *Rethinking Agency: Developmentalism, Gender, and Rights* (Madhok 2013a).

5. Interview with Sathin Gulab, Village Bhavni, Gram Panchayat Bhavni, Tehsil, Jumwa Ramgarh, Jaipur. Interviewed 24 December 1998. See also Madhok (2013a).

6. In their narratives, Truth is increasingly seen as synonymous with justice and justice is articulated in terms of women's rights, and the credibility of the state becomes inextricably linked (in their narratives) to its commitment and ability to not only protect the Truth but also the interconnected set of moral principles; equality, justice, and rights, which are seen as components of Truth. Thus, the truth, as articulated by the sathins is that women have rights, but that powerful interests in the community subvert these rights and in doing so interfere with the *Truth*.

7. In documenting their rights narrative over their twenty year participation in this development programme, I found that there was a distinct pattern in their thinking and speech practices which could be plotted in terms of three distinct 'stages'. The initial contact with rights based ideas produced in their wake considerable moral dissonance and suspicion which in turn gave way in time to a 'new-found faith' in a state-centric discourse of rights and finally, in the face of serious failings of the state, they are forced to weave their own theoretical and practical defence of the idea of rights independent of the state.

8. Cecoedecon noted by many to be one of the largest recipients of foreign funds. Interview with Sunny Sebastian, Rajasthan correspondent for the *The Hindu*, February 2004, Jaipur.

9. Interviewed in 2004, Kotkhawada, Phagi Panchayat, Jaipur. This is an extract from a longer interview with Prem Bairwa.

10. Interview with Manohari Devi, field worker 'Marudhar Ganga Society', Village Baodi, Tehsil Gopalgarh, Panchayat Samiti Osian, District Jodhpur, caste Meghwanshi (Dalit caste).

References

Abu-Lughod, L. 2002. 'Do Muslim Women Really Need Saving? Anthropological Reflections on Cultural Relativism and Its Others', *American Anthropologist*, 104(3): 783–90.

———. 2010. 'The Active Social Life of "Muslim Women's Rights": A Plea for Ethnography, Not Polemic, with Cases from Egypt and Palestine', *Journal of Middle East Women's Studies*, 6(1): 1–45.

Agnes, F. 1997. 'Protecting Women Against Violence? A Review of a Decade of Legislation 1980–89', in *State and Politics in India*, pp. 521–65. New Delhi: Oxford University Press.

Alcoff, L. 1995. 'The Problem of Speaking for Others', in J. Roof and R. Wigeman (eds), *Who Can Speak: Authority and Critical Identity*, pp. 97–119. Urbana: University of Illinois Press.

Asad, T. 2000. 'What Do Human Rights Do? An Anthropological Enquiry', *Theory and Event*, 4(4): www.muse.jhu.edu/journals/theory_and_event/v004/4.4asad.html

Brett, A.S. 2003. 'The Development of the Idea of Citizen's Rights', in Q. Skinner and B. Strath (eds), *States and Citizens*, p. 98. Cambridge: Cambridge University Press.

Brown, W. 1995. *States of Injury*. Princeton, NJ: Princeton University Press.

———. 2000. 'Suffering Rights as Paradoxes', *Constellations*, 7(2): 230–41.

Burchill, G. 1996. 'Liberal Government and the Techniques of the Self', in A. Barry, T. Osbourne, and N. Rose (eds), *Foucault and Political Reason*, pp. 19–36. London: Routledge.

Butler, J. 1997. *Excitable Speech: A Politics of the Performative*. London and New York: Routledge.

Chatterjee, P. 2004. *The Politics of the Governed: Reflections on Popular Politics in Most of the World*. New York: Columbia University Press.

Cheah, P. 2006. *Inhuman Conditions: On Cosmopolitanism and Human Rights*. Cambridge, MA: Harvard University Press.

Comaroff and Comaroff. 2012. *Theory from the South: Or, how Euro-America is Evolving Toward Africa*. Boulder, CO: Paradigm Publishers.

Crenshaw, K. 2000. 'Were the Critics Right About Rights? Reassessing the American Debate about Rights in Post-Reform Era', in M. Mamdani (ed.), *Beyond Rights Talk and Culture Talk*, pp. 61–74. Cape Town: David Phillip Publishers.

Darwall, S.L. 1977. 'Two Kinds of Respect.' *Ethics*, 88(1): 36–49.

Escobar, A. 1995. 'Encountering Development: The Making and Unmaking of the Third World', *Princeton Studies in Culture/Power/History*. Princeton, NJ: Princeton University Press.

Foucault, M. 1994. *Ethics: Subjectivity and Truth*. Edited by Paul Rabinow. London: Penguin.

Gandhi, N. and N. Shah. 1992. *The Issues at Stake: Theory and Practice in Contemporary Women's Movement in India*. New Delhi: Kali for Women.

Goodale, M. 2006. 'Introduction to "Anthropology and Human Rights in a New Key"', *American Anthropologist*, 108(1): 1–8.

Goodale, M. and S.E. Merry (eds). 2007. *The Practice of Human Rights: Tracking Law Between the Global and the Local.* Cambridge: Cambridge University Press.

Grewal, I. 2005. *Transnational America: Feminisms, Diasporas, Neoliberalisms.* Durham: Duke University Press.

Jenkins, R. and A.M. Goetz. 1999. 'Accounts and Accountability: Theoretical Implications of the Right to Information Movement in India', *Third World Quarterly*, 20(3): 603–22.

John, M.E. 1996. 'Gender and Development in India, 1970–90s: Some Reflections on the Constitutive Role of Contexts', *Economic and Political Weekly*, 37(41): 3071–7.

———. 1998a. 'Feminisms and Internationalisms: A Response from India', *Gender and History*, 10(3): 539–48.

———. 1998b. 'Feminism in India and the West', *Cultural Dynamics* 10(2): 197–209.

———. 2002. 'Feminism, Poverty and Globalization: An Indian View', *Inter-Asia Cultural Studies*, 3(3): 351–67.

Kapur, R. and B. Crossman. 1996. *Subversive Sites. Feminist Engagements With law in India* New Delhi: Sage Publications.

Kiss, E. 1997. 'Alchemy or Fool's Gold? Assessing Feminist Doubts over Rights', in M.L. Shanley and U. Narayan (eds), *Reconstructing Political Theory: Feminist Perspectives*, pp. 1–24. London: Polity Press.

Kumar, R. 1999. 'From Chipko to Sati: The Contemporary Indian Women's Movement', in N. Menon (ed.), *Gender and Politics in India*, pp. 342–69. New Delhi, Oxford University Press.

Levitt, P. and S. Merry. 2009. 'Vernacularization on the Ground: Local Uses of Global Women's Rights in Peru, China, India and the United States', *Global Networks*, 9(4): 441–61.

Madhok, S. 2009. *Five Notions of Haq: Exploring Vernacular Rights Cultures in Southern Asia.* New Working Paper Series, Gender Institute, London School of Economics.

———. 2010. *'Rights Talk' and the Feminist Movement in India*, pp. 224–42. New York: Routledge.

———. 2013a. *Rethinking Agency: Developmentalism, Gender and Rights.* Delhi and London: Routledge.

———. 2013b. 'Action, Agency, Coercion: Reformatting Agency for Oppressive Contexts', in S. Madhok, A. Phillips, and K. Wilson (eds), *Gender Agency and Coercion*, pp. 102–21. Basingstoke: Palgrave MacMillan.

Mamdani, M. (ed.) 2000. *Beyond Rights Talk and Culture Talk: Comparative Essays on the Politics of Rights and Culture.* Capetown: New Africa Books.

Mani, L. 1989. 'Contentious Traditions: The Debate on *Sati* in Colonial India', in K. Sangari and S. Vaid (eds), *Recasting Women: Essays in Colonial History*, pp. 88–126. New Delhi: Kali for Women.

Menon, N. 1999. 'Introduction', in *Gender and Politics in India*, pp. 1–36. New Delhi: Oxford University Press.

———. 2004. *Recovering Subversion: Feminist Politics Beyond the Law.* Urbana: Indiana University Press.

Merry, S.E. 2009. *Human Rights and Gender Violence: Translating International Law into Local Justice.* Chicago: University of Chicago Press.

Mignolo, W.D. 2000. 'The Many Faces of Cosmo-Polis: Border Thinking and Critical Cosmopolitanism', *Public Culture*, 12(3): 721–48.

Murray Li, T. 2007. *"The Will to Improve": Governmentality, Development and the Practice of Politics.* Durham and London: Duke University Press.

Phadke, S. 2003. 'Thirty Years On: Women's Studies Reflects on the Women's Movement', *Economic and Political Weekly*, 8(43): 4567–76.

Povinelli, E.A. 2011. *Economies of Abandonment: Social Belonging and Endurance in Late Liberalism.* Durham: Duke University Press.

Rai, S.M. 2002. *Gender and Political Economy of Development.* Oxford: Polity Press.

Rajan Sunder, R. 2003. *The Scandal of the State: Women, Law and Citizenship in Postcolonial India.* Durham: Duke University Press.

Ram, K. 2000. 'The State and the Women's Movement: Instabilities in the discourse of "rights" in India', in A.M. Hildson, V. Mackie, M. MacIntyre, and M. Stivens (eds), *Human Rights and Gender Politics: Asia-Pacific Perspectives*, pp. 60–82. New York and London: Routledge.

———. 2008. 'A New Consciousness Must Come: Affectivity and Movement in Tamil Dalit Women's Activist Engagement with Cosmopolitan Modernity', in P. Werbner (ed.), *Anthropology and Cosmopolitanism: Rooted, Feminist, and Vernacular Perspectives*, pp. 135–58. Oxford, NY: Berg Publishers.

Spivak, G.C. 1999. *A Critique of Postcolonial Reason.* Cambridge: Harvard University Press.

Wilson, R. (ed.). 1997. *Human Rights, Culture and Context: Anthropological Perspectives.* London: Pluto Press.

PART II

NORMATIVE SOURCES AND
INTELLECTUAL TRADITIONS

5

Human Moral Obligations, Dharma, and Human Rights

Shashi Motilal

The Western liberal conception[1] of human rights has become an entrenched part of our conceptual scheme for explaining, justifying, and criticizing the individual and state. However, many thinkers have also criticized the relevance of such a conception, particularly as a means of achieving global social justice. One of the concerns has been the question of whether such a conception can justify a set of human rights universally agreed upon by the international community which is diverse in its social, political, religious, and cultural set up. What is being sought is a concept which can be the 'norm' guiding an international moral code of human conduct. The question is can the Western liberal conception of human rights, where such rights are understood as universal moral claims that an individual can make against other individuals or the State (simply by virtue of the fact that he/she is human), fit this role?

In his chapter 'Conditions of an Unforced Consensus on Human Rights', Charles Taylor (2011) explains what it would mean to come to 'a genuine, unforced international consensus on human rights' in terms of the Rawlsian notion of 'overlapping consensus'[2] where, as he puts it,

> [D]ifferent groups, countries, religious communities, and civilizations, although holding incompatible fundamental views on theology, metaphysics, human nature, and so on, would come to an agreement on certain norms that ought to govern human behaviour. Each would have its own way of justifying this from out of its profound background conception. We would agree on the norms while disagreeing on why they were the right norms, and we would be content to live in this consensus, undisturbed by the differences of profound underlying beliefs. (Taylor 2011: 105).

Although Taylor raises the pertinent question of whether the traditional Western liberal conception of human rights could be that 'norm' around which an international consensus could form, he is quick to candidly express his doubts, especially in the face of the criticism and opposition that such a notion has evoked from cultural relativists. He candidly states that, 'we can't assume without further examination that a future unforced world consensus could be formulated to the satisfaction of everyone in the language of rights'. (Taylor 2011: 106). The aim of my paper is to explore the traditional conception in forging an unforced consensus to arrive at a universal norm of human rights. I develop the concept of 'human moral obligation' as a more promising candidate that would fit the role of the 'norm' that Taylor is seeking. My claim is that the concept of human moral obligation, which I derive from some aspects of the concept of *dharma* as it is found in the ancient Hindu philosophy and religion, is suitable for the role since it or something similar, along the lines of a broad notion of moral obligation, is to be found in the major ethical and religious systems of the world; this makes it a more basic concept than the concept of human rights which clearly has had its roots in the narrow Western liberal democratic form of political set up having its own share of conceptual problems.[3] Despite the many differences that the major world ethical and religious systems express in terms of their differing, sometimes even conflicting, metaphysical, theological, and other commitments, a minimalistic notion of obligation in some form is admitted and this could serve as the core element justifying a uniform system of moral code, defining and determining an international code of conduct. A concept of moral obligation derived from the vast and variegated foundational background of different metaphysical, ethical, and religious systems of thought would support and justify such a concept of human moral obligation while at the same time would also allow for the plurality of multi-dimensional belief systems to be found in the world community. Such a notion, therefore, is more likely to succeed in building the international consensus that we are trying to seek without undermining the cultural diversity supporting it. If we can admit such a concept of human moral obligation, the concept of human rights may no longer be relevant, or only relevant in so far as it would stand for the legal rights afforded by a legal system needed to enforce the system of human moral obligations. Of course, it goes without saying that the ideal legal system (the legal system as it ought to be, that is, a just and fair legal system) would need to be in conformity with the accepted notion of human moral obligation. In attempting to achieve my aim in the paper, I proceed as follows.

First, I give a brief description of the traditional Western conception of human rights, followed by the cultural relativist criticism, which renders it, in my opinion, a weak candidate for the role of the norm on which an international agreement could be reached.[4] Next, I give a brief account of the concept of dharma, and excluding some of the metaphysical baggage surrounding the notion of dharma, such as caste hierarchy, I propose to derive and develop a more general concept of human moral obligation from this idea. Lastly, I attempt to briefly outline the relation that the concept of human moral obligation will have to a legal system on the one hand and the foundational base of differing religious, metaphysical, and cultural background on the other.

The Traditional Western Notion of Human Rights and the Cultural Relativistic Critique

It is widely held that social justice can be achieved when people in society actually enjoy human rights, that is, can make claims that are moral—and maybe legal claims—against other individuals/institutions for what morally belongs to them by virtue of being human. Some rights that people enjoy can be justified on grounds such as law, custom, religion, tradition, culture, etc. But these are contingent aspects of social life, and may not always pass the test of moral scrutiny. Human rights have typically been admitted by appealing to something more permanent in human beings, something without which human beings would not be human, inalienable to human nature—their 'being human', their 'human-ness', which may be their human dignity, their rationality, their autonomous powers of thinking, their ability to use and understand language, engage in higher powers of thinking, their capacity for suffering, or their having 'capabilities' in the Sen-Nussbaum sense. If human rights are the inalienable rights that people have simply by virtue of being human, can securing human rights (understood in some such sense) alone ensure social justice? This 'individualistic' conception of human rights, with its roots in the largely Western political system of liberal democracy, has come under criticism from various quarters, amongst which the cultural relativist critique is perhaps the strongest. The main contention of the cultural relativist is that such a conception of human rights is not universally present in all cultures, for example, some pre-modern Western cultures and Non-Western cultures do not subscribe to it. Alasdair MacIntyre presents a strong critique of the concept in his book *After Virtue* (1981) where he concludes that there are no human rights because all attempts to give good reasons for the belief in human rights have failed. Belief in human rights is like 'belief in witches or unicorns' (MacIntyre 1981). Speaking of ancient and medieval societies, the question has often been raised as to whether the traditional Western conception of a human right is to be found in the Hindu society of ancient India.

Raimundo Panikkar (1982), while considering this question, has expressed scepticism towards the efficacy of human rights in bringing about social agreement amongst culturally different societies. He examines some of the basic assumptions underlying the traditional Western conception of human rights, and shows their weak points. According to him, the Western discourse on human rights assumes the following propositions, which are incorrect or dubious, at best.

(1) There is a universal human nature different from the rest of reality and that this is known through reason.

(2) The concept of human rights also implies dignity of the individual which in turn implies:

  a. A distinction and separation between the individual and society.
  b. Autonomy of humankind vis-à-vis, and often vs. the Cosmos.
  c. Resonances of the idea of man as micro-cosmos and reverberations of the conviction that man is *imago dei* [image of God], and at the same time the relative independence of this conviction from ontological and theological formulations.

(3) The underlying assumption of a democratic society which implies:

  a. That each individual is seen as equally important and thus equally responsible for the welfare of society. Each has a right to stand by his or her convictions.
  b. That society is the sum total of individuals whose wills are sovereign and ultimately decisive, and there is no instance that is superior to society.
  c. That rights and freedom of the individual can be limited only when they impinge upon the rights and freedom of other individuals, and therefore majority rule is traditionally justified. (Panikkar 1982: 80–3).

Panikkar closely examines these assumptions and rejects them as highly implausible. According to Panikkar, there is no universal concept of human rights because humankind presents a 'plurality of universes of discourse' and that if we want to extend the validity of a concept 'beyond its own context we shall have to justify the extrapolation'. (Panikkar 1982: 84). This he thinks is a difficult and complex matter.

Panikkar agrees that there certainly is a universal human nature, but this nature is not 'segregated and fundamentally distinct from the nature of all living beings and/or the entire reality'. (Panikkar 1982: 89). Also, any one interpretation of this 'universal human nature' may not apply entirely to human nature. He also accepts that human dignity is important and cannot be undermined in any way. However, he is of the opinion that the 'person' must be distinguished from the 'individual'. Explaining this distinction he says, 'The individual is just an abstraction, that is, a selection of a few aspects of the person for practical purposes. My person, on the other hand, is also in "my" parents, children, friends, foes, ancestors, and successors. "My" person is also in "my" ideas and feelings and in "my" belongings'. (Panikkar 1982: 90). Such an idea of a person has its repercussions on the idea of rights and here Panikkar has to say the following:

> Rights cannot be individualized in this way.... Rights cannot be abstracted from duties; the two are correlated. The dignity of the human person may equally be violated by your language, or by your desecrating a place I consider holy, even though it does not 'belong' to me in the sense of individualized property.... An individual is an isolated knot; a person is the entire fabric around that knot, woven from the total fabric of the real.... Certainly without the knots the net would collapse; but without the net, the knots would not even exist. To aggressively defend my individual rights, for instance, may have negative, i.e. unjust, repercussions on others and perhaps even on myself. The need for consensus in many traditions—instead of majority opinion—is based precisely on the corporate nature of human rights. (Panikkar: 1982: 90–1).

About the last assumption of democracy Panikkar says that human rights afford the means of protecting the dignity of individuals in such a set up, but in a hierarchical one, which need not necessarily be oppressive, the particular human being cannot defend his or her rights by demanding or exacting them independently of the whole. And, when considered in the context of the whole, the right may not even sustain (Panikkar 1982: 91).

Referring to the cultural relativist, Taylor says, 'They see something dangerously individualistic, fragmenting dissolvent of community in this Western legal culture [of human rights]' (Taylor 2011: 106–7). Thus, there seems to be some problem with the traditional conception of human rights, particularly in its individualistic connotation, that does not make it a fit candidate for the role of the 'norm' on which an unforced consensus of the international community can be sought. Clearly, the notion of human rights needs to be reviewed and reconsidered for this role.

It is to be noted that the international doctrine of human rights understood as a legal tradition has always been supported by a philosophical foundational base and it is my conviction that the foundational approach to the enterprise of seeking international consensus is fundamentally correct. None of the aspects of human nature which provide the philosophical justification for the concept of human rights—for example, human dignity, human rationality, autonomy, basic sense of equality, etc.—can be denied and neither are they in conflict with each other. The problem lies not with identifying some human trait which is universally and essentially present in all human beings, but in treating this trait as 'a justification for an individual claim that I can make on others', which is what the language of rights amounts to. What is problematic, in my view, is the notion of a human right as being a moral claim that one individual has over others in society in abstraction from the 'person' that she or he is. On my account, as humans we do share a common trait or common nature and that is our individual and collective sense of moral responsibility or moral obligation to our self as a person and to every other being, human or non-human. The notion of human moral obligation that I am trying to develop is normative and is construed along lines of the notion of dharma as is delineated in classical and modern Hindu religion and ethics. I would like to briefly put forward an account of the notion of dharma in the next section and then go on to delineate the concept of human moral obligation which, as I understand it, could be divested of much of the metaphysical baggage associated with the notion of dharma, while at the same time be powerful enough to form the norm defining an international moral code of conduct.

The Concept of Dharma[5]

Ancient Indian philosophy conceives of the relation between the individual and society and their connection to morality in terms of dharma. The concept of dharma is a polymorphous concept which in its diverse though not unrelated senses has remained a dominant and pervasive concept in the Hindu way of life. Over a period of several centuries it acquired wide ramifications of meaning and was used in different contexts including the metaphysical, moral, religious, artistic, social, political, legal, etc. Hence no single definition suffices to encapsulate its meaning which is to be understood from the context in which it has been used. One of the important aspects of this concept is encapsulated in the following lines:

dhāraṇād dharmam ity āhur dharmo dhārayati prajāḥ
yaḥ syād dhāraṇa saṃyuktaḥ sa dharma iti niścayaḥ

[Dharma is that which maintains the social order. Dharma ensures
well-being and progress of humanity. Dharma is surely that which fulfills these objectives]. (*Mahābhārata* Karṇaparva, 49.50).

According to Kane, in the course of its long history, the main meaning of dharma came to be 'the privileges, duties and obligations of a man (or woman) his (or her) standard of conduct as a member of the Aryan (Hindu) community, as a member of one of the castes, as a person in a particular stage of life.'[6]

It has been maintained in ancient Indian philosophy that human life is enmeshed in imperfections which bring about suffering. Thus, the quest for perfection and the resulting end to suffering was considered to be the *summum bonum* of life. It was also held that following one's dharma was the only and the most effective way to reach this desired goal. For Hindus, the *Dharmaśāstras*, or Dharma Texts, both described and prescribed a person's duties and responsibilities in terms of their gender, caste, and stage in life (student, householder, forest dweller, or holy wanderer). According to Kanada, author of the Vaiśeṣika Sūtra, doing one's prescribed duties not only led the individual to material prosperity (*abhyudaya*), but also to spiritual enhancement (*mokṣa* or *niḥśreyasa*): yato 'bhyudaya niḥśreyasa siddhiḥ sa dharmaḥ (Vaiśeṣika Sūtra 1.1.2) (that is dharma which leads to material prosperity and spiritual enhancement). In fact, it was held in Hindu ethics that dharma if properly practised was the surest means to universal welfare (*sarvabhūtāhita*), which should be the goal of all cosmic processes. But, what was important was that this was a goal which was not to be realized in isolation by an individual. In fact, in the Vedic culture, there is no idea of an isolated individual as every existence is conceived as an element (*piṇḍa* or *vyaṣṭi*) in the totality (*brahmāṇḍa* or *Samaṣṭi*) or as one with the totality.[7] The purpose is to create an ideal society that affords its members the means to develop towards perfection and liberation.

Dharma has both an ontological dimension and a normative dimension. In its ontological dimension, it is 'the cosmic ordering principle that upholds and promotes the evolution of the universe as a whole and each of its individual parts'. (Holdrege 2004: 213). Dharma constitutes the nature of a thing (*svabhāva*) and its disposition (*guṇa*). Thus the dharma of fire is to burn and that of water is to quench thirst. As Sri Aurobindo puts it, 'Everything indeed has its Dharma, its law of life imposed on it by its nature' (Sri Aurobindo 1959: 104). Though the dharma of each individual is distinct and specific to itself, no individual has an isolated and independent nature. Everything partakes in the totality (*samaṣṭi*) as its member or part (*vyaṣṭi*) (Sri Aurobindo 1959: 340).

Dharma also regulates the functioning (*karma* or course of action) of everything in the entire Cosmos, thereby sustaining it. This regulation is needed most for the self-conscious human being (*puruṣa*) who is bestowed by nature with free will and responsibility. It is 'the cosmic ordering principle that regulates every aspect of individual, social, and cosmic life, finding expression on the human plane in a comprehensive system of sociocultural norms and duties' (Holdrege 2004: 238). Thus dharma serves as a foundation to morality. A virtue or dharma is posited as a norm of conduct to be followed, and it is also the prescribed duty to perform.

In traditional Hindu ethics, dharma is ultimately dependent upon the cosmic order for its normative power. The reference to a transcendental order is necessary to guarantee the unconditionality, universalizability, and infallibility of dharma. However, dharma as a moral norm is not rigidly absolute. It admits of 'wise-relativity', as Sri Aurobindo puts it (Sri Aurobindo 1959: 92). There are many situations where the transgression of dharma is allowed. Such crisis situations (*dharmasaṃkaṭa* or *āppatih*) demand deviations, known as *āpaddharma*. Otherwise it is non-violable. These situations have been categorized and codified to eliminate arbitrariness and subjectivism. Thus, there is room for exceptions without giving up on the absolute, eternal, and inviolable nature of dharma.

Dharma is fixed and yet evolving. In the words of Sri Aurobindo, 'Dharma is fixed in its essence, but still it develops in our consciousness and evolves and has stages; there are gradations of spiritual and ethical ascension in the search for the highest law of our nature'.

(Sri Aurobindo 1959: 104). This implies that our moral consciousness is constantly evolving until the state of perfection is reached.

Dharma as a normative principle enjoins or prescribes 'privileges, duties, and obligations' at two different levels—those that are common or universal (*sādhāraṇa dharma*), that is, incumbent on all people; and those that are specific, depending on one's gender, caste, and life-stage (*svadharma*). The first, which are shared by all people, would include the virtues of compassion for all creatures, patience, lack of envy and greed, generosity, non-violence, etc. The second set of privileges, duties, and obligations are different for different individuals and also for the same individual in different situations or stations of life. They are classified under *svadharmas, varṇāśramadharmas, kuladharmas, yugadharmas*, etc. Thus there is a wide variety of dharmas.

The Hindu view of life admits of four stages in life (*āśramas*), four social orders (*varṇas*), and four objects of life (*puruṣārthas*). The scheme of four puruṣārthas, namely, *dharma* [righteousness], *artha* [material wealth], *kāma* [desire], and *mokṣa* [liberation] encompass all the different aspects and stages of human existence—individual, social, and cosmic. Of the four puruṣārthas the concept of dharma is assigned the first place in order of preference since it must regulate artha and kāma so that they could lead one to mokṣa, the highest goal of life. What this implies is that the acquisition of material resources (artha) and their enjoyment (kāma) both require proper management through dharma. Without being regulated by dharma they are not puruṣārthas. It is to be noted that Hinduism espouses an organic view of society and a relational understanding of the human person. A person is not an isolated individual but is to be defined as a member of both a family and community having specific responsibilities at different stages in his or her life and as determined by gender, by kinship group into which one is born—that is, one's caste—and by one's individual abilities. Caste hierarchy, of course, has been one of the most oppressive features of Indian society; but it has been, and continues to be, challenged by many (for example, Gandhi) on the basis of resources internal to Hinduism.

Human Moral Obligations in the Light of Dharma

The classical view about human rights takes them to be moral claim rights expressing a three term relation between a claimant (human in this case), a good or value, and a duty bearer (natural or a non-natural person like a state or a state agency) (Hinsch and Stepanians 2006: 119). This understanding of human rights is problematic to the extent that it shows the concept itself to be otiose. It is an indubitable fact that there are certain values—that is basic values, for example, life itself. Being a value, it is inherently prescriptive, imposing a certain obligation on everything which is capable of upholding it (that is, preserving it). Thus it is a moral obligation on every being which is capable of preserving life that that being does preserve life and not do anything which violates it in any form except under exceptional circumstances. Thus, the relation is a two-termed relation between a value and those that are morally obliged to uphold that value. It goes without saying that there is a plurality of such values and we have different obligations (perfect and imperfect obligations) to uphold these values. Also, that human moral obligations are moral obligations that humans have towards other humans in their individual capacities as well as members belonging to groups. In other words there is also a collective sense of human moral obligation which enjoins us as members of groups to look after the welfare of the group.[8] The underlying idea is that, that is the way the world order under the Cosmic Order is supposed to be, or rather ought to be, though that is not how it actually is.[9] Human moral obligations are not upheld due to many reasons.[10] If everyone acted according to the dictates of human moral obligations then we would have an ideal world order— the perfect world, the utopian order that is sought after. Since that is not so, society needs a distributive and retributive system to take care of the benefits and burdens of the co-operative as well as the non-cooperative efforts of people in society. Such a system is afforded by the law of the land which gives its people the right to make claims against others who have defaulted in making good their obligations towards them. The claim-rights system which expresses a three-term relation between a claimant, a good, and a duty bearer is thus the relation expressed by the system of positive/legal rights and duties. In fact, human moral obligations act as guidelines to build such a legal system while at the same time providing moral justification to it. Any legal system would be morally justified if it had the backing of moral obligations, otherwise it would itself be morally wrong. It is in this sense that there are 'bad laws' which need to be reviewed and changed. It is to be noted that it is in this sense that both humans and non-humans including natural and non-natural things can fall within the purview of the law of the land implying that normally animals, historical monuments, cultural artifacts, etc. also have the legal right to be preserved or not to be desecrated. It follows that if at the moral plane, there are no claim rights as human rights are envisaged to be, and if such claim rights are only rights afforded by a legal system in place, then human rights as moral claim rights become redundant. The so called human rights are only legal rights or positive rights albeit to be supported by a sense of moral obligation which forms the under grid supporting different legal systems. Our common sense of moral obligation may be derived from different religious, philosophical, socio-political, and cultural belief systems, but as moral obligations towards oneself and everything else in the cosmos, they would have a minimalist common meaning. Such a sense of moral obligation is admitted by most, if not all belief systems.

Every human being thus has a human moral obligation to himself/herself, as well as to other beings (both human and sub-human), to treat each with dignity and respect, as every being is an integral part of the cosmic whole. This is his basic moral obligation or what is termed as *sādhāraṇa* dharma in the Hindu context. These basic human moral obligations are present in every human being from birth and ought to be fulfilled, although the fact is that because a human being is a slave of his passions and because he is free, at times he is misled and does what he ought not to do and/or fails to do what he ought to do. This results in what are called 'human rights violations' in the language of human rights.

Like dharma, basic human moral obligations have a constitutive as well as a regulative aspect in our lives. In their constitutive aspect, they make us what we are as a species and regulate our life as it ought to be *vis-à-vis* the other elements in the entire cosmos. If and when these basic moral obligations are fulfilled by all towards all, there would be no need for individuals to make claims against one another, for example, to be treated with respect and dignity.[11] It must also be kept in mind that besides human beings, no other being (for example, a non-human animal) is capable of actually making such claims, and yet in a sense, it too has a place in the cosmos. Therefore, what is construed as a 'right', that is, a claim of a sort, would unfairly exclude non-human animals unless one can argue for the rights of animals in the same sense, which is difficult, I think, to say the least. On the other hand to say that as humans we have moral obligations even towards non-human beings would spell out a more cordial relationship between humans and the non-human world. This relationship between human and everything non-human is a pervading theme in traditional Indian philosophy expressed in the idea of the relationship between the *piṇḍa* (part or element) and the *brahmāṇḍa* (the Cosmos or the Whole). Thus, the so called 'basic right to life' as an individual moral claim is better understood as a moral obligation where each being's existence is assured because of moral obligations that all humans must fulfil and not merely because it can make a claim for itself. Moreover, a claim right is always a right against someone/something who/which has a duty to respect and fulfil that right. But so far as basic rights are concerned, the rights holder also has a similar duty towards others who have similar rights. We would need to say that each person has both a right against another and a duty towards him too. It is surely less complicated and parsimonious to think that everyone has an obligation towards all others to treat each other with dignity and respect, not to unnecessarily harm one another, etc. Thus, in their regulative aspect, human moral obligations serve as the foundation of morality since they are instrumental in regulating the action of human beings.

Besides the basic human moral obligations which all human beings have *qua* human being, and which afford life and dignified existence to all beings, there are other moral obligations that one has by virtue of the personal and social roles that one enters into throughout one's life.[12] For example, as a parent, I have the moral obligations associated with being a good parent and my child must eventually learn about his obligations towards me, as a parent. When we each fulfill these obligations, there is no need for rights. Obligations determined by social roles are affected by cultural determinants and since cultures differ in different societies, the social role which determines human moral obligations would be different in different cultures. For example, most societies would want to grant that elders of the society must be respected by the younger. But the expression of respect for elders is culturally determined. In some cultures, such as in the Hindu culture, we touch the feet of our elders but this is not a practice in non-Hindu cultures. Again on the same score, there may be practices in the latter that are alien to the former. It would be wrong to believe that in non-Hindu cultures, where the young do not touch the feet of their elders, the right of the elders to be respected is being violated by the younger generation. The so called right to be respected, or rather, the respect that they deserve, is by and large given to them in both cultures but expressed in different ways. In fact, it would be odd to say that elders in a society can claim respect. Respect is earned by doing respectful deeds where the other person feels obliged to treat you with respect. It is human moral obligation of the young to respect the elderly and for them to reciprocate by love and affection. Equally odd would it be to say that the young have a right to be loved. Such sentiments between generations are better understood along lines of human moral obligations, otherwise construing them as rights will lead to an unnecessary proliferation of rights.

Human moral obligations do not depend on any empirical order which accounts for their authoritative and obligatory character. In that sense, they are different from legal rights and duties that are enforced by some existing empirical order. Like dharma, human moral obligations are dependent on the Cosmic Order for their normative power. Deriving their obligatory nature from the Cosmic Order guarantees their unconditional, universal, and infallible character.[13] But this does not mean that human moral obligations are absolute and admit of no exceptions. Like dharma, they admit of 'wise relativity' or exceptions. Our human moral obligations are *prima facie* duties which can be overridden by other duties depending on the nature of the exceptional circumstance.

Thus, human moral obligations are fixed and yet evolving with the evolution of moral consciousness in human society. Along the lines of Sri Aurobindo's philosophy, one can believe that this evolution continues until perfection is reached. The idea is that we can perpetually try to make ourselves into morally better beings. As human moral obligations are not static, they are different for different individuals and also for the same individuals in different situations. Depending on where one is, 'one's station in life' including one's personal, professional, social, and political roles, one's human moral obligations will be determined.[14]

To the question—how are human moral obligations known—the answer is that the basic obligations (which may be positive or negative) like not to unnecessarily harm others, to have respect and dignity for the inherent worth of every being, not to intentionally deceive others, etc. are inherent in human nature and common to all human beings. To say this is to say that a human being is essentially a morally good being. The evil in him has external causes that he cannot overcome because of weakness of will. This sentiment is echoed in the writings of many modern Indian philosophers like Gandhi, Sri Aurobindo, Rabindranath Tagore, and others. Regarding social role-related obligations, these are acquired by sources in society, like parents, teachers, elders, friends, etc., are deeply influenced by culture, and are expressed differently in different cultures.

Our human moral obligations, like the notion of dharma, form the backbone of our social moral existence. They are the indices that tell us how we should live our lives by regulating our actions and desires. If actions are not regulated by an understanding of our human moral obligations, then they cannot be virtuous. For example, material wealth is an economic value, the equitable distribution of which is made possible by the regulatory force of human moral obligations. Wealth not acquired in this way and/or desires not fulfilled in accordance with the regulatory authority of our human moral obligations will result in what are called 'violations of human rights' in the rights discourse.

Dharma, in the Vedic context, is not only an end to being a puruṣārthas (end or goal of life); it is also a means of mokṣa (liberation). At this point, I do not want to say that the complete fulfillment of human moral obligations will lead us to the attainment of liberation in any transcendental sense, but if a world in which there are no violations of the so called human rights is a desirable world, then fulfilling our human moral obligations is surely a means of attaining such a world. It is definitely a means of achieving social and global justice.

So far in developing the concept of human moral obligations I have tried to show some affinities of this concept with the notion of dharma in traditional Indian philosophy. But there are some important and crucial differences. First, let me emphasize that my development of human moral obligations (both basic and role determined obligations) do not presuppose a caste hierarchical social structure with links to a theory of karma, rebirth, and the notion of retributive justice in any way. The model that I am proposing is certainly not committed to a hierarchical social structure in terms of caste or race distinctions, although distinctions of gender and class cannot be so easily offloaded. In any case, admitting gender and class distinctions need not necessarily result in discriminatory practices in any derogatory sense. In that sense, the model that I am suggesting offloads some of the metaphysical and soteriological commitments of Hindu philosophy without giving up on its basic metaphysical assumptions of the nature of the self (the Atman and Brahman and the relation between them). The 'metaphysical baggage' which can be offloaded from the concept of human moral obligation was an integral part of the belief system of people of ancient India of Hindu faith since it was related to the concept of dharma itself. Similar metaphysical commitments may be part of the belief systems of people of other religious faiths or again the same metaphysical commitments may persist in the belief systems of present day followers of the Hindu faith. But, so long as these different people can agree on the common norm of human moral obligations, we would have an 'unforced consensus' in Taylor's terms or a Rawlsian 'overlapping consensus'. I am thus led to believe that people having different religious faiths with conflicting and opposing metaphysical commitments may be convinced about a minimalistic concept of human moral obligation, that about such a concept there could be an international 'overlapping consensus', and that such a concept would help us outline a universally acceptable moral code of human conduct. The moral code of conduct would be universally acceptable since that would be defined and determined by the 'overlapping consensus' on the concept of human moral obligation.

But what is most important here is to understand how the concept of human moral obligation would actually encounter and explain cultural plurality and diversity while retaining the intercultural common grounding I seek for it. How do the cultural and moral differences of diverse cultural communities get expressed to give room for cultural identities to stay intact or at least discernibly different? Here, I would like to fall back upon some ideas found in Charles Beitz's recent work *The Idea of Human Rights* (2009). What Beitz wants to say in the context of human rights, I wish to employ and exploit in the context of human moral obligations.

Explaining 'intercultural agreement' in the context of theories of natural rights and agreement theories, Beitz states that the concept consists of the following three elements[15] (Beitz 2009: 74–5):

(1) A 'common core' which is the minimum to which all members of a cultural community would agree;
(2) an 'overlapping consensus' amongst people belonging to diverse cultures; and
(3) 'progressive convergence'.

There are many culturally different human communities with different, sometimes even conflicting and opposing, belief systems. But, in each community, there is a sense of moral obligation present which forms the common minimum core to which all members of the community agree. Different communities, through a process of 'overlapping consensus' and 'progressive convergence', are able to arrive at a norm which I claim is not that of a universal notion of human rights, but a universal sense of human moral obligation understood as the sense of moral obligation that humans owe, not only to other humans, but to the entire Cosmos. 'Progressive convergence' I would understand in the same sense as Beitz as 'intercultural agreement that arises not from the actual contents of existing moral cultures, but instead from the contents of these cultures as they might develop or evolve under pressures for adaptive reinterpretation'. He talks of 'the best available elaboration of the basic normative materials of these cultures for the circumstances of modern life'. (Beitz 2009: 88). Thus, it is the practical constraints of global modern living which drive us to the unforced consensus that Taylor talks about. This also leads us to the tripartite levels that Taylor thinks is what we should distinguish in our conceptual model. At one level is the 'norm' which defines and determines the international code of morally acceptable conduct and this norm is provided by the concept of human moral obligation and not by the traditional notion of rights. This norm itself is derived from or is the outcome of an 'overlapping consensus' at the basis of which is the vast and variegated system of different, and sometimes conflicting, belief systems.[16] This forms a second level in the model, and yet at another level, the third level, the norm itself gets expressed in the form of legal systems which state laws which enforce the code of conduct on individuals by ascribing to them legal rights and legal duties. The legal system of one state can differ from the legal system of another state in the specific laws that it enacts, but it would count as a 'just and fair' legal system only if it is in consonance with the norm arrived at by the processes of 'overlapping consensus' as well as 'progressive convergence'. Thus, there is the norm at one level, its philosophical justification at another level, and its legal expression at a third level. None of this overrules the fact that the norm itself gets expressed in culturally different behaviour which can be morally evaluated in terms of the internationally agreed upon norm.

In another respect also, the idea of human moral obligations is important in that it links closely with the idea of human agency. After all, duties are to be done and obligations must ensue in actions. They are what one 'must do'. Rights are claims. They are not things we do, rather in making a claim, we are waiting for something to be done to us or for us, either by other individual(s) or some institution, even if it is only a negative duty they may be performing. But, it might be asked—in fulfilling my human moral obligations I am doing something for others, how am I doing something for myself—what rights are guaranteed to us? It must be remembered that we have a moral obligation towards ourselves too—to protect and promote our well-being—which makes killing in self-defence also morally correct. In fact, my moral obligation to protect myself is a stronger motive for action than my right to do the same. Also, it is because I have this moral obligation towards myself that there is the law to safeguard this obligation providing me the legal right to protect myself. Therefore, in doing our duties, we do things for ourselves in the long run. It is true that when others (that is, other than myself) fulfil their human moral obligations, my interests will be taken care of, but what if they fail to do so? In other words, how do we ensure a universal fulfilment of human moral obligations? Is it to be legislated from above or do we rely on the moral compass of members of society? The approach needs to be two-pronged. One, to generate the sense of human moral obligations in people (both in the individual and collective sense) and the moral motivation to fulfil them, and second, to have a legal system based on a strong moral foundation to take care of cases where these obligations are not fulfiled. In that sense, human rights as legal rights act as fall back mechanisms when we fail to fulfil our moral obligations. I do not have a detailed road map to put forward at this point, but I firmly believe that it would need to come from within our moral conscience. There are practical considerations to be taken into account but from the theoretical point of view, I think that in fulfilling our human moral obligations, we are making conceptual space for social justice, because to understand and act on our human moral obligations is nothing but treating people as they deserve to be treated, giving them what is due to them, and this I take to be the core of social justice.

* * *

In my view, if human moral obligations are admitted as binding on every human being, then we can dispense with the language of human rights, although legal rights would have to be admitted as fall back mechanisms. One of the reasons why the concept of human rights was admitted, calling for basic moral rights which every human being had by virtue of being human, was because it was thought that the law of the land itself could be unfair (for example, the laws that allowed apartheid). If the law of the land is in conformity with our human moral obligations, it would not be unfair. Where individuals fail to abide by their human moral obligations, legal rights could be appealed to, to rectify the wrong done. Cultures which justify so called human rights violations on grounds of cultural and moral diversity, and on grounds that there is no universal and uniform notion of human rights, have laws which at best need to be reinterpreted or at worst discarded. They are morally wrong in the first place because they are not in conformity with the basic human moral obligations which in essence transcend all cultural differences. The violations in question are violations of laws which themselves are violations of basic human moral obligations.

Thus, I believe we can do without the notion of human rights since it carries with it the baggage of individualism and is feasible only on the ability to make claims for one self in abstraction from the human relations in which we are intrinsically entrenched and the roles that we are inextricably tied up in. The language of human rights has no advantage over the language of human moral obligation. On the contrary, the latter helps us to keep out of problems that the former implies. To know and fulfil our human moral obligations is the need of the global human community and that is the point of an 'unforced consensus'.

Notes

1. I am grateful to Prof. Jay Drydyk for drawing my attention to the point that it is a certain conception of human rights that I am examining and rejecting in my paper. Human rights, in my opinion, are legal or positive rights afforded by the State Law as back up measures to achieve social and perhaps global justice too, when human moral obligations fail to be fulfilled.

2. The chapter by Prof. Drydyk in this volume argues for the position that Taylor's 'unforced consensus' is different from Rawls's 'overlapping consensus' in an important sense, although Taylor himself does not seem to understand this. Here, I take Taylor on his own admission that it is like Rawls's 'overlapping consensus'.

3. Such philosophies, that is, the various ancient Indian philosophical systems, are diverse in many aspects of their philosophies, but they (barring the materialists) broadly share the principles defining and delineating the concept of dharma.

4. In my account of the cultural relativistic critique of the concept of human rights, I have concentrated more on pointing out the reasons why it fails to be universally acceptable than on the obvious fact that there is cultural plurality and diversity, which cannot be ignored.

5. In this section, I have tried to give a brief account of the concept of dharma (including its metaphysical underpinnings) as it is found in some primary and secondary sources. In the next section, where I explain the concept of human moral obligation, I also make clear the aspects of dharma that I do not subscribe to, for example, the caste system.

6. Kane (1974), as quoted in Vasudha Narayanan (2001). It is to be noted that the definition does not include the term 'right'. In the early Vedas the word 'dharma' appears many times and in later texts it means 'religious ordinances and rites' or sometimes 'fixed principles or rules of conduct'. When paired with other words, dharma can mean 'merit acquired by the performance of religious rites' and 'the whole body of religious duties'—view of Vasudha Narayanan as quoted in Harold Coward. 2005. *Human Rights and the World's Major Religions, Vol. 4: The Hindu Tradition*, p. 32. Westport, CT: Praeger.

7. This idea is pervasive in the Vedic texts. I have not found a single verse referring to this idea quoted in any secondary source on the subject matter.

8. At the outset I would like to state that human moral obligations include both perfect and imperfect obligations, as these are standardly understood in the literature. I also believe that these moral obligations would be determined by one's circumstances, abilities, and to whom these obligations are due. In this sense both individuals and collectives like the state and state agencies can be said to have moral obligations.

9. It is true that materialists would not believe in a Cosmic order and the subjectivists and emotivists would be disinclined to believe in any objectively real order in the world, but I think that there is enough evidence of some sort of order expressed in the natural world as expressed in the dharma (natural dispositions) of things; perhaps there is more order than there is disorder, and this prompts me to believe that there is real objective order in things and this is one facet of the Cosmic Order which is constitutive as well as normative in nature.

10. The reasons may be both internal as well as external to the person. If one fails in one's obligations due to reasons outside one's control then the individual cannot be held morally responsible for his action/inaction and may be acquitted.

11. Since one has a basic human moral obligation to oneself too, for example, to preserve one's existence, self-respect, dignity, etc., when these are threatened, one can indeed take action in self-defence. This would mean that I ought not to harm animals except in self-defence. In such a circumstance, the moral obligation not to harm another would not be a *prima facie* obligation overridden by another; there would be no such obligation because he who wilfully harms deserves no protection.

12. I think the idea of 'role determined human moral obligations' is very important but largely unexplored in this context. Throughout our lives we are playing different roles and related to these are different responsibilities which must be fulfilled. These would create different obligations which would be morally binding on us.

13. I admit that there could be other causes of convergence among moralities like enough commonalities in our moral psychology, or the fact of the presence of human reason, but that there is a transcendental source like the Cosmic Order needs to be admitted too so that the convergence rests not merely on contingent matters of fact.

14. A role, it is to be noted, is different from social categories like caste, class, gender, race, etc. One can do without the latter, although to some extent it would be difficult to off load gender and class differences.

But, one cannot ignore in any way the roles that we are in, or choose to be in, during different stages of our lives.

15. Beitz himself is critical of this attempt on the part of the naturalists and the agreement theorists and thinks that the problem of human rights needs a 'fresh start'. I, however, think that there is a lot that makes sense in the three elements and can be effectively used to understand 'intercultural agreement'.

16. The belief systems would comprise of different beliefs including metaphysical beliefs about human nature, religious and ethical beliefs, sociopolitical and cultural beliefs, etc.

References

Beitz, C. 2009. *The Idea of Human Rights*. Oxford: Oxford University Press.

Coward, H. 2005. *Human Rights and the World's Major Religions, Vol. 4*. Westport, Connecticut: Praeger Perspectives.

Donnelly, J. 1982. 'Human Rights and Human Dignity: An Analytical Critique of Non-Western Conceptions of Human Rights', *American Political Science Review*, 76: 303–16.

Hinsch, W. and M. Stepanians. 2006. 'Human Rights as Moral Claim Rights', in R. Martin and D.A. Reidy (eds), *Rawls's Law of Peoples: A Realistic Utopia?* Oxford: Oxford University Press.

Holdrege, B. 2004. 'Dharma', in S. Mittal and G. Thursby (eds), *The Hindu World*, pp. 213–48. New York: Routledge.

Kane, Pandurang Vaman. 1974. *History of Dharmasastra, Vol. II, Part I*, 2nd edition, p. 3, Poona: Bhandarkar Oriental Institute.

Mahābhārata Karṇaparva. www.sacred-texts.com/hin/mbs/mbs08049.htm (accessed 31 July 2013).

Lipner, J. 2000. 'A Hindu View of Life', in J. Runzo and N.M. Martin (eds), *The Meaning of Life in the World Religions*. Oxford: One World Publications.

MacIntyre, A. 1981. *After Virtue*. Notre Dame, IN: University of Notre Dame Press.

Narayanan, V. 2001. 'Hindu Ethics and Dharma', in J. Runzo and N.M. Martin (eds), *Ethics in the World Religions*, pp. 177–95. Oxford: One World Publications.

Panikkar, R. 1982. 'Is the Notion of Human Rights a Western Concept?' *Diogenes*, 30(75): 75–102.

Rawls, J. 1971. *A Theory of Justice*. Cambridge, MA: Harvard University Press.

Rawls, J. 1993. *Political Liberalism*. New York: Columbia University Press.

Rouner, L.S. (ed.). 1988. *Human Rights and the World's Religions.* Notre Dame, IN: University of Notre Dame Press.

Sri Aurobindo. 1959. *The Foundations of Indian Culture, 1st edition.* Pondicherry: Sri Aurobindo Ashrama Press.

Taylor, C. 2011. *Dilemmas and Connections: Selected Essays.* Cambridge: Harvard University Press.

6

Autonomy and Human Rights in Ancient and Modern Indian Buddhism

Gordon Davis

There are many ways to debunk the claim that traditional Western and Indian values diverge when it comes to matters of individual autonomy and other human rights ideals. It might suffice to point out that while the discourses of rights and justice that one finds in Gandhi or Ambedkar were absent in classical Indian philosophy, likewise the discourses of rights and justice that one finds in Kant, Mill, and Rawls were absent in classical and medieval Western philosophy. Rather than radical cultural difference, what we find is that the evolution of modern statehood saw rights-based frameworks emerge out of earlier, embryonic conceptions of individual dignity, conceptions with roots in both traditions. These particular rights-based frameworks were often either legal or legalistic, and when we distinguish legal rights from moral rights, a broader range of values needs to be considered in order to determine whether pre-modern reflections on dignity and justice amount, in some cases, to a tacit acknowledgement of human rights ideals.

But a debunking of the claim to Western exceptionalism with respect to understanding autonomy and rights could go deeper than this. The key ideas of the Enlightenment in the West were not based on Plato, Aristotle, or the Stoics; those Western icons were rather heroes of an earlier so-called 'renaissance'. The Enlightenment went beyond Greco-Roman ideas and ideals, for better or for worse. Those who take it to have been for the better might put it this way: the Enlightenment not only went beyond the confines of the Christian faith, but also beyond Greco-Roman ideas about fate, metaphysical teleology, natural hierarchies and the tragic outcomes of hubris, among other ideas and beliefs. Partly by developing explanations for these beliefs, modern thinkers exposed these and other forms of false consciousness, and arguably fostered liberating new ways for understanding humanity and its place in nature. However, this more literal process of 'enlightenment' was not rooted exclusively in Western ideas;[1] arguably a similar ideal of enlightenment had already put down roots in ancient Indian thought—in the common cause of *Vedānta* and Buddhism against false consciousness.

In evoking an ideal of spiritual enlightenment in this context, I may be suspected of equivocating with the word 'enlightenment'. But I shall argue here that the relationship between the Buddhist concept of enlightenment and the modern one is closer than is often recognized, and also that the relationship between enlightenment and individual autonomy is closer in Buddhist thought (and perhaps also in Vedānta) than is often recognized.

I shall also argue that while philosophical trends come and go in every tradition, some values are universal and normatively valid in ways that various traditions have recognized and undertaken to defend philosophically. Some would expect universal values, if there are any, to be ideals of success or well-being that are (potentially) 'facilitated by' rights, rather than turning out to be the rights themselves. Such an expectation would be strongest among those who accept an 'instrumental' view of the value of rights. But my first task here will be to lay out an alternative to instrumental and intrinsic (or 'status-based') explanations of the value of rights. It may partly be due to unawareness of this alternative that many have overlooked the relevance of autonomy and rights to some classical Indian conceptions of ethics.

Before outlining this alternative account of the value of human rights, I will say a couple of things about my methods in appealing to Buddhist ethics as a source of evidence for universalism about the value of autonomy. First of all, I make no assumption about there being anything special, or epistemically privileged, about moral perspectives that are rooted in Buddhism. Evidence of moral insight from other philosophical traditions, for example those in China that predated the arrival of Buddhism, would be similarly revealing. But more importantly in the present context, much of what we discover in Buddhist axiology—that is to say, ethics in the broadest sense—is discernible in Advaita Vedānta thought. Arguably it is precisely in those convergences between Buddhism and Hinduism (for example, between the Yogācāra school of Mahāyāna Buddhism and early Advaita Vedānta, which overlapped in the period 800–1000 CE) that intellectual autonomy took a form that balanced individual rights with the value of enlightenment in a way that foreshadows modern conceptions of autonomy and human rights.

Secondly, I should be clear about the manner and purpose of my citing of Buddhist texts here. In discussing Buddhist sources, I will draw on texts that offer moral insights at increasing levels of generality. After an initial discussion of the classical doctrine of *anatta/anātman*, I begin with anecdotes from the Pāli Canon; I will then consider Ambedkar's generalizations about the ethical principles they invoke; and finally I will consider the relevance to autonomy (and especially, freedoms of thought and expression) of central values and ideals, such as those of *prajñāpāramitā* (perfection of wisdom), *tathāgatagarbha* (a universal individual potentiality for enlightenment), *brahmavihāra* (an attitude that combines compassion and even-handedness), and *nirvāṇa*. The anecdotes suggest that certain rights were tacitly accepted in ancient Indian Buddhist contexts. Meanwhile, the principles and ideals provide potential justifications for such rights. What is important, in terms of assessing a universalist claim, is not whether these rights were made legally explicit, but whether a justification was and is available from within the conceptual resources of multiple traditions. It is better evidence of universalism to see independently evolved rationales for rights in a world where most societies ignore them than to see a legal framework of rights imposed throughout the world, but without any actual or potential justification to go along with it.[2]

A Non-Kantian Notion of Autonomy Common to Modern Westerners and Ancient Buddhists: how Appearance Matters when the Appearance of Choice Differs from Reality

It is important to be clear at the outset that 'autonomy' will not be used here in a Kantian sense, even though later on I will refer to some of Kant's specific ideas about human rights. The ethical convergence I claim we can find across these otherwise widely differing cultural contexts is one that treats Kantian moral premises as more peripheral to the modern Western context than is sometimes assumed to be the case (and *a fortiori*, I shall marginalize Judaeo-Christian voluntarism); and on the Indian side, for present purposes, we can similarly marginalize certain instances of moral rigorism, such as can be found in some monastic orders (not to mention parallel instances of voluntarism in Hindu and Buddhist traditions).

It will also be important to keep in mind that in emphasizing convergence, I do not wish to underestimate the distinctive contribution of certain Buddhist insights, overlooked or neglected in the West, which can inform the process of improving Western theories of ethics, justice, and rights. One example I wish to highlight here at the outset is that which goes by the simple name *anatta* (in Pāli) or *anātman* (in Sanskrit)—the doctrine of 'no-self' or 'non-self'. It is worth mentioning here, since it is incompatible with Kantian autonomy but compatible—though perhaps not obviously so—with the notion of autonomy favoured in what follows.

Kant treated the Leibnizian conception of the highest good as a beneficial but illusory ideal,[3] but treated free will *qua* autonomy as something that is not illusory in that way—that is, he treated autonomy as having a kind of objective reality with respect to the metaphysics of personhood. I will argue that we can stand this position on its head, and still retain a place for autonomy in the axiology that validates human rights ideals. Autonomy 'as a feature of persons' (*qua ontological*) is at best a beneficial but illusory ideal; but *qua beneficial*, we may be able to construe autonomy *qua value*, without fully indulging the ontological illusion. Meanwhile, ethical conceptions of the highest good can be taken seriously, without our relying on any such metaphysics of personhood.

The Western philosophical tradition has been slow to articulate forms of reductionism and eliminativism about personhood—and even slower to see the potential moral significance of these forms of metaphysical revisionism. In relation to free will and autonomy, it is only in recent years that free will sceptics have proposed multi-level treatments combining benign propagations of illusion with normatively sensitive judgments as to when such illusions can and should be lifted.[4] But treatments of this kind have been developed since the beginnings of Buddhist philosophy. At their foundation is the doctrine of anatta/anātman, which challenges the notion of autonomous agency, yet without undermining the robust ethical foundations of Buddhism.[5] Charles Goodman, for example, has argued that pleasures of various kinds are rightly treated as having value within certain Buddhist perspectives, and their having value can be interpreted in a robust sense with direct relevance to moral priorities; and yet, some kinds of pleasure rest on illusions about the source, meaning, and durability of those pleasures (Goodman 2009: 48–50; 82–4; 124 ff). Pleasure for the proverbial 'brain-in-a-vat' is still pleasure; and similarly, a feeling of autonomy can have value even when the social and psychological basis for this 'autonomy' turns out to be different than what agents generally assume it to be.

Rather than offering a detailed defence of this suggestion here, I will offer a metaphor with three variations, to illustrate three different ways of practising and valuing autonomy. Autonomy is generally presumed to have value as both a means and an end—even if, for some, that end is more akin to the sort of defeasible intrinsic value that is often attributed to pleasure, knowledge, and artistic activity. As a means, it can be a direct or indirect means to goods such as wisdom, virtue, and happiness, *inter alia*. If we were to represent autonomy as a stairway, or the construction of a stairway, there should be value and personal fulfilment in both the making of the stairway, and in where it leads.

Imagine, first of all, building a spiral stairway that encircles a 'Babelian' tower, a tower that one decides to build but never to finish—with the aim of reaching ever higher into the sky. One can enjoy the process of making design choices; but one cannot enjoy the result, both because the work is never finished and because eventually it reaches so high that one cannot even enjoy the vista, which ultimately disappears from view. Compare a second stairway, within a stairwell of one's own design, connecting an underground tool locker with the main floor of a house. This stairway enables one to use one's tools to improve the design of one's house; but when the point is reached where no further work is required, the house can be enjoyed, while the stairwell can be left unused—or even filled in with concrete, if the owner wishes. The first stairway is built without any justifiable end or aim, while the second is built with such a specific aim in mind that its value (only as a means) is quickly exhausted. The intrinsic value of any autonomous choices made by the builders is open to doubt; and even a metaphysically real autonomy—if there were such a thing—would turn out to be ethically idle.

A third stairway could be described, one that corresponds to what it would be like to operate within a phenomenology of autonomy, and metaphorically speaking, one that leads ultimately from that phenomenology to a higher wisdom, meanwhile enabling the strenuous effort of climbing to culminate in something akin to *eudaimonia*. Here we can imagine a path leading from the foot of a steep hill, to a high promontory. At first the hill appears not to have any paths or trails, so one must make one's own path. The process of identifying the right rocks to form a natural path would be an intrinsically interesting challenge, and finding the best way to scale them may be pleasing. Even more intrinsically worthwhile is the vista one can enjoy at the top. And this would be no less true if that vista revealed what one had not noticed initially: that the rocks on one's 'natural stairway' must have been placed there by someone previously. It is not just that the sense of wisdom and achievement compensates for the puncturing of the illusion of autonomy (that is, the false sense of having blazed a new trail). The 'phenomenology' of one's experience of putative autonomy need not involve regret. On the contrary, like an avid experimentalist always willing to pursue unlikely hypotheses, one who has reached the promontory can exercise her abilities by descending and ascending, exploring the phenomenology of autonomy while tempering this with the wisdom attained at the higher vantage point.

Some will notice a resemblance between this last example and the parable of the raft, often used by Buddhists to explain that when one reaches nirvāṇa, the vehicle (the teachings, methods, efforts, analyses, etc.) can be seen to contain half-truths and potentially misleading assumptions, albeit useful ones for the purpose of steering a course towards nirvāṇa. Some Buddhists say that the raft becomes dispensable, but Damien Keown points out that in some versions of the parable, the enlightened traveller is meant to retain the raft; and in a Mahāyāna context, this is true even if it does indeed contain half-truths (Keown 2001: 95–105; 149–54). Likewise, our climber does not leave her path unused, even after realizing it is not 'her own' path; and the phenomenology of 'autonomy' can be revisited, sometimes without scare quotes—for instance, for the purpose of inculcating the aspiration to autonomy in fellow citizens or fellow travellers.

In some ways, Kantian autonomy is most akin to that of our first example of a stairway builder. For Kant, the goals of knowledge and eudaimonia are outweighed by the imperative of autonomy, which is made sacrosanct by its correspondence with a putatively real freedom in the agent (that is, in a diachronically continuous self). This kind of freedom can be represented, perhaps, by the open space into which the tower can be indefinitely extended, and the lack of any constraints on design details. The kind of autonomy that I shall argue to be relevant to justifying human rights, on the other hand, is one that we explore, enjoy, and occasionally transcend, but all this from within one or another form of the good life. I hope to show that this approach does not entirely instrumentalize the value of autonomy, even though its instrumental roles—or rather the instrumental roles of the value—are ethically as important as the value itself. As for the confidence with which we can speak of 'justification' and 'importance' here, this may be reinforced by the intercultural convergence we find with respect to autonomy and rights, and the role of both in axiology—or so I shall argue.

Qualifying the Intrinsic Value of Rights Without Instrumentalizing Autonomy

There is always a danger of triviality if we claim to find intercultural convergence on ideals of human rights that are weakened or watered down—either as a result of accounting for only very general categories of rights or as a result of making rights 'political, not metaphysical', in Rawls's phrase. If rights are thought of as political necessities rather than 'ethical' or 'comprehensive' values, intercultural convergence, at least in the modern world, may seem less surprising and less interesting. To ensure that we are investigating the possibility of a non-trivial convergence, we should begin with a Western model that is comprehensively and foundationally ethical.[6]

One of the most robust defences of the ethical standing of human rights in recent years is that of James Griffin, articulated in his recent book *On Human Rights* (Griffin 2008). His approach is in some ways rooted in the liberal utilitarian synthesis of John Stuart Mill, but Griffin replaces the utilitarianism with a more pluralistic account of value that he calls simply a 'teleological' approach. Griffin allows that interpersonal trade-offs can be morally justified with respect to any value and any person or group of persons—which brings him closer to utilitarians than to liberals and libertarians—but he argues that (i) sacrifices of liberty and autonomy require a higher threshold of compensating gains than other infringements of people's interests; and (ii) the overall *telos* of the good life is not just a matter of happiness in a subjective sense, but also includes other values, such as knowledge and understanding, but especially—and deserving special social and political protection—personal liberty and autonomy.

In partial contrast to liberty, autonomy is more a matter of being able to set one's own priorities, make up one's own mind, and judge how to organize one's beliefs, standards of evidence, and reasoning. Autonomy is a more fundamental value than liberty, insofar as the absence of external constraint on action that constitutes liberty would be of little real value without autonomy of thought and purpose. (This is not to say that other intellectual values, perhaps promoted by educational institutions, cannot be expected to temper the range of exercise of intellectual autonomy; and more generally, autonomy is subordinate to axiological pluralism, no matter how fundamental it may be in relation to human rights.) Now, distinguishing liberty from the more general concept of freedom, we can paraphrase Griffin's position on the most fundamental human rights in this way: freedom of thought and conscience is integral to autonomy, while freedom of speech and expression is the most crucial link between autonomy and liberty.

As for the rights themselves, in both their abstract and institutionalized forms, these are largely instrumental, but not just in relation to the orientation of law and public policy towards prosperity and happiness—rather, they are also instrumental in relation to autonomy itself. This might make Griffin's view sound like one of the many variations of the instrumental conception of the value of human rights. But the difference is that autonomy has a degree of intrinsic value in his view (an overrideable degree, in this respect akin to pleasure), and autonomy is an ideal of freedom that is presupposed by anyone who regards a protected personal space as a human right and not merely a convenient legal right. Both kinds of right are basically devices, but their constitutive aim, and not just their indirect impact, is intrinsically valuable.[7] Griffin tries to explain a wide range of fundamental rights on the basis of autonomy, liberty, and their interaction; but I will focus here mostly on the central cases of rights of conscience, thought, and expression.

Another way of seeing Griffin's approach as constituting a distinctive justification of free speech rights is as follows. On the one hand, the freedom to make up and express one's own mind does not seem a mere ingredient in producing a more enjoyable life, such that we would willingly exchange that freedom for more enjoyment (if such extra gains were available in that way). On the other hand, this freedom does not seem to have value apart from its contribution to quality of life; or at least, having a right to free speech would seem to add little or nothing to a life in which that was the only benign feature (in other words, a miserable life, short not only of happiness but of human rights, with the exception of this one right). Can the value of this freedom, though, be neither instrumental nor intrinsic? An alternative view emerges when we disambiguate 'freedom', separating the sense of a socially or politically protected right to free speech from the sense of autonomy, the ability to decide on one's own priorities and long-term plans, on one's own terms as much as possible. The former is instrumentally valuable, the latter intrinsically valuable. And while the right to free speech is instrumentally valuable, it is not merely an indirect means of bringing about greater overall desire-satisfaction or other benefits of a more prosperous society; rather, it is a means of gaining greater autonomy, which has intrinsic but not absolute value.

Free speech is not only a means to autonomy, nor only a means to happiness (whether directly or via autonomy), but also a means of promoting other people's happiness, especially when it enables a richer discourse in public debate to help improve public policy. For some, admittedly, this raises worries about a right to free speech becoming limited by a duty of public speech. But Griffin is not alone in allowing trade-offs between the personal and social uses of this freedom—here he is in the company of Kant and Mill, for example.

This raises the question of the place of Griffin's approach within the modern Western tradition of rights discourse. I have presented his approach as an alternative to two mainstream views of the value of rights; but those two views have been mainstream primarily in the past few decades, and if we take in a broader sweep of the tradition since the Enlightenment, this third view can be seen to have played a significant role in the development of liberal thought. This is particularly true in the case of Kant and Mill, different as they are in their ethical approaches. Kant's defence of the right of free speech rests primarily on the importance of scholars' contributions to healthy public debate; and although he thus instrumentalizes free speech, he does not instrumentalize the autonomy it promotes (Kant 1996: 17–22). As a utilitarian, Mill's instrumentalist remarks about free speech are less surprising; but like Kant, he treats the resulting autonomy as having intrinsic value, albeit as part of a conception of happiness. (Of course, whereas Mill speaks of happiness, Kant speaks of a more elusive 'highest good', and whereas Mill implies that the requirement of respecting autonomy may be defeasible in some contexts, Kant does not; but despite these differences, they joined with perhaps the majority of Enlightenment thinkers in trying to steer modern ideals away from the opposite poles of narrow libertarianism and narrow hedonistic utilitarianism.)

The other instrumental function that Kant, Mill, and Griffin all recognize is the function of extending and promoting general knowledge and understanding within society, and this is the aspect of their thought that brings them closest to the primary—epistemic—meaning of 'Enlightenment'. In the last section, I will return to this notion of Enlightenment, noting some inflections in this concept that are due to figures such as Spinoza and Schelling—whose emphasis on the experience of breaking through epistemic barriers (as well as on autonomy) highlights a partial convergence between modern Western values and ancient Buddhist ones.

Canonical Anecdotes and Ambedkar's Reflections on Buddhist Values

If we see autonomy as contributing to a kind of eudaimonia, and if we consider the parallels between Buddhist enlightenment and something like Aristotle's more esoteric conception of eudaimonia (the more spiritual form that he thought more fit for Gods),[8] we may wonder whether the Buddha's discourses also show signs of acknowledging the importance of autonomy. And it turns out that there is indeed some recognition of this in classical *buddhavacana* scripture. Though I am only aware of a few relevant anecdotes, some reflections concerning autonomy—if not also concerning rights—can be found in scriptures that discuss the dangers of domination, manipulation, and arbitrary authority.

For example, in the Pāli Canon's *Mahaparinibbana Sutta*, the Buddha warns monks not to treat any teaching as a dogma, and in particular not to treat any high-ranking monk as an authority; those who wish to become Buddhists should rely on their own judgment to choose what to believe (David 1899–1921: 73–9).[9] Secondly, in a section of the *Vinaya* scriptures, the Buddha notes that students should feel free to disagree with their teachers (Gombrich 2009: 15–16).[10] Thirdly, the *Samaññaphala Sutta* tells the story of a slave who decries the injustice of his position and status, and in the continuation of the sutta, the Buddha argues that the slave deserves at least the option of becoming a monk (which would in effect be freedom, since monks were not required to remain members of the order). It is made clear that liberation in itself is a good thing, whether the slave enters monastic life or not, and at the end of the sutta, this liberation is used as a metaphor for enlightenment (Florida 2005: 112).[11]

Some might argue that these texts give a misleading impression of the importance of autonomy in Buddhism, on the grounds that only Enlightenment has intrinsic value and to endorse autonomy in these contexts is just to endorse something that will, on occasion, instrumentally conduce to enlightenment. This concern, however, underestimates the tight connection between autonomy and enlightenment. When Griffin offers a list of the most pervasive forms of heteronomy, he includes 'indoctrination, brain-washing, domination, manipulation, conformity, conventionality, false consciousness [and] certain forms of immaturity'. (Griffin 2008: 151). Overcoming these is not merely instrumentally useful, but intrinsically part of cultivating autonomy. Moreover, to overcome all of these would be tantamount to enlightenment itself. This is more than just a Mahāyānist claim (Mahāyānist in the sense that the Mahāyāna generally regards enlightenment as the overcoming of epistemic obstacles like these, rather than the purgation of desire or craving). It is a familiar theme in both the Theravāda and the Mahāyāna that intellectual independence and spiritual self-reliance are key elements in enlightenment.[12]

Ambedkar echoes the Pāli Canon's indictments of heteronomy in several passages in his detailed exposition of Buddhist doctrine, *The Buddha and his Dhamma*, the last work he wrote before his death in 1956. He writes, for example, that:

> [What] requires morality to be made sacred and universal...[is the need] to safeguard the growth of the individual. Under the struggle for existence or under group rule the interests of the individuals are not safe. The group set-up prevents an individual from acquiring consistency of mind...[and also] leads to discrimination and denial of justice...[and to] stratification of classes. Those who are masters remain masters, and those who are born in slavery remain slaves. Owners remain owners, and workers remain workers...This means that there can be liberty for some, but not for all...there can be equality for a few, but none for the majority. What is the remedy? The only remedy lies in making fraternity universally effective. What is fraternity? It is...another name for morality. This is why the Buddha preached that Dhamma is morality; and as Dhamma is sacred, so is morality. (Ambedkar 2011: 173).

Ambedkar here addresses at least three of Griffin's 'enemies of autonomy': domination, conformity, and false consciousness. The themes of domination and conformity (and emancipation) are obvious; but regarding false consciousness, one aspect of this danger is brought out in Ambedkar's language. We may notice the description of morality as having to be made sacred; Ambedkar thereby avoids the wishful thinking that takes morality to be intrinsically sacred. He is promoting a kind of transparency about the origins of moral systems that is similar to the Buddha's use of the raft metaphor to describe his own teachings—that is, to highlight the elements of invention and utility in the structure of the eightfold path and other prescriptive frameworks.[13]

Various moral principles in Buddhism are said to have this provisional status, including even the cherished principle of *ahiṃsā*:

> [T]he Buddha made a distinction between Principle and Rule. He did not make Ahimsa a matter of Rule. He enunciated it as a matter of Principle or way of life. In this he no doubt acted very wisely. A principle leaves you freedom to act. A rule does not. Rule either breaks you, or you break the rule. (Ambedkar 2011: 183).

While the provisional status of some moral principles may make them conventional rather than objectively normative, this does not mean that all of the ethical values underlying them are conventional. It seems to me that Ambedkar is faithful to classical Buddhism in representing enlightenment itself as objectively normative—though he famously identifies nirvāṇa/nibbana with ethical engagement and an awareness of ethical value, to a degree that many other Buddhist philosophers do not:

> [U]nderlying [the Buddha's] conception of Nibbana…[is] the happiness of a sentient being as distinct from the salvation of the soul [after death]…[14] [He] does not say that the passions must be extinguished completely. [He] says, do not add fuel to the flame…Nibbana means enough control over passion so as to enable one to walk on the path of righteousness…Nibbana is another name for righteous life… [And quoting the Buddha from *Samyutta Nikaya* III:], "Rooted in Nibbana…the righteous life is lived." (Ambedkar 2011: 127–8).

Finally, in challenging the belief in miracles and other superstitions, Ambedkar turns to false consciousness more explicitly. (When Ambedkar refers to the importance of being free, in the first sentence below, it would seem that he has a practical rather than a metaphysical freedom in mind, since his point is that a practical freedom of inquiry leads to an understanding of causation which is all-encompassing, explaining even human behaviour.)

> What is the use of man's existence, if he is not free? What is the use of man's intelligence, if he continues to believe in supernatural causes?... There cannot be any event which is supernatural in its origin. It may be that man is not able to discover the real cause [of events]...But if he has intelligence, he is bound one day to discover it. In repudiating supernaturalism, the Buddha had three objects. His first object was to lead man to the path of rationalism. His second object was to free man to go in search of truth. His third object was to remove the most potent source of superstition, the result of which is to kill the spirit of inquiry. [The] doctrine of Kamma and Causation is the most central doctrine in Buddhism. It preaches Rationalism, and Buddhism is nothing if not rationalism. (Ambedkar 2011: 133).

In referring to 'Kamma' (or karma), Ambedkar might seem to be reintroducing the sort of trans-generational retribution he rejects elsewhere; but since he clearly has no intention of doing this, it might be better to think of the relevant doctrine here as that of dependent origination, sometimes known as 'conditioned genesis' (*pratītyasamutpāda*)—or indeed as something simply along the lines of Kant's generic causal principle (that every event has an efficient cause).

In these passages, other 'enemies of autonomy' are identified. Besides domination, conformity, and false consciousness, we see charges of manipulation and indoctrination brought against the dissemination of superstitions. Griffin also mentioned 'immaturity'; certain forms of immaturity seem to be recognized here as obstacles to enlightenment, insofar as it may show a lack of maturity and realism, for example, to suppose that complete cessation of ethical engagement—and what Ambedkar calls passion—is both possible and desirable.[15] (Meanwhile I hesitate to identify maturity with rationalism, though one wonders if all Ambedkar means by 'rationalism' here is the will and capacity to break through false consciousness in a broad sense.)

In general, the highlighting of autonomy in these passages provides a way of explaining and justifying the anecdotes cited earlier from the Pāli Canon. This autonomy clearly calls for a degree of independence from social institutions and from one-sided educators and educational methods, not to mention the basic liberties alluded to in the tale of the freed slave.[16] It seems clear, at least from Ambedkar's exposition, that this autonomy would not only conduce to enlightenment, but also to a kind of personal eudaimonia—that is, the sort of telos that Griffin considers the foundation of his ethical justification of human rights.

The Foundations of Autonomy in Buddhist Values and Ideals

The fact remains that most contemporary Buddhist ethicists who address the topic of human rights treat them—as well as autonomy itself—as at best instrumentally justified, in relation to either the promotion of the spiritual path or the cultivation of compassion.[17] It seems quite possible, however, that Ambedkar was closer not only to a Millian view along the lines of what we saw in Griffin's approach, but also to Buddhist ideals, in his treatment of autonomy as having intrinsic value. However, how could we judge who is more faithful to so-called 'canonical' Buddhist principles and ideals? This may be impossible; but rather than hoping to judge who is more faithful, we can at least attempt to judge whether the teleological account of autonomy is a plausible fit within traditional Buddhist ethics, per- haps as plausible as competing views. Here I refer to 'ethics' in the broadest sense of axiology—so that we should consider the normative elements, not only in precepts forbidding killing and theft, but also in concepts such as tathāgatagarbha (a universal individual poten- tiality for enlightenment), brahmavihāra (a sort of master virtue of which compassion is the prime example), nirvāṇa, and its Mahāyāna equivalent, prajñāpāramitā (perfection of wisdom).

At the peak of its philosophical sophistication in early medieval India, about fifteen hundred years ago, Mahāyāna Buddhism was heavily influenced by the Yogācāra school, a school whose ideas have only partially survived in some branches of Buddhism in Tibet and Japan today. But many of the Indian texts have survived in their entirety, and although they are not always considered in this light, they can be read as presenting a powerful case for autonomy, lib- erty, and equality. Some of the most famous texts defend a form of metaphysical idealism, and have often been compared to Berkeley and Kant (Garfield 2002b); but I will be highlighting other themes—in particular, the tathāgatagarbha, which represents a certain conception of the universal nature of personhood, and related concepts.

This term was primarily used to stress that every individual has the capacity to become an enlightened being, but its use in the Yogācāra context tended towards an understanding of the equal dignity of all persons irrespective of their spiritual affiliation or soteriological prospects (Sutton 1991; Williams 2009: Chapter 5). (*Garbha* means embryo, and *tathāgata*, an epithet of the Buddha, refers in effect to the ultimate ineffable state of being of one who is enlightened.) Three aspects of Yogācāra thought account for this egalitarianism and explain the naturalness of construing the ethical implications in terms of values of liberty and autonomy. First of all, two of the supreme virtues in this tradition are the so-called brahmavihāras of *karuṇā* (compassion) and *upekkha* (often translated as 'equanimity', but since this English term has connotations that clash with the emotive overtones of karuṇā (compassion), it may be better to think of it as even-handedness or impartiality). The impartiality that is implied in these virtues is meant to be directed towards all sentient beings; but combined with the notion of tathāgatagarbha, it has a particular application here to fellow humans and what is owed to every individual. However, might we owe, to every person we meet, a forced march to a monastery, or do we rather owe each person a protected personal space, with a significant degree of liberty and autonomy?

The second aspect of the Yogācāra, which helps to answer this question, is its scepticism about the eightfold path and about definitions of nirvāṇa. Preconceptions about the path can be obstacles to enlightenment, and preconceptions about the ultimate goal can be misleading. Genuine enlightenment, prajñāpāramitā (the perfection of wisdom), often requires that preconceptions—even erudite Buddhist ones—be challenged, revised or abandoned.[18] And it is no longer taken for granted that the monastery is where this wisdom may be best cultivated. The sage Vimalakīrti has more success as someone immersed in the worlds of family and business affairs (McRae 2004); and in one of the key texts on the tathāgatagarbha doctrine, the central sage is Queen Śrīmālā.[19] Moreover, such figures are depicted as expecting their interlocutors to devise their own arguments and make up their own minds.[20]

This shows that autonomy is regarded not as an elite achievement, but as a starting point to which everyone is entitled. (Incidentally, Vimalakīrti's interlocutors include men and women of all classes in society.) Now, there is a third aspect of Yogācāra, although a more problematic one for anyone who has struggled with the ethical implications of pantheism or other radical forms of monism, which appears to strengthen the 'right' or 'entitlement' that all individuals can claim by virtue of their sharing the nature of the tathāgata. This is the aspect of fundamental non-duality, which many Mahāyāna Buddhists regard as entailing a fundamental equality between sages and supposedly 'embryonic' sages. The 'embryo' referred to in tathāgatagarbha is thus in one way illusory; each person is already no different than an enlightened person. Hence if a Buddha is assumed to carry supreme dignity, so is everyone else.

Due to its frequent identification with *buddhadhātu*, the tathāgatagarbha is often translated as 'Buddha-nature'; and both in English and in Sanskrit this has probably added weight to the individual dignity it is meant to convey. However, in temporarily refraining from using this translation, we can more clearly see how similar this Yogācāra perspective is to its philosophical cousin in the medieval Hindu world, the Advaita Vedānta school. Not only is this suggested by the role of non-duality just noted, but some Yogācāra texts even dare to call the purified garbha the *ātman*. There are ways of squaring this with the Buddhist doctrine of anātman, so perhaps the meeting of minds here cannot be complete.[21] But, since Hindu Advaita is after all a form of Vedānta, it would be worth exploring the degree of overlap between the ideals of equality we have just noted in Buddhist sources and those that Advaitins could have and perhaps did notice in the Upaniṣads, which feature similar scenarios in which different classes of people and unconventional views are encouraged to interact and learn from one another without manipulation or coercion.

These considerations suggest that it is not merely the Buddhist context, but also certain aspects of the ancient Indian context more generally, that produced a powerful way of justifying human rights, or at least those rights that are most relevant to autonomy. As it happens, there is also a Sanskrit term that means something close to the 'right' of an individual (*adhikāra*), but there is actually little to be gained by scrutinizing its uses here (Bilimoria 1993). This is because, insofar as we are considering whether the validity of rights claims holds only within Western contexts or perhaps holds universally, we should focus more on the scope of justifications for underlying values such as autonomy and equality. It might turn out that while the modern Western context saw the specification of detailed rights, the ancient Indian context gave rise to an articulation of the correct justification for such rights (perhaps analogously: Babylonians had the most detailed mathematical formulas, whereas the Greeks had the proofs). However, if we see philosophers working independently, in markedly different cultural contexts—in this case, in ancient India and in the West—but arriving at similar reasons for holding similar values, this may constitute stronger evidence for a kind of modest moral universalism.

* * *

The best candidates for values that are universally valid, with some prospect of support from the Buddhist insights just canvassed, are the moral impartiality that is captured in the brahmavihāra framework and the twin aims of wisdom and the alleviation of suffering that the ideal of nirvāṇa comprises, especially in its prajñāpāramitā form. Yet, it is the belief that suffering is best reduced via wisdom that makes autonomous reflection a key value in both ancient Buddhist and modern Western ethics, and in some contemporary explanations of the value of human rights. Whether these convergences constitute grounds for taking autonomy to be a universally valid ideal remains to be seen.

It may be that autonomous reflection is the only reliable way of fostering the kind of wisdom that is partly constitutive of eudaimonia. If something like Griffin's pluralistic conception of the good life corresponds to a universally attractive ideal, then in this way autonomy might be a universally valid value as well. (It remains true, as noted in Section I, that no ontic claim about autonomy needs to hold at the level of objective psychology for the aspiration to autonomy to serve in this role.) The success of this line of reasoning would depend on whether the close relation between enlightenment and the aspiration to autonomy is as close as Griffin and Ambedkar suggest, in their very different ways. Meanwhile, there is another way to strengthen the case for a close relation along these lines—namely, to argue that Buddhist enlightenment and modern enlightenment are variations on the same basic aspiration to overcome false consciousness.[22]

To claim a close kinship here will naturally seem far-fetched inso-far as conceptions of Buddhist enlightenment are limited to the most rarefied and mystical forms of nirvāṇa. But I have already alluded to the Mahāyāna notion of *bodhicitta*, a non-mystical form of *buddhatta/buddhatva*[23] that is sometimes regarded as both ethically and sote-riologically superior to what some Mahāyāna texts pejoratively refer to as the '*nirvāṇa* of the *arhat*' (due to its disengaged nature). This form of enlightenment remains closer to ordinary consciousness on the one hand, but involves a radical moral impartiality on the other hand. Though remaining connected to common sense, it sets off a chain of purgations of false belief (reminiscent of Descartes or—as already mentioned—Berkeley and Kant), while filling the void with impartial compassion (reminiscent of Hutcheson or Hume). It is not complete without action—but here we might compare the dedicated and self-sacrificing social engagement of a Condorcet or a Saint-Simon, insofar as their Enlightenment predecessors laid the groundwork for such engagement by treating transcendental forms of consciousness as having implications for an engaged form of moral impartiality.

It might be objected that a better translation of 'buddhatva' than enlightenment would be awakening and that the rhapsodic con-notations of religious awakening fit awkwardly with the modern Western ideal of enlightenment. But of course, apart from some Zen depictions of so-called 'sudden enlightenment', Buddhists have not intended any such rhapsodic connotations. And meanwhile, we might consider what 'enlightenment' really means in the Western context. To take just one source, Kant considered enlightenment to involve a shaking off of comfortable preconceptions and the purgation of erroneous beliefs (Kant 1996)—transformations, in other words, that equally invite the metaphor of awakening, one he himself used, moreover, in referring to his emergence from 'dogmatic slumbers' as a young reader of David Hume.

Some might also object, more fundamentally, that traditional Buddhists sought a different form of knowledge, with a different purpose. Buddhist enlightenment was experiential rather than theoretical, it is often said, and it served no purpose beyond itself, such as research programs, public works, and technological applications. In response, we should consider, on the one hand, that Buddhist philosophers theorized about enlightenment by distinguishing ultimate truth from conventional truth in ways that prefigured the primary/secondary quality distinction and Kant's distinction between the noumenal and the phenomenal (and different traditions have different views—within Buddhism—on how close this philosophizing comes to enlightenment itself) (Garfield 2002b). As for the alleged tendency to social or technological instrumentalism in the Western context, the kind of knowledge pursued in light of the distinctions just mentioned hardly qualifies as an example of this. Such instrumentalism may have motivated Condorcet, but—for better or for worse—did not motivate Berkeley, Hume, Rousseau, Kant, Hegel, or even Mill. (Indeed, this is a gross understatement when it comes to Berkeley and Rousseau.)

More interestingly, we are apt to overlook the experiential aspects of philosophical insight that many of these Enlightenment figures highlighted. Hume often remarked on the philosopher's access to mindful repose, not surprisingly in contexts where his scepticism reached the point where only the ancient ideal of *ataraxia* retained any validity for him. Spinoza reached a similar point, and since in his case this came via reflecting on causal necessity and metaphysical non-individuation, the parallel with Buddhist enlightenment is perhaps even closer. Finally, there are those Enlightenment figures, such as the post-Kantian idealist Friedrich Schelling, who elevate aesthetic experience to a kind of hyper-philosophical status, construing it as an experience that is both transcendentally self-conscious (thus exhibiting a kind of autonomy) and yet beyond any subject-object duality. In all of these instances, parallels with both Buddhist and Advaita Vedānta philosophical ideas have been unduly neglected. (Moreover, all of the Western philosophers just mentioned, along with Schopenhauer, Nietzsche, Russell, Bergson, and William James, were either sceptics or reductionists about personal identity, revealing another partial convergence with Buddhist philosophy, although many of these philosophers were influenced by Buddhist reflections on anatta/anātman—hence my acknowledgement of the prior and distinctively Buddhist contribution to our understanding of the metaphysics of personhood, in the first section. It is for another occasion to add more detail as to how these quasi-Buddhist views on personhood were combined with an emphasis on autonomy as a social and political value (in the case of Spinoza), as a moral value (Schelling) and as a prudential value (Nietzsche and others).

I will close by remarking that a wide-ranging convergence along the above lines might be a mixed blessing for contemporary ethical theorists who are transculturally sensitive but also interested in the prospects for moral realism or universalism. If a reappraisal of early modern philosophers in the West revealed them to have what are virtually (quasi) Buddhist sensibilities, the shared commitment to overcoming false consciousness 'via autonomy' might just be thought to rest on a mistake that somehow infected both traditions. On the other hand, the fact that ancient Buddhism and modern Western philosophy do not exhibit the same sensibilities—apart from a few of the points of contact noted here—might be thought to strengthen an argument for the universal validity of that commitment. In other words, even in contexts where divergent conclusions might be expected, a significant convergence is discernible in regard to the importance of autonomy, *qua* prudential value. This might, in turn, help to explain why some aspects of human rights discourse are discernible not only in ancient Buddhist contexts, but perhaps elsewhere as well.

Notes

1. As is well-known, the pre-renaissance transplantation of science and mathematics from Indian, Persian, and Arab contexts was a major factor.
2. I am not speaking here of moral concerns about a creeping liberal global hegemony, but rather about the difficulty of drawing ethical or meta-ethical conclusions from such trends.
3. Leading, at least, to the illusion that we can know the source of this highest good—though Kant's own use of the term 'illusion'

(*transzendentale Illusion*) was too strong even in the case of Leibniz's theological conception of the highest good, since he did not quite rule out its metaphysical possibility (Grier 2001).

4. As, for example, in the work of Saul Smilansky (Smilansky 2000) and Derk Pereboom (Pereboom 2001).

5. Damien Keown (Keown 2001) and Charles Goodman (Goodman 2009) have done much to show how moral ideals, far from being undermined by the non-self doctrine, are in fact strengthened by it— for example, via its implications for impartiality.

6. Not that there is any reason, in general, to begin from Western rather than Indian or other perspectives; on the contrary, the model suggested by the third metaphor above captures a certain Buddhist perspective, and I thought it worth starting there. But at this point, I turn to a conception of autonomy that is formulated in terms of 'human rights'.

7. This is nonetheless not an 'intrinsic view' or 'status-based view' of rights; what has intrinsic value, rather, is autonomy, seen as part of *eudaimonia*; rights remain instrumentally valuable in relation to this telos. Wenar (2005) suggests a similar hybrid of intrinsic and instrumental views, but leans more towards a status-based view, *qua* normative explanation.

8. In Book Ten of the *Nicomachean Ethics*.

9. This is the sixteenth sutta in the *Digha Nikaya*.

10. Gombrich cites *Vinaya* I: 46 and 49. It may be that a student cannot disagree in any way he pleases; rather, he can correct his teacher—which admittedly suggests a duty as much as it does a right.

11. The *Samaññaphala Sutta* can be found in David 1899–1921, Volume I (*Digha Nikaya, Sutta* 2).

12. A famous image sometimes invoked in this connection is that of the solitary rhinoceros, in the Pāli Canon, as a symbol of the arhat who has achieved independence from social norms and pressures.

13. I do not mean to imply that Ambedkar held, and nor do I wish to suggest that all values relevant to moral thought and discourse are merely conventional, nominal or 'constructed'. Even if morality in its socially operationalized form is constructed, it would ideally be constructed out of objective prudential values—an example of which I discuss presently.

14. Similarly, the well-known Buddhist scholar Robert Thurman calls the third noble truth (the truth that nirvāṇa is attainable) 'the truth of happiness' (Thurman 2005). This is indeed an equation one finds in central texts such as the *Dhammapada*. As I indicate at the end of this section, however, it can be clearer to call this wide notion of happiness

eudaimonia, to distinguish it from narrower conceptions oriented around subjective contentment or desire-satisfaction.

15. This is one of those intriguing points on which Ambedkar allowed Mahāyāna elements to take precedence over Theravāda elements, in his syncretistic approach. It is a Mahāyāna belief that the earlier (Theravāda) Buddhist ideal of ethical and conative disengagement was intended only for certain preliminary meditative purposes, and that the more mature ideal of the bodhisattva retained a central role for ethical engagement at all advanced levels of spiritual progress.

16. It is also worth mentioning, in this connection, Ambedkar's highlighting of the initially controversial nature of the Buddha's allowing for followers to exit and re-enter the monastic order as a matter of personal choice (Ambedkar 2011: 261); this contrasts with the former absence of a right within some Christian orders to exit them—a feature of convents, for example, that was heavily criticized by Enlightenment figures.

17. In relation to compassion, see Garfield 1998 and Chappell 1999; in relation to spiritual aims, see Keown 1998 and Inada 1998; those who are sceptical about even an instrumental justification include Ihara 1998 and Junger 1998. An exception is Sevilla 2010, who considers something closer to a 'status-based' justification.

18. This is perhaps most strikingly expressed in the *Laṅkāvatāra Sutra* (see Sutton 1991).

19. Paul 2004. The setting here is not one of those in which a woman turns out to be a male bodhisattva in disguise; Śrīmālā is in fact a woman and a layperson.

20. In the case of Śrīmālā, it is rather that the Buddha—in talking to whom Śrīmālā becomes the central sage in the story—allows her to explain the Dharma 'as she wishes' (Paul 2004: 21). Meanwhile, a concern may remain among Western liberals, for example, that autonomy is granted here merely to play an instrumental role, and that one ends up with a duty, rather than a right, to pursue wisdom. This might only worry libertarians, however. Recall that Kant treated the free expression of ideas as a duty; and we have been considering views like Griffin's, where autonomy and wisdom are not only rights, but also goods worth promoting in society. Meanwhile, nothing that has been recounted here, in the Buddhist context, precludes autonomy remaining part of the experience of enlightenment, and/or part of the *eudaimonia* of wisdom (provided this is compatible with anātman; see below).

21. For Yogācārins, 'ātman' in this sense is just a potentiality, so it cannot be an individuating feature of a person (nor can it be individuating when

it is actualized). The Buddhist doctrine of anatta/anātman/non-soul would thus remain sound. (Whether the doctrine, in that form, might be reconciled with Advaita Vedānta—but not with other schools of Hindu thought—is a fascinating question that continues to be debated.)

22. Worries might persist about how an aspiration to overcome false consciousness can be combined with an aspiration to a kind of autonomy that has no ontic reality. But recall the analogy from Section I: in climbing the mountain—motivated by the prospect of blazing one's own trail—the second aspiration serves the first, since it enables one to see more clearly how the trail came into existence; and this enlightenment does not reverse the value already found in the process of discovery.

23. The original Pāli and Sanskrit terms for enlightenment. On *bodhicitta*, see Williams, 2009: 194–200.

References

Ambedkar, B.R. 2002. *The Essential Writings of B.R. Ambedkar*. Edited by V. Rodrigues. New Delhi: Oxford University Press.

———. 2011. *The Buddha and his Dhamma: A Critical Edition*. Edited by A.S. Rathore and A. Verma. New Delhi: Oxford University Press.

Aristotle. (trans. by D. Ross and rev. by L. Brown). 2009. *Nicomachean Ethics*. Oxford: Oxford University Press.

Bilimoria, P. 1993. 'Is *Adhikāra* Good Enough for Rights?', *Asian Philosophy*, 3: 1–13.

Chappell, D. 1999. 'Buddhist Peace Principles', in D. Chappell (ed.), *Buddhist Peacework: Creating Cultures of Peace*, pp. 199–232. Boston: Wisdom Publications.

David, T.W.R. (trans.). 1899–1921. *Dialogues of the Buddha, Volumes 1–3*. London: Oxford University Press.

Fiske, A. and C. Emmrich. 2004. 'The Use of Buddhist Scriptures in B.R. Ambedkar's The Buddha and his Dhamma', in S. Jondhale and J. Beltz (eds), *Reconstructing the World: B.R. Ambedkar and Buddhism in India*. New Delhi: Oxford University Press.

Florida, R.E. 2005. *Human Rights and the World's Major Religions, Volume 5: The Buddhist Tradition*. Westport, CT: Praeger.

Garfield, J. 1998. 'Human Rights and Compassion: Towards a Unified Moral Framework', in D.V. Keown, C.S. Prebish, and W.R. Husted (eds), *Buddhism and Human Rights*, pp. 111–40. Surrey, UK: Curzon Press.

———. 2002a. 'Three Natures and Three Naturelessnesses: Comments Concerning Cittamatra Conceptual Categories', in *Empty Words: Buddhist*

Philosophy and Cross-Cultural Interpretation, pp. 109–27. Oxford: Oxford University Press.

———. 2002b. 'Western Idealism through Indian Eyes: A Cittamatra Reading of Berkeley, Kant, and Schopenhauer', in *Empty Words: Buddhist Philosophy and Cross-Cultural Interpretation*, pp. 152–69. Oxford: Oxford University Press.

Gombrich, R. 2009. *What the Buddha Thought*. London: Equinox.

Goodman, C. 2009. *Consequences of Compassion: An Interpretation and Defence of Buddhist Ethics*. Oxford: Oxford University Press.

Grier, M. 2001. *Kant's Doctrine of Transcendental Illusion*. Cambridge: Cambridge University Press.

Griffin, J. 1996. *Value Judgement: Improving our Ethical Beliefs*. Oxford: Clarendon Press.

———. 2008. *On Human Rights*. Oxford: Oxford University Press.

Hooker, B. 2000. *Ideal Code, Real World*. Oxford: Clarendon Press.

Ihara, C. 1998. 'Why There Are No Rights in Buddhism: A Reply to Damien Keown', in D.V. Keown, C.S. Prebish, and W.R. Husted (eds), *Buddhism and Human Rights*, pp. 43–52. Surrey, UK: Curzon Press.

Inada, K. 1998. 'A Buddhist Response to the Nature of Human Rights', in D.V. Keown, C.S. Prebish, and W.R. Husted (eds), *Buddhism and Human Rights*, pp. 1–14. Surrey, UK: Curzon Press.

Junger, P. 1998. 'Why the Buddha Has No Rights', in D.V. Keown, C.S. Prebish, and W.R. Husted (eds), *Buddhism and Human Rights*, pp. 53–96. Surrey, UK: Curzon Press.

Kant, I. 1996. 'An Answer to the Question: What is Enlightenment?', in *Practical Philosophy* (edited and trans. by M. Gregor), pp. 17–22. Cambridge: Cambridge University Press.

Keown, D.V. 1998. 'Are there Human Rights in Buddhism?', in D.V. Keown, C.S. Prebish, and W.R. Husted (eds), *Buddhism and Human Rights*, pp. 15–42. Surrey, UK: Curzon Press.

———. 2001. *The Nature of Buddhist Ethics*, 2nd edition. New York: Palgrave.

McRae, J., (trans.) 2004. 'The Vimalakīrti Sutra', in *The Sutra of Queen Śrīmālā of the Lion's Roar/Vimalakīrti Sutra*, pp. 75–199. Berkeley, CA: Numata Center for Buddhist Translation and Research.

Mill, J.S. 2001. *Utilitarianism*, 2nd edition (edited by G. Sher). Indianapolis: Hackett.

Paul, D.Y. (trans.). 2004. *The Sutra of Queen Śrīmālā of the Lion's Roar/Vimalakīrti Sutra*. Berkeley, CA: Numata Center for Buddhist Translation and Research.

Pereboom, D. 2001. *Living without Free Will*. Cambridge: Cambridge University Press.

Queen, C. 2004. 'Ambedkar's Dhamma: Source and Method in the Construction of Engaged Buddhism', in S. Jondhale and J. Beltz (eds), *Reconstructing the World: B.R. Ambedkar and Buddhism in India*, pp. 132–50. New Delhi: Oxford University Press.

Sevilla, A.L. 2010. 'Founding Human Rights within Buddhism: Exploring Buddha Nature as an Ethical Foundation', *Journal of Buddhist Ethics*, 17: 214–52.

Siderits, M. 2006. 'Buddhist Reductionism and the Structure of Buddhist Ethics', in P. Bilimoria, J. Prabhu, and R. Sharma (eds), *Indian Ethics: Classical Contemporary Challenges*, pp. 283–95. Aldershot, UK: Ashgate.

Smilansky, S. 2000. *Free Will and Illusion*. Oxford: Oxford University Press.

Sutton, F.G. 1991. *Existence and Enlightenment in the Laṅkāvatāra Sutra: A Study in the Ontology and Epistemology of the Yogācāra School of Mahāyāna Buddhism*. Albany: SUNY Press.

Thurman, R. (trans.). 1976. *The Holy Teaching of Vimalakīrti: A Mahāyāna Scripture*. University Park: Pennsylvania State University Press.

———. 2005. *Thoughts on Buddhism*. Toronto: CBC Publications.

Wenar, L. 2005. 'The Value of Rights', in M. O'Rourke (ed.), *Law and Social Justice*, pp. 179–209. Cambridge, MA: MIT Press.

Williams, P. 2009. *Mahāyāna Buddhism: The Doctrinal Foundations*, 2nd edition. London: Routledge.

7

Human Rights, Indian Philosophy, and Patañjali

Shyam Ranganathan

We live in a world coloured by the Western intellectual tradition. One of the theses of this tradition is an old Platonic idea, that we are essentially our souls—'soul' being another word for 'mind'. Call this the mentalist account of personal identity. The apparent motivation for this was the idea that while our bodies might change over time, our minds (our values, beliefs, aspirations) stay the same. Buddhists, of course, make short work of this: the Pali Canon is filled with reminders that any reason we have to doubt that our body is our self over time give us ample grounds to criticize our identification with our minds (Sacred Text Internet Archive, *Milindapañha*). However, if we do believe that we are our mind, what individuates us?

The answer from liberals, from Hobbes to Mill, is that it is our preferences that individuate us and our life's challenge is to figure out what it is that makes us happy in the long run. Of course, this is the source of our difficulty: if what makes us happy puts us on a course of collision with each other, then the pursuit of our autonomy creates strife. Liberals call this the 'state of nature'.

Marxists are famous for criticizing mentalist accounts of the (human) self; we are material they tell us. In the *Economic and Philosophical Manuscripts*, Marx famously argued that we are primarily members of the human species, and while humans are animals, there is something special about humans: we can objectify ourselves in our products as a means of self-reflection. Capitalism is bad because it gets us to give up our objectifications (us) for wage labour; higher pay means better-paid slaves. The real problem is that the human worker is deprived of the ability to treat his/her products as a means to self-reflection and instead must treat it as a means to survival. The end result is our self-alienation.

It would be nice if the Marxist alternative were a genuine alternative to the Platonic tradition of mentalism. To see whether it is, let us start with an objective account of mind and body. Practically, most agree that their body is their skin and everything under; they can part with their hair and nails without losing their body it seems, but tearing skin and anything underneath it is a wound and an incursion into a body. The objective mental correlate to a body is its complement: everything outside of the skin. All of reality from one's own point of view could hence be divided into one's own body and one's mind. We could reject this way to carve up reality into the body and mind, while retaining the uncontroversial idea that one's body is one's skin and everything under, but then the mind as something distinct from the body disappears into oblivion, for it is neither the body, nor the complement of the body. (One might assume that the mind is not the complement of the body as such, but some small part of it. Call this the petite option. But this option presents us with no objective boundary that separates our mind from the rest of the complement of the body.) But if the mind is not to disappear into oblivion, then it is the complement to the body. Death, we could say, is the ultimate failure of the mind (the complement of the body) to maintain the functioning of the body, despite bodily change. Alternatively, put another way, death is the body without a complementary mind. In death, what mind a body has, fails to intervene and coordinate with the body to maintain health. If this is the right account of the distinction between bodies and minds, then it seems that the Marxist view that we are our products, or that we can objectify ourselves in our artefacts, confuses our personal identity with some part of our mind. If the Marxist account of the self is the paradigm Western account of the materiality of the self, and the Platonic account is the paradigm mentalist account of the self in the West, then the Western tradition seems to characterize the self as mental.

The bifurcation of reality into our body and mind may seem implausible: even if we go down the road of understanding that our mind is the complement to our body, our mind quickly decomposes into a public world with other living bodies in it. This undermines treating the complement to the body as our mind. If the complement of our body is our mind, then clearly our minds are not our self, for the mental world is filled with other beings too. Similarly, our bodies are not completely us, they are filled with waste products and diseases that we can remove while maintaining our identity. The trouble is that personal identity can survive radical changes in how our body and mind presents over time to the point that it seems that the equation of the self with anything that can be known objectively is mistaken.

Such challenges pose no problem for a Yoga account of personal identity. Accordingly, we are neither our minds, nor our bodies. Rather, we are non-natural abstractions with an interest in abstracting from content (objects). Put another way, a person is a self-directed abstraction from content (objects). To be non-natural is to be the opposite of what is natural; the natural (*prakṛti*) is defined by causality (*guṇa*). Natural objects are best studied empirically; their behaviour can be fully explained by external causation. (The *Yoga Sūtra* recognizes three general varieties of such causes: inertia (*tamas*), activity (*rajas*), and illumination (*sattva*).[1] According to the *Yoga Sūtra*, we cannot understand persons as objects of nature, for while natural objects are best accounted for by external forces and conditions, such forces are an impediment to the authenticity of a person (Ranganathan 2008: II.18, III.36). (If I push you into doing something, I do not thereby know you, but rather what I did. If I want to know you, I have to allow you an environment where you are not coerced; your behaviour under such contexts can be understood as authentic. That is because the behaviour is a matter of self-direction, and self-direction moves away from objects that could otherwise undermine self-direction.) To understand a person (*puruṣa*) as a non-natural abstraction is to understand them as not explainable by external coercion or conditions. Rather, they are explainable by internal explanations: choice, responsibility, and obligation. These are ethical concepts. However, if such external conditions are spatiotemporal, it follows that persons are not spatiotemporal. This may seem strange, but we live this whenever we change our temporal and spatial context while retaining our identity. Travel shows we are not spatiotemporal. Non-spatiotemporal objects are universals. It follows that people are universals.

Now that we understand in what sense people are understandable (via ethical concepts), the rather obtuse idea that people are self-directed abstraction from content ought to make some sense. To call people self-directed abstractions from content is to understand a person as (ideally) the explanation for their relationships with other things in their environment, including other people. This is to recognize that people as a matter of self-regulation have an interest in regulating their relationships with objects in their environment. Hence, we are self-directed abstractions from content with an interest in abstracting from content.

Here we come to know the essential difference between persons and non-persons: to abstract from content is the essence of criticism, and as people are self-directed abstractions from content, the essence of a person is criticism. This criticism consists in putting a certain critical distance between oneself and one's object of inquiry. Hence, we could identify persons with the freedom to move. Non-persons are not critical. They are not essentially free to move.

When we live an authentic life, elements that are amenable to a naturalistic analysis function in conjunction to express the authenticity of the individual. A life well lived is a life where our body and mind (as the complement) are coordinated to reflect our essence (Ranganathan 2008: I.2–3). This involves taking responsibility for ourselves and everything in our minds.

In lay terms, the idea of abstraction from content is as simple as having an interest in being able to get up and move to another locale, such as the other room. When we cannot do this, illness sets in. Death (of the body) is the ultimate personal failure to abstract from content (it is as though the mind is abstracting from the body). Nevertheless, philosophically, the idea of the abstraction from content defines formal logic; what makes logic different from epistemology, or the empirical sciences, is that it allows us to abstract from all content. To abstract from all content is to move away from particulars to universals, from times and places to kinds of times and places. We can be logical about going grocery shopping, doing our chores, or planning policy.

Mentally, when we fail to abstract from content, we identify with our thoughts and beliefs; if I feel sad, I incorrectly define myself by the sadness, or correlatively, if I feel angry, I believe myself to be angry. An example of failing to abstract from mental content is the person watching a movie and identifying themselves with the experience. It would seem that when the movie is over, the observer no longer exists for the observer was the movie, which is absurd. Identifying with physical content comes about when one decides that one's body, as it is, regardless of its state of repair, is oneself. If I identify with my body, and my body has an excess of some pathogen, then I would have to identify the pathogen as part of me. Alternatively, if my body were characterized by a challenge, perhaps a wound or an extra burden, I would thereby identify with the wound and the burden, take those away and the former me is dead. While I recognize that this urge to identify with one's bodily condition is pervasive, it is a mistake (Ranganathan 2008: I.4).

One way to see why identifying with one's mind or body is a mistake is to consider the prospects of medicine. Medicine is possible because doctors rely on an idealization of the patient, relative to which the doctor can criticize the body or mind of the patient. The doctor succeeds in diagnosing illness in proportion to her ability to distinguish the person, as an ideal, from the full set of mental and physical symptoms they present.

We can also see that failing to abstract from content causes problems in mundane concerns. If I cannot abstract from my money, I cannot distinguish it from myself, and if I cannot distinguish it from myself, I cannot invest it wisely without thereby considering myself dead. If I cannot abstract from my current finances, I cannot form plans to change things for myself; I would be defined by my bank account or my pocket's worth of change—now and forever.[2] I call these cases of having an interest in abstracting from our minds, bodies, and wealth, the *a priori* or *subtle* (*sūkṣma*) cases.

Similarly, if I am interested in someone as a friend, or perhaps romantically, it's not going to go well if I do not give that person some space. If I want to get to know the characteristics of an object in my environment, I cannot understand it without being able to control my relationship with it and this involves examining the object from differing perspectives, which in turn presupposes my ability to abstract from the object. If I cannot know objects, I cannot value them or protect them. I call these cases of having an interest in abstracting from other people and objects of interest the *a posteriori* or *gross* (*sthūla*) cases.

If I want to see what these considerations have in common, it is that we have an interest in abstracting from content. What it is to abstract from content is to be critical. To be critical is to put some distance between yourself and an object of inquiry.

What the *a priori* (*sūkṣma*) and *a posteriori* (sthūla) cases show is that rationality in the *a priori* and in the *a posteriori* cases amount to the same thing.

This is an alien thought in the Western tradition. Going back to Plato's Divided Line in the *Republic*, through the Medievals, and most all modern philosophers, the common line has been that there is a difference between empirical knowledge and knowledge of reason, and they report to differing criteria. Empirical knowledge concerns our senses, while rational knowledge concerns reason. This leaves things rather mystical: why just two kinds of knowledge— why not three? No explanation is given, and the question is treated as moot.

However, if the story I am telling is correct, empirical knowledge and rational knowledge are really two differing applications of the same directive: that we ought to abstract from content. I cannot see what I do not separate myself from, and I cannot reason if I do not allow myself to separate from particular cases.

Our interest in abstracting from content and its ability to account for knowledge as such also shows something else to be a myth: scepticism is a failure of knowledge. Since Plato, Western philosophy has viewed scepticism as a threat to knowledge. Anything is better than doubt for the archetypal Westerner—even faith. But if the account I have been recommending is correct, scepticism is not a threat to knowledge; to know is to practice disbelief. If I cannot leave the room I am in, I have little reason to believe it is real. But when I leave this room, I no longer believe it. My leaving the room (and hence, not having beliefs about it anymore) shows me that it is real, my beliefs about the room do not.

I believe that these are all very basic considerations in philosophy, essential to finding our feet in the discipline. But it is also the *Yoga Sūtra*. Patañjali writes that 'Yoga is the control of the (moral) character of thought', which in contemporary terms is the idea that yoga (discipline) is being critical about what we think (*citta-vṛtti-nirodhaḥ*) (Ranganathan 2008: I.2). When we accomplish this, we, as knowers, live as abstractions (*svarūpe vasthānam*) (Ranganathan 2008: I.3), and if we fail to be critical and live a life as abstractions, we identify with the force of other things (*vṛtti-sārūpyam-itaratra*) (Ranganathan 2008: I.4). To fail to abstract is to give up our autonomy and thereby be guided by extraneous influences.

What say us about the ideal life? According to Patañjali, the goal is *kaivalya*, commonly translated as 'isolation', but equally well put as 'autonomy'. But this autonomy or isolation is impossible so long as there is any residual selfishness (Ranganathan 2008: IV.24–29). If the Yoga account is correct, the liberal idea that what we want is us, is mistaken, for our preferences are motives we can distinguish ourselves from. Liberalism is the selfishness to get rid of. However, so is the idea that we are definable by our species, language, ethnicity, caste, gender, or sexuality. This is not to say that our sexuality, language, ethnicity, nationality, and species are not important features of our lives, but if we are going to value these features of our lives (like money we can invest), we have to know them, and we cannot know what we cannot abstract from. But if we can abstract from them, we are not them. Ergo, if I can know my species, I am not my species, it does not define who I am. This is important, I believe, for it shows that the rights that we have are not granted to us by our biology but constitute who we are as persons. Some persons are humans, but not all things human are persons, and not all persons are human. However, the types of rights that we ought to be interested in are personal rights and this goes for Indians as well. Put more basically, we are our rights, which is to say our normative freedom, and this normative freedom consists in being able to abstract from content. But as this freedom is abstract and abstractive, it is a confusion to identify it with a species, such as humanity, our products, minds, or bodies.

As a means to make the case for personal rights, I shall consider the only plausible reason for thinking that humans are special, or that the personal and the human are somehow coextensive. This is the thesis that thought is linguistic. I shall argue that this is the source of unsatisfactory political options. The Yoga alternative allows us to understand ourselves as our personal rights, constituted by a critical concern for the truth and personal integrity.

Stereotyping the West

Do we have 'human rights' by virtue of being human, or is human biology irrelevant? The claim that it is our humanness that grants us these rights is absurd; a tumour can be human, as can my hair, but a human tumour or hair, independently of a person, has no rights—and even with a person, they have no rights (Marquis 2007). Now we see why: to be a person is to be the kind of thing that warrants a certain type of respect; simply being human is insufficient, for something can be human and impersonal. In response, one might claim that being human is insufficient, but necessary to have the kind of rights that are worthy of discussion under the heading of human rights. However, this position is not obviously true. As evidence, consider the following: if I were to inject into you a substance that systematically changed your DNA so that you wake up from a coma with extra limbs and teeth, and are no longer genetically human, do you continue to have the kinds of rights that you cherished as human rights? (For those who believe this is farfetched, I invite you to consider that gender is something that can be reassigned through surgery and hormonal therapy; advances in gene therapy are afoot—the ability to change our species may be soon.) If these rights are earned by virtue of being human, it seems that you no longer have them for you are no longer human. If the only thing that stops me from mistreating you is that you are human, then I could mistreat you now as I have seen to it that you are not human. However, if the rights that you called 'human' are really the types of rights that persons have independently of their species, then depriving you of your membership in the human species may not deprive you of your personal rights.

This is the question of moral standing: who counts? This is an area of moral philosophy that gets little play in the Western philosophical tradition, but I believe is at the heart of many Indian philosophy. Indeed, if I were to stereotype Western moral philosophy, I would say that it barely addresses the question of moral standing (the considerations that differentiate those who are morally significant from those items that are not). Instead, the answer to the question is often assumed or not seriously defended: it is humans that count, and for the most part, only humans. This is not to claim that some philosophers of a Western heritage have not taken to defending non-human animals in ethics (Regan 2004; Singer 1990). Peter Singer notably draws on the influential moral philosopher, Jeremy Bentham (Bentham 1988). However, Bentham is one of two famous Utilitarians in the Western tradition; the other is J.S. Mill. Mill rejects equating non-humans with humans. On his account, humans are more important for they can experience 'happiness', while non-human animals can only experience 'pleasure': 'It is better to be a human being dissatisfied than a pig satisfied; better to be Socrates dissatisfied than a fool satisfied'. (Mill 1863: Chapter 2). Mill's argument for this is non-existent,[3] but this is easily overlooked against the backdrop of Western anthropocentrism. Utilitarianism in the Western tradition is not obviously on the side of non-human animals, and with very little argument or none at all, it can ride on the coattails of Western anthropocentrism. Kant, the West's spokesperson for Deontology, is decidedly uninterested in non-human animals. He tells us that the only reason we should be nice to non-human animals is that if we are mean to them, we may develop habits of cruelty that we can visit on humans (Kant 1974, 5: 298–303; 1996, 6: 443). The upshot of this is that if we can find a way to torture puppies while being nice to human infants, there would be nothing wrong with torturing puppies on Kant's account (Wood 1998: 194–5). Aristotle, the Western spokesperson for virtue ethics, defined ethics as learning how to get along in one's city state (*Ethics*: I.3); this is not a welcoming account of ethics for non-free humans, let alone, non-humans. So, here is the tally: out of the three big moral theories in the West (Utilitarianism, Deontology, and Virtue Theory), the famous defenders are decidedly anthropocentric in bent, with the lone exception of Jeremy Bentham.

In South Asia, the question of who counts, morally, gets far more play. This surfaces in the extensive concern in South Asian philosophy with the nature or essence of the self (*ātmā*), whether we have one, and what its positive or negative characteristics are. The history starts in the Vedas with scant comments about the origins of the Gods, and culminates in Upanishadic reflections on the metaphysical foundations of reality. Here, we find the self-discussed by itself, but also in relation to the world-self, *Brahman*. In the *Chāndogya Upaniṣad* (VI.8.7), we find the self and Brahman related via the famous formula *tat tvam asi* (that you are). An important discussion on the self that sets the stage for later treatments can be found in the *Kaṭha Upaniṣad*, and in particular the famous story of Nachiketa. Nachiketa is sentenced to death by his father and arrives in the abode of the God of Death, Yama, who is absent. Upon return after three days, Yama, offers the young boy three boons to make up for his lack of hospitality. The most exacting of the boons the boy asks for is an account of what happens to a person after they die. Yama's response involves positing the reality of a self, distinct from cognitive and perceptual faculties (*Kaṭha Upaniṣad*: I.1). Around, or shortly after the time, as the formation of the more sophisticated accounts in the Upanishads (circa 500 BCE), we find the development of Buddhist, Jain, and other responses to the question of the self. After this point, virtually every school of Indian philosophy takes it as its task to explain the self. The options abound: Buddhists deny the enduring reality of the self, but the continuity of responsibility, nihilist deny both, while realists defend the reality of the self. Some realists defend a unitary account of the self, according to which individuality is an illusion (such as *Advaita Vedānta*), while others (*Yoga, Sāṅkhya, Viśiṣṭādvaita Vedānta, Dvaita Vedānta, Nyāya, Vaiśeṣika*, and *Pūrva Mīmāṃsā*) defend or assume individuality. Accounts of obligations and rights of such individuals are tied to these metaphysical accounts.

So it is that in Asian philosophy, and South Asian philosophy in particular, questions of the essence of the self are central; such questions are often treated as essential to the explication of dharma: duty or morality. Unsurprisingly, given the depth of importance, this question is given in South Asian and Asian philosophy, there are a variety of answers to this question. In general, it is pretty clear that Asian philosophers do not, as a whole, assume that humanity is coextensive with personhood. Indeed, those who use the technical term '*puruṣa*' (person) for describing their philosophy criticize (almost as a category) the identification of a person with their species or biology. Patañjali in the *Yoga Sutra* calls this conflation of a person with their biology the vice of *asmitā*, or egotism (Ranganathan 2008: I.17). While Vedāntins tend to uphold the propriety of animal sacrifices, they often argue that ultimately, all sentient beings are essentially the same or equal (Rāmānuja 1996: III.i.25; Śaṅkara 1962: III.i.25). Madhva holds that individuals differ constitutionally, not in accordance with species, but with character (Madhva/ Ānandatīrtha 1993: I.17). Buddhists, who are famous for the no-self view (*anātmā*) identify moral standing with the lack of a self, which is tantamount to sensitivity to the outside. This constitutes the conditions for *duḥkha* (discomfort) that are transcended through compassion. Similarly, Jains appear to understand persons as anything that is sentient; they hence restrict action to avoid infringing upon the rights of others (Sūtrakṛtāṅga 1987: I.xi.7–10). This culminates in a meditative fast unto death that Jains traditionally distinguish from suicide: suicide is something we do—fasting to allow others their rights is not doing anything.

We could use 'human rights' to talk about what Indian philosophers have had to say about the kind of rights that we think humans have. More often than not, we would find philosophies that provide us reason to be critical of conflating the biological category of humanity with personhood.

Humanism is not unique to the Western tradition. Confucius, the famous philosopher of Asian philosophy, was a humanist; he valued *jen* (or humanity) as the source and arbitral of questions of value. There is not anything nearly so humanistic and influential in the South Asian traditions. In Europe, the tradition of privileging the human has a long history. It starts with the ancient Greeks, who had one word for thought, opinion, and word/language: *logos*. This is a linguistic accident: many languages have words for these various concepts, but Greek has one word for all of these concepts. Sanskrit, for instance, has no word that simultaneously expresses both concepts: *śabda* (word) or thought (*citta*)—you have to choose which you mean and one does not allow a free ride for the other. This conflation of thought with word and language is indicative of a certain attitude that the Greeks apparently had: to think is to employ language. With few premises, this idea that thought and word amount to the same thing entails the conflation of the category of being human with the category of persons. The premises are as follows:

(1) If one can think, one can use a word, and if one can use a word, one can think (logos).
(2) If one is a person, one has rights.
(3) If one has rights, then one can think.
(4) If one thinks (logos) then one uses words (logos).
(5) If one uses words, then one is human.
(6) Therefore, if one is a person and has rights, then one is human.

The first premise is an explication of the idea of logos. The second premise, that persons are constituted by their rights, is the claim that persons are essentially free, which is tantamount to saying that persons are by definition responsible. It is not easy to deny this, for if we deny people their rights in practice (such as a right to their agency), they cease to exist. This is death. Therefore, it is a metaphysical constraint on persons that they have rights, or we should say that people are their rights. Take away their rights, and you take them away.[4] This is something on which moral philosophers tend to agree. The third premise (if one has rights, one can think) is likely something that philosophers agree too. As being unable to think is a limit to personal freedom, so we must grant that to be a person is to be able to think as they are essentially free (as per the second premise). The fourth premise might be understood as a decomposition of the first premise (it is one of the two conditionals that comprise the bi-conditional of the first premise). The fifth premise is an empirical generalization: language it seems is a primarily human thing. Through the logical rules, hypothetical syllogism and exportation, the series of conditional claims results in the conclusion. This gets us to the idea that to be a person is to be human. The argument is, in logical terms, valid (if the premises are true, the conclusion has to be true). But is it sound (that is, are the premises true)?

I do not doubt that some of these premises may appear controversial to someone. Many of these premises have been disputed in the history of Indian philosophy. For instance, the debate on whether persons are free or not goes to the very heart of ancient Indian philosophy, where philosophers disputed whether or not *kriyā* (agency) characterizes persons. Buddhists, Jains, and many so called 'Hindu' philosophies such as Yoga, Nyāya, Vaiśeṣika, Pūrva Mīmāṃsā, and some versions of *Vedānta* took the view that persons are agents, which is to say free to act and choose. This is to deny that people can be deprived their freedom, and thereby their rights, and continue to be persons. Others, such as the *Ājīvikas*, along with *Sāṅkhya*, and *Advaita Vedāntins*, deny that agency (hence freedom, and hence rights) defines persons. Rather, persons who are for the most part unfree (Śaṅkara 1991, 2: 11), on this account and by some fluke come to understand themselves as mere passive observers in an externally determined world (cf. *Sāṅkhya Kārikā*). Philosophers on the side of agency usually paid homage to the importance of ethics (*dharma*) while those who denied agency usually had critical views of ethics, as when Ādi Śaṅkara, the famous Advaitan, said that even dharma (duty) is an evil for someone interested in *mokṣa* (liberation) (Śaṅkara 1991 commentary on Gītā 4: 21). Both sides tended to agree that consciousness or thought is an attribute of persons, and so they would not deny the connection between personhood and thought. What Indian philosophers never seriously entertained was the question of whether species defines personhood, nor did they as a group seriously entertain the idea that in order to think one requires language. They typically did not affirm that all animals can speak language, and so they would, as a group, affirm the fifth premise as a generality.

So we come to the culturally particular and absolutely non-universal claim that there is an essential connection between thought (citta)[5] and word (śabda) embodied in the Greek idea of logos. Add this one toxic premise into the mix of otherwise defendable premises and one gets the speciesism that defines the West, the speciesism that conflates personhood with being human. Given the importance Greek culture was given in Western civilization (whether in its Christian, Islamic, or secular forms), logos and the associated speciesism has had a profound impact on the West. All religious traditions and cultures that look back on the Greeks typically share this orientation. Call this package, typified in the argument, *Westernism*.

I think that the idea that Westernism is innocent is a mistake. One way to look at it is to believe that it is the foundation of humanism.

However, this is naive. If one takes seriously the connection between thought and language, in a world of linguistic diversity, this conflation puts people between the rock and hard place of two unpalatable options. Either hold on to the pretence that one's thought transcends one culture and language, in which case one must view people who speak differing languages with suspicion, and ultimately requiring conversion to one's own linguistic culture, or give up on the idea that one's thought transcends one's language and accept linguistic relativism. There seems to be a third option: assume that we are all the same—that despite our seemingly superficial cultural differences, there is something fundamentally similar about our minds due to our shared humanness. This is the Kantian option. However, the identification of thought with language, and the reality of radical linguistic difference, makes this option implausible. (Even linguists such as Noam Chomsky who hold that all human languages are produced by a deep generative grammar do not claim the obviously false thesis that languages as a rule have words that have the same meaning. See Chomsky 1975.) I call this more liberal option 'naive universalism'. Therefore, I propose that the West as propped up by Westernism has yielded three options: colonialism/imperialism (whether in soft missionary forms, or hard political forms), relativism (in academic forms), or naive universalism that ignores the reality of our differences. Asian powers that have attempted to emulate the West (Imperial Japan, or perhaps modern China) typically emulate these options. Given the insecurity that Westernism breeds, it has a way to create a veneer of uniformity that it can then take to be evidence of its naive universalism. Given the imperial history of the West, and the fact that it has overrun the Earth, it has culturally altered everywhere so that when it interacts with former colonies in post-colonial times, it seems to find seeming reflections of its own culture, which it can interpret as evidence for naive universalism. No wonder naive universalism in its liberal form comes on the heels of Western imperialism; this is something that Sonia Sikka's paper outlines in detail.

The upshot? Unless one values colonialism/imperialism, relativism, or naive universalism, one should probably reject the premises that there is a connection between language and thought. If one rejects this, one no longer has the key premises in the argument for the conflation of personhood with humanity that I called Westernism. One might balk at this claim; indeed, it would seem, all we need to do is reject some premise in the argument to deny its strength. But the identification of language with thought is the odd thesis. The remaining theses have been entertained by Indian philosophers: the idea that we have rights (freedoms) is core to Jain, Buddhist, and Yogic morality. Indeed, there is no way to explicate the Buddhist idea of Four Noble Truths (the idea that we can put an end to suffering by abandoning maximizing preferences for a Buddhist program of harm reduction), the Jain idea of mokṣa amounts to realizing our essential motion (dharma on their account), or the Yogic idea that success in Yoga comes from meditating on the ideal person who never had any trouble (Ranganathan 2008: I.24), without taking seriously the idea that freedom is native to agents. Our rights are nothing we acquire; rather, we actualize them, on these accounts.

Indeed, given the extensive attention of Indian philosophers to mokṣa, it is strange to claim that Indian philosophers were not interested in rights. The idea that we are essentially free is something that is vigorously defended by these and other Indian philosophies as they criticize bondage (saṃsāra), either as an illusion or an incursion into our interests. The idea that our personhood is defined by these freedoms (2) is certainly Yoga (Ranganathan 2008: III.50), but other kindred philosophies as well. The idea that to be free is to think freely (3) is certainly part of the Jain value of anekantavada (non-one-sidedness) (cf. Koller 2000), but seems to be part of many Indic philosophies that identify liberation with a life such as ours but without trouble (Madhva/Ānandatīrtha 1904; Rāmānuja 1991; Śaṅkara 1962). Indeed, the idea that we are defined by jñāna or knowledge (a view held by many Vedānta schools) is arguably an Indic way of establishing the connection between personal identity and thought. The idea that (5) speaking language is a largely human thing is an empirical claim, which may or may not be true, but is certainly something one can attest to regardless of one's geography. Rather, it is (1) and (4), the connection between language and thought, that is alien to Indic philosophy. For anyone to claim that it is a starting point for rational discussions is to confuse Greek culture with what is rational.

Cross Cultural Research

The idea that language and thought have a close connection is commonly assumed in the Western tradition but rarely defended. Philosophers who are part of the so-called 'linguistic turn' in the West have often assumed this premise as part of a research project, but this is not the same as defending the thesis. My own view is that the thesis is a bust (Ranganathan 2007: 2011). I argue that no workable account of translation that explains successful academic practices can get off the ground with the linguistic account of thought. But my reasons for thinking that the thesis is mistaken stretch back to my interest in accounts of Indian philosophy. Here we meet a strong tradition of scholarship, commonly called 'Indology,' that treats the study of all things Indian—even Indian philosophy—as the fitting object of social scientific study. Hence, the primary means of studying Indian philosophy is on this account: not philosophy itself, but philology or linguistics, social sciences that study language. No doubt, linguistics is a social science and if the study of Indian philosophy could be reduced to linguistics, then we would do well to let linguists be the ones who tell us about Indian philosophy. But why should we think that the best way to get to Indian philosophy is via linguistics? We would think this if thought and language amount to the same thing. This is the assumption of logos.

Given the cultural peculiarity of logos as an assumption, the insistence of scholars to put language first in their study of non-Western cultures is an expression of a strange ethnocentrism. It is ethnocentric on two fronts. First, the assumption itself is original to one culture only (the ancient Greeks) and hardly universal as far as theorizing about thought is concerned. Secondly, the conflation of thought with language creates and reifies ethnocentrism, in so far as it identifies what one thinks with one's language. In the face of this, we might wonder if there is any positive evidence about the success of the linguistic orientation to thought. There is certainly plenty of evidence concerning the problems it causes in research. The problems are a consequence of the methodology of confusing language with thought. It leads to the mistaken view that studying language is the best means of studying thought. But the ethnocentrism of identifying thought with language sows many problems, including the idea that the thought of the other is forever frozen in their language, and inexpressible in ours.

As an example, consider the failure of Orthodox Indology to account for moral philosophy and ethics in the Indian tradition. The argument goes: if there is an Indian word that means what the Western word 'ethics' or 'moral' means, then we could translate Indian texts using that word as texts of ethics. The closest philosophical analogue to 'ethics' or 'morality' in Indian literature is 'dharma'. In fact, the term 'dharma' is ubiquitous in Indian literature and philosophy. No school of philosophy in South Asia passes the opportunity to say something about dharma, and the term is used prominently in many traditions. Given the prominence of this term, it would seem that Indian philosophy is nothing if not obsessed with moral philosophy. It would certainly be convenient for purveyors of Western imperialism, in either political or cultural forms, to make this rich tradition of Indic normative philosophy disappear, for then they could hold that Western political intervention in South Asia was necessary to fill a vacuum of serious reflection on ethics and politics. The way the rich tradition of Indian moral theorizing disappears is via the claim that 'dharma'—the most plausible linguistic correlate to morality of ethics in the Indian tradition—has too many meanings. The bulk of the meanings are not 'morality' or 'ethics'.

Orthodox Indology generates this conclusion by conflating the meaning of a word with its use. This violates a basic distinction in the philosophy of language between meaning and use. For any given meaning of a word, there are innumerable uses of this word: hence, the idea that there are too many uses of a word for it to have a single meaning is absurd. This is basic stuff in the philosophy of language. But Orthodox Indology has not heard about this basic distinction. According to Orthodox Indology, the objectivity of the meaning of a word is just what it is used for in a context, and given that there are so many different uses for a term such as 'dharma,' it follows that there is no one meaning for this term. As I noted, this does not pass philosophical muster. By parity of reasoning, one would have to conclude that 'good' does not have a single meaning for it is used for far too many things. However, Orthodox Indology is not a branch of philosophy concerned with its own history, it is social science. Given this conflation of meaning with use, Orthodox Indology generates the conclusion that there are too many meanings for 'dharma' for it to be translatable into English, or for it to be accurately characterized as a single concept. The late eminent Indologist Wilhelm Halbfass summarizes this view:

> Numerous statements have emphasized the fullness of meaning and the complexity of *DHARMA*, as well as the difficulty of translating it or of even adequately paraphrasing it…. It has been repeatedly emphasized that the concept of *DHARMA* is so difficult to define because it ignores or transcends differences which are essential or irreducible for Western understanding—differences between fact and norm, cosmos and society, physics and ethics, etc.
>
> (Halbfass 1988: 311–13).

I could continue to pour scorn on the conflation of meaning with use that allows for this conclusion, but what often does not get enough attention is that this approach to Indian thought results in a bad account of Western thought. In short, Halbfass's pretence about Western thinking could not be more mistaken.

The dichotomy between fact and norm, cosmos and society, physics and ethics, is an influential dichotomy that begins with Hume (taken up in earnest by Kant), but one that is certainly absent in classical and ancient Western philosophy and is not a permanent fixture in subsequent Western philosophy. For a doctrine that violates and transcends these supposed essential distinctions to the Western understanding, one should look no further than what many consider the foundational text of Western civilization, Plato's *Republic*. In the *Republic*, Plato argues for a theory of justice that sees the soul and society as analogously composed, and equally capable of being just. Moreover, the normative importance of justice is a function of the good, which in Book VI, Socrates argues is the Form of the forms, which is to say that it is the ultimate ideal object and ground of reality, and that all facts, including physical facts, are constituted by goodness, even if indirectly. (Plato's notion of the good thus is similar to the Vedic notion of *Ṛta*, the forerunner to numerous subsequent theories about dharma in the Indian tradition.) It was this theory that allowed Plotinus in *The Enneads* (I.8) to argue that matter is Evil, because, unlike the world of Ideas, matter is far removed from the good. This reduction of the physical to the evaluative can be found in Aristotle as well, to the extent that teleology is woven into his basic physical notions such as causality and his biological classifications. For instance, Aristotle's view that man has a rational principle (*Ethics*: I.13) is not a descriptive generalization, but a normative claim about what is normal in humans: if a human being presents a lack of rationality, on Aristotle's account, this human fails to be human in some essential respect. Biology is thus not a matter of brute fact for Aristotle, it is an evaluative matter that takes into account the teleology of organisms. Aristotle's writing on nature parallel his writing on ethics, and in this respect, Aristotle's thinking about facts and values parallels many discussions of dharma in the Indian tradition.[6] Closer to our time we need look no further than the tradition of Utilitarianism, that identifies goodness with pleasure, happiness, or the conditions of biological thriving. Utilitarianism, a mainstay of recent moral enquiry, rejects the physics-ethics distinction to the extent that it attempts to reduce ethical considerations to basic facts about the empirical world that can be studied through natural sciences, including physics.

Halbfass's comments are exemplary of the disappointing side of South Asia Studies: against the backdrop of a general ignorance of Western philosophy, India and its intellectual tradition is compared with the West. The trouble, of course, is not that Halbfass is a bad Sanskritist: no one would believe that. I certainly do not. The trouble is that he operates on the non-philosophical assumption that accessing Indic thought is about accessing Indic languages. But any philosopher who teaches introductory philosophy knows this is false: native speakers of English who are philosophy students do not thereby know the right answer to what the good is because they are proficient in the use of the word 'good'. Students could quote the Oxford English Dictionary if they like, but its definition of good, linguistically respectable as it may be, hardly settles the question of what is good. The real issue is that philosophical questions are not settled by knowing what our words mean and that is because to a great extent, the question is 'how' we are to define our words. As G.E. Moore noted, for any definition of 'good', we might ask if the definition is correct (Moore 1903).

This applies to the concept of a 'person' as well. If it turns out that most speakers of 'English' believe that to be a person one must be human, and if this makes its way into the OED, it hardly settles the philosophical question of what is a person. This is because philosophy is not a social science. Answers to philosophical questions are normative and are not reducible to common opinion or its historical artefact, language. There is hence no way to address the question of what 'dharma' is independently of being involved in thinking about how we ought to think about dharma, or morality. Linguistics is neither necessary nor sufficient for understanding philosophy. But if the linguistic facts do not settle philosophical questions, linguistic expertise may not be necessary to understand Indian philosophy.

How do we define 'dharma,' or 'ethics'? I think that this question is moot; it is up to linguists to define these terms for that is their job. However, if we assume that thought is language, then we inflate the value of linguistic assessment.

Rejecting the connection of thought and language is as easy as rejecting the conflation of meaning and use; if we can draw a distinction between these two, then we can recognize that we use language to express thoughts without thoughts thereby being linguistic. This has practical implications. First, we can see that words with differing meanings can express the same thoughts. 'I am writing this essay' and 'Shyam Ranganathan is writing this essay' express the same thought when expressed by me, even though the meaning of the words included in these sentences are different. This would not be plausible if thought is linguistic. Second, we can see that though human language is important for humans to think, it is only instrumentally important. This shows why philosophers are correct for not assuming that native speakers of English who know the meaning of the English word 'good' thereby know the answer to the question of what is good. Third, it shows that accuracy in translation is not about matching words with the same meaning. Rather, if the object of translation is the preservation of thought, then we have to relativize translation to some practical purpose. In the case of philosophy, it is the philosophical purpose that counts. Hence, 'ethics' and 'dharma' can have the same philosophical significance, though their linguistic meaning is different, in so far as they share the same philosophical purpose to articulate moral theories. This unlocks Indian philosophy from the prison of logos. Indians do not need to look to the West for inspiration for their normative theorizing, for normative theorizing, and philosophy as such, is not ethnic. Philosophers anywhere are capable of that kind of thing, and India has a rich tradition of philosophy. The linguistic account of thought, however, treats thought as ethnic, and if the word 'ethics' or 'rights' are words of English, it seems we are stuck looking to the West for proprietary accounts of ethics and rights.

Yoga and Rights

In the last two sections, I have argued against the guilty premise in Westernism: the conflation of thought with language. This allows for the conflation of the category of persons with humans given other non-culturally peculiar premises, but it also creates insecurities: those who are not linguistically like us are a threat, it seems, to the universality of our own thought. Worse, it creates an inappropriately insecure variety of scholar, one who takes no care in reporting the intellectual history of what they take to be their (Western) tradition, but excessive attention to linguistic detail in the studied (South Asian) tradition. This excess generates strange comparisons and biases based on a lack of knowledge of two different kinds: a lack of knowledge of mother tongue (scholarship tongue) tradition, and a misunderstanding of the studied tradition that comes from a fixation on microscopic detail to the detriment of macroscopic meaning. In the Indological case, this lack of knowledge expresses itself in the low bar set for knowledge of the mother tongue tradition, and a misguided emphasis on linguistic details of the studied linguistic tradition that leaves high level generalities unnoticed, such as shared philosophical functions amongst words with differing linguistic meanings such as 'ethics' and 'dharma'. The double standard sets up an apartheid: the mother tongue tradition of normative theorizing about 'rights' or 'ethics' gets legitimized without critical review, and no amount of evidence can allow the studied tradition to show that it has, within it, a rich tradition of addressing normative questions under the heading of 'dharma'.

The same type of double standard arises in the political context: the native tradition is treated as right by default and the studied tradition is a threat, to be revered as another (relativism), or to be run over (imperialism). In the case of moral standing, this double standard shows up in a similar apartheid to the case of scholarship: 'we' are treated as persons by default and without much critical review ('we' being humans) and non-human others are put under a microscope, probed, vivisectioned, and studied in great detail as different. We too can be put under a microscope, probed, vivisectioned, and it would become apparent that we are not so different from our non-human cousins, but somehow, we are spared those indignities and assumed to be persons while non-humans are assumed to be non-persons. Worse, this question begging double standard generates a most absurd ideological barrier to the evidence: it assumes that any quality we have as persons are by definition human, and accuses those who interpret non-humans as persons as guilty of *anthropomorphism* (Frey 1980).

The root of the double standard is the conflation of thought with language; if what is thinkable is what I can say, then anyone else who cannot say what I say is at a disadvantage, whether this is a studied tradition or non-human animals. I, and those like me, are treated as paragons of rationality, but for no other reason than my inability to understand.

The conflation of thought and language is a special case of failing to be critical. To fail to be critical is to identify ourselves with our thoughts; as language characterizes part of our cultural identity, identifying thoughts with our cultural identity is a means of identifying ourselves with our thoughts. What is far more critical is to put some distance between ourselves and our language, and what we find then is that we can continue to think even while we are critical of linguistic meaning and language. This is the norm in philosophy as a discipline. This is because philosophy is where we practice the manipulation of thoughts as a means of maintaining our autonomy. This is how yoga as a project is conceived, according to Patañjali.

Historically, philosophy was not distinguished from the empirical sciences in the West; indeed, the empirical sciences were called 'natural philosophy'. Things changed when scholars recognized that the variety of explanation appropriate in cases of nature is not philosophical; philosophy abstracts from contexts and delivers considerations of wide applicability. Empirical explanations are context bound.

For example, a physicist could provide an account of our universe, and ours only, and thereby make a contribution to physics. But in philosophy, it would not do to provide an account of our universe only. The metaphysician needs to provide an account of universes, as such, in order for the account to be admissible as a philosophical account of universes. The same ought to be the case in ethics and political philosophy; merely describing how we assign rights in the context of human society, though sociologically relevant, is not a philosophical project. And it ought not to be a philosophical project, for how we assign rights in practice may not be just.

The asymmetry between natural and non-natural explanations has to do with the direction of fit. In the case of natural explanations, we want to know how objects behave, subject to contingent limitations: causality. In the case of philosophy, we want to understand something in abstract from its contingent limitations. In the *Yoga Sūtra*, this difference is enshrined in the distinction between nature (prakṛti) and people (puruṣa).

The difference is instructive: some objects can only be understood in terms of limitations. Others such as us could be treated as objects of empirical research, but this is to understand us in terms of contingent limitations. These limitations are not necessarily a reflection of our choices. I could, for instance, pick you up and operate you as a puppet, and while this would reveal something about your pliancy and weight (biological considerations), it would not be a great way for me to get to know you, for the behaviour you display would be a function of coercion (causality) and not a matter of self-direction. To know you is to know the object that is you that is self-directed. To see this involves giving up on treating you as an object understandable in terms of external constraints.

The upshot is that a person could be treated as an object of nature, and understood purely from the outside. But in proportion to our failure to treat a person as a person, we fail to see who they are. When people are free, they abstract from elements in their environment. When they fail to do so, illness sets in (Ranganathan 2008: II.34). People have an interest in abstracting from content, and moreover that ideally they have the right to do so. As this is what is essential to being a person, then all people have an interest in being able to abstract from content. This entails that our interests do not collide, for colliding against each other (traffic accidents) is another way for us to not abstract from content (cf. Ranganathan 2008: IV.29–30). So for any person to have their interests protected is for all persons to have their interests protected (Ranganathan 2008: II.30–1). Unlike the liberal model, where we are what we want and we must compromise part of who we are to maximize our preferences, Yoga entails that our freedom is uncompromising. But as each one of us has the same interests, each one of us has an interest in vigorously pursuing it now; waiting for a Messiah is like waiting for Godot. Hence, Patañjali holds that '(Success in yoga is) near for those who are intense...and is also proportional to the degree of intensity: feeble, moderate or above measure'. (Ranganathan 2008: I.21–2)

The *Yoga Sūtra* specifies three practices as essential to yoga: *tapas* (austerities), *svādhyāya* (self-criticism), and *Īśvarapraṇidhāna*. We are familiar with tapas, what is packaged in our consumerist world as yoga. But the importance extends beyond its marketability; to undertake austerities is to be committed to abstracting from one's perceptions of oneself. This is necessary if we maintain our freedom as people who can abstract from content. Self-criticism is essential in order for us to understand the proper and healthy boundaries that ought to mediate our relationships with others. Īśvarapraṇidhāna means meditating on the Lord, a special person untouched by troubles (Ranganathan 2008: I.24). It is not a creator God. Meditating on Īśvara puts the seeds of omniscience in us (Ranganathan 2008: I.25). What is this? Religious fervour? Faith? I think these are mistaken interpretations. To meditate on Īśvara is to think critically about the person who never made any mistakes. However, this is to meditate on the abstract conditions of autonomy. Īśvarapraṇidhāna is hence the practice of moral philosophy. The reason that this latter activity is important is that it requires us to be critical about criticism itself; if we cannot be critical about criticism itself, we cannot perfect ourselves as abstractors from content.

In order to jump start this program of self-improvement, the *Yoga Sūtra* recommends five political objectives that ought to be endorsed and maximized 'throughout the world, irrespective of station at birth, country or place, time or custom'. (Ranganathan 2008: II.31) These rules are abstaining from harm (*ahiṃsā*), truthfulness (*satya*), abstinence from theft (*asteya*), sexual restraint (*brahmacharya*), and unacquisitiveness (*aparigrahā*). These are invaluable to civil society, but also to personal growth. The order is instructive: a fidelity to truth over harm reduction would permit factors in our world that are not in our interest, hence, we ought to be committed to a safe world before we insist on its objectivity. This reflects the yogi's insight that the objectivity of the world is a social construction based on our decisions and that a failure to put safety first is irresponsible. Next, we ought to be concerned with truth as something objective, something of which we can be critical. This is part of what is involved in putting it after safety. Next we ought to be respectful of 'personal' property. Marx points out that capitalists often confuse personal property with private property; private property is excess wealth that can be used in the service of generating more wealth. I think given the critical view that Patañjali takes of acquisitiveness, he doesn't have much regard for private property. However, people need things to survive, we humans could use a good toothbrush (or neem stick); we shouldn't deprive each other of that kind of thing. Clothing, food, and shelter certainly fall into this category. We have a right to these as persons. Next we ought to be mindful of ourselves as entities requiring restraint: this is *brahmacharya*. I think the idea that it implies abstinence from sexual relationships is misleading as we do not need to abstain from sexual relationships to control our own sexuality or to be self-restrained. Rather, when we control our sexuality, we are our own masters; it not only protects others from unwanted advances, it also protects ourselves from losing a grip on ourselves. None of this entails that any specific sexual orientation is expected of us or more desirable. If anything, the approach provides ample grounds for criticizing the heterosexist preference for heterosexual relationships on the grounds of it being natural. If it is natural, it is not personal. Sexuality, as an expression of our personhood, is self-directed and hence has no foundation in nature. To treat sexuality as natural (coercion from the outside) is to confuse sex with rape; sex is an expression of personhood, rape is not. Finally, we ought to be critical of acquisitiveness for a culture of acquisition confuses the value of our lives with stuff, and the more we confuse the two, the less we can abstract from content. Neo-liberal economics that places an emphasis on consumerism is to be avoided.

Problems with the Yoga Account

On the Yoga account, rights are not natural: they are ethical. Rights are identical with who we are, and whether they are observable or not concerns whether we have created a world that is amenable to autonomy. Talk of rights is not empty drivel; genuine rights (freedoms) capture who we are ideally. Nature is something we ought to criticize as distinct from us. Just because something is natural does not mean that it is good for us; disease is natural, it is not good for us.

A world structured by yoga is a world in which people are free, and this freedom is measured by our mutual mobility. Everyone's interests coincide, for a failure of autonomy (mobility) in the case of one party constitutes a hurdle to another's mobility. The quality of life is thereby measurable by an individual's freedom to move; in proportion to an individual's inability to move, they are owed aid and intervention. This allows us to recognize that not all interests count as personal rights. Plants have an interest in thriving, but this thriving requires being rooted, which is an example of failure to abstract from content. Persons, in contrast, need to move around as an expression of their autonomy; the animal kingdom (comprised of organisms with an interest in mobility) is the natural correlate of persons.

The Yoga account, as I understand it, provides some reason to be sympathetic with Liberal and Marxist accounts of human freedom. Liberals are correct for valuing freedom and understanding freedom in terms of choice. Marxists are correct for being suspicious of private property and for favouring personal property. Both accounts are mistaken as they are mentalist: they identify personhood with something mental, whether a product of our efforts or our preferences, and this is a mistake for personal identity is not reducible. Correlatively, both are mistaken for the speciesist preference of humans over non-humans. The problems that we face now are a threat to people who have an interest in abstracting from content, regardless of species: overcrowding, environmental disasters, and war are not just problems for humans.

A society arranged on principles articulated by Patañjali would encourage mobility of all sorts. Justice, on this account, is the freedom to move. Failures of a society to deliver the basic requirements of health would be a failure to promote mobility. Healthcare is on this account a right, not a privilege. Education, in so far as it aids mobility, would be a right. If income is necessary for mobility, then a minimum income necessary for the requisite personal property would also be a right.

Some might argue that our species is not something that we can abstract from: if I am human, that is who I am. This confuses what abstraction is—if I cannot critically distinguish between my interests as a person and those of my species, I act like most humans who pursue policies that seem to put humans first and the result is short term gains for anthropocentric projects and long term environmental disasters of all sort that come back to haunt us humans. Short-sighted thinking identifies my interest with my species. This entails that our interests as people requires an interest in promoting the type of world that makes room for diversity in species and one that is mutually safe. As persons are by definition non-natural, their interests are not reducible to what they are condemned to by nature, but rather what conforms to their ideal interest in abstracting from content. All of this entails that humans ought to not only take a role in stewardship of the environment, but also care for non-human species as an extension of their understanding of our shared personal essence. This may involve intervening and altering the nature of species of persons so that they could coexist with minimum harm. It is hence not an objection to Yoga that many beings, owing to their species, have aggressive instincts that cause them to violate precepts of yoga; if these are natural, they ought to be altered.

Another possible objection is that the Yogic account apparently leaves caste untouched, and we know that caste is an evil. This is mistaken. The Yogic account does not treat caste as a final object of social arrangement; indeed, our main political objectives defy caste boundaries on Patañjali's account. But the idea that we are defined by what we do or our ancestry has no obvious grounding in the Yogic account of the self as self-directed abstraction from content.

One might worry about Yoga's approach to historical injustices. Yoga is highly critical of memories. Memories, the *Yoga Sūtra* teaches us, are like *saṃskāras* (tendency impressions) that come about by a personal choice to identify with an experience. This is a problem for it is a failure of rationality. However, if we do not remember historical injustices it seems that we are bound to repeat them. The problem with this criticism is that it draws no distinction between knowing about a historical injustice and remembering it. To know about a historical injustice is to move away from it; to remember it is to retain the experience of it. Indeed, if memories are the retention of experienced content, and if the content is a historical injustice, then keeping the memory alive is a way to perpetuate the injustice. Historical injustice requires knowledge, but this means criticism, which is only possible if we can move away from the object of interest. In the case of historical injustice, the object of interest just is the historical injustice. Therefore, what we need to do in order to change the world for the better is not remember the bad things, but know they are things of the past, which allows us to be critical about them.

Religion, and especially Indic versions that are identified by remembered traditions (*smṛti*), are apparently on the chopping block. This would seem to render a Yogic constitution strange in the Indian context. Patañjali for his part notes that religion is something that we have to come up against in our critical self-study: in this practice we come to identify our chosen deities (*iṣṭadevatā*) (Ranganathan 2008: II.44). The idea that we can choose our own deities is Indic, but the idea that the identification of our chosen deity is part of self-study is important, for it shows that religious affiliation is a choice and we bear personal responsibility for it. Deity choice is not to be confused with conforming to community expectations or history, and as it is personal, it would be inappropriate for us to force such a choice on others. Proselytizing is a mistake.

Finally, one might worry that Yoga provides no resources for dealing with social conflict. Dealing with social conflict is necessary to minimize injury and violations of personal rights. Patañjali for his part recognizes that conflict is something that the Yogi must overcome via a philosophical wisdom that responds appropriately to opposition. If Yoga is the promotion of our interests in being free abstractors from content, and if abstraction from content is the essence of logic, then opposition to Yoga is ill-logic. People who are illogical should not be treated as autonomous, but significantly compromised. In such cases, making changes in the environment that serve to maximize everyone's autonomy is in everyone's interests. Surmounting opposition is about understanding that our interests coincide.

* * *

The study of Indian philosophy and Indian contributions to ethics and human rights is fraught with obstacles. These obstacles are what Patañjali' would have called 'engrossment with presuppositions; (Ranganathan 2008: I.42). We often presume theses such as the linguistic foundations of thought in an effort to understand things Indian, and this causes and generates its own cast of problems. Getting rid of Western baggage in the study of Indian philosophy is essential, but the Western baggage is nothing more than the idea that our species defines our rights as persons, and the correlative idea that thought is linguistic. Certainly, if we observe current affairs, these ideas are everywhere, but to assume that this reflects something essential about personhood is to ignore the culturally specific origins of these theses and the intervening centuries of Western political campaigns to homogenise the world.

It could be possible to misinterpret these arguments and assume that if logos and Westernism are particularly Western doctrines, and they are wrong, then there is something constitutionally wrong or bad about Westerners. This would be ignorance; if persons are self-directed abstractions from content, then all of our interests are the same, regardless of where we live. We might naively identify with our ethnic origins, national boundaries, religious or caste identities, or the like, but this confuses the source of our freedom and our abiding interests: our self, the person. The person is not the mind (what we believe) or our bodies (how we seem), but self-directed abstraction from content. The more people are conditioned by their environment, culture, or upbringing, the less free they are. Yoga is the project of turning the tide of coercion into our mutual benefit by abandoning antagonism as part of a project of personal freedom.

If Patañjali's account is correct, we ought to dream together, like Vishnu reclining on the cosmic serpent. As Vishnu, we would not judge our interests in terms of the species we belong to, recognizing friends and companions regardless of their species: snakes, eagles, monkeys, beauty herself (*Padma*) are welcome. In dreams, we can change how things appear to us if they are not in our interests. If we fail to dream our reality together, we treat the status quo as ideal, and thereby give up criticism, which is our autonomy. Dreaming about a different kind of world, with the appropriate space for us all is the challenge of living and this challenge cannot be accomplished if we do not survive. We need to take care of ourselves as dreamers, and this requires respect for autonomy. As we survive and dream, we change how things are; those who cannot dream die by attrition.

Notes

1. The term 'guṇa' has been translated in many ways. As one author notes, in the Sāṅkhya tradition that Yoga is a spin-off from, guṇas are the constituents of nature. (K.B. Ramakrishna Rao. 1963). Calling them substances is a mistake, as nature is primarily a realm of causality (Ranganathan 2008: IV.3).

2. Some might wonder if the term 'detachment' is a synonym for what I mean by abstraction. I do not think so; abstraction is consistent with the Sanskrit idea of kaivalya: a state that arises when one has been cleansed of all selfishness by dharma (Ranganathan, 2008: IV.29–31). Detachment is something that occurs when we stop caring. They are not the same idea.

3. The closest thing to an argument (in *Utilitarianism*) for this claim is Mill's theory (presented in Chapter 2 of *Utilitarianism*) that the relative worth of pleasures is only measurable by those who have had experience of both pleasures. It does not follow from this that sensory pleasures are less or that non-human animals are incapable of intellectual pleasures.

4. Niraja Jayal's case for legal rights points to a seemingly different idea of rights as they play a role in defining the statelessness of displaced people. Without legal rights, displaced people have no place to call home. The case for rights from Yoga is a case for personal rights: the freedoms that constitute us as individuals. The yogi has great sympathy for such displaced people however, for in lacking legal rights, people's ability to abstract from content is limited.

5. There are many ways to render the term 'citta'. *Consciousness* or *mentality* is commonly paired with this term. *Thought* may not be a perfect correlate, but this is probably because the idea of thought as developed in the Western tradition is fairly provincial. In general, it is wise not to

get too fussed about translating words in terms of same meaning; that requirement disappears if one criticizes the identification of thought with linguistic meaning. If one believes that translation depends upon pairing up words with the same meaning, then translation is pretty much impossible given syntactic and semantic variations across languages.

6. For an account of Aristotle's teleological notion of causation see D. Charles. 1991. For a discussion of Aristotle's normative conception of biology, see Irwin's illuminating discussion of how Aristotle's thinking on ethics parallels his thinking about nature and biology (T.H. Irwin 2000).

References

Bentham, J. 1988. *The Principles of Morals and Legislation*. Buffalo, NY: Prometheus Books.

'Chāndogya Upaniṣad.' (edited and trans. by M.F. Müller). 1900. *The Upaniṣads. Volume 1, Sacred Books of the East*, pp. 1–144. Oxford: Clarendon Press.

Charles, D. 1991. 'Teleological Causation in the Physics', in L. Judson (ed.), *Aristotle's Physics: A Collection of Essays*, pp. 101–28. Oxford: Clarendon Press.

Chomsky, N. 1975. *Reflections on Language*, 1st edition. New York: Pantheon Books.

Frey, R.G. 1980. *Interests and Rights: The Case Against Animals*. Oxford: Oxford University Press.

Halbfass, W. 1988. *India and Europe: An Essay in Understanding*. Albany, NY: State University of New York Press.

Irwin, T.H. 2000. 'Ethics as an Inexact Science: Aristotle's Ambitions for Moral Theory', in B.H. and M.O. Little (eds), *Moral Particularism*, pp. 100–29. Oxford: Clarendon Press.

Īśvarakṛṣṇa. (edited and trans. by S.S. Suryanarayana-Sastri). 1948. *Sāṅkhya Kārikā*, 2nd revised edition. Madras: University of Madras.

Kant, I. 1974. (trans. by J.H. Bernard). *Critique of Judgement*. London: Hafner Press, Collier Macmillan.

———. (trans. by M.J. Gregor). 1996. *The Metaphysics of Morals*. New York: Cambridge University Press.

'Kaṭha Upaniṣad'. (edited and trans. by M.F. Müller). 1900. *The Upaniṣads. Volume 2, Sacred Books of the East*, pp. 1–21. Oxford: Clarendon Press.

Koller, J.M. 2000. 'Syādvāda as the Epistemological Key to the Jaina Middle Way Metaphysics of Anekāntavāda', *Philosophy East and West*, 50(3): 400–7.

Madhva/Ānandatīrtha. (trans. by S. Subba Rau). 1904. *(Brahma Sūtra Bhāṣya) Vedānta Sūtras with the commentary of Sri Madhwacharya*. Madras: Thompson and Co.

Madhva/Ānandatīrtha. (edited and trans. by K.T. Pandurang). 1993. *Mahabhārātatātparyaṇirnaya*. Chirtanur: Srīman Madhva Siddhanton-nanhini Sabha.

Marquis, D. 2007. 'An Argument that Abortion is Wrong', in R. Shafer-Landau (ed.), *Ethical Theory: An Anthology*, pp. 439–50. Malden, MA: Blackwell Publishing.

Marx, K. (trans. by M. Milligan). 1959. *Economic and Philosophical Manuscripts of 1844*. Moscow: Moscow Progress Publishers.

Mill, J.S. 1863. *Utilitarianism*. London: Parker, Son, and Bourn. www. ebooks.adelaide.edu.au/m/mill/john_stuart/m645u/ (accessed 17 July 2013).

Moore, G.E. 1903. *Principia Ethica*. Cambridge: Cambridge University Press.

Plato. 1966. 'Republic', in E. Hamilton and H. Cairns (eds), *The Collected Dialogues of Plato, Including the Letters. Bollingen Series 71*, pp. 575–844. New York: Pantheon Books.

Plotinus. (trans. by S. Mackenna). 1969. *The Enneads*, 4th edition. London: Faber.

Rāmānuja. (trans. by Svami Adidevanada). 1991. *Śrī Rāmānuja Gīta Bhāṣya*. Madras: Sri Ramakrishna Math.

———. (trans. by George Thibaut). 1996. *(Śrī Bhāṣya/Brahma Sūtra Bhāṣya) Vedānta Sūtras with the commentary of Rāmānuja*. Delhi: Motilal Banarsidass.

Ranganathan, S. 2007. 'Translating Evaluative Discourse: The Semantics of Thick and Thin Concepts', PhD dissertation, York University.

———. 2008. *Patañjali's Yoga Sūtra: Translation, Commentary and Introduction*. Delhi: Penguin.

———. 2011. 'An Archimedean Point for Philosophy', *Metaphilosophy*, 42(4): 479–519.

Rao, K.B. Ramakrishna. 1963. 'The Guṇas of Prakṛti According to the Sāṁkhya Philosophy', *Philosophy East and West*, 13(1): 61–71.

Regan, T. 2004. *The Case for Animal Rights*. Berkeley, CA: University of California Press.

Milindapañha. 'The Questions of King Milinda.' www.sacred-texts.com/bud/milinda.htm (accessed 17 July 2013).

Śaṅkara. (trans. by G. Thibaut). 1962. *The Vedānta Sūtras with the Commentary by Śaṅkara*. New York: Dover Publications.

Śaṅkara. (edited and trans. by Gambhirananda). 1991. *Bhagavadgītā with the commentary of Śaṅkarācārya*. Calcutta: Advaita Ashrama.

Singer, P. 1990. *Animal Liberation*, 2nd edition. New York: New York Review of Books; Distributed by Random House.

'Sūtrakṛtāṅga'. 1987. (edited and trans. by H.G. Jacobi). 1987. *Jaina Sutras*, pp. 235–436. Delhi: AVF Books.

'Uttaradhyayana'. (edited and trans. by H.G. Jacobi). 1987. *Jaina Sutras*, pp. 1–234. Delhi: AVF Books.

Wood, A. 1998. 'Kant on Duties Regarding Nonrational Nature', *Proceedings of the Aristotelian Society Supplement*, LXXII: 189–210.

8

Human Rights and Political Toleration in India: Multiplicity, Self, and Interconnectedness[1]

Ashwani Peetush

I would argue that given the plurality and diversity of both the domestic and global environment political toleration is critical to issues of justice and human rights. Indeed, toleration is one of the cornerstones of any just modern society. Yet, the ideal of toleration is usually thought to originate from within, and most often justified from a European historical and philosophical context. It is thought to be a response to societal conflict and the Wars of Religion in the West, which is then exported to the rest of the world, by colonialism (ironically), or globalization. The West, once again, calls upon itself to teach the rest of the world how to be more ethical. I think that this not only plays into the hands of cultural and ethical relativists, but that this picture is far from accurate; it ignores rich indigenous sources for political toleration that already exist and have existed in India for millennia. In this chapter, I explore three central and predominant ideas in India as providing justification for distinctly Indian forms of toleration. I examine how toleration, and indeed, more strongly, respect and recognition for difference and pluralism, emerge through three influential Indian self-understandings: the theory of *anekāntavāda* or non-absolutism as a response to multiplicity; the concept of *ātman* or self; and the idea of *pratītyasamutpāda* or interconnectedness.

In contrast to various Euro-Western legal and political ideals that may have little resonance, I think indigenous sources offer a far more promising alternate ground upon which to build an overlapping convergence on basic human rights in India. Of course, how such ideals are justified, articulated, and practiced may be varied, and this is desirable. Values, norms, and legal practices that resonate with people's self-understandings and traditions have a better hope of success than those that are externally imposed. As Jacques Maritain (1948) argued and Rawls later developed: what is crucial in a global convergence on human rights norms is to arrive at an agreement on basic ethical standards, such as freedom from discrimination, civil and political freedom, equality before the law, assuring the basic necessities of life such as food, shelter, clothing, and education for all, without the insistence that these can only be justified from a Euro-Western metaphysical, philosophical, or legal framework. As Sarvepalli Radhakrishnan (1955), Gadamer (Pantham 1992), and James Tully (1995) contend: the purpose of such convergence is not uniformity in diversity, but rather, unity in diversity. Perhaps the lessons that one can draw from the Indian context might be helpful to the neo-colonial bent of mind that continues to thrive in the West.

Indeed, I would argue that simply because a community is not organized around Euro-Western liberal legal and economic principles, or does not articulate these in the language and discourse of individual rights and private property, or because a community may be organized around more substantive views of the good life, does not mean that it does not have ethical standards against various abuses such as rape, torture, genocide, and slavery. It does not mean that such communities do not have ethical ideals such as care and compassion, trust, respect, justice, and fairness. In addition, it does not mean that such societies do not have respect for the life, integrity, and basic well-being of their members. Europeans did not invent morality or justice (to which the history of European Imperialism, colonialism, fascism, slavery, and current forms of Western neo-liberalism bear testimony). Difference does not necessarily entail opposition; to be non-liberal does not mean to be anti-liberal.

Now, I recognize that texts and traditions are internally diverse and contested; they speak with a multiplicity of voices and are formed by histories of conflict and struggle between the powerful and the oppressed. As such, I would argue that there are and can be no 'raw' uninterpreted texts or traditions, free from the histories of such power struggles. We are, thus, always in a position of having to interpret and reinterpret, to invent and reinvent, to construct a coherent account that puts texts and traditions in their best possible light, given what we have come to learn about ourselves. As such, my aim here is not to recover the 'original intentions' or 'original meanings' of the various authors and texts I examine. I am suspicious of those who make such claims, as interpretation is deeply implicated in a web of teleology. However, my development is not purely anew, of course; I would contend that it has historical and philosophical precedence. Where my interpretation does diverge from tradition and constructs justification anew, I find nothing to lament. My view is that traditions do in fact change and must in the face of arguments about basic equality and justice. Indeed, as responsible citizens of the world, we must be agents of such change. If certain ideas and practices do not stand up to what we know about the integrity of sentient beings, then they must be contested and, ultimately, dropped, no matter how sacred. This is as it should be; in the face of oppression and domination, we must dream and build better worlds.

Let me also point out that I am in no way arguing that India has a perfect or ideal history of tolerance or anything of this nature. My task here is to seek, and if need be, explicitly construct, sources for toleration and other basic values required to frame issues of justice and human rights from within various Indian traditions. But, moreover, I should point out that various contradictory values and practices always exist in large and complex societies. Indeed, Locke himself justified the theft of indigenous land on a liberal basis because natives did not have a notion of private property and representative government, and Mill justified the colonization of India because Indians did not understand the key value of individual autonomy. Neo-liberals continue to interpret liberalism in a manner that leads to some of the grossest economic inequalities in history, despite Rawlsian liberals who insist that individual freedom is meaningless without certain basic social and economic conditions. If it is legitimate for Westerners to debate, reconstruct, and reimagine the nature of liberalism and human rights, why should not the same freedom be afforded to other traditions? To ask this is not to deny the critical importance of human rights and freedom in the name of some abstract ethical relativism or 'Western Imperialism' or parochialism as the West would charge; it is to demand the freedom that Westerners repeatedly arrogate for themselves. Nor is it the demand for some kind of exceptionalism accountable only to itself, as some Western nations repeatedly claim for their countries. The demand is for a seat at the table, to which formerly colonized nations surely have a right and something for which they have paid in full—on all fronts.

Political Toleration: From Enduring to Respecting the Other

Let me start with the idea of toleration in the context of issues of justice and religious and cultural diversity. Tolerance is regarded as an ethical virtue; it requires choosing to restrain ourselves from hindering that with which we do not agree. As a political value, toleration requires adopting such a virtue at a societal or national level towards those with whom we diverge regarding their self-understandings, institutions, and beliefs. Minimally, toleration is a species of endurance: I make the choice to put up with and endure you, your people, and your beliefs. The reasons for why I may do so are varied, culturally, historically, and conceptually. It may be a concern for your individual autonomy and the importance of freedom of conscience. It may be for pedagogical reasons, knowing that belief is difficult to coerce. It may arise from a form of compassion, or a form of epistemic humility, as well as scepticism about what we can know about the world.

Political toleration exists on a continuum; it resides between a *modus vivendi* on the one side and recognition and respect on the other end. Enduring differences may be the result of a kind of modus vivendi (Rawls 1999); a form of stability that is sustained by a balance of power. I leave you alone, I put up with and endure you, your people, your beliefs, out of pragmatic necessity; this is because you have equal power and are a potential threat to my well-being, as I am to yours. This fits particularly well with a Hobbesian contractual view of moral and political relations; the potential threat that others represent gives rise to mutual agreement on basic legal and political rules of interaction and the limits of individual and collective freedom, as well as the limits of tolerance. The toleration that emerges out of such practicality is rather tenuous; it is grounded in self-interest and lasts as long as there is a balance of power. It is not genuinely an ethical form of toleration, as I do not interfere only because I lack the power to overthrow you.

At the other end of the continuum exist more robust forms of toleration that are tied to recognition and respect of differences, of plurality, as legitimate forms of being in the world. No one perspective embodies all that is valuable and worthy of pursuit in life. Such forms of toleration are also, at times, connected with a sense of epistemic humility. That is, an acknowledgement that what we can come to know is often limited and that our self-understandings may not be the only legitimate perspectives. Even though your practices may not be in accord with my own, I do not interfere with you not simply because I respect your autonomy, but because your practices and understandings may be as legitimate as my own. This opens the door for dialogue and the attempt to understand the other.

These more robust forms of tolerance would suggest that we provide an environment that is hospitable not only to individual differences, but collective differences as well, so that these are not suffocated by poverty and prejudice. Along these lines, drawing on First Nations traditions, James Tully (1995) remarks that the weaving together of different threads brings about the strength of a cloth. For these forms of toleration, as recognition and respect, understanding and respecting difference and diversity is not simply for its own sake, but because difference and diversity represents the horizon, breadth and richness, and potential of the human spirit. This potential is understood pluralistically.

Before we turn to such forms of toleration in the Indian tradition, I should point out that toleration does not imply that we value or tolerate everything. What we value requires a critical engagement with the other; this is a project in which we learn not simply about others, but ourselves also. And it may be that even after the best effort at understanding, we may not consider particular practices to be of value, and sometimes we may think that they are blatantly unjust. We have a framework for such judgments: although human beings and cultures are different in numerous ways, we also share much in common. As Amartya Sen (2009) and Martha Nussbaum (2006), as well as many others, argue, we share basic needs, such as food, shelter, nurturance, love, the opportunity for social engagement, play, and meaningful work. Certain kinds of actions and practices can threaten the most basic of such needs.

The Multiplicity of Reality: Anekāntavāda and Ahiṃsā

The acknowledgement of the legitimacy and value of differing self-understandings other than our own has deep historical and conceptual roots in the ideas of ahiṃsā or non-violence and anekāntavāda or non-absolutism; these develop in response to the view of multiplicity as an inherent aspect of reality. I would argue that it is difficult to overestimate the value of these ideas. They continue to permeate Indian landscapes and constellations of thought and practice; indeed, they structure many of the various self-understandings from Aśoka to Gandhi to the lives of present-day villagers in India.

How does one deal with competing claims when it comes to comprehensive questions about meaning and purpose, and the nature of the self and its relation to the divine? One response is to show why others are wrong and why we are right; this is the approach that many people take, especially when it comes to philosophical and religious claims. The anekāntavāda theory is entirely different: it attempts to show that various competing claims may only appear contradictory; such claims need to take into account the *nayas* or perspectives of the person making such claims.

This particular theory grows out of an overarching ethical commitment to ahiṃsā, which is thought to be fundamental to enlightenment for the Jaina school. The emphasis on the value of ahiṃsā greatly influenced both the Upaniṣadic and Buddhist traditions, although their metaphysical justifications for non-violence differ. Jaina ontology divides the world into two basic categories, of which there may be innumerable manifestations: the *jīva* (self) and *ajīva* (matter); the essence of jīva is perception, knowledge, bliss, and energy, and ajīva includes the mind, the senses, and speech. The basic ontological division is thus between consciousness/sentience on the one hand and matter on the other. The nature of the self is bliss and omniscience, yet it is enmeshed in matter (as gold in ore). The aim of existence is to free the self from this bondage; the greatest hindrance to this aim is causing violence, in all its forms. The perfection of the self lies in the pursuit of knowledge and ethical virtue, of which non-violence is the highest form. Violence, however, is not limited to action that physically harms other living beings, but also consists of thought and intention, and applies to the entire realm of one's existence and attitude, including how one intellectually approaches the differing viewpoints of others.

Indeed, since on the Jaina view, reality is thought to be composed of an innumerable/infinite number of modifications of jīvas and ajīvas, each with an innumerable number of qualities and modifications, knowledge of such a reality is almost always limited and partial. As Malliṣeṇa argues in his celebrated work of logic entitled the *Syādvādamañjarī* (a thirteenth century commentary on the famous work of Jaina philosopher Hemachandra):

> [S]tandpoints are infinite because of an entity's infinite modifications and because of the standpoint-view of the speaker's meanings which are satisfied by one modification, and so the elders say: "As many are the ways of speaking about a thing, so many are the statements of the standpoint-method." (Malliṣeṇa 1979: 268).

Malliṣeṇa thus argues that the truth of a particular claim must thus be indexed to substance/subject, time, space, mode/quality (Malliṣeṇa 1979: 264). Hence, the Jainas emphasized the idea of anekāntavāda or the thesis of not-one-sidedness. On this view, truth claims must be qualified by perspective, by the term *syāt* or conditionally. The resulting doctrine of *syādvāda* or conditional predication takes into consideration the multisided and multidimensional nature of reality. Thus, instead of asserting that *x* is *y*, on this account, it is thought that one could only assert that from such a perspective, *x* is *y*, or that, conditionally, *x* is *y*. This is to take into consideration the multisided and multidimensional nature of reality.

The Jaina approach to divergent views about the nature of existence provided a model of thinking about differences that fostered a sense of mutual tolerance and respect among various schools in ancient India. Certainly, it was grounded in a sense of epistemic humility, although, at the same time not being a form of relativism, as reality exists as a unitary whole, yet it is multisided. One must thus approach other perspectives not necessarily as false, but as, perhaps, only partially true—let me point out that, significantly, the same attitude is adopted towards one's own view. Therefore, differences may not necessarily be seen as opposing or contradictory or wrong (or inherently evil, needing to be destroyed or colonized), but simply a description of reality from another, equally legitimate, although incomplete, perspective—which could be said to be true of one's own point of view. As Siddhasena Divākara (fifth century) argues in his Sanmati Tarka (1973),

> 1.28...A man who holds the view of the cumulative character of truth (Anekāntajña) never says that a particular view is right or that a particular view is wrong. (Saṅghavi and Doshi, 2000: 23)

for,

> 1.23...every naya [aspect, standpoint] in its own sphere is right, but if all of them arrogate to themselves the whole truth and disregard the views of rival nayas then they do not attain the status of a right view. (23)

as,

> 1.25...if all the Nayas arrange themselves in a proper way and supplement to each other, then alone they are worthy of being termed as "the whole truth" or the right view in its entirety. But in this case they merge their individuality in the collective whole. (20)

Thus, one ought not to immediately condemn others' views, but try and see these for what they may have to offer. In fact, the Jainas attempted to synthesize the Advaitan view that reality is monistic pure consciousness with the Buddhist ideas that reality is constantly in flux. The Jaina affirmed that things, qua their substance/essence, or *svabhāva*, are unchanging, yet, their forms or modes are constantly in flux (Divākara, 1973: 269–71).[2] Hegel, much later, would develop a similar intuition whereby the synthesis of thesis and antithesis give rise to a higher or more complete truth.

The theory of anekāntavāda had an enormous impact on Indian self-understandings. Indeed, Gandhi was not only influenced by an Advaitic reading of the Upaniṣads, but he was also strongly influenced by the Jaina interpretation of the principle of ahiṃsā and the theory of anekāntavāda.

> I am an *Advaitist* and yet I can support *Dvaitism* (dualism). The world is changing every moment, and is therefore unreal, it has no

permanent existence. But though it is constantly changing, it has something about it which persists and it is therefore to that extent real. I have therefore no objection to calling it real and unreal, and thus being called an *Anekāntavādi* or a *Syādvādi*.... It has been my experience that I am always true from my point of view, and am often wrong from the point of view of my critics. I know that we are both right from our respective points of view. And this knowledge saves me from attributing motives to my opponents or critics.... I very much like this doctrine of the manyness [sic] of reality. It is this doctrine that has taught me to judge a Musalman [Muslim] from his standpoint and a Christian from his. Formerly I used to resent the ignorance of my opponents. Today I love them because I am gifted with the eye to see myself as others see me *and vice versa*. I want to take the whole world in the embrace of my love. My *anekāntavād* is the result of the twin doctrine of *Satya* and *Ahiṃsa*. (Gandhi 1981: 30).

The theory of anekāntavāda continues to mould popular ideas of how to understand differences and tolerance to this day in India. This can be seen, for example, in how the theory is made accessible by the ancient Jain metaphor used to discuss various pursuits of truth: *andhagajanyāyaḥ* or that of a group of blind men attempting to determine what an elephant is from their various perspectives. The fellow closest to the elephant's feet declares that an elephant is like a pillar, the one who strokes its ears argues that an elephant is like a fan, the person who grasps its tusk deems the elephant to be like a pipe, the one who strokes its trunk believes it to be tree-like, the one who caresses its belly argues that the elephant is like a wall, and the man who squeezes its tail thinks the elephant is like a rope. The descriptions the blind men provide are, of course, partially true but incomplete. Yet, they take their partial knowledge as the absolute truth and become engaged in a heated debate over the essence of the elephant. They take their partial knowledge as a description of the whole, which they are unfortunately unable to see. As such, they are unable to recognize or appreciate, much less even tolerate, each other's view. Although this story has its origins with the Jainas, both the Upaniṣadic and Buddhist schools, and later the Sufi schools, have their own versions.

Thus, I would argue that the theory of anekāntavāda gives rise to a particularly strong form of tolerance based on the ethical consideration of ahiṃsā or non-violence as applied to differences. The other is not someone to be overcome and beat down with argument, or worse, converted or slaughtered by the sword; the other is someone with whom we need to be fully and actively engaged. In addition, the ethical justification for tolerance here is grounded both at the level of epistemology and metaphysics. This is a particularly strong form of tolerance interpreted as giving due consideration to the other since it is based on the axiom that the other's view may indeed be correct, given her perspective. As such, it requires us to place ourselves on equal footing with that of the other, as, in the end, our views may be either plain wrong, or, at best, incomplete, as we ourselves occupy a limited and partial naya on reality as it is. That is, it is not simply that we have epistemic limits on what we can know to be true, and, thus, we should refrain from attacking the other, but, that rather, the truth itself can be plural or innumerable or infinitely modified. Multiplicity is an inherent feature of reality. This is something that we must understand if we are to make any progress in acquiring knowledge.[3]

The Self as other: Ātman

The school of Advaita Vedānta and its interpretation of the Upaniṣadic concept of self or ātman has had an enormous impact on modern Indian self-understandings. Its metaphysical conception of the self, drawn from the Upaniṣadic texts, is different from the Jaina school; this conception provides a justification for tolerance and respect on a distinct basis. Let us take a closer look. On the one hand, the self as jīva, that is, the self of ordinary experience, is unique. It is the *ahaṃkāra* or I-ness (or I-maker). This is the self as a psychophysical entity, as an individual, a person with a unique history and characteristics, capacities, abilities, likes and dislikes, and needs. The ethic of enlightenment that goes along with this picture is, in one sense, staunchly individualistic; the individual is responsible for her own emancipation, it cannot be granted or given to her, as an act of grace. It has to be earned through work and merit, or karma, on the basis of individual effort.

On the other hand, according to the Advaitic or non-dual reading of the Upaniṣads, although the self of ordinary experience (the jīva) is unique, the self at an ontological level, the real self (the ātman) is the same in all things. It is characterized as pure consciousness, as *draṣṭā*, the seer, or *sākṣin*, the witness. Ātman here is not understood as a kind of substance or mind that lies behind experience, like a type of Cartesian soul/ego; rather, ātman is the state of seeing, or awareness, or the presence of consciousness in-itself, individuated. Furthermore, on the Advaita account of the self, although the self, persons, and the world are experienced as a multiplicity, they are ultimately grounded in brahman or the unity and the wholeness of being. Brahman is the substrate of existence or reality; the manifest world is a partial glimpse of this enduring wholeness of existence upon which it is founded and for which it has its source. Brahman thus both transcends and is immanent in the world (as is the spider to the web).

The goal of existence is the realization of the ultimate identity of the self and Brahman; *mokṣa* or enlightenment is the experience of the oneness or wholeness of infinite being as the nature of oneself, or the self as other, and the other as self. It is the inward realization of something that is there all along, which is pure consciousness. The theistic conceptions that arise from this view are rather different from those of Abrahamic religions: God is not distinct from the self, but, indeed, God is one's deepest self, as one's very own nature. As the Bṛhadāraṇyaka Upaniṣad asserts: ahambrahmāsmi, I am Brahman (1.4.10). That is, it is I that is God; God is not outside us, but is our higher self, which we share in common. God is not apart from ourself, not some external reality who created and judges us, but rather, the most intimate and best part of ourselves.

Let us see how one might justify various ethical values on this view: it is not simply out of fear of karmic consequences that one fulfils one's *sādhāraṇa* dharma or duty to uphold universal values such as dāya or compassion or ahiṃsā, but rather that, on a deeper level, the self is intimately connected to the other. To harm the other is to harm the self. As the Īśa Upaniṣad says: 'he who sees all beings in his own self and his own self in all beings does not feel revulsion by reason of such a view'. (Radhakrishnan 1953: 572). This is precisely the reason why there are negative karmic consequences of harm. Indeed, it is the practice of virtues such as compassion in everyday life, while stemming from the wholeness and unity of existence that leads to its ultimate realization. For, in the practice of compassion, not only does one empathize with the suffering of another, but one experiences that suffering as one's own. The boundaries of the individual self become more permeable, as one begins to see the self as the other and the other as self, even though this may start at the level of the jīva or everyday self, it leads to a recognition of the identity of the same ātman in both the self and the other.

Now, tolerance, especially theistic, has been historically and conceptually grounded in an Advaitic interpretation of the Upaniṣads in a number of ways. In one respect, it follows the idea of the self, qua jīva, or the self of ordinary experience, as being a unique individual, with a specific set of needs, likes, and dislikes. The seeker's make-up and spiritual needs, her characteristics, or *guṇas*, determine the *mārga*, or path, from the many available, given what suits her unique nature. As Rāmakṛṣṇa (Abhedânanda 1903), a central figure in the Bengal and Hindu Renaissance who combined *bhakti*, or devotion, with the Advaita school, explains,

> As one can ascend to the top of a house by means of a ladder or a bamboo or a staircase or a rope, so diverse are the ways and means to approach God, and every religion in the world shows one of these ways. (quoted in Abhedânanda 1903: 10)

for:

> As a mother, in nursing her sick children, gives rice and curry to one, and sago and arrowroot to another and bread and butter to a third, so the Lord has laid out different paths for different people suitable to their natures.... Dispute not. As you rest firmly on our faith and opinion, allow others the equal liberty to stand by their own faiths and opinions. (quoted in Abhedânanda, 1903: 73–4).

Rāmakṛṣṇa's chief pupil Vivekānanda, a neo-Vedāntin, also laid out the implications of this view by quoting verse seven of the Śiva Mahimnaḥ Stōtram in his address to the Parliament of Religions in Chicago in 1893, 'As the different streams having their sources in different places all mingle their water in the sea, so, O Lord, the different paths which men take through different tendencies, various though they appear, crooked or straight, all lead to Thee. (Vivekānanda 1999: 20–1)'.

Thus, individuals cannot be coerced to follow a path that they did not choose, which is not of their making. This not only violates their integrity, but will not work, for each has specific needs. As such, each should be allowed to work out his/her salvation in his/her own way, at his/her own pace. This sort of reasoning accounts for wide acceptance and tolerance of a large variety of divergent doctrinal differences and practices among Hindus. It also explains in part why Hindus do not proselytize and why their conversions are difficult. It is interesting to note that tolerance here is grounded on a model similar to the liberal model: respect for individual freedom requires a tolerance of difference, but this is in a rather different metaphysical context.

Indeed, religious pluralism and freedom is not simply a theoretical matter, but plays a vital role in the way that Hinduism is practiced. It is not only thought to be perfectly legitimate to be a devotee of Kṛṣṇa, Veṃkaṭeśavara, Rāma, mother Kālī, or any of the other various manifestations, but it is not unusual to find non-Hindu deities, such as that of Jesus or Mary in Hindu altars. Many Hindus will pray in a church or at a Sufi shrine without the least bit of hesitation. There are some communities in India that define themselves as Hindu-Muslims or Muslim-Hindus; members of the Salam Girasia Rajputs traditionally have both a Hindu and Muslim name for each person in the community (Parekh 2008).

Apart from such diversity being grounded in the acceptance of individual differences, tolerance is further grounded on the idea that various paths lead to the same ultimate destination—the various streams merge in the same sea. Although methods and practices may diverge, the end goal is the same. A famous passage in the Ṛgveda states that 'The wise speak of what is one in many ways' (*ekaṃ sad viprā bahudhā vadantyaghniṃ yamaṃ mātariśvānamāhuḥ*) (Ṛgveda 1.164.46).[4] In the Bhagavad Gītā, Kṛṣṇa, an Avatāra, in discussing with Arjuna the question of which path is best suited for enlightenment, says: 'In whichever way men take refuge in me, I love them. All men, Arjuna, follow my path' (*ye yathā māṃ prapadyante tāṃs tathaiva bhajāmyaham*) (The Bhagavad Gītā 4.11). At the time when the Gita was composed, there was a rich diversity and pluralism in thought and practice: there were yogic ascetics, Buddhists, Jainas, brahmanical sacrificers, philosophical dualists, monists, theists, atheists, and so on (Davis 2008: 371). Kṛṣṇa proclaims that these divergent paths are all his and lead to ultimate realization. On this sort of view, then, the idea that there is only one true path or religion is intrinsically flawed. Hence, one must be respectful of others' understandings and practices.

Historically, despite the rise of religious extremism and Hindu nationalism post-independence, as Bhikhu Parekh argues, Hindus have generally shown a great deal of respect and tolerance towards other religions. At times when Jews were being persecuted by Christians in Europe or treated unjustly in Muslim countries, they were welcomed in India. They were given official patronage and financial support; in the Hindu kingdom of Cochin, they were provided their own self-governing district. Indeed, Christians arriving in the fifth century, Muslims in the eighth, and the Zoroastrians in the tenth, were all embraced with freedom of religious belief (Parekh 2008).

Of course, I am not asserting that the history of India is, even prior to British colonization, free from sectarian religious tensions and violence. However, it is less than that found in other contexts. Moreover, we should note that it is not that Hindus tolerate all differences. Often, one hears the slogan 'unity in diversity', as a common theme in contemporary India, both in religion and politics. That is, perspectives that unconfusedly and unmistakably infringe on basic ethical values, around which there must be unity, are not regarded as legitimate and constitute the limits of toleration.

But, for a tradition that has been able to deal with such diversity for much of its history, how is it that violence grounded in religious doctrine and practice seems to be on the rise, fuelled by Hindu nationalism? I think that one of the key things to note here is that current forms of Hindu nationalist movements developed during and after British colonialism, where Hinduism became much more of a reified identity, a political marker, that is strategically pitted against Muslims, for example, by the British Raj, in an attempt to divide and conquer. Many Indian political theorists, such as Ashis Nandy and T.M. Madan argue that such movements have little to do with the soteriological aspirations of Hinduism at all; rather, they are political instruments to attain power and privilege.

In his insightful study of Hindutva nationalism, Partha Chatterjee (1998) shows that current Hindu national movements are rather odd. What one may think of as theocratic movements are anything but theocratic. Unlike the older Hindutva conception that developed around independence, like the Hindu Mahasabha, new movements rest on purely political and secular agendas. Apart from a few voices, Hindutva movements do not seek to ground theocratic institutions on Vedic injunction; they do not seek religious education, or censorship of science, or the teaching of evolutionary theory, or anything of the like. Instead they distinguish themselves from Islamic fundamentalists in this manner; they pride themselves on being the voice of rationality, secularism, and reason, and attack their opponents as 'pseudo-secularists'. Indeed, one wishes that perhaps these nationalists were more religious and took to heart some available sources for tolerance in the Hindu tradition. In short, I would argue that Nandy is right here; Hindutva represents the instrumentalization of religion for the sake of political power.

I should also mention that the Advaitic reading of the Upaniṣads has been used not only to ground tolerance, but also to ground basic notions of equality. Indeed, many contemporary critics, including Gandhi, argue that the caste system and the oppression of women with its hierarchical underpinnings are inconsistent with the central teachings or spirit of Hinduism or Advaita. Infact, Gandhi's objections against the caste system were often based on ideas of equality grounded in Advaitic notions of ātman or on the idea that the same self exists in all; thus, there can be no inherent superiority or inferiority of one individual or group over another (Government of India 1969: 103–7).

Certainly, the caste system has a long history of being criticized and contested on various grounds indigenous to Indian traditions. It is not that somehow British liberals showed Indians the utter incivility of such a system (as some might have it); in fact, to the contrary, the British reified the system as it was to their advantage, not to mention the external 'caste' system they imposed on India, in which they were the superior race, and thus had a natural right to rule over the inferior Indians (N.B. Dirks 2001). In present day India, caste discrimination has much the same status as racism against Blacks in America and the history of slavery; although, discrimination by caste is deemed unconstitutional and there are stringent laws against such discrimination, it continues to exist socially despite affirmative action plans and reserved seats for members of oppressed castes in government and educational institutions. I contend that the battle against the caste system in India is making headway, as is the battle against racism that Blacks currently experience in America. I think that arguments grounded in indigenous sources, such as the Upaniṣads, are likely to have the strongest impact, as they resonate with people's self-understandings.[5]

Interconnectedness as Pratītyasamutpāda

The third central idea from which toleration emerges is pratītya-samutpāda or dependent origination in various Buddhist perspectives. Although these views share much in common with the Jaina and the Advaitan and other Upaniṣadic schools, they also diverge in important aspects. They emphasize ahiṃsā and tolerance, but they frame these notions in the theory of *anātman* or no-self, and pratītyasamutpāda or the theory of interconnectedness. While Buddhists agree with Advaitans that the self of ordinary experience (the jīva) is unreal, most think there is nothing that underlies this experience. On dominant Buddhist interpretations, there is no ātman or pure consciousness, so to speak. The self is merely an aggregation (*skandhas*) of physical, mental, perceptual, and volitional processes, along with the processes of consciousness. There is nothing over and above these processes that we can call a self, as there is no river over and above the flowing of the water. Indeed, according to the theory of pratītyasamutpāda or interconnectedness, nothing has essence (svabhāva) or separate or unique existence. Existence is marked by a continual process of change that is the result of interactions of various processes. Suffering and violence is a result of clinging on to the delusion of self as separate and permanent. Virtues such as ahiṃsā help one to overcome this delusion.

The ever-changing stream we associate with the self is closely intertwined with the stream of others, given pratītyasamutpāda or the interconnected nature of reality. With the realization of this interconnection, as the Dalai Lama asserts, we begin to understand that our interests converge in a profound sense:

> We begin to see that the universe we inhabit can be understood in terms of a living organism in which each cell works in balanced cooperation with every other cell to sustain the whole. If just one of these cells is harmed, as it is when disease strikes, that balance is

harmed, and there is danger to the whole…. Such an understanding of reality also allows us to see that this sharp distinction between self and others arises largely as a result of conditioning…. Indeed, within this picture of dependently originated reality, we see that there is no self-interest completely unrelated to others' interests. Due to the fundamental interconnectedness which lies at the heart of reality, your interest is also my interest. Thus my happiness is to a large extent dependent on yours. From this, it becomes clear that "my" interests and "your" interests are intimately connected. In a deep sense, they converge. Because of this, if we wish for our own happiness, we have to consider others. (The Dalai Lama 1999: 46–9).

Thus, my reason for respecting you, or, at least putting up with or tolerating your views in the minimal sense and not inflicting harm on you, or depriving you of the basic means of economic subsistence, is that to harm you is to harm myself in some deep sense. On the Advaita model, we share this deeper sense of self, while in the Buddhist picture, even though there is no such same self in common, the ever-changing stream we associate with the self is intimately tied to the stream of others, given the web-like nature of reality.

This organic model is in stark contrast to the liberal contractualist view in which ethical and political norms arise on the basis of separation of self from other. On the contractual picture, it is because you present a threat to me that I agree to contract with you and give up some of my freedom, as long as you do the same, whereas on the organic model, the other is seen as intimately connected, and thus her interests are not separate from one's own. Nevertheless, I think that both approaches can converge on some of the same basic norms. Of course, there will be differences. For example, the self of Indian theorizing is not limited to the human being, but, includes non-human animals and the environment. There is no reason to assume, a priori, that when there are divergences, it is somehow the liberal contractualist who is always in the right. Perhaps, it is the West that has something to learn from India here.

Indeed, I would argue that one of the earliest articulations of political toleration emerges from the principle of ahiṃsā or non-violence interpreted as a political principle, in contrast to merely an individual ethical virtue. This is first developed by the Indian Buddhist emperor Aśoka (269–32 BC), and later by Gandhi. I contend that this is one of

the first appearances—if not the first—of the idea of political toleration as such. As early as the third century BC, Aśoka's edicts declared
respect for all perspectives, philosophies, and religions as an implication and requirement of the principle of ahiṃsā. Here the idea of
non-injury is explicitly related to the positive aspect of respecting,
recognizing, and honouring others' dharma or philosophy/religion
at a political level:

> King Priyadarshi honors men of all faiths, members of religious
> orders and laymen alike, with gifts and various marks of esteem. Yet
> he does not value either gifts or honors as much as growth in the
> qualities essential to religion in men of all faiths. This growth may
> take many forms, but its root is in guarding one's speech to avoid
> extolling one's own faith and disparaging the faith of others improp-
> erly or, when the occasion is appropriate, immoderately. The faiths
> of others all deserve to be honored for different reasons. By honoring
> them, one exalts one's own faith and at the same time performs a
> service to the faith of others. By acting otherwise, one injures his own
> faith and also does disservice to the faith of others. But if a man extols
> his own faith and disparages another because of devotion to his own
> and because he wants to glorify it, he seriously injures his own faith.
> Therefore concord alone is commendable, for through concord, men
> may learn and respect the conception of Dharma accepted by others.
> King Priyadarshi desires men of all faiths to know each other's doc-
> trines and to acquire sound doctrines. Those who are attached to their
> particular faiths should be told that King Priyadarshi does not value
> gifts or honors as much as growth in the qualities essential to religion
> in men of all faiths. Many officials are assigned to tasks bearing this
> purpose—the officers in charge of spreading the Dharma, the super-
> intendents of women in the Royal household, the inspectors of cattle
> and pasture lands, and other officials. The objective of these measures
> is the promotion of each man's particular faith and the glorification of
> Dharma. (Rock Edict XII; Nikam and McKeon 1959: 51–2)

Now, one of the interesting things to note here is that political
toleration, recognition, and respect for various philosophical and
religious doctrines and practices arises from principles internal to these
Buddhist traditions, not despite them. This is radically different,
both conceptually and historically, from how political toleration
and the related notion of secularism emerged in Europe. As the
quintessential political ideal, toleration grows out of the bloodshed

of the Reformation and the Thirty Years Wars (1618–48). It emerges from religious factions within Christianity and its inability to cope with internal differences as a result, in part, of claims to absolute truth. The birth of political neutrality and the separation of Church and state, secularism, and indeed liberalism itself, have roots in this bloody conflict. But this is not the case here. Āsoka realizes the importance of tolerance as it is intrinsic to Buddhist practice. Indeed, it is after his conquest of Kaliṅga and the horrors of war, for which he himself was responsible, that Āsoka constructs a political interpretation of āhiṃsa; he expands the principle from a personal virtue to a political virtue. Toleration emerges as a result of ideas central to dominant philosophical and religious doctrines and practices, not as an antidote to them.

What this means is that one needs to be careful when one attempts to graft Western forms of toleration to the Indian context, which may lack relevant similarities. As Nandy (2004) points out, to presume to teach tolerance through secularism to Indian villagers is not only indicative of Western arrogance, it misses something crucial. Not only does it smack of a grave historical irony, it ignores rich and diverse sources that have existed and continue to exist in Indian self-understandings. These are most likely to succeed, as they resonate most with people's senses of self. And while secularism is an absolute necessity in the Indian context, particularly due to the kinds of reified and dangerous communal identities that continue to exist post-independence, one needs to investigate which forms of secularism will have the most favourable outcome. As Sarvapalli Radhakrishnan, a philosopher and former President of the Republic of India, argues:

> When India is said to be a secular state, it does not mean we reject the reality of an unseen spirit or the relevance of religion to life or that we exalt irreligion. It does not mean that secularism itself becomes a positive religion or that the state assumes divine prerogatives. Though faith in the Supreme is the basic principle of the Indian tradition, the Indian State will not identify itself with or be controlled by any particular religion. We hold that no one religion should be accorded special privileges in national life or international relations for that would be a violation of the basic principles of democracy and contrary to the best interests of religion and government.... No group of citizens shall arrogate to itself rights and privileges which it

denies to others. No person should suffer any form of disability or discrimination because of his religion but all alike should be free to share the fullest degree in the common life. This is the basic principle involved in the separation of Church and State. The religious impartiality of the Indian state is not to be confused with secularism or atheism. Secularism as here defined is in accordance with the ancient religious traditions of India. It tries to build up a fellowship of believers, not by subordinating individual qualities to the group mind but by bringing them into harmony with each other. The dynamic fellowship is based on the principle of diversity in unity which alone has the quality of creativeness. (Radhakrishnan 1955: 202).

On the Indian model of secularism and state neutrality, impartiality is interpreted as equal or an even-handed treatment respect of all religions; the state does not favour one over the other but recognizes the importance of religion in the life of each citizen. Rajeev Bhargava has explored these ideas in detail in his various works (Bhargava 2010). This model of secularism is unlike the case of France (and Quebec), where secularism has been interpreted as a complete wall of separation model, where religion ought to play no part in the political or the public sphere of life (thus, for example, forbidding the *hijab* in public schools on such a basis and throwing children off soccer teams because of their turbans). On the Indian version then, religious belief is accepted as something that may be a constitutive part of the lives of citizens, and the manifestations of such an identity are accepted as a part of the public sphere. As Radhakrishnan argued, such a model of secularism, and, indeed, respect for diversity and pluralism, is rooted in and emerges from the ancient historical, conceptual, and political self-understandings and traditions of India, three of which I have explored here.

* * *

The problems that India faces, such as gender inequality, casteism, ableism, religious extremism, communal violence, poverty, and pollution, are not unlike the problems faced by other nations around the globe. India has modernized, liberalized, industrialized, corporatized, and, as such, individuals are open to various standard threats by the state and numerous neo-liberal multinational corporations. Indeed, there is a growing collective global consciousness, a raised aware-ness, of the sorts of abuse and exploitation to which the weak are vulnerable. It would be unwise, to say the least, not to make use of the economic, legal, and political insights of others. However, one needs to remember that such solutions need to be articulated and under-stood in the vernacular. Importantly, we should take advantage of the freedom to avail ourselves of the distinct rich indigenous sources and self-understandings that may help to guide and sustain our futures—a freedom often denied to the colonized imagination. To the dismay of some Westerners, there is no singular historical and conceptual trajec-tory along which modernity and ethical progress move forward and there is no place where this is more obvious than in India, where the ancient continues to live alongside the modern. In building a greater India and a stronger republic, in dreaming together, we must not only imagine our futures, we must imagine and reimagine our pasts, weaving threads from the fabric of those who have dreamed before us.

Notes

1. Previous versions of this chapter were presented at the Canadian Philosophical Association, as well as the Human Rights and India workshop sponsored by the Social Sciences and Humanities Research Council of Canada. I would like to thank participants for their com-ments and suggestions. I would also like to thank Haripriya Parivrajika, Joseph LaRose, Yasaman S. Munro, Judy Pelham, Renata Cristi, Rebekah Johnston and Jordon DeLonge. In addition, I am grateful to Roger Gilman, Sarah Lucia Hoagland, Daniel T. Rakus, and the late James Graff, for earlier insightful and engaging conversations on human rights.
2. 'There cannot be a thing which is devoid of its modifications of birth and decay. On the other hand, modifications cannot exist without an abiding or eternal something—a permanent substance, for birth, decay and stability (continuance)—these three constitute the character-istic of a substance of entity'. (Divākara 1973: 269).
3. For an illuminating discussion of the ethical and political implications of the Jaina view, see also Ram-Prasad. (2007: 1–50).
4. The full verse is:

> indraṃ mitraṃ varuṇamaghnimāhuratho divyaḥ sa suparṇo gharutmān |
> ekaṃ sad viprā bahudhā vadantyaghniṃ yamaṃ mātariśvānamāhuḥ ||
> (Ṛgveda 1.164.46).

5. For insight into the idea of tolerance in the context of Upanisadic traditions, see also Sharma (1979) and Kirloskar Steinbach (2002).

References

Abhedânanda, Swâmi. 1903. *The Sayings of Ramakrishna*. New York: The Vedânta Society of New York.

'Bhagavad Gītā.' www.sacred-texts.com/hin/bgs/bgs04.htm (accessed 12 June 2012).

Bhargava, R. 2010. *The Promise of India's Secular Democracy*. New Delhi: Oxford University Press.

'Bṛhadāraṇyaka Upaniṣad.' http://is1.mum.edu/vedicreserve/upanishads/fifteen_upanishads_11_brihadaranyaka.pdf (accessed 31 July 2013).

Chatterjee, P. 1998. 'Secularism and Tolerance', in *Secularism and Its Critics*, pp. 345–79. New Delhi: Oxford University Press.

The Dalai Lama, His Holiness. 1999. *Ancient Wisdom, Modern World: Ethics for a New Millennium*. Great Britain: Little, Brown and Company.

Davis, R.H. 2008. 'Tolerance and Hierarchy: Accommodating Multiple Religious Paths in Hinduism', in J. Neusner and B. Chilton (eds), *Religious Tolerance in World Religions*, pp. 313–17. West Conshohocken, PA: Templeton Foundation Press.

Dirks, N.B. 2001. *Castes of Mind*. Princeton, NJ: Princeton University Press.

Divākara, S. 1973. 'SanmatiTarka', in S. Radhakrishnan and C.A. Moore (eds), *A Sourcebook in Indian Philosophy*, pp. 269–71. Princeton New Jersey: Princeton University Press.

Gandhi, M.K. 1981. *Young India. Volume 7*. Ahmedabad: Navajivan Publishing House, New Order Book Company.

Government of India. 1969. *The Collected Works of Mahatma Gandhi, Vol. XXXV*. India: Publications Division, Government of India.

Jaini, P. 1979. *The Jaina Path of Purification*. Berkeley: University of California Press.

Kirloskar-Steinbach, M. 2002. 'Toleration in Modern Liberal Discourse with Special Reference to Radhakrishnan's Tolerant Hinduism', *Journal of Indian Philosophy*, 30: 389–402.

Kymlicka, W. 1995. *Multicultural Citizenship: A Liberal Theory of Minority Rights*. Oxford: Clarendon Press.

Madan, T.N. 1998. 'Secularism in Its Place', in R. Bhargava (ed.), *Secularism and Its Critics*, 297–320. New Delhi: Oxford University Press.

Malliṣeṇa. 1979. 'Syādvādamañjarī', in S. Radhakrishnan and C.A. Moore (eds), *A Sourcebook in Indian Philosophy*, pp. 260–8. Princeton New Jersey: Princeton University Press.

Maritain, J. 1948. 'Introduction', in UNESCO (ed.), *Human Rights: Comments and Interpretations, a symposium*, pp. 1–9. www.unesdoc.unesco.org/images/0015/001550/155042eb.pdf (accessed 18 May 2010).

Nandy, A. 1998. 'The Politics of Secularism and the Recovery of Religious Toleration', in R. Bhargava (ed.), *Secularism and Its Critics*, pp. 321–44. New Delhi: Oxford University Press.

———. 2004. 'A Billion Gandhis', *Outlook India*, 21 June 2004. http://www.outlookindia.com/article/A-Billion-Gandhis/224252 (accessed 5 September 2013).

Nikam, N.A. and R. McKeon (ed. and trans.). 1959. *The Edicts of Asoka*. Chicago and London: The University of Chicago Press.

Nussbaum, M. 2006. *Frontiers of Justice: Disability, Nationality, and Species Membership*. Cambridge, MA: Harvard University Press.

O'Flaherty, W.D. (trans.). 1981. *The Rig Veda*. New York: Penguin Books.

Pantham, T. 1992. 'Some Dimensions of the Universality of Philosophical Hermeneutics: A Conversation with Hans-Georg Gadamer', *Journal of Indian Council of Philosophical Research*, 9: 123–35.

Parekh, B. 2000. *Rethinking Multiculturalism: Cultural Diversity and Political Theory*. Cambridge, MA: Harvard University Press.

———. 2008. 'Hindu Theory of Tolerance', in P. Bilimoria, J. Prabhu, and R. Sharma, *Indian Ethics*, pp. 337–50. New Delhi: Oxford University Press.

Radhakrishnan, S. (ed. and trans.). 2000 [1953]. *Īśa Upaniṣad*, pp. 565–78. New Delhi: Harper Collins Publishers.

———. (ed. and trans.). 2000 [1953]. *The Principal Upanisads*. New Delhi: Harper Collins Publishers.

———. (ed. and trans.). 2000 [1953]. *Vajrasūcika Upaniṣhad*, pp. 933–8. New Delhi: Harper Collins Publishers.

———. 1955. *Recovery of Faith*. New York: Harper and Brothers Publishers.

Ram-Prasad, C. 2007. *Indian Philosophy and the Consequences of Knowledge*. Hampshire, Guildford: Ashgate.

Rawls, J. 1993. *Political Liberalism*, 1996 paperback ed. New York: Columbia University Press.

———. 1999. *The Law Of Peoples: With The Idea of Public Reason Revisited*. Cambridge, MA: Harvard University Press.

'Rgveda.' www.sacred-texts.com/hin/rvsan/rv01164.htm (accessed 12 June 2012).

Saṅghavi, S. and B. Doshi. 2000. *Siddhasena Divākara's Sanmati Tarka with a Critical Introduction and an Original Commentary*. Ahmedabad: L.D. Institute of Indology.

Saṅkara, A. (trans. by S. Mayeda). 1992. *Upadeśasāhasrī*. Albany: SUNY Press.

Sargeant, W. (trans.). 1994. *The Bhagavad Gita*. New York: State University of New York Press.

Sen, A. 1998. 'Secularism and Its Discontents', in R. Bhargava (ed.), *Secularism and Its Critics*, pp. 454–85. New Delhi: Oxford University Press.

———. 1999. 'Human Rights and Economic Achievements', in J.R. Bauer and D.A. Bell (eds), *The East Asian Challenge For Human Rights*, pp. 88–99. New York: Cambridge University Press.

Sen, A. 2009. *The Idea of Justice*. Cambridge, MA: Belknap Press of Harvard University Press.

Sharma, A. 1979. 'All Religions Are: Equal? True? Same?: A Critical Examination of Some Formulations of the Neo-Hindu Position', *Philosophy East and West*, 29(1): 59–72.

Taylor, C. 1989. *Sources of the Self: The Making of the Modern Identity*. Cambridge, MA: Harvard Univesity Press.

Taylor, C. 1999. 'Conditions of an Unforced Consenses on Human Rights', in J. Bauer and D. Bell (eds), *The East Asian Challenge for Human Rights*, pp. 124–44. Cambridge: Cambridge University Press.

Tully, J. 1995. *Strange Multiplicity: Constitutionalism in an Age of Diversity*. Cambridge: Cambridge University Press.

Vivekananda, Swami. 1999. *Chicago Addresses*. Delhi: Advaita Ashrama.

PART III

SOCIAL PRACTICES AND APPLIED CONTEXTS

9

The Rights of Man

A Gandhian Intervention

Bindu Puri

This chapter attempts to reconstruct a lesser known interjection into human rights discourse. M.K. Gandhi, who spent most of his life fighting for the rights of the exploited and dispossessed—against racial discrimination in South Africa and for the political and economic rights of colonial Indians—made the following response to the 1948 UN Committee drafting the *Universal Declaration of Human Rights*:

> [A]ll rights to be deserved and preserved come from duty well done. Thus the very right to live accrues to us only when we do the duty of citizenship of the world. From this fundamental statement perhaps it is easy enough to define the duties of man and woman and correlate every right to some corresponding duty to be first performed. (GandhiServe Foundation, Vol. 95: 137).

The same views were expressed by Gandhi to the framers of India's Constitution:

> Fundamental rights can only be those rights the exercise of which is not only in the interest of the citizens but that of the whole world.... Rights cannot be divorced from duties. This is how *satyagraha* was born, for I was always striving to decide what my duty was. (Publications Division, 1961: 230)

This Gandhian intervention appears perplexing for two reasons. First, because of its rejection of the central idea of the 1948 Declaration that human rights are 'indefeasible imprescriptible' moral rights belonging to man *qua* man. Second, because it correlates moral rights belonging to the human subject not with corresponding duties in an object, but with duties in the subject itself. In contemporary human rights discourse, a right has three distinct elements: First, it has a *subject*: the holder or bearer of the right.... Second, it has an *object*: the person against whom right is held.... Third, it has a *content*: what it is the right thing to do or to have done' Contemporary human rights discourse proceeds on an understanding of the relationship between rights and duties which is significantly different from the Gandhian one; in terms of that discourse if A has a right that something be done by the person B against whom that right is held, A has a claim on that person such that it can be said that: 'A's claim against B that B do X is logically equivalent to B's duty toward A to do X: claims and duties are in this way correlative. (Sumner 2012: 358–9)

This paper will attempt to reconstruct Gandhi's position on human rights and justice, why he rejects the idea of rights of man qua man, and what he means by speaking about rights as being meaningless without correlative duties. It will also attempt to bring out the epistemic virtues inherent in the Gandhian methodology of securing individual rights through the practice of satyagraha.

Founding International Legal Human Rights in the Moral Rights of Man *qua* Man

It must be admitted that the idea of human rights as unconditionally belonging to man qua man has been met with philosophical hesitation from those other than Gandhi. There has been philosophical opposition to both the conception of indefeasible moral rights of man qua man, which traces back to Bentham's famous critique of the idea of natural rights of man, and to the international legal practice of human rights. At this point it makes sense to examine the meaning of the term 'human rights' in contemporary philosophical and political discourse. In contemporary usage, 'human rights' refers to the international legal rights that are the focus of international human rights practice. Such human rights practice is based on a consensus expressed in a set of documents that contain both the statement and moral foundation of human rights. These documents are: the *Universal Declaration of Human Rights* (1948), the *International Covenant on Civil and Political Rights*, and the *International Covenant on Economic, Social, and Cultural Rights*. International human rights practice refers to the sum total of the institutional and organizational efforts to promote human rights, including the jurisprudence of the European Convention on Human Rights, the activities of treaty bodies, and the UN Human Rights Council; it also includes foreign aid policy, access to loans and credit, and memberships in multilateral institutions conditional on meeting international human rights standards.

There are two key points of contention in contemporary philosophical discussion concerning the conception of human rights and international human rights practice. The first is whether it is possible to understand international human rights as an attempt to realize universal moral rights through international law. This suggests that international human rights can only be justified if there are philosophical arguments supporting the existence of unconditional moral rights which are due to man qua man simply by virtue of being human. The second issue concerns the justification of the practice of international human rights. Is it justifiable to define human rights *a priori* and subsequently administer them through non-democratic institutions and interventionist global politics? The first question that arises is whether it is necessary to have international legalization of human rights as opposed to domestic legalization; if this is answered in the affirmative, a number of issues remain:

(a) the questionable legitimacy of institutional efforts to implement legal human rights; (b) the questionable legitimacy of legal human rights norms themselves, given the apparent deficiencies of the processes by which they are created and specified; and (c) the supremacy problem (the controversial nature of the claim of international human rights law to override even the most fundamental domestic law). (Buchanan 2012: 291).

Buchanan for instance suggests that there is a need for a 'social moral epistemology of international legal human rights' (Buchanan 2012: 290). He raises questions such as whether the contemporary international human rights practice has relevant 'epistemic values' and just how well do international 'legal-institutional processes perform in addressing scope and conflict problems' (Buchanan 2012: 291).

Gandhi addressed both these issues in his early responses to the 'rights of man'. First, in his view, there were no arguments to establish that there could be unconditional rights held by all humans simply by virtue of their humanity. It appeared that, for Gandhi, individual moral rights were to be earned by the performance of individual duties. Second, Gandhi raised the problem of administration of such rights. In *Hind Swaraj* itself, Gandhi criticized administration of justice through a third party with the figure of the judge as the measure of justice. He argued in 1909 that men become 'unmanly' by asking 'a third party' to mediate between them. 'Surely, the decision of a third party is not always right. The parties alone know who is right'. (Parel 1997: 61). It could be said that on the Gandhian view courts of law increased enmity by treating the two parties as antagonists and the judge as the third party. It may have been this difficulty with the idea of third party justice which led Gandhi to suggest an alternative method for securing rights for the individual, that is, the practice of satyagraha. The methodology of satyagraha was based upon the idea that an individual earns his/her moral rights by performing his/her duty of non-violent resistance to injustice while choosing to defer to the opposing other. It can be argued that the practice of satyagraha, while it expressed a commitment to giving opposing others their due, also exemplified an uncompromising adherence to epistemic values in an insistence/*agraha*, on truth. It may be noted that this insistence on truth worked well in the powerfully contextualized Gandhian practice of securing rights; the careful attention to truth made it possible to sort out conflicting claims to rights in the Gandhian satyagrahas. However, the epistemic virtues of satyagraha notwithstanding, it cannot be denied that Gandhi's response to the 1948 human rights committee puts him in opposition to liberal arguments for the human rights of man qua man.

There have been numerous and vastly different approaches to grounding human rights in the moral rights of man qua man. These can be framed along two basic lines: consequentialist and deontologist. Bentham famously dismissed 'natural rights' as 'simple nonsense'. He argued that the idea of 'imprescriptible or…indefeasible, means nothing unless it exclude[s] the interference of the laws'. (Bentham 2012: 278). In his view, the idea of the rights of man qua man was meant to 'keep up a spirit of resistance to all laws' (Bentham 2012: 277). By contrast, J.S. Mill was sympathetic to the rights of man; he argued powerfully in *Utilitarianism* that 'the essence of the idea of justice, that of a right residing in an individual' (Mill 2012: 292) is what testifies to the 'more binding obligation' of the moral rules that constitute justice. Mill suggested that the 'characteristic sentiment of justice' is 'simply the natural feeling of resentment, moralized by being made coextensive with the demands of social good' (Mill 2012: 295). He takes 'vengeance' and 'retribution' as 'closely connected with the sentiment of justice'. (Mill 2012: 293). Individual claims to rights and the insistence that justice be done has a certain urgency due to the idea of 'retribution', which is a sentiment, according to Mill, that is consistent with the promotion of social utility; Mill argues that claims for individual rights can be seen as consistent with the principle of social utility. However, critiques of consequentialist approaches reveal that a counter example can always be proposed in which the overriding of a human right of an individual will promote social utility (Williams and Smart 1973: 97–8). Thus, it may seem that rule consequentialism rather than act consequentialism is more hospitable to human rights. There are, however, longstanding perceptions of formidable difficulties with utilitarian and consequentialist approaches to human rights. 'In short utilitarianism has forgotten rights…. If it speaks of rights at all it could only say all men have one and the same right, namely that all men should try to increase the total happiness. And this is a manifest misuse of language'. (Carritt 2012: 343).

It may appear that deontologists possess better moral grounds for the rights of man qua man. A prime source of the arguments of many contemporary liberal deontological moral views on human rights is the philosophy of Immanuel Kant and the ideal of a human being as an 'end' in a 'kingdom of ends'. Kant claims that persons possess a certain dignity as rational beings, making it inappropriate to treat them as mere means rather than ends in themselves. Closely allied with the idea of human beings as ends in themselves, is that of legitimate entitlement to individual rights, implying an absence of servility or dependence on the kindness of any other. In terms of the expectation of empathetic inclinations from the other, any such expectation is taken by Kant to be servility to that other. J.B. Schneewind observes that 'a society built around the virtues of benevolence and kindness is for Kant a society requiring not only inequality but servility as well'. (Schneewind 1992: 311). Kant makes this point clearly:

> Many people may take pleasure in doing good actions but conse- quently do not want to stand under obligations toward others. If one only comes to them submissively they will do everything; they do not want to subject themselves to the rights of people, but to view them simply as objects of their magnanimity. It is not all one under what title I get something. What *properly belongs to me* must not be accorded to me merely as something I ask for. (Schneewind 1992: 311; emphasis mine).

Kant distinguishes between perfect and imperfect duties; the former have correlates in the rights or entitlements of others. Such rights 'properly' belong to human subjects simply by virtue of their status as human subjects.

The philosophical difficulty with Gandhi's position on human rights is locating his arguments vis-à-vis the long tradition of lib- eral philosophical argument which seeks to ground international human rights in the moral rights of man qua man. The evaluation of Gandhi's response to the idea of moral rights is complicated by his relentless and lifelong practice of securing the 'fundamental rights of the people' (GandhiServe Foundation Vol. 51: 327). In this paper I will examine both Gandhi's understanding of rights as correlative to duties and his practice of securing the moral rights of individuals (through satyagraha) in vastly different contexts.

Gandhi: Rights and Duties

There is something that seems confounding about Gandhi and contemporary human rights discourse in relation to political philosophy. And at first, the Gandhian opposition to the moral rights of man qua man seems perplexing given the fact that he engaged in a lifelong struggle for basic human rights. Second, the complete neglect of Gandhi and his human rights movements by contemporary philosophical human rights discourse; it is almost as if nothing that Gandhi said and did was of philosophical significance to that discourse.

The Gandhian moment of self-transformation, which it is claimed marked the transition from man to *mahatma*, was related to a sense of the violation of the basic human rights of the self. This moment, often noted by commentators, was the incident at Pietermaritzburg Railway Station in South Africa where Gandhi was physically thrown out of a first class railway compartment despite possessing a valid ticket. In his *Autobiography*, he related his thoughts that night:

> I began to think of my duty. Should I fight for my rights or go back to India.... I should try, if possible, to root out the disease and suffer hardships in the process. Redress for wrongs I should seek only to the extent that would be necessary for the removal of the colour prejudice. (Gandhi 1968: 166)

The importance of rights was therefore evident to Gandhi as early as the 1893 incident; indeed, it appears that Gandhi thought in terms of human moral rights at that time. One may note the following comment from Gandhi: 'It is true that the Indians in South Africa are not poor and hungry. But man cannot live by bread alone. Money has no value before human rights. And the South African Government does not give these rights to Indians there'. (GandhiServe Foundation Vol. 97: 332). It can therefore be argued that Gandhi's opposition to human rights discourse concerned the fact that he did not accept the philosophical presuppositions of the early liberal conception of human rights as set forth in the 1948 Declaration, rather than a failure to understand the importance of rights to human dignity. In this context it should be noted that it was not the human rights specified in the Declaration that Gandhi likely opposed; this will become clearer when we consider the kind of rights for which Gandhi led satyagrahas. It further becomes evident from consideration of the resolution on Fundamental Rights and Economic Changes passed in the 1931 session of the Indian National Congress (GandhiServe Foundation Vol. 51: 327). It is significant that this resolution was largely formulated by Gandhi and Nehru.

It is the central argument of this paper that Gandhi was opposed to some of the basic suppositions of the Declaration of 1948 and the subsequent covenants on human rights: (i) the notion of unearned rights to which man is entitled qua man; (ii) the methodology of addressing injustice through the mediation of a third party; and (iii) the modern universalism which philosophically grounds a large part of liberal thinking about equality. It can be argued that modern universalism, on which the liberal state is largely based, organizes general responsibility to produce a public space within which individuals can interact as abstract equals, relegating all that which is incompatible with such equality to the private sphere. In the public sphere equality before the law and majoritarian democracy provides individuals third party justice with the judge as the measure of such justice. It is this thinking which is enshrined in all the declarations of the universal rights of man. Gandhi conceived of both the state and justice in a radically different way. The ideal Gandhian state was a *ramrajya*, which Gandhi often described as a state that secured justice for the weakest of the weakest. The Gandhian methodology of securing rights through satyagraha and *ahimsa* was meant to contest domination without seeking to set up a new dominating major centre.

Gandhi and the Contents of the Human Rights of Man

That Gandhi understood the importance of rights to human dignity and further that he was not opposed to the human rights enumerated in the 1948 Declaration becomes clear if we examine the following categories of human rights in the context of the Gandhian movements.

The April 1917 satyagraha at Champran demonstrates the value that Gandhi placed on the rights of the person, including life, liberty, and security of the person (UNDHR 1948, Article 3), privacy and freedom of movement (Articles 12 and 13), ownership of property

(Article 17), prohibition of slavery (Article 4), and freedom from torture or cruel, inhuman, or degrading treatment or punishment (Article 5). Under the *tinkathia* system the tenant farmers were under the control of European planters. They were subject to extortion, enhanced rents, arbitrary punishments, imprisonment at the hands of planters, etc. It was a result of Gandhi's satyagraha that the Champaran Agrarian Bill was introduced in November 1917.

Gandhi also clearly placed great value on the rule of law and associated rights, including: equal recognition before the law and equal protection of the law (Article 7), effective legal remedy for violation of legal rights (Article 8), impartial hearing and trial (Article 10), presumption of innocence (Article 11), and prohibition of arbitrary arrest (Article 9). From February 1919 to April 1919 Gandhi led the first all India satyagraha movement. A country-wide *hartal* was organized to secure withdrawal of Rowlatt Act; the Rowlatt Act was framed to enable some offences to be tried expeditiously before High Court judges with no right of appeal. It provided for preventative detention and continuous detention and included provisions against the publication or circulation of seditious documents.

In regard to political rights, such as freedom of expression and association (Articles 19 and 20), the right to take part in government (Article 20), and periodic and genuine elections by universal and equal suffrage (Article 21), we can refer to Gandhi's Quit India resolution in 1942 and also to his work in this regard between 1942 and 1947.

The Bardoli satyagraha is an example demonstrating Gandhi's understanding of the importance of economic and social rights, including the right to an adequate standard of living (Article 25), just and favourable remuneration (Article 23), the right to join trade unions (Article 23), the reasonable limitation of working hours (Article 24), and free elementary education (Article 26). In 1927 the revenue department of the Bombay government enhanced the assessment in Bardoli taluq by 22 per cent and in some cases it was raised by as much as 60 per cent. The Bardoli peasants claimed that this rate was unjust as it was fixed without full investigation and that the tax department's report was inaccurate. As the peasants were unable to pay the raised taxes, it was decided, at a conference organized by the congress in Bardoli, to withhold the enhanced portion of the taxes.

Sardar Vallabhai Patel, who was invited to lead the satyagraha, set forth the demands of the peasants for an enquiry and their refusal to pay the enhanced taxes. The *satyagrahi* peasants submitted willingly to the penalties of arrest and seizure of their lands. The government appointed the Broomfield committee, thereby granting an impartial inquiry into the enhancement of the tax; the forfeited lands were restored to the peasants, and the satyagrahi prisoners were released. Other examples of Gandhi's work in this area include the Ahmedabad Textile Workers Movement (1917), the Kheda satyagraha (1918), and the salt satyagraha (1930). And finally that everyone has a right to participate in the cultural life of the community (Article 27). In connection with this last right and with all the other human rights categorized in the UN Declaration, it is important to recall the resolution on Fundamental Rights and Economic Changes passed in the 1931 session of the Indian National Congress (GandhiServe Foundation, Vol. 51: 327). This resolution was introduced by Gandhi and co-drafted by both Gandhi and Nehru. The preamble to this resolution stated that one of the chief aims was to 'enable the masses to appreciate what *swaraj*...will mean to them.... The congress, therefore, declare that any constitution which may be agreed to on its behalf should provide, for the following' (GandhiServe Foundation, Vol. 51: 327). Though it is not possible to enumerate all of the twenty provisions here, it may be noted that they included every provision stated in the much later UN Declaration and related covenants. Some of which are as follows:

(1) Fundamental rights of the people, including:
   a. freedom of association and combination;
   b. freedom of speech and press;
   c. freedom of conscience and free profession and practice of religion, subject to public order and morality;
   d. protection of culture, language and scripts of minorities;
   e. equal rights and obligations of all citizens, without any bar on account of sex;
   f. no disability to attach any citizen by reason of his or her religion, or caste, or creed, or sex in regard to public employment, office of power or honour, and in the exercise of any trade or calling;

g. equal rights to all citizens in regard to public roads, wells, schools and other places of public resort;

h. right to keep and bear arms in accordance with regulations made in that behalf;

i. no person shall be deprived of his liberty nor shall his dwelling or property be entered, sequestered, or confiscated, save in accordane [sic] with law.

(2) Religious neutrality on the part of the State.

(3) Adult suffrage.

(4) Free primary education.

(5) A living wage for industrial workers, limited hours of labour, healthy conditions of work, protection against the economic consequences of old age, sickness, and unemployment. (GandhiServe Foundation, Vol. 51: 327–8).

From the previous accounts of the rights that occupied Gandhi's attention it seems possible to argue that his own specifications of individual moral rights and his struggle for such rights came fairly close to the contents of the human rights listed in the 1948 Declaration, subsequent discourse, and international practice of such rights. However, if Gandhi's specifications for the contents of human rights were not significantly different from that of contemporary human rights discourse and practice, then why should he have expressed any dissent to the framers of the 1948 Declaration?

As previously suggested, it is possible that his dissent concerned the fundamental presuppositions of the Declaration of Human Rights rather than the human rights contained within the Declaration itself. In fact, it is possible to further argue that Gandhi's dissent was primarily related to his opposition of the idea that justice could be granted by a third party and the related conception that an abstract equality before the law was sufficient to secure justice to the vulnerable.

Gandhi proposed an alternative conception, that of human rights as earned by individual human subjects through a process of growing into a sense of justice. For Gandhi such a sense of justice consisted minimally in developing the capacity to give all others their due. One way that Gandhi seemed to believe it was possible to give others their due was by deferring to all equally, whether the other was a relative, friend, or unjust opposing person or state. Satyagraha was the Gandhian method of securing rights by performing one's duty of resisting injustice while deferring to the unjust other. Justice could not be secured by creating institutions to put general responsibility and abstract equality before the law into place in the public sphere. It could only be secured by assuming individual responsibility to resist injustice, and through an 'equality of deference' to all others (Skaria 2011: 206).

Gandhi, in his opposition to the 1948 Declaration, seemed to be arguing primarily against the notion of an unconditional individual entitlement to responsible or just behaviour from others when he suggested that the rights of an individual are conditional on his or her previous performance of duty:

> I would say that there is nothing like a right. For one who has no duties there are no rights either. In other words, all rights emanate from duties—if there is no duty, there is no right either. When I do my duty, it brings some result and that is my right.... Suppose I work for the whole day and earn eight annas—I get those eight annas as my right. How did I have that right? Because I worked. If I do not work and take eight annas, I appropriate that amount, I do not have it as my right. I can have a right only when I fulfil my promise to work and that too sincerely in thought, word, and deed. But if I do not work with my heart in it, if I exploit the employer and deceive him because he is not noticing it, then it is a sin. (GandhiServe Foundation, Vol. 97: 377).

Gandhi seemed to be arguing that an individual has no unconditional rights qua man. The right to responsible behaviour from others must be earned by doing justice to all others with whom he or she comes into contact or conflict. Every individual must earn the right to responsible behaviour from others by developing the human capacity for, at the very least, a minimal sense of justice while negotiating a relationship with them; note above the requirement of 'sincerity' and the use of the term 'sin' in connection with the appropriation of an unearned moral right.

I argue that one way Gandhi's arguments concerning the precedence of duties over rights can be understood is if we reconstruct Gandhi's ideas as using the notion of duty in the metaphorical, rather than the contractual, sense. Gandhi may have been using the familiar idea of an individual's duty emerging from a contractual obligation to his or her employer to express a primary insight about justice. Perhaps he was using the term 'duty' in order to indicate that the central insight in any conception of justice is the idea of 'fairness'; certainly, he argued that it was part of a man's *swabhav* (nature; own most orientation) to be bound by a unilateral obligation to give all others their due. For instance, in an essay he had written about the swabhav of man he argued,

> 'My ethics not only permit me to claim but require me to own kinship with not merely the ape but the horse and sheep, the lion and leopard, the snake and the scorpion…. The hard ethics which rule my life, and I hold ought to rule that of every man and woman, impose this unilateral obligation upon us.' (Prabhu and Rao 1967: 424).

Gandhi invoked 'kinship' in the context of man's nature as involving a unilateral obligation to the other because it was a good example of giving others their due. Also, in relations of kinship conflicts were most likely to be refigured by love or deference to the other even in the context of continued resistance. It should be noted that Gandhi often used the word *paropkar*. He used this term, for instance, in the Gujarati edition of the *Hind Swaraj* during his critique of modern medicine (Parel 1997: 62–3). Paropkar is derived from two words: *par* and *upkar*; the term 'par' means the other or not one's own and the term 'upkar' means to do good to. In the Gandhian view, the primary set of moral rules that constituted justice concern giving all others their due and thereby growing into an individual sense of justice. More importantly, it seemed that for Gandhi all other rules of justice followed from this basic and primary rule.

However, this giving of what is due, to every human and non-human other, ought not to be confused with the idea of 'just dessert', which often entails vengeance and retaliation. Retaliation had no place in Gandhi's understanding of justice, which will be further clarified in the next section when I discuss the technique of securing justice through satyagraha. However, one may note the following comment made by Gandhi in the context of his attempts to secure a redress of rights violations in South Africa in 1896: 'Our method in South Africa is to conquer this hatred by love…. We do not attempt to have individuals punished but, as a rule, patiently to suffer wrongs at their hands'. (Publications Division, 1961: 43). The non-violent resistance to unjust others while voluntarily deferring to them rather than harbouring retaliation or revenge was part of what was legitimately due to the human and non-human other in a Gandhian notion of justice.

For Gandhi, if any human being was to be in a position to make moral rights claims on any other being, or even the state, he or she had to 'do justice' to that other. In an important sense an individual's own humanity, his or her authentic existence as a moral being (that is, his or her swabhav as a human being), consisted in recognizing that there was something due to a human or non-human other, whether opponent or friend. Gandhi's central insight about giving a person his or her due was that 'getting one's due' as a human being was something that emerges out of the process of giving others their due.

It seems clear that on this view, getting one's due in terms of one's basic moral rights emerged out of the process of giving others their due and therefore could not be thought of purely in terms of arriving at some 'good' end state. On Gandhi's view, individual moral rights could not be understood purely in consequentialist terms as arriving at a 'good' end state by any means whatever. This may be the reason that Gandhi incorporated circularity in his conception of justice in the metaphorical terms of an individual subject performing his duties and earning his rights. As Gandhi was leading a mass movement, it was perhaps far easier for him to convey his central insight about justice, that of the primacy of doing justice to others, in the comparatively simpler terms of duties and rights. One might think, then, that 'not giving a person or opponent their due' would in itself be a way of granting that one's life and actions became not only unjust, but inhuman such that there was no longer anything 'justly' due oneself *qua* human being. Gandhi seemed to be acutely aware of the possibility of injustice in individual demands for justice that proceeded without giving others their due: 'no one can deny the fact that if the practice of seeking justice through murders is established amongst us, we shall start murdering one another for what we believe to be justice'. (GandhiServe Foundation, Vol. 51: 316–17).

Gandhi provided examples ranging from the intimacy of personal relationships, largely those of kinship, to social relations in order to explain this sense of justice as consisting primarily in giving a spouse, a child, a friend, and society in general what was due them:

> As a young man I began life by seeking to assert my rights, and I soon discovered that I had none—not even over my wife. So I began by discovering and performing my duty by my wife, my children, friends, companions, and society, and I find today that I have greater rights, perhaps, than any living man I know. If this is too tall a claim, then I do not know anyone who possesses greater rights than I. (GandhiServe Foundation, Vol. 79: 293).

In interpreting Gandhi's emphasis on rights as correlative with duties as a metaphorical expression of his primary insight concerning the nature of justice as consisting primarily in giving others their due, I am going against other fairly important interpretations. Judith M. Brown, for instance, has argued that in stressing duties Gandhi was merely expressing a metaphysical commitment to the ancient Hindu concept 'of *dharma* or duty'. In Brown's view, since Hindu society was centred on the ethics of dharma it 'had no rights discourse.... Dharma meant not just the religious duty of the individual but also of the status group: its objective was making a human society that would conform to an underlying order and balance in the universe (*rta*)'. (Brown 2000: 88–9). According to Brown, it was a commitment to such a metaphysics that led Gandhi to 'stress on duties rather than on rights, and on the mutual interdependence of individuals and groups if the whole was to function morally'. (Brown 2000: 89). She argues that this tradition of *rta* and dharma, to which Gandhi was an heir, 'saw no problem with the basic inequalities between individuals, and did not address issues of social change and conflict'. (Brown 2000: 88).

I shall argue that Gandhi was terribly interested in removing inequalities between people in the enforcement of individual rights and in securing social justice to the vulnerable. It may therefore be possible to unpack the Gandhian idea of earning individual moral rights by examining two alternative notions which Gandhi often used in connection with rights and justice: moral confidence and respect. Gandhi argued for the intimate connection between respecting oneself and respecting 'others':

> Where there is egoism, we shall find incivility and arrogance. Where it is absent, we shall find a sense of self-respect together with civility.

> The egotist thinks too much of his body.... He who holds his self-respect dear acts towards everyone in a spirit of friendship, for he values other's self-respect as much as he values his own. He sees himself...in line with others. The egotist keeps aloof from others and, believing himself superior to the rest of the world, he takes upon himself to judge everyone and in the result enables the world to have a measure of his smallness. (Murti 1970: 36).

This might indicate that part of what Gandhi saw as doing justice to others or giving others their due was that of according them the respect which one holds dear to oneself. One might agree with the deontologists that man qua man was an end worthy of respect; however Gandhi suggests that one cannot have a sense of one's own self-respect or self-worth qua being a person while at the same time wilfully undermining or violating the self-respect of others. An authentic and stable sense of self-worth must be derived from one's independent evaluation of one's own accomplishments, goodness, sense of doing the right thing, etc. One's sense of doing the right thing or accomplishing something cannot be dependent or based entirely on comparisons with others as having accomplished less or having done wrong; this basis of self-worth is too precarious as it always depends on perceiving the smallness of others, which is surely a thing beyond one's own control. Further, doing justice by others, giving them their legitimate human due, was a precondition to one's own sense of self-respect and consequently the source of the legitimacy of one's claims to basic human rights as part of the self-respect due to oneself as a moral being.

This also concerned Gandhi's idea that the relations between citizens were extensions of the relations within the family. In an important sense, Gandhian justice could not be based on equality before the law, but on an 'equality of deference'. (Skaria 2011: 206). One's own sense of self-respect was a consequence of having a minimally developed sense of justice or capacity to defer to and respect others whom it became one's duty to resist when unjust. Gandhi stressed man's duty to resist injustice rather than seeking third party intervention: 'The relationship of the government and its subjects is that of father and son, not of master and slave. It is the duty of the son to resist injustice on the part of the father'. (Skaria 2011: 212). The example of Prahlad, the son of the demon king, was often invoked by Gandhi: 'By disobeying…his father's order for the sake of truth, Prahlad not only remained staunch in *satyagraha* but did his duty as a son'. (Skaria 2011: 212). By choosing to defer to the unjust other, one demonstrated one's equality to that other. By resisting the other while deferring to them, one compelled the other to accept that deference responsibly. That is, one thereby compelled the other to respect one's basic human rights redress the injustice etc.

Another notion Gandhi sometimes used in this regard was that of moral confidence. Gandhi often argued that the legitimacy of individual and group claims to rights derived from the moral confidence that came from a sense of having done justice to others and from an equality of deference to all others. Hence, in 1922 in the context of withdrawing civil disobedience after the incident at *Chauri Chaura*, where an unruly mob had killed twenty-three policemen, he stressed the need for Indians to regain moral confidence which had been lost by the violence. For Gandhi it could only be legitimate to press for human rights after such confidence had been re-earned by the individuals concerned: 'By strict discipline and purification we regain the moral confidence required for demanding the withdrawal of notifications and the discharge of prisoners'. (Murti 1970: 162). It is possible to argue that one's self-worth or self-respect could, for Gandhi, only come from a moral confidence in the legitimacy of one's claim to basic human rights; such moral confidence in turn depended on the confidence in having done justice to others with whom one lived or was in conflict. However, the moral confidence of having done justice to others and thereby being worthy of getting one's due from others depended strongly on knowing how things really were in the world. A certain moral realism and a close connection to truth was, therefore, an important constituent of the Gandhian idea of justice.

Securing Justice: Firmness (*Agraha*) on the Truth (*Satya*)

In his efforts to secure the rights of Indians in South Africa Gandhi developed a method of securing individual human rights to the vulnerable or exploited. This method, which he called satyagraha, was suggested by him to the Indian National Congress on 4 September 1920. Satyagraha is a combination of the words 'satya', meaning truth, and 'agraha', meaning firmness. It has often been translated as truth force or the force that is generated by firmness on truth. Gandhi recognized that this method marked 'a definite change in the policy which the country had hitherto adopted for the vindication of the rights that belong to it and its honor'. (Publications Division, 1961: 245). It is apparent that Gandhi formulated a very clear methodology, powerfully contextualized to the local contexts of individual rights claims, to secure justice for an oppressed individual. Therefore it can be argued that Gandhi's second difficulty with the formulation of human rights in the 1948 Declaration is the idea that human rights could be secured by means of legitimate 'guardianship' in the form of international law and international arbitration; that is, by an abstract equality before law and third party justice with international covenants serving as the measure of justice. Gandhi experimented in South Africa and India with the effort to secure human rights for individuals living in those states by making petitions to the government in Britain. His experience seemed to convince him that there could be no once removed guardians of the rights of man. His argument concerning the essential reciprocity of an individual's rights and duties by its suggestion of circularity in the conception of justice seemed to indicate that an individual alone was responsible for any affirmative action for securing his or her basic human rights, either individually or collectively. This was a movement away from modern universalism's emphasis on general responsibility as an adequate provision for securing justice to the vulnerable or subordinate. It is possible to argue that Gandhi's repeated insistence that the rights of an individual emerge from his or her own performance of duties was meant to indicate that justice could be secured only in the context of an individual's own responsible and localized engagement with asserting his or her rights while remaining just to the other with whom he or she was in conflict.

One reason why Gandhi may have appeared to contextualize the practice of securing moral rights to the individuals involved in the specific cases was his clear recognition of the connection between truth and justice. Since Gandhian justice was, at a primary level, about giving all others their due, it was important that rights claims were made in a context and manner in which it would be possible to arrive at the truth between the conflicting parties. For an oppressed rights claimant to give 'others' their due, to do justice to and by others, means at the very least that when in conflict with them he or she must try to know the other's perspective and arrive at the truth of the matter by examining how things really are. Note that if rights are defined in an *a priori* manner and administered by international bodies removed from the context of the alleged rights violation, then it becomes almost impossible to do justice to the alleged rights violating other. For international arbitrating institutions cannot do justice to the rights subject and allegedly rights violating others without knowing where the truth lies between the conflicting parties. It is progressively difficult in third party justice to develop epistemic values in rights securing procedures.

Another reason that Gandhi may have opposed an international guardianship of human moral rights may have been his own strong moral sense of the inseparable connection between means and ends. For Gandhi, rights and freedom could only be secured by the individual rights claimant through the process of engaging in a non-violent affirmation of his or her freedom and rights through a just resistance to the unjust other. The process of this engagement itself empowers the rights claimant and heightens their sense of justice. Hence, there could be no resulting increase in rights without the active participation of the individual rights claimant. Note in this context the difficulties with the idea that democracy can be granted as an end goal or political institution to a subjugated people by international arbitration and interventions. The very democratic processes put in place by international bodies are likely to degenerate into autocratic and dictatorial processes unless the individuals themselves engage in the processes by which democracy is actualized in political processes.

Satyagraha was Gandhi's suggested methodology to individuals and collectives who wanted to secure freedom, justice, economic, and political rights. 'Passive resistance is a method of securing rights by personal suffering; it is the reverse of resistance by arms'. (Parel 1997: 90). According to Murti (1970: 22), 'This is the literal meaning of satyagraha—insistence on truth, and force derivable from such insistence…. We shall find too, on further reflection, that conduct based on truth is impossible without love. Truth-force then is love-force. We cannot remedy evil by harbouring ill-will against the evil-doer'.

Gandhi appears to have been making at least two relevant points about the nature of justice in stressing certain features of satyagraha. First, that satyagraha is an insistence upon truth. 'Its root meaning is holding on to truth, hence truth-force'. (GandhiServe Foundation, Vol. 19: 206). The very conception of satyagraha as a truth force generating a power for the securing of justice to individuals makes the connection between justice, truth, and rights apparent in Gandhi. Second, the insistence upon truth was a non-violent insistence. 'A gentleman writes to ask me whether one should take to violence if one's rights are not granted. We cannot secure our rights through violence'. (GandhiServe Foundation, Vol. 97: 376). This reflects first that Gandhi believed that the only way to get at the truth in a situation was through non-violence and even love of the conflicting other and second, that the choice of non-violent resistance reflected an equality of deference. Making the choice to defer to the other while resisting him or her is *swabhavik* (natural) to man, however it was also an expression of the individual's equality to the unjust other in his or her complete rejection of the hierarchies of power by choosing deference over violence. Incidentally, such a choice also safeguards the rights claimant from making moral mistakes in cases of errors of judgment where the truth could be entirely on the side of the alleged rights violator.

It is important to elaborate two points that Gandhi made about the nature of justice. First, Gandhian justice clearly involved truth. For Gandhi there could be no legitimate process of securing rights or of getting justice without taking care of the epistemic values of the procedure to secure such rights or justice. It is noteworthy that one of the chief difficulties in contemporary international human rights practice is evaluating the truth of conflicting claims about human rights violations. It seems self-evident that the moral strength of a human rights claim depends on its connection with how things are as a matter of fact in the world, or that part of the world about which the claim has been made. Gandhi framed his method to secure individual moral rights almost entirely from the perspective of truth or remaining close to certain realism in moral matters.

One may take note of the component ideas that were constitutive of the Gandhian process of satyagraha:

(1) Gandhi insisted on addressing rights violations with the active participation of the alleged victims of injustice in the same context in which the claimed rights violations had occurred. In all his satyagrahas there was no redressal of a rights violation or perpetuation of injustice that proceeded from a geographical distance. This made it easier to evaluate truth claims of both the oppressed and oppressor.

(2) Gandhi insisted that close attention be paid to the facts in the context of cases of alleged injustice before embarking on a satyagraha. This becomes clear if we reflect upon the Gandhian practice of making a detailed study of the empirical facts of the case at the place or site where the injustice had occurred before advising on the satyagraha. For instance, in the case of the Champaran satyagraha, Gandhi met with Raj Kumar Shukla, a peasant from Champaran, almost a year before he embarked upon the satyagraha; he waited a year before embarking on the Champaran satyagraha in order to make a detailed inquiry into the conditions of the peasants and the position of the planters. On 11 April 1917, as a first step, Gandhi met the relevant 'other'—Mr Wilson, the Secretary of the Planters Association—and on 13 April he met Mr Morshead, Commissioner of the Tirhut division. Both of these 'others' were hostile to him and refused to give him information. On 16 April, Gandhi set out on elephant back for Iasanlipathi to talk to affected peasants and by noon that day he reached Chandrahia, one of the villages which supplied the indigo to the Motihari factory. It was here that he was served with a notice asking him to leave the district which he resisted, agreeing to submit to suffer 'the penalty for disobedience' (GandhiServe Foundation, Vol. 15: 336). He said clearly that 'my desire is purely and simply for a genuine search for knowledge. And this I shall continue to satisfy so long as I am left free'. (GandhiServe Foundation, Vol. 15: 336–7).

(3) Gandhi insisted on the central role of the rights claimant in undergoing the difficulties and pain associated with the insistence on the rights in question; satyagraha was a method of

securing rights through individual suffering. This was not meant to glorify pain or recommend martyrdom, but a theoretical and practical manoeuvre intended to privilege individual responsibility over the general responsibility enshrined in the institutions of the modern liberal state with its allegiance to modern universalism. Gandhi was always aware of the possibilities of untruth and therefore wanted the burden of error to rest on the claimant. This helped to discourage untruth in the form of false claims to right violations and also detracted from the possibility of abdication of individual moral responsibility by the rights claimant in case any mistake in judgment had been made.

(4) As satyagraha was structured around doing justice to the opponent, it was most important to keep the possibility of arriving at the truthful solution of the conflict open by incorporating dialogue with the other into the resistance itself. Note, for example, the following comment by Gandhi: 'It is a principle of satyagraha that if there is an opportunity for talks with the party against whom satyagraha is being offered, then talks should be tried'. (GandhiServe Foundation, Vol. 51: 321).

(5) Since satyagraha was defined as insistence on truth, there was no theoretical inconsistency in withdrawing from a satyagraha if it was found that truth lay on the other side.

The constituent ideas of satyagraha brought out what Gandhi saw as one of the critical demands of justice—its close connection with truth. This made it difficult for him to accept a universal conception of the human rights of man qua man which necessarily functioned at a distance from the sites of right conflicts.

The second point about satyagraha is the fact that it was conceived as a non-violent adherence to truth which revealed Gandhi's commitment to what he thought was the primary element in any conception of justice, which was giving the other his or her due. As getting one's due from others was dependent, in a Gandhian framework, on attempting to do justice to the other, the conditions of the methodology of asserting individual moral rights became most important. Such assertion was necessarily contextual with the violated and violator negotiating with each other in a manner that the person claiming his or her rights was in a position to do justice to the other. There were many constituents to this doing of justice in a Gandhian sense. First, giving the other minimal respect in the form of an equality of deference, of civility, and of kindness. Second, giving the other his or her due by respecting their physical integrity as a person by remaining non-violent while insisting upon one's rights. Third, giving the other his or her due by remaining non-violent thereby expressing a faith in the possibility that truth might well lie in the others' understanding of the case. Fourth, giving the other his or her due by not assuming oneself qua oppressed to be in the right but searching for the truth by examining the local empirical facts of the case in a detailed manner.

The central Gandhian argument that getting justice from others depends crucially on doing justice to others seemed to have tied questions of Gandhian justice firmly to truth. This led Gandhi to insist on contextual treatments in cases of conflicts about justice and also led him to stress the idea that justice could be secured best at the local levels where it is possible for involved parties to evaluate their conflicting claims to rights by essentially and locally verifiable claims about how things really were. This perhaps was one of the reasons for Gandhi's hesitation at the idea of the 'charter of rights' whose 'guardian' (GandhiServe Foundation, Vol. 88: 150) would be international bodies far removed from the local sites of conflicts about justice. For Gandhi such geographical and theoretical space between an alleged rights violation and international arbitration made it difficult to ensure epistemic values in human rights practice.

* * *

Gandhi's rejection of the central idea of the *Universal Declaration of Human Rights* (UDHR) (1948)—the concept of human rights as inalienable moral rights belonging to man qua man—may appear odd given Gandhi's central role in the history of the struggle for basic equality and freedom for the oppressed and vulnerable members of society. However, as has been demonstrated, Gandhi's requirements for human rights were not dissimilar from what was stipulated in the UDHR and his objection was more concerned with the presuppositions of the document than its actual content. He contended that human rights are not solely a matter of individual entitlement, rather they also involve unilateral duties and obligations toward others; this is a requirement of justice. In this light, others must not be viewed as adversaries with differing interests, but as kith and kin, towards whom we have foundational duties; duties toward others are extensions of kinship relationships. This is a requirement for one's sense of self-respect and is the source of legitimacy of one's claims to basic human rights. Finally, justice as satyagraha cannot be attained through third-party adjudication, removed from local contexts. Justice requires non-violent resistance and concrete local engagement, where one has direct access to the situation and the facts, unabstracted from the local context.

References

Bentham, J. 2012. 'Selection from "Anarchical Fallacies"', in D. Jeske and R. Fumerton (eds), *Readings in Political Philosophy: Theory and Applications*, pp. 274–81. Canada: Broadview Press.

Brown, J.M. 2000. 'Gandhi and Human Rights: In Search of True Humanity', in A.J. Parel (ed.), *Gandhi, Freedom, and Self-Rule*, pp. 87–101. New Delhi: Vistaar Publications.

Buchanan, A. 2012. 'Human Rights', in D. Estlund (ed.), *The Oxford Handbook of Political Philosophy*, pp. 279–97. New York: Oxford University Press.

Carritt, E.F. 2012. 'Selection from "Ethical and Political Thinking"', in D. Jeske and R. Fumerton (ed.), *Readings in Political Philosophy: Theory and Applications*, pp. 341–3. Canada: Broadview Press.

Gandhi, M.K. 1968. *The Selected Works of Mahatma Gandhi, Vol. 1: An Autobiography*. Ahmedabad: Navajivan Trust.

GandhiServe Foundation. 'Collected Works of Mahatma Gandhi (CWMG)', Vols 1–97. www.gandhiserve.org/e/cwmg/cwmg.htm.

Mill, J.S. 2012. 'Selection from "Utilitarianism"', in D. Jeske and R. Fumerton (eds), *Readings in Political Philosophy: Theory and Applications*, pp. 282–95. Canada: Broadview Press.

Murti, V.V. Ramana (ed.). 1970. *Gandhi: Essential Writings*. New Delhi: Gandhi Peace Foundation.

Parel, A.J. (ed.). 1997. *Gandhi: 'Hind Swaraj' and Other Writings*. Cambridge: Cambridge University Press.

Prabhu, R.K. and U.R. Rao (eds). 1967. *The Mind of the Mahatma*. Ahmedabad: Navajivan Publishing House.

Publications Division (ed.). 1961. *The Collected Works of Mahatma Gandhi (in 100 volumes)*. India: Publications Division, Ministry of Information and Broadcasting, Government of India.

Rawls, J. 1971. *A Theory of Justice*. Cambridge, MA: Harvard University Press.

———. 1999. *The Law of Peoples*. Cambridge, MA: Harvard University Press.

Schneewind, J.B. 1992. 'Autonomy, Obligation, and Virtue: An Overview of Kant's Moral Philosophy', in P. Guyer (ed.), *The Cambridge Companion to Kant*, pp. 309–41. New York: Cambridge University Press.

Skaria, A. 2011. 'Relinquishing Republican Democracy: Gandhi's Ramarajya', *Postcolonial Studies*, 14(2): 203–29.

Sumner, L.W. 2012. 'Rights', in D. Jeske and R. Fumerton (eds), *Readings in Political Philosophy: Theory and Applications*, pp. 357–71. Canada: Broadview Press.

United Nations Declaration of Human Rights (UNHDR). 2012. 'The United Nations Declaration of Human Rights (1948)', in D. Jeske and R. Fumerton (eds), *Readings in Political Philosophy: Theory and Applications*, pp. 269–73. Canada: Broadview Press.

Williams, B. and J.J.C. Smart. 1973. *Utilitarianism: For and Against*. Cambridge: Cambridge University Press.

10

Invoking Human Rights

Dalits and the Politics of Caste Violence in Gujarat

Gopika Solanki

The body of literature on the vernacularization of human rights discourses suggests that nongovernmental organizations (NGOs) play a role in appropriating and adapting this framework to demand and promote social justice in local contexts, often merging the local and the global (Goodale and Merry 2007; Kennedy 2004). It is argued that the legitimacy of these organizations, the politics of donor assistance, NGOs' embeddedness within local societies, NGOs' relationship with the political elite, the content of these organizations' ideas, and the strength of existing hierarchies and norms all influence the success of these processes, and that the efforts of NGOs are often more successful when international rights norms resonate with local values (An-Na'im 2001; Levitt and Merry 2009). Dalit[1] groups in India have successfully merged human rights values with national legal structures. A number of influential NGOs for Dalit human rights in Gujarat have addressed caste violence through litigation and by working towards improving the implementation of the law criminalizing everyday and ritualistic violence against Dalits and Adivasis,[2] namely the Scheduled Castes and Scheduled Tribes (Prevention of Atrocities) Act, 1989 (henceforth, POA).[3]

The POA defines atrocity as an offense and lists a variety of practices of caste discrimination and humiliation as criminal offences under sections 3(1) and 3(2). It also imposes exemplary punishment; endeavours to erase practices of caste discrimination, exploitation, and violence; gives financial assistance to victims to realize justiciable rights; and makes provision for the relief and rehabilitation of victims of violence under Rule 12(4) of the Act. Under the rules laid down for the implementation of this Act in 1995, state governments must create special courts to try these cases. This law co-exists with the Protection of Civil Rights Act of 1955 (henceforth, PCR), but as early as 1995 we find that offences of caste discrimination and violence are largely recorded under the POA.[4]

Scholars have argued that exclusive and excessive reliance on the law and legal platforms to operationalize human rights norms and address questions of social justice and equality does not adequately address the complex dilemmas that accompany resistance to inequality and discrimination. They suggest that liberal legalism reduces the role of politics by relying on courts, not open-ended political processes, to determine interpretive frames, and limits the normative aspirations of the left (Brown and Halley 2002; Hastrup 2003; Rosenberg 1991). In the context of this debate, this chapter engages with the following question: under what conditions is the privileging of legal action an effective resource for human rights organizations that aim to redress caste discrimination?

The Puzzle of the Atrocity Act in Gujarat

In 2012, the National Campaign on Dalit Human Rights (NCDHR), along with other organizations working on Dalit rights (such as India-based Western NGOs, Navsarjan Trust, the Behavioural Science Centre, and Janvikas) organized public meetings across India to discuss potential reforms to the POA. The NCDHR also coordinated the National Coalition for Strengthening Scheduled Castes (SCs) and Scheduled Tribes (STs) (POA) Act. During a meeting at Ahmedabad,

Western Gujarat, Dalit writers, intellectuals, former members of
Dalit Panther, retired bureaucrats, political party workers, lawyers,
NGO workers, litigants, and lay persons raised key dilemmas: the
state is a routine violator of human rights of Dalits, yet it must be held
accountable; the law does not adequately protect against private or
retributive violence before or after dispute resolution, but judicial
resolution is still necessary. Participants were pessimistic about many
structural barriers to legal mobilization, but remained optimistic
about the potential of the law. These contradictions and complexities
surrounding the Atrocity Act, as the law is called in popular parlance,
are supported by data.

Patterns of cases registered under the POA, shown in Table 10.1,
bring to light the politics of crime registration and highlight the
complexities previously discussed. In general, states with high levels of crime report higher crime rates against Dalits and Adivasis;
southern states, with better governance records, are also more likely
to report crimes. However, to compare the prevalence of caste violence, it is useful to group states with comparable densities of SCs,
because demography influences parties' mobilization of Dalits and
how the POA is implemented.[5] Four categories emerge when we
group states according to the number of SCs in relation to the total
population. The states with the highest levels of Dalit populations are
Uttar Pradesh (21.7 per cent), Punjab (28 per cent), and West Bengal
(23 per cent); Uttar Pradesh records the highest crime rate. States
where SC and ST populations range from 15 to 18 per cent are Bihar,
Odisha, Andhra Pradesh, Madhya Pradesh, Rajasthan, Karnataka,
and Tamil Nadu; the rate of registration of crimes against SCs and
STs is high in Madhya Pradesh and Rajasthan, both of which are
considered less developed states with a history of poor governance.
Gujarat, Assam, Kerala, and Maharashtra comprise the third category of states with populations ranging between 7 and 10 per cent
of the total population. In the remaining states, SC populations are
numerically marginal, and lower crime rates are recorded.[6]

Among states where the SC population ranges between 7 and
10 per cent of the total population, such as Assam (6.9 per cent),
Maharashtra (10 per cent), Kerala (9.8 per cent), and Gujarat
(7.1 per cent), Gujarat records the highest number of crimes registered under the POA.

Table 10.1 Records of crimes against SCs registered under the POA Act, 1989, in states where SCs make up 7–10 per cent of the total population

Year	State	SC population: in lakh as per 2001 census and as a percentage of the total population	Number of cases registered under the POA Act, 1989, per state	Total number of cases registered in India under the POA Act, 1989	Number of cases registered per lakh population as per 2001 census
2001	Gujarat	36.0 (7.1)	446	14,758	12.20
	Maharashtra	98.8 (10.3)	187	14,758	1.89
	Kerala	31.2 (9.8)	135	14,758	4.32
	Assam	18.3 (6.9)	N/A	14,758	N/A
2002	Gujarat	36.0 (7.1)	1192	26,177	33.11
	Maharashtra	98.8 (10.3)	812	26,177	8.21
	Kerala	31.2 (9.8)	469	26,177	15.03
	Assam	18.3 (6.9)	N/A	26,177	N/A
2003	Gujarat	36.0 (7.1)	1056	20,290	29.33
	Maharashtra	98.8 (10.3)	870	20,290	8.80
	Kerala	31.2 (9.8)	335	20,290	10.73
	Assam	18.3 (6.9)	N/A	20,290	N/A

Table 10.1 (Continued)

Year	State	SC population: in lakh as per 2001 census and as a percentage of the total population	Number of cases registered under the POA Act, 1989, per state	Total number of cases registered in India under the POA Act, 1989	Number of cases registered per lakh population as per 2001 census
2006	Gujarat	36.0 (7.1)	991	26,665	27.60
	Maharashtra	98.8 (10.3)	1017	26,665	10.30
	Kerala	31.2 (9.8)	364	26,665	11.65
	Assam	18.3 (6.9)	282	26,665	15.45
2007	Gujarat	36.0 (7.1)	1038	29,825	28.80
	Maharashtra	98.8 (10.3)	1146	29,825	11.60
	Kerala	31.2 (9.8)	477	29,825	15.30
	Assam	18.3 (6.9)	125	29,825	6.80
2008	Gujarat	36.0 (7.1)	1228	33,367	34.10
	Maharashtra	98.8 (10.3)	1172	33,367	11.90
	Kerala	31.2 (9.8)	519	33,367	16.60
	Assam	18.3 (6.9)	104	33,367	5.70
2009	Gujarat	36.0 (7.1)	1180	33,426	32.80
	Maharashtra	98.8 (10.3)	1072	33,426	10.80
	Kerala	31.2 (9.8)	467	33,426	14.90
	Assam	18.3 (6.9)	0.0	33,426	0.00

2010	Gujarat	36.0 (7.1)	1008	32,569	28.00
	Maharashtra	98.8 (10.3)	1107	32,569	11.20
	Kerala	31.2 (9.8)	583	32,569	18.70
	Assam	18.3 (6.9)	7	32,569	0.40
2011	Gujarat			33,719	
	Maharashtra				
	Kerala				
	Assam				

Source: Data compiled from the Annual Report of the National Commission for Scheduled Castes (2004–5); 2006–10 reports filed under Section 21(4) of the Scheduled Castes and the Scheduled Tribes (Prevention of Atrocities) Act, 1989, Ministry of Social Justice and Empowerment, Government of India; 2011 records from the National Crimes Records Bureau. Crime figures for Uttar Pradesh are available up to September 2003. Uttaranchal figures exclude the quarter ending June 2002. No data is available for Assam for years 2001–3.

These results are striking for several reasons. We find that, on average, the number of cases registered per lakh (100,000) as per the 2001 census is also high for Kerala. However, this can be explained by the state's record in human development and that it has the highest levels of literacy and social awareness, as these factors strongly correlate with high levels of legal mobilization and legal awareness. Maharashtra has a history of caste riots, but it also has a history of anti-caste discrimination and social movements. In addition, a strong civil society, and several lower caste-based parties (such as the Republican Party of India (RPI) and the Bahujan Samaj Party (BSP) are present in Maharashtra; still, its rate of crime registration is lower than that of Gujarat. Gujarat does not have a history of anti-caste discrimination movements, and lower caste-based parties are not politically significant in state politics. The state has a history of caste violence and caste riots; since the 1990s, Gujarat has been the stronghold of the Bharatiya Janata Party (BJP), a Hindu nationalist party. The BJP has converted anti-caste violence into anti-Muslim violence (Shani 2007) and has selectively appeased lower castes while continuing to pursue a rigid vision of a caste-differentiated society. Nonetheless, Gujarat demonstrates higher levels of crime registration under the POA.

An alternate explanation for the data,[8] and more frequent mobilization of the POA in Gujarat, is that the effectiveness of judicial redress results in higher conviction rates under the POA. Table 10.2 outlines the disposal rates of crimes against Dalits in state courts. Although only about 15 to 20 per cent of total cases pending before the judicial system result in final outcomes (as pendency rates are high), the nationwide conviction rate under the POA has decreased from 34.1 per cent in 2001 to about 29.6 per cent in 2010.

Gujarat has the lowest conviction rate of crimes against Dalits and Uttar Pradesh has the highest. Also, the conviction rate is much lower in Gujarat than it is nationally. Final judicial decisions are the outcome in 11.3 per cent of cases (Annual Report of the NCSC 2004, 240–2). The rate of conviction in Gujarat was 3.7 per cent in 2001 and 6.3 per cent in 2009. Anecdotal evidence from Gujarat also supports this trend.[9]

These data raise the following question: what explains the high rate of mobilization of the POA Act in Gujarat despite the area's

Table 10.2 Disposal of Cases of Crimes against SCs and STs before the Courts, 2001–9

State	SC population as percentage of total population	Conviction rates in IPC (Indian Penal Code) cases			Conviction rates in special cases		
		2001	2005	2009	2001	2005	2009
Uttar Pradesh	21.1	54.9	58.6	54.0	49.2	49.6	52.4
Gujarat	7.1	24.7	30.9	41.1	3.7	3.9	6.3
Maharashtra	10.2	13.1	11.7	9.6	1.8	5.9	6.5
Kerala	9.8	50.0	51.2	57.1	4.8	13.9	9.9
India	16.2	40.8	42.4	41.7	34.1	29.8	29.6

Source: Data adapted from Ramaiah (2011: 161).

low rate of convictions? Drawing upon the idea that the political environment shapes legal and social policy outcomes, I suggest that given the rise of Hindu rights in Gujarat in the aftermath of caste-based violence and its capture of state power since 1995, the political context of Gujarat has constrained Dalit rights organizations' ability to bring about radical social change and limited their mass appeal on many issues. In response, most organizations working on Dalit rights have increasingly turned to the law to safeguard and advance Dalit rights; they have specially focused on the implementation of laws penalizing caste violence on the ground and have integrated national and international human rights norms into their discourses and strategies. Their efforts have increased rights consciousness and Dalit assertiveness and resulted in piecemeal and ad hoc processes of change, but they have failed to realize the transformative potential of embedding human rights values in the realm of the state and society.

Outlining Political Developments in Gujarat and the Context of Caste and Hindutva Politics[10]

During the independence movement, Gujarat was a stronghold of nationalist politics. Lower-caste groups and Adivasis adversely affected by the taxation policies of the British government mobilized in support of the nationalist movement, but were not meaningfully integrated into the leadership or organization of the Indian National Congress (or Congress party) (Hardiman 1981). The support for the Gujarati nationalist movement came mainly from upper and middle castes, especially Patidars, Brahmins, and Baniyas. Congress strong-man Sardar Patel, who led nationalist campaigns in Gujarat, kept alive the idea of a strong, united, masculine, military nation as an ideal—a nationalist ideal—that was appropriated later by the Hindu right-wing BJP (Bharatiya Janta Party) and its affiliates, together known as the Sangh Parivar.[11] Following independence, the Congress Party in Gujarat was led by upper-caste groups, and it maintained ties with Hindu revivalist organizations such as the Arya Samaj. It also maintained policies such as land reforms in Saurashtra under the slo-gan 'land to the tiller', which redistributed land to Patel peasants, not to Dalit landless labourers, and did not challenge caste politics. Patel peasants emerged as successful economic players in Gujarat politics.

In 1967, the Gujarat Congress Party split; the conservative fac-tion, the Morarji Desai-led Congress entered into an alliance with the Hindu right-wing Jana Sangh party (the predecessor of the BJP). Politically excluded groups, Dalits, and Adivasis, many of whom were first-generation recipients of the Indian state's reservation policy for the advancement of SCs and STs, had begun to mobilize during this time. The early 1970s saw the beginning of the deinstitution-alization of the Congress Party at the national level; Indira Gandhi began concentrating power in the party, side-lining regional leaders who might challenge her power, and expanding the social support base of the party with the slogan 'remove poverty'. In Gujarat, as a result of national deinstitutionalization, the Congress party under Madhavsinh Solanki stitched together an electoral alliance popularly referred to as KHAM (backward castes, religious minorities, and Dalits and Adivasis), and began to field electoral candidates from these groups; their numbers rose from 38.7 per cent of candidates in 1967 to 68.6 per cent in the 1980 Legislative Assembly election. These groups also began to dominate state patronage driven public-sector undertakings and government boards (Sheth 1999).

The upper castes responded violently to the perceived loss of polit-ical power, economic patronage, and social dominance, and turned to the political outfits of the Hindu right. In 1981 and 1985, the Congress-led government's proposal to implement reservations in educational posts for economically and socially backward castes was met with anti-lower-caste violence in Ahmedabad and other administrative units of the state. The purpose of the upper-caste violence was to oust the Congress government, which was led by lower castes, Adivasis, and Muslims. The violence subsided only when the Chief Minister was forced to resign. This moment marked the demobilization of Dalit politics in Gujarat: the countermovement affected the Dalit and Adivasi state employees' unions, the nascent Dalit Panther,[12] and textile workers' unions. In 1986, the Dalit and non-Dalit youth activists working with the Behavioural Science Centre and unionizing bonded landless labourers in Golana (a village in north Gujarat) were fired at by upper-caste strongmen. Four workers were killed, eighteen were injured, and Dalit houses were burnt. The youth activists realized that both routine and retributive violence were actively used to weaken Dalit movements. They pursued upper-caste landlords in the Supreme Court for thirteen years and placed the legal enforcement of anti-caste discrimination legislation high on the agenda of Dalit emancipatory politics.[13] India opted for economic liberalization in 1993; since then, civil society organizations have multiplied and some of the politicized Dalit activists have formed and worked for NGOs. Currently, some of the largest NGOs working on Dalit human rights at local and international levels, such as Navsarjan Trust and Janvikas, are headed by activists who share this history.

Throughout the 1990s, in the aftermath of caste riots and to prevent the loss of power, the upper castes turned to the Sangh Parivar, which realized that the numerical strength of the upper castes was not sufficient for electoral victory. However, in keeping with its ideology of building a Hindu nation, the Sangh Parivar began to promote an alternative socio-political alliance that stressed Hindu unity, attempting to bring Dalits and Adivasis into its fold and demonizing the Muslim as 'the other'. The deinstitutionalization of the Congress Party, the absence of strong leftist politics, the rise of an aspirational upper caste and middle class that aligned with the Hindu right, and the closure of Gujarat's textile mills (which provided a political base for solidarity between Muslim and lower-caste workers in unions) further eroded these groups' solidarity. The BJP and its affiliates also attempted to include these groups by providing social services; by opening schools, hostels, medical clinics, and forest dwellers' organizations in tribal areas; by training its youths to uplift the lower caste, prevent religious conversions, and carry out *shuddhi* (purification) programmes for converted Tribals (including Dalits and Adivasis who act as foot soldiers in the BJP's ideological programmes); and by directing public violence against Muslims rather than Dalits; thus breaking the solidarity between lower-caste, Adivasi, and Muslim groups (Shani 2007; Sud 2007). Between 1990 and 1995, in unstable coalition governments, the BJP intermittently ruled the state. And in 1995, it came to power. The strategy of orchestrating public violence against minorities, especially Muslims and Christians, for electoral gains was used in Gujarat in 1998. In 2002–3,[14] when the police failed to prevent such violence and conduct arrests, government prosecutors intimidated and bought off witnesses, state ministers led rioting mobs and exhorted people to loot, murder, and burn, and local media fuelled rumours of mythical counter-attacks by Muslims. Some of the Dalits and Adivasis, targets of violence in the 1980s, now participated in anti-Muslim violence, affirming in some ways the success of the BJP's strategy of Hindu unity.

The assimilation of lower-caste groups into the Hindu identity by the Hindu right is an unfinished, uneven, and internally inconsistent project of Hinduization, involving 'contestation and construction' and a desire to include Dalits in the Hindu project, all the while maintaining upper-caste hegemony of the state and society (Sud 2007).[15] Being in government has enabled the Hindu right to build a popular consensus around exclusionary politics and to unevenly channel the benefits of public goods and services to some Dalit sub-castes, leaving out more vulnerable sub-castes among Dalits (Sud 2007). Dalit politics in Gujarat face different challenges: while some sections of Dalits have benefitted from state patronage, the state's neo-liberal policies have prevented the entry of Dalits into the public sector as jobs are no longer filled, but rather contracted. As a result, Dalits' access to employment in the public sector has been blocked. Economic liberalization in Gujarat has also strengthened the economic clout of dominant castes and adversely affected the urban and rural poor; routine civic life for many Dalits and Adivasis is marked by caste-based segregation and discrimination as well as private violence against Dalits. In other words, the success of the Hindu right's project has strengthened upper-caste dominance and the Hindu right's militant authoritarianism on the ground has narrowed the scope for Dalit protest and opposition, weakened the resistance against caste-based and communal violence, and politically co-opted and fragmented Dalit and backward caste groups.

As a result, a new kind of Dalit politics emerged in the 1990s. Three trends characterize it: a re-routing to and containment within the cultural sphere (especially through the promotion of Dalit litera-ture),[16] a shift from Dalit movements to NGOs and 'NGOization', and the use of courts to address issues ranging from routine gover-nance to social justice. Dalit groups are constrained by the political manoeuvres of the Hindu right and the lack of a mass base, similar to many other rights-based NGOs that also emerged in Gujarat in the 1990s.[17] In this chapter, I focus on the programmes of Navsarjan Trust, as it is one of the largest organizations working on Dalit rights in Gujarat, and it was established and staffed by Dalit workers. In addition, it sees legal mobilization and legal advocacy as central to addressing caste violence.

The POA and the Question of the State

Studies[18] point to a lack of political will and institutional short-comings when explaining low rates of conviction in atrocity cases. Activists[19] suggest that there is little political and social support for government interventions to reduce caste inequality and there is much resistance to policies that may actually help reduce caste inequality. Institutional factors—delays in framing charges and police investiga-tions, incomplete investigations, perjury in court, police and judicial bias exercised through discretion, compromises between the parties, the prevalence of bonded labour, and the economic dependence of Dalits on perpetrators of violence—also explain the low conviction rates in cases of caste violence (National Coalition for Strengthening SC & ST POA Act, 2010).[20] The following sections discuss these political and institutional factors.

The POA in the Police *Chowky* (Station House) and NGO Activism

Scholars have argued that while the law has the capacity for symbolic change by communicating positions on ideological issues and shaping values, its instrumental effects are evident when legislation and court rulings affect the behaviour of citizens, officials, and organizations (Rosenberg 1991). Scholars have also focused on changes in police behaviour—reporting, investigations, and arrests—as they impact convictions (Goldstein 1977). In the Indian context, studies and reports show that high rates of acquittal in POA cases are due to loopholes in police investigation. The police harass and detain Dalit members who file cases, force the parties to compromise, refuse to record the case, ask for bribes to register and investigate a case, refuse to apply the relevant act, conduct incomplete and shoddy investigations, and fail to act as per the law. Police are also pressured in politically sensitive cases and often collude with political bosses to dilute cases. Documents are often forged, post-mortem reports or DNA tests can be falsified or go missing; corruption is an everyday part of the legal process. Local police stations are often staffed by police officers who, embedded in social ties, safeguard the interests of their own castes. Police officers also tend to implicate vocal Dalit activists in criminal cases.[21] Direct and indirect caste discrimination colours the attitude of the police and often results in converting POA cases into private vendettas. Even when Dalit respondents manage to overcome internal conflicts and hurdles to legal action, they may face hostility from within the state judicial machinery, which can respond with coercion and its own rhetorical, political, and legal arsenal. As Raju Solanki, an activist with the Council for Social Justice, suggests:

> Casteism is all-pervasive. It shows itself in the way in which the legal machinery thinks of the Atrocity Act.... All progressive legislation in India is derided, referred to as the misuse of law. In most cases, the police call the POA an extortion law—implying that Dalits use this law to force forward castes to attempt a compromise and offer money in exchange for dropping the case by turning hostile in court.[22]

Besides, the state government also maintains vigilance over the registration of crimes under the POA and controls crime registration in order to maintain its political agenda of assimilative and authoritarian forms of Hindu unity.[23]

How do state-level Dalit human rights groups respond to the judicial and administrative machineries' unresponsiveness? Dalit organizations pursue a rights-based approach to legal mobilization and institutional reform, and prioritize accessibility, including access to legal processes, institutions, information, and redress or complaints mechanisms. Their intervention in a large number of disputes and a cross-pollination of ideas across platforms enables them to generate expertise. To cite just one example, Navsarjan has offices in many districts of Gujarat and monitors crimes against Dalits. Local newspapers report atrocity cases and Navsarjan workers initiate contact with families if they hear that no crime has been registered. In Navsarjan's field offices, victims' families can approach civil society organizations. The activists monitor cases and hold local public meetings, where they list aloud cases that remain under investigation. They monitor the implementation of POA provisions, insist on a senior police officer's presence while registering a crime to prevent corruption, ensure proper investigation, and hold the police accountable. They actively resist the state's human rights violations and torture while in custody. For instance, a young Dalit man, picked up under suspicion of burglary, died while in police custody. His family suspected torture. The police attempted to hand over the body to the family after the post-mortem report exonerated the police. Navsarjan activists, along with the victim's family, insisted on an official inquiry, sat outside the police station in an overnight public demonstration, and refused to leave the police station with the body until an inquiry had been initiated.

Group mobilization is another strategy. In Sayla Taluka, in the Surendranagar district of Gujarat, Anil, a Dalit man who had served in the military, built his house at the outskirts of the Dalit *mohalla*, the segregated area where Dalits lived. His house, near the panchayat office, was as big as the houses of dominant castes, and he was often derided as an upstart keen to challenge upper-caste dominance. Unlike some of the village's Dalits who worked as agricultural labourers in the fields of upper castes, he had a 'government' job with a pension; hence, he could not be harassed through economic boycott. From the balcony of the panchayat office, some local village youths routinely sexually harassed Dalit girls who walked past the building: whistling, using derogatory language, and attempting to molest them. Anil,[24] who was working in his house one morning, reprimanded the local youths. That afternoon, the local youths shot him dead in retaliation. In the aftermath of the shooting, Dalits in the village feared that violence targeting other Dalits may continue and that the case may be treated as one of private vendetta, rather than one of caste violence motivated by caste prejudice. Dalits in Sayla Taluka approached the Dalit rights organization Navsarjan.

On 13 April, the organization planned a big rally. The Dalit community took care of the food and organized a *mandap* for public meeting. Navsarjan distributed pamphlets in all the district's villages that highlighted the facts of the incident and explained the Atrocity Act. Some upper-caste leaders of the village declared that Dalit peoples would face severe retributive violence if the public meeting went ahead (*Bhega thaya to mari nakhshu*). The police were informed of this development.

On the day of the public meeting, Dalit people (including a large number of Dalit women) and other supporters began arriving in the thousands. The organizers were aware of the possibility of 'tension'; the police officials had spoken to the organizers and warned them that a curfew might be declared if any violence occurred during this meeting. The village was divided across caste lines and, in this instance, the Other Backward Classes (OBCs) living in the village decided to support the Dalit mobilization and joined the rally. Political leaders got news of the public meeting, and Dinesh Parmar, an ex-MLA (Member of Legislative Assembly) of the Congress party, attended the rally and declared political support. The Rajkot-based BJP MLA also attended the public meeting. On the day of the meeting, Anil's wife addressed the meeting and narrated the sequence of events that had led to Anil's death. She also gave context to the crime and narrated earlier incidents of caste prejudice. Anil's economic advancement was seen as a challenge, and he had been threatened several times for not deferring to the power of upper castes. Prominent local Dalit leaders and members also spoke of practices of untouchability prevalent in the area, cited other recent cases of atrocities against Dalits in Gujarat, and gave information about the Atrocity Act. Dalit leaders and organizers distributed literature on laws and public schemes for Dalits and on Dr Ambedkar's views on the elimination of caste prejudice; they also provided information about the legal procedures for filing cases under the POA and shared details about the activities of the National Campaign on Dalit Human Rights. Such meetings serve many purposes: they send a message of Dalit organization to dominant castes, prevent backlash, generate media interest to publicize the incident and related issues, assure other Dalits of political support, spread legal awareness, shape legal consciousness, and send a message to political parties to rein in elites who threaten violence.

The POA in Courts: Some Glimpses into NGO Interaction with the Judicial System

Dalit activists and organizations have evolved successful counter-tactics against these obstacles, which has led to a greater understanding of the law and political, administrative, and judicial processes. The judicial system offers many challenges as well, and activists attempt to challenge and check judicial immunization, minimize judicial discretion, and implement accountability. However, the Hindu rights ideology has also captured state institutions, and lawyers and activists suggest that about three-fourths of Gujarat's higher judiciary share the ideology of the Hindu right.[25] In addition, personal and political connections between judges, police, and dominant elites often result in the subversion of justice. In a well-publicized case of six teachers' gang rape of a minor girl from a deprived and vulnerable background, two of the teachers were known to have political connections with rival political parties, and one of the teachers was the nephew of a state minister. The director of Navsarjan, Manjula Pradeep, who intervened in the case and helped the girl through counselling and the legal process, consistently had to ward off 'political requests' to accommodate the nephew of the minister. If the girl's father accepted money, a witness would lie during the trial, and the case would be dismissed due to the lack of evidence. However, Navsarjan resisted the pressure, and the girl, assured by the organization's support, refused to compromise. The accused were convicted in the district court.

NGOs help to prepare witnesses for trial, ensure and track media coverage, provide legal research, and deal with police pressure and touts wishing to mediate between parties, violence and backlash, and political interests. Frequently, the victims are defended by state-appointed prosecutors, who often are unprepared, uninterested, and do not meet their clients; cases fall through because of legal technicalities. 'In many cases, the perpetrators are acquitted because the prosecutor does not even cross-examine the accused.'[26] In one case, a presiding judge made casteist comments informally to the victim, and the organization filed a complaint and succeeded in effecting the transfer of the presiding judge. NGOs such as Navsarjan maintain a list of lawyers who can step up at such times and take over the case. Dalit organizations file applications to change the prosecutor and to appoint special prosecutors under the POA. Given that conviction rates are low, Dalit groups often organize informal public hearings where victims can describe in public their experiences with the judicial system. Juries consisting of prominent citizens, human rights activists, police officials, retired judges, and Dalit intellectuals are appointed. The judges presiding over the informal hearings and testimonies analyse the cases, highlight the lack of implementation of the POA, and offer a set of recommendations for the government.[27] These exercises are also routinely carried out in Gujarat districts and at the state level.

The Dominant Elites and the POA

In the context of the POA, mobilization of the law is likely to produce coercion from the state and counter-mobilization from the entrenched elites. The elites resist by using private violence or accessing state officials, power, and money. Despite the myth of misuse of the POA, not all cases of atrocities are even reported by Dalits. From the standpoint of litigants, filing cases under this act is often costly, lengthy, and cumbersome; bargaining between parties often occurs before and after the court has ruled; and initiation of a legal case, or even the resolution of disputes, does not necessarily eliminate private violence, but rather can exacerbate it under certain conditions, deflecting from legal action. In many atrocity-prone districts of Gujarat, Navsarjan has formed human rights committees comprising eminent social workers, judges, public servants, and educationists, largely from Dalit, but also from other communities.

These committees speak to civic associations in the area and spread awareness through social networks. They represent Dalit interests in cases filed under the Atrocity Act and advise local people on how to access legal aid. For instance, they meet with the police officials who refuse to register cases and follow up on legal complaints and filings. To the families of victims, they offer legal and other advice, referrals to other resources like medical facilities, and assistance in accessing legal aid and the compensation that is due to them.

The government of Gujarat denied the prevalence of incidents of the social boycotting of Dalits until 2006, when grassroots activists forced this issue into the open. In the Anand district of the village of Sojira, the president of the *gram panchayat*, the *sarpanch*,[28] was a Dalit. The village's panchayat office was rented out regularly for social events, but Dalits had never succeeded in doing so. When the Dalit sarpanch went to book the hall for his daughter's wedding, he was denied permission on the grounds of untouchability. The Dalit sarpanch filed a case under the Atrocity Act for practices of untouchability. The village panch decided to announce in public the social boycott of Dalits (*saad padavyo*). The Dalits in the village, facing the brunt of this boycott, contacted Dalit human rights organizations; but in the end, the village's factions decided to compromise, as the Dalits could not live with the hardships. The size of the village's Dalit population, the political clout of different communities, the social and economic ties between different social groups in the village, and the terms of the negotiation affected whether or not the dispute was fought until the very end. See the following illustrations from cases registered at Navsarjan:

> The whole village gathered and they announced the boycott over [the] loud speaker. We could hear everything from here. They said that *dheda*[29] are against development and that we have to give them punishment.... If any dheda points at us, we will cut off their fingers. If they speak to us, we will cut off their tongues. It went like this from 9 p.m. till 11 p.m. We made a call to the Chuda police station but they said that no one was available.... At the end of the meeting, they sounded the drum.[30]
>
> Social boycott has enormous consequences. Dalit families would be forced to go to the next village or even further, if nearby villages also joined in the social boycott, to get milk for children or to even

buy salt; daily labourers would have to migrate as they would not be hired by their employers in the village, sick Dalit children would not be able to reach the hospital as no one will drive them there. And the threat of violence to the group would always loom large.[31]

At times, Dalits are forced to migrate in large numbers, with their cattle, and camp in the district collector's office, abandoning their properties, fields, crops, to ask for resettlement as they feared for their lives in the village.[32]

Navsarjan conducted a study and identified 17 current cases of social boycott (Paleaz n.d.). The organization publicized the results through the media. They wrote letters to the National Commission for Scheduled Castes, the National Commission for Scheduled Tribes, the regional office of the SC Commission in Ahmedabad, the Chief Minister, MLAs, and the national and state human rights commissions. The government of Gujarat was forced to acknowledge this in its 2006 annual report to the federal Ministry of Social Justice and Empowerment.

While legal mobilization is a focal point of Dalit groups' strategies, these groups also attempt to address social and political exclusion, taking into account Dalits' lack of representation in economic development, position in the caste hierarchy, limited access to basic goods such as health and education, and the effect of all these factors on legal mobilization. Recognizing the power of social and economic dominance in perpetuating caste dominance and inequality, Navsarjan and other organizations offer employment training to Dalit youths, encourage them to leave traditional caste occupations, help foster an entrepreneurial spirit, and mobilize around the state government's failure to distribute federal funds to Dalit and Adivasi students.[33] To increase children's access to educational opportunities, local NGOs have established revolving libraries, children's rights groups, and residential schools for Dalit children. However, the scale of these interventions does not compare with the scale of the state's non-intervention. The government of Gujarat, for instance, fails to distribute federal grants to students from Dalit, Adivasi, and Muslim groups.[34] These organizations have initiated campaigns for the implementation of government schemes to recognize and distribute land, conducted campaigns for minimum wages, and made visible crimes against Dalit women.

NGO support encourages legal mobilization among Dalits and Adivasis. For many litigants, to even engage with the state's legal system involves acquiring the legal language and learning to navigate the legal system, despite the fact that the legal system may not return a favourable decision, and retributive violence may accompany legal mobilization. Participants in the dispute often become informal political entrepreneurs, replicating and using elsewhere their new legal knowledge, strategies, and experience. They share legal strategies, skills, and documents with others; they create connections (*olkhan*) with legal, state, and political actors, which might be useful in other contexts; and their aspirations change as they become aware of new possibilities. These enterprising litigants may become frequent users of the legal system and, thus, pursue their cases in legal arenas. Many of litigants also volunteer with local Dalit rights groups or participate in other activities.

It is argued that any legislation or intervention addressing racial discrimination must be multifaceted and must operate at multiple levels to address individual and structural discrimination. Because attempts to change discrimination must address the root cause of stigma and limit the power of dominant groups to shape cognitive frames, narrowly conceived interventions will fail to change contextual factors (Link and Phelan 2001). Marc Galanter, who followed the Untouchability Offenses Act, and later the PCR between 1950 and 1980 in India, highlighted that these laws were underutilized despite high levels of awareness of these Acts among Dalits. Conceding the role of institutional factors in the poor implementation of these Acts, he suggested that an increase in the strength of public-spirited lawyers (especially Dalit lawyers), enhancement in the scale and quality of legal services, and the emergence of civil rights organizations specializing in litigation would lead to effective implementation and, subsequently, high mobilization of these laws (Galanter 1989). For Galanter, the latter factor was important; he especially noted the role of the Harijan Sevak Sangh in mobilizing and supporting cases at the grass-roots level. However, we find that the presence of civil society organizations and cause lawyers on their own have proved inadequate mechanisms for the effective implementation of these laws in practice. In contrast, explaining the success of the POA in Uttar Pradesh, several reports point out that Uttar Pradesh, where SCs make up

21.7 per cent of the population, records the highest number of cases under the POA, even when compared to other states with similar concentrations of SC population.[35] In Uttar Pradesh, governing parties such as the BSP are ethnic parties with extensive lower-caste mass appeal and base, and the BSP has made the strict implementation of the POA Act one of its priorities. The party has backed up this legislation by implementing job quotas and distributing land to its core constituency of *Chamar* voters, not as patronage granted to co-ethnics, but as fulfilling a programmatic agenda. However, realizing that the 'character of the state' needed to change in order to implement the POA, the BSP attempted to 'forge a subaltern-friendly state' by disciplining the bureaucracy through the use and threat of transfer. Once in power, the BSP transferred 62 Indian Administrative Service (IAS) and 105 Indian Police Service (IPS) officers. The scale of transfer was greater during the BSP's second round in office (Guha 2009: 97–8). Thus, the BSP succeeded in neutralizing entrenched bureaucratic resistance and installed its own favoured bureaucrats to implement its key policies, including the effective implementation of the POA; the result is evident in the data.

In contrast to the situation in Uttar Pradesh, this chapter demonstrates that Dalit human rights groups in Gujarat have used the law, court arena, and adjudication process as a productive encounter between the state, social organizations, individuals, and groups. They have used the adjudication process not only to provide Dalit individuals with protection and legal access, but also to spread human rights norms and to demand that local police and court officials enforce accountability. Groups in Gujarat have sidestepped the state and its limited response by spurring national campaigns to reform and implement the POA Act. However, the chapter also points to the structural factors limiting the potential of this strategy. Dalit organizations are successful in ensuring legal awareness and supporting legal mobilization, but are constrained by the nature of the state and the political field. The gains made through civil society activism, such as state accountability and increased legal awareness and mobilization, are ad hoc; institutional transformation proves to be elusive.

The next section, outlining women's legal consciousness, offers a potential route towards thinking about the possibility of breaking this deadlock experienced by civil society, for these women activists offer a glimpse of what James C. Scott calls 'a "shadow history" which remains to be written for political action, for this experienced history often contains many little traditions' with sub-strata of different values which offer 'a pattern of profanations—symbolic reversals of the existing social order'. (Scott 1977).

The Many Avatars of the Atrocity Act

This section of the paper focuses on the political agency of Dalit women and demonstrates how Dalit women's rights committees, through their interventions, have used the Atrocity Act (1989) and, in doing so, have broadened the human rights approach from a legalistic approach to a developmental enterprise. They effected this change by establishing conceptual links between human rights and different conceptions of poverty and development and between law, social hierarchies, and social policies; in doing so, they have challenged the capture of the public distribution system and public policies by the elites and dominant castes, demanded accountability from state administrations, and offered different routes to challenge caste discrimination.

Literature on Dalit women's rights has highlighted women's oppression at the intersection of caste, class, and gender. However, recent studies, especially those on the political participation of Dalit women, highlight their agency in processes of political mobilization and social change (Ciotti 2012). Focusing on the Dalit and Bahujan women activists' role in the BSP and leadership in Uttar Pradesh, Manuela Ciotti presents a counter-image to the portrayal of Dalit women as victims of untouchability and violence—one of claim-makers stressing the politics of difference (Pandey 2006). She demonstrates how lower-rung women BSP leaders have recast the notion of *seva*, or service, often associated with upper-caste notions of charity, to negotiate contemporary politics; in doing so, these women have often acted as legal and political entrepreneurs (Krishna 2003), linking the poor with state agencies, politicians, and bureaucrats. In addition, Ciotti suggests that based on upward class mobility, women's agency is not reducible to unproblematic versions of sanskritization; to a mimicry of women's activism in India; or to an ethically driven, emancipatory Dalit project from the standpoint of the oppressed. Rather, their agency is rooted in and constrained by contemporary Indian party politics, economic policies, statecraft, the upward class mobility of sections of Dalits, and developmental practices. In a similar vein, this paper highlights the agency of Dalit women's groups associated with NGOs to link law, social policies, and human rights approaches.

In a different body of literature, one touching on legal consciousness, Sally Merry argues that human rights are transplanted on the ground through rights-based social services and human rights activities. Discussing the processes of localizing transnational knowledge of human rights (Merry 2006: 179), Merry demonstrates how the appropriation of human rights in vernacular contexts allows individuals to enrich and add to their perception of injustice and to demand accountability from the state for injury to this rights-conscious self. In a similar vein, Marc Galanter (1983), drawing on Clifford Geertz, has argued that law should be seen 'as a symbol of legal and cultural meanings…[that] affects us primarily through communication of symbols—by providing threats, promises, models, persuasion, legitimacy, stigma and so on'. (Galanter 1983: 127). While citizens' experiences of law and legal institutions shape how they perceive the law, citizens can also stretch the boundaries of legal knowledge and widen their frame, using law in society. Merry, in *Getting Justice and Getting Even: Legal Consciousness among Working Class Americans*, argues that law 'consists of a complex repertoires of meanings and categories understood differently by people depending on their experience with and knowledge of law. The law looks different for example, to law professors, tax evaders, welfare recipients, blue collar homeowners and burglars'. (Merry 1990: 5). Looking at the communication pattern of Dalit women's human rights groups, we find how the promises of the Atrocity Act influenced rights consciousness and contributed to citizenship practices and political participation.

Many NGOs working on Dalit rights in Gujarat have facilitated women's rights committees, some comprising exclusively Dalit women, others crossing caste lines. These committees began as an initiative of Dalit women who were socially active in their villages; some had received paralegal training from NGOs, some had attended meetings on aspects of *panchayati raj*, and others had accompanied their relatives or friends to NGO offices to address legal issues. Many such women initially came together to address issues of governance in their residential areas and then expanded the scope of their work. They often meet twice or thrice a week, in visible public spaces in the village.

The women's rights groups of Dalit women associated with NGOs in Gujarat act as doorstep courts and political entrepreneurs, and adjudicate, or at times arbitrate, in cases pertaining to women:

> The fact that a group of Dalit women can sit in the middle of the village and decide on disputes in itself has a powerful impact on the politics of exclusion in the village. Initially we had taken up issues concerning Dalits—we had conducted a survey of our areas and identified problems of lack of water, inadequate sewage facilities, and approached the panchayat to solve these issues. We also act as a go between; women come to us if they need to obtain BPL [below poverty line] cards, or if they need to get caste certificates; often they don't know which government offices to go to and we help them. Recently, many *sarpanch* have been coming to us. In the village school next door, a schoolgirl was raped by her teacher. The *sarpanch* was a Dalit and he knew about our work and asked us to help. We took up the issue—we were with the family and insisted on her medical check-up and treatment and worked with the police to register the case. Now village *sarpanchs* from other areas also approach us or refer to us similar cases of crimes against women and domestic disputes.[36]

The Lack of Access to Public Goods is Injustice Under the Atrocity Act

A letter addressed to the National Human Rights Commission (NHRC) on 28 March 2010 reads as follows:

> We are part of the Dalit Women's Rights Committee functioning from five villages of the Chotila block of Surendranagar district in Gujarat. We want to bring to your attention that Dalits are denied access to water in 150 villages of Gujarat due to caste discrimination in violation of Articles 14, 15, 17 and 21 of the Indian constitution. In our villages, Dalit areas do not have *pukka* [paved] roads. We do not have our own burial grounds and are not allowed to use

cremation grounds of the dominant castes in violation of the Atrocity Act, 1989. We request you to follow up with the Government of Gujarat to address these violations of Dalit human rights in Gujarat.

Addressed to the National Commission for Scheduled Castes, the Chief Minister, and the Gujarat Home Minister on 9 April 2011, another letter raises a similar set of issues:

In August 2010, Dalits holding BPL cards were granted free plots of land in the *Gareeb Kalyan Mela* [Social Welfare Gathering] by the Government of Gujarat. Seven families were to be given plots measuring 30 ft by 30 ft to construct houses. We have followed up on the government's announcements with the sarpanch, Block Development Officer, District Development Officer, District Collector, and the Chief Minister's Office. We want to let you know that it has been seven months since this policy was announced and Dalits are under pressure to transfer this land to dominant caste interests for meager sums (*jameen babte daban thayu chhe*). This is a crime under the Atrocity Act, 1989.[37]

Another letter addressed to the Deputy Superintendent of Police, Bhavnagar lists the action required to follow up on recently filed cases under the Atrocity Act (1989) as well as in general cases of crimes against women:

We are writing to ask you about the status of investigation in the following cases of crimes against women and Dalit women in our locality: Rape and murder of a woman named Kokilaben on 7 April 2009; kidnap of 17 yr. old Varshaben on 2 January 2009; severe injury due to domestic violence to Nitaben on 30 May 2009.[38]

The letters demonstrate that Dalit women have found different ways to talk about law, justice, and their associated claims. They see the Atrocity Act as an integrated and cross-cutting element of political participation and development on the ground, rather than just stand-alone legislation. In these letters, we find that the normative ideas of the Atrocity Act become the marker to highlight forms of violence pervading everyday aspects of rural governance and undermining the implementation of social policy. These and similar letters draw attention to the way in which dominant caste groups use violence, intimidation, and discrimination to funnel policy benefits intended for the whole village.

We find here that Dalit women's committees' awareness of legal categories and rules shape the framing of caste-based prejudice and their characterization in public discourse and grievance articulation to the state. Two issues framed women's sense of injustice. The first is the disjuncture between the equal citizenship promised in law and enshrined in the rhetoric of panchayati raj and the intentional distortion of policies in practice due to prevailing caste norms. The second issue is generalized everyday experiences of caste-based exclusion and injustice, which Dalit women challenge by using the ethical frame of the law. An enhanced sense of social citizenship and Dalit identity, a willingness to take action, and political decentralization offer these women space for participatory action. For many women's committees, the law provides the means not only to challenge specific violations of human rights but also to draw attention to political and social norms of caste equality that should accompany governance. Legal mobilization is substituted by proactive legal appeals based on equity, fairness, and the identification of unjusticiable caste violence (that could be justiciable in the future) affecting quality of life.

Women's human rights committees have a fair knowledge of the law and legal systems themselves and of their limitations in the face of social realities. They realize that law in and of itself may have limited effectiveness as an instrument for social change, depending on the context. In a caste-based structure, the law can be ignored with impunity or interpreted with bias. In some correspondence, women make visible the politics of compromise and its social ineffectiveness as well as the role of the police in diluting the promise of the law, thus silencing their grievances; they also stress the importance of state accountability in such matters, as the following complaints to the district officials suggest:

> In the village of Lakshmipura, in the Palanpur district, the street lights were not working, and when we [the women's group] approached the panchayat, we were beaten and told [by the panchayat members] "have you heard of light in your areas?" We had gone to file an atrocity case but the police mediated and worked out a compromise and the case was not filed…. There are ten houses of Dalits and the 500 Rabaris and 100 upper castes in the village and the Dalits saw

no choice but to compromise. However, the lights have yet to be installed and we would like to ask you about the kind of action taken by you in this matter.[39]

Similarly, in another letter, a group of women write:

We are a group of women from Bavla taluka, Dhandhuka district. We are writing to let you know that our human rights are violated. To begin with, we only get water for an hour every day and the water does not reach our area. The pipeline that delivers water to the village is controlled by the sarpanch who is a Rabari [OBC] and he controls the valve. The Dalit residential areas are located at the end of the village and the water reaches there last. If the water valve is switched off earlier, the water does not reach us. This village has always practiced untouchability in matters related to water—we were not allowed to fill water from other wells in the area. The practice of untouchability with respect to access to water is a crime as per the Indian constitution. Such incidents are punishable under the Atrocity Act and we urge you to take into consideration our application and give us justice.... The gram panchayat is caste-ridden and ineffective and Dalit women's names are not included in the final list of beneficiaries living below the poverty line that are eligible for schemes like *Indira Awas*, Widow pension, *Jawahar Rozgar Yojana*, and other schemes that are part of the Integrated Rural Development Programmes. Their names do not figure in the list of names.

The Mahila Adhikar Panch (Women's Rights Council) of Parali village in Limbdi Taluka of Surendranagar district wrote to the President of the Village Council, District Collector, District Health Officer, Primary Health Care Centre, and the Deputy Superintendent of the Police in that area on 18 August 2008:

We want you to know that there are many atrocities against us... sewage water is emptied near the Dalit area and since past few years, we have been sick with malaria, TB, and chikungunya.... We want you to know that the legal minimum wage is Rs 100 a day but we are only paid Rs 40 a day. The dominant castes in the village tell us that starvation is the tactic to break your resistance—we will neither employ you, if you protest, nor will we allow you to go outside the village to look for employment elsewhere (we will break your legs if you venture outside in search of employment—*bahar jasho to tantiya bhangi nakhshu*)...sexual harassment of Dalit women is routine in our village and if we complain, the police come to the village and leave after *chai-pani* [bribes] with the dominant castes. The Atrocity Act is meant to protect us.

In these letters, Dalit women highlight how elites corner the benefits of development resources intended for legitimate development ends and use force, intimidation, and indirect discrimination to implement policies in a way that protect their own interests. The women highlight caste lines' influence on access to goods and services; as their letters suggest, the distribution of public goods is intrinsically tied to social contexts and the Dalits' political and social struggle. The quest for equitable redistribution of overall gains is a political as well as legal imperative. However, accountability deficits at every level continue to prevent the aggregate gains of development from being translated into human well-being for the poorest sectors of society.

Anupama Rao has argued that the legal-bureaucratic recognition of Dalits through legislation such as the POA Act 1989 recodes everyday and symbolic forms of violence against Dalits as 'atrocities' and that such legislation contains the possibilities of emancipation and conflict; for through its regulatory function, law helps 'the subaltern to enter into circuits of political commensurability and into the value regime of being human'. (Rao 2009: 264). At the same time, it marks the Dalit subject as an exceptional, historically marginalized subject, and re-encodes Dalit vulnerability as crucial to Dalit identity. It invites retributive violence from upper castes and cements the boundaries between groups. Thus, for Rao, the foundation of liberal legality, with its emphasis on universality and equality, makes criminal law an inadequate tool to end caste violence (Rao 2009). However, a more generous reading of women's human rights committees demonstrates the possibility of a more transformative vision that goes beyond the law. Women's human rights committee members understand that formal legal mechanisms are important instruments for change; they also suggest that human rights need to be seen as open-ended, flexible, and capable of application in diverse situations and in ways not limited to adjudication in courts and tribunals. While human rights are interpreted in a formal legalistic manner by NGOs that parent these groups, women's rights groups on the ground discuss the ways in which they challenge caste discrimination through demanding societal relations and their work; in doing so, they foreground Dalit women's agency in the process.

As Dinaben Vanakar, the paralegal worker at Navsarjan who initiated women's committees in villages, shared:

> At first we formed a committee and worked with Dalit women.... Soon, women from other caste groups began to come for help. Here is where the issue of untouchability came in, and we had the opportunity to apply the Atrocity Act in our village through our court, not the sarkar's [state] court.... What is the purpose of the Atrocity Act? Ultimately, we want to live in a society where this type of caste violence is eliminated. That is what we achieve through our committee also. In order to challenge the practice, we would offer tea and water to them [referring to caste Hindus who would approach them for help] when they would approach us [to challenge untouchability]... we could see them hesitate, thinking about possible sanctions from other villagers, but then they had come for help form us...most people then would take the tea and water offered by us. Over time, they were forced to confront their practice of untouchability and mingle with us...over time we also began to work with some women from dominant castes.... This idea took off and we now have some mixed women's human rights committees in some villages.[40]

We find here that Dalit human rights NGOs have taken a broad approach to address the symbolic and instrumental aspects of the law: they use an adjudication process as a productive encounter between state and society, thereby demonstrating that the formal legal underpinnings of a rights-based approach intrinsic to the Atrocity Act can assist in challenging discrimination, but that accountability of crimes also needs to be realized through many other avenues and mechanisms, including monitoring, reporting, public debate, and greater citizen participation in public service delivery. These NGOs enjoy a degree of success in engaging with formal legal processes, in ensuring the implementation of the Act, and in generating rights awareness among Dalits, but the efforts and advancements that they produce occur within a broader political context hostile to their core agenda, thus limiting their ability to bring about institutional change. Besides, Dalit groups have failed to revive and conjoin to legal activism that demobilized Dalit movement and to substantively challenge the ideological and material projects of the Hindu right; therefore, legal reforms and interventions have failed to address structural inequality effectively or enduringly. While we find that women's collectives' imaginative use of law opens up new spaces for political action, these spaces are still largely within the frame of access to state and good governance; overall, these strategies have yet to realize a transformative effect on everyday forms of power relations in society.

Notes

1. The literal translation of this term means oppressed, broken. It is a self-referential term to refer to the group seen to fall outside the caste system. The term Scheduled Caste is used to refer to Dalits in official discourse.

2. The Indigenous peoples of India; they are officially referred to as Scheduled Tribes.

3. Articles 17, 23, and 25(2) (b) of the Constitution of India (1950) enjoined the state to provide protective recognition to Scheduled Castes. Article 17 abolishes the practice of untouchability in India. Article 23 prohibits traffic in humans and forced labour. Article 25(2) (b) provides for throwing open Hindu religious institutions of public character to all Hindus, in order to address the social practice of barring Dalits from temple entry. In response, the Parliament of India passed the Untouchability (Offenses) Act, 1955, to give effect to Article 17, and in 1965, it appointed a committee to examine untouchability as well as the economic and educational status of Dalits. The committee submitted its report in 1969, and based on this report the Government of India introduced the Untouchability (Offences) and Amendment and Miscellaneous Provisions Bill in the Lok Sabha in 1972. In 1976, the Protection of Civil Rights Act (PCR), 1955, was introduced as an amendment, making caste discrimination and violence offences punishable by law, and making the eradication of untouchability a statutory duty of state governments. The law was largely ineffective in practice, and Dalit groups across the country called for a more comprehensive and punitive law. As a result, the Scheduled Castes and Scheduled Tribes (Prevention of Atrocity) Act was enacted in 1989, and the rules were framed in 1995.

4. For instance, only 633 cases were recorded nationwide under the PCR in 2002. In Gujarat, under the PCR, 46 cases were recorded in 1998,

37 in 1999, 26 in 2000, and 19 in 2001 (see NCRB, New Delhi, Crime in India annual reports; as cited by the National Commission for Scheduled Castes, First Annual Report 2004–5: 241–2).

5. Population density is an important variable for understanding the mobilization strategy of political parties seeking to organize ethnic groups (Chandra 2004: 15).

6. Annual Report of the National Commission for Scheduled Castes, 2004–5: 241–2.

7. Data unavailable for 2004 and 2005.

8. It may be argued that advances in education and occupational status can explain higher levels of reporting of crimes, but the educational and occupational status of Dalits in Gujarat is lower than that of states that have achieved near universal basic education, such as Kerala, Tamil Nadu, and Himachal Pradesh (National Scheduled Caste Commission Annual report 2004–5: 116). In 2002–3, the drop-out rate of Dalit school children in primary education was 26.6 per cent in Gujarat as opposed to zero per cent in Kerala and 8.6 per cent in Maharashtra; the drop-out rate for Dalit children in high school was 75.5 per cent for Gujarat, 23.6 per cent for Kerala, and 58.7 per cent for Maharashtra (Annual Report of the National Commission for Scheduled Castes, 2004–5: 123).

9. Small-scale studies undertaken by the Navsarjan Trust and the Council for Social Justice in Gujarat report that of the 14,242 cases of atrocities against SCs and STs completing trials in several district sessions courts in Gujarat from 30 January 1990 to 30 July 2007, 91.8 per cent ended in acquittals, 3.9 per cent in compromise, and a mere 2 per cent in convictions (National Coalition for Strengthening SC & ST POA Act 2010: 25).

10. The term *Hindutva* refers to political Hinduism, based on the idea that Indian state and society should be organized according to exclusivist 'Hindu' norms.

11. The Sangh Parivar refers to the BJP and its affiliates, including its ideological nucleus, the Rashtriya Swayam Sevak (RSS) Dal; its religious and proselytizing wing, the Vishwa Hindu Parishad (VHP); its students wing, the Akhil Bharatiya Vidyarthi Parishad (ABVP); and its women's wing, the Rashtriya Sevika Samiti (National Service Committee).

12. Interview with Raju Solanki, Council for Social Justice. 19 June 2008. Ahmedabad.

13. Interview with Martin Macwan, Founder, Navsarjan. 10 August 2012. Ahmedabad.

14. On 27 February 2002, a train car carrying a number of Hindu nationalist activists was burned during the halt at the Godhra station

in Gujarat. Fifty-seven Hindu nationalist activists died in the fire. These activists were returning from a popular agitation to build a temple at a site in Ayodhya, north India, where a 400-year-old mosque, Babri Masjid, was illegally burned down by Hindu right-wing mobs in 1992. The Hindu right interpreted the incident at Godhra as Muslim provocation. The train-burning triggered three days of retaliatory attacks on Muslims in Gujarat, killing more than 2,000 Muslims and displacing thousands more; the state administration was complicit in the attack (Narula 2003).

15. Valjibhai Patel, a prominent Dalit activist who was part of the Dalit Panthers in Gujarat explains:

> The BJP and the Chief Minister of Gujarat practice worst forms of paternalistic politics—they announce *gareeb kalyan melas* (gatherings for the welfare of the poor), in which the Chief Minister, like the royalty of yesteryears, distributes paltry benefits to few poor Dalit families. Mind you, these are actually government schemes that the people have the right to access, but these are announced like the Chief Minister's *daan dakshina*, alms, amidst much fanfare and publicity, to the helpless families in order to secure their (and the rest of the hopefuls') loyalty to the party and the Chief Minister.... However, Dalits are not integrated into the Hindu order envisaged by the BJP. Under this party, ritualistic Brahminism is part of state policy. For instance, the state government has for many years announced training for Dalit priests in Hindu rituals, serving a dual purpose—continuing the policy of untouchability as Brahmin priests will not have to officiate at Dalit social functions. [In addition], such practices Hinduize Dalits and Adivasis while confining them to their place within the caste hierarchy. (Interview with Valjibhai Patel, 11 August 2012. Ahmedabad).

16. Personal communication with activist and scholar Achyut Yagnik. 17 June 2008. Ahmedabad.

17. Minority rights groups recently mobilized the courts to ask the Modi government to implement the federal government's scholarships for economically deprived minority groups. The government of Gujarat has challenged the constitutional validity of this scholarship scheme, arguing that it violates constitutional equality. The court ruled against the Modi government and upheld the validity of the scheme (*The Hindu*, 7 May 2013).

18. See '20 Years of the Scheduled Castes and the Scheduled Tribes (Prevention of Atrocities) Act, 1989: Report Card. National Coalition for Strengthening SCs and STs (POA) Act'. Vashista Printers: Delhi. April 2010.

19. Interviews with Valjibhai Patel, P.K. Valera, August 2012, Ahmedabad.
20. See 'Broken People: Caste Violence against India's "Untouchables"', 1998, New York: Human Rights Watch; 'Struggle against Social Terrorism: Human Rights Movement of Gujarat,' compiled by Raju Solanki, 2009, Council for Social Justice.
21. For instance, in the Ved village of Panchmahals, a Dalit woman and her son, carrying pots of water, spilled water on the road. A retired police officer, passing by, reprimanded them for polluting the road. The young man defended himself. The police officer hit the boy with an iron rod and called the nearby police station and informed them of the incident. When six to ten Dalit villagers registered the case under the Atrocity Act at the police station, the police charged the people, arrested and kept in custody three Dalit villagers, and filed a case against them under Section 333 of the Indian Penal Code, 1860, for voluntarily causing grievous hurt to deter a public servant from his duty. The Dalits of the area contacted local NGOs, which took up the matter with higher officials, and local media and newspapers, which covered the event; they also organized a meeting between Dalit leaders from Ved and the area's deputy superintendent of police. This pressure led to the filing of cases against police constables who had assaulted Dalit villagers under Section 133 of the Indian Penal Code, 1860, for abetment of assault by a police officer while on duty, obstructing the police. However, the cases against all parties continued; the three Dalit members of Ved were released on bail, as was the retired police officer. Other constables who were part of the incident were transferred to other police stations. (Manubhai, Navsarjan Trust, 12 August 2012, Ahmedabad).
22. Interview with Raju Solanki, Council for Social Justice. 19 June 2008. Ahmedabad.
23. Interview with Kirit Waghela, Navsarjan Trust. 16 July 2011. Ahmedabad.
24. The victim's name has been changed to protect confidentiality.
25. A senior government attorney shared with me on conditions of anonymity: 'Lawyers know which way the verdict is going to swing the minute she comes to know which judge is assigned to the case. Most of the judges in the Gujarat High Court share the RSS ideology and it is an open secret'. 18 July 2012. Ahmedabad.
26. See 'Struggle against Social Terrorism'. (2009: 7).
27. Such a hearing was held on 31 March 2008 by the Centre for Dalit Human Rights, Navsarjan's legal wing. See, for instance, Navsarjan Trust's 2008 report 'Justice Undelivered: Public Hearing on the Lack of Enforcement of the POA in Gujarat'.

28. Sarpanch is the democratically elected head of the village-level institution of local self-government. The 73rd and 74th amendments to the Indian Constitution have introduced a three-tier system of political decentralization and devolved several administrative functions to the gram panchayat, the village assembly, and to elected office bearers of village-level institutions.

29. *Dheda* is an illegal, derogatory caste-based term used to refer to Dalits in Gujarati.

30. An interview with Kishorbhai Parmar, reported in 'A Legally Immune Form of Discrimination: Report on Socioeconomic Boycott of Dalits in Gujarat'. Navsarjan Trust (2009: 1).

31. Interview with Kirit Waghela, 15 July 2011. Ahmedabad.

32. Interview with Kanti Parmar, 17 June 2012. Ahmedabad.

33. The government of Gujarat, for instance, fails to distribute federal grants to students from Dalit, Adivasi, and Muslim groups. See, for instance, the news item: 'The govt. not using the central grants for welfare of SC/ST and minorities', *Gujarat Samachar*, 8 July 2008. NGOs lobbied with opposition MLAs to raise this issue in the state assembly. Congress MLAs Sahilesh Parmar, Chandu Dabhi, and Amit Chavda raised this issue in the assembly and met Social Justice and Law Minister Fakir Waghela.

34. NGOs in Gujarat had to approach the High Court to order the government to release scholarship funds to minority students (Prakash 2013).

35. For instance, SCs make up 23 per cent of the population in West Bengal and 28 per cent in Punjab.

36. Interview with Dinaben Vanakar, 20 July 2011. Ahmedabad.

37. Letter written by the women's committee based in Viramgaum district, Gujarat.

38. See also *Dalito par thata atyachar babate Jaher sunawani* (Public Hearing of Atrocity Cases and Crimes against Women), Place: Yashwant Rai Natya Gruha. Bhavnagar. 30 March 2012. Unpublished pamphlet.

39. This letter dated 8 October 2010 was addressed to the District administration and the State Human Rights Commission, Government of Gujarat.

40. Interview with Dinaben Vanakar, 17 August 2012. Ahmedabad.

References

An-Na'im, A.A. 2001. 'Human Rights in the Arab World: A Regional Perspective', *Human Rights Quarterly*, 23(3): 701–32.

Bob, C. 2007. 'Dalit Rights are Human Rights: Caste Discrimination, International Activism, and the Construction of a New Human Rights Issue', *Human Rights Quarterly*, 29(1): 167–93.

Brown, W. and J. Halley. 2002. 'Introduction', in W. Brown and J. Halley (eds), *Left Legalism/Left Critique*, pp. 1–37. Durham, NC: Duke University Press.

Cali, B. and S. Mackled-García (eds). 2006. *The Legalization of Human Rights: Multi-Disciplinary Perspectives on Human Rights and Human Rights Law*. London: Routledge.

Chandra, K. 2004. *Why Ethnic Parties Succeed: Patronage and Ethnic Head Counts in India*. New York: Cambridge University Press.

Ciotti, M. 2012. 'Resurrecting Sewa (Social Service): Dalit and Low-Caste Women Party Activists as Producers and Consumers of Political Culture and Practice in Urban North India', *Journal of Asian Studies*, 71(1): 149–70.

Galanter, M. 1983. 'The Radiating Effects of Courts', in K. Boyum and L. Mather (eds), *Empirical Theories about Courts*, pp. 117–42. New York: Longman.

———. 1989. *Law and Society in Modern India*. New York: Oxford University Press.

Goldstein, H. 1977. *Policing a Free Society*. Cambridge, MA: Ballinger.

Goodale, M. and S. Merry (eds). 2007. *The Practice of Human Rights: Tracking Law Between the Global and the Local*. Cambridge: Cambridge University Press.

Government of India, Ministry of Social Justice and Empowerment. 2004. 'Annual Report on the Scheduled Castes and the Scheduled Tribes (Prevention of Atrocities) Act, 1989 for the Year 2004'. www.socialjustice.nic.in/policiesacts1.php (accessed 13 March 2013).

———. 2005. 'Annual Report on the Scheduled Castes and the Scheduled Tribes (Prevention of Atrocities) Act, 1989 for the Year 2005'. www.socialjustice.nic.in/policiesacts1.php (accessed 13 March 2013).

———. 2006. 'Annual Report on the Scheduled Castes and the Scheduled Tribes (Prevention of Atrocities) Act, 1989 for the Year 2006'. www.socialjustice.nic.in/policiesacts1.php (accessed 13 March 2013).

———. 2007. 'Annual Report on the Scheduled Castes and the Scheduled Tribes (Prevention of Atrocities) Act, 1989 for the Year 2007'. www.socialjustice.nic.in/policiesacts1.php (accessed 13 March 2013).

———. 2008. 'Annual Report on the Scheduled Castes and the Scheduled Tribes (Prevention of Atrocities) Act, 1989 for the Year 2008'. www.socialjustice.nic.in/policiesacts1.php (accessed 13 March 2013).

———. 2009. 'Annual Report on the Scheduled Castes and the Scheduled Tribes (Prevention of Atrocities) Act, 1989 for the Year 2009'. www.socialjustice.nic.in/policiesacts1.php (accessed 13 March 2013).

————. 2010. 'Annual Report on the Scheduled Castes and the Scheduled Tribes (Prevention of Atrocities) Act, 1989 for the Year 2010'. www.socialjustice.nic.in/policiesacts1.php (accessed 13 March 2013).

Government of India. 2006. 'National Commission for Scheduled Castes, First Annual Report 2004–2005'. www.ncsc.nic.in/pages/view/219/218-first-annual-report (accessed 25 February 2013).

Guha, S. 2009. 'Ethnic Parties, Material Politics and the Ethnic Poor: The Bahujan Samaj Party in North India.' PhD dissertation, McGill University.

Hardiman, David. 1981. *Peasant Nationalists of Gujarat: Kheda District 1917–1934*. New Delhi: Oxford University Press.

Hastrup, K. 2003. 'Representing the Common Good: The Limits of Legal Language', in R.A. Wilson and J.P. Mitchell (eds), *Human Rights in Global Perspective: Anthropological Studies of Rights, Claims and Entitlements*, pp. 16–32. London: Routledge.

Human Rights Watch. 1999. *Broken People: Caste Violence against India's Untouchables*. New York: Human Rights Watch.

Kennedy, D. 2004. *The Dark Sides of Virtue: Reassessing International Humanitarianism*. Princeton, NJ: Princeton University Press.

Khagram, S., J.V. Riker, and K. Sikkink (eds). 2002. *Restructuring World Politics: Transnational Social Movements, Networks and Norms*. Minneapolis: University of Minnesota Press.

Krishna, A. 2003. 'Whatever Is Happening to Caste? A View from Some North Indian Villages', *Journal of Asian Studies*, 62(4): 1171–93.

Levitt, P. and S. Merry. 2009. 'Vernacularization on the Ground: Local Uses of Global Women's Rights in Peru, India and the United States', *Global Networks*, 9: 441–61.

Link, B. and J.C. Phelan. 2001. 'Conceptualizing Stigma', *Annual Review of Sociology*, 27: 363–85.

McCann, M. 1994. *Rights at Work: Pay Equity Reform and the Politics of Legal Mobilization*. Chicago: University of Chicago Press.

————. 2006. 'Law and Social Movements: Contemporary Perspectives', *Annual Review of Law and Social Science*, 2: 17–38.

Merry, S. 1990. *Getting Justice and Getting Even: Legal Consciousness among Working Class Americans*. Chicago: University of Chicago Press.

Narula, S. 2003. 'Compounding Injustice: The Government's Failure to Redress Massacres in Gujarat', *Human Rights Watch* 15(4): 4–69. www.hrw.org/reports/2003/india0703/India0703full.pdf.

National Coalition for Strengthening SCs & STs POA Act (NCSPA). 2010. *20 Years Scheduled Castes & Scheduled Tribes (Prevention of Atrocities) Act Report Card*. New Delhi: NCSPA.

Paleaz, Jenny. (n.d.) 'A Legally Immune Form of Discrimination: Report on Socioeconomic Boycotts of Dalits in Gujarat', www.navsarjan.org/Documents/Social%20Boycott%20Report%20-%20Jenny%20Paleaz.doc/view (accessed 14 March 2013).

Pandey, G. 2006. 'The Subaltern as Subaltern Citizen', *Economic and Political Weekly*, 41(46): 1779–88.

Prakash, C. 2013. 'Religious Minorities in Gujarat Can Breathe a Small Sigh of Relief', *Human Rights India*. www.humanrightsindia.blogspot.ca.

Ramaiah, A. 2011. 'Growing Crimes against Dalits in India despite Special Laws: Relevance of Ambedkar's Demand for 'Separate Settlement', *Journal of Law and Conflict Resolution*, 3(9): 151–68.

Rao, A. 2009. *The Caste Question: Dalits and the Politics of Modern India*. Berkeley: University of California Press.

Rosenberg, G. 1991. *The Hollow Hope: Can Courts Bring About Social Change?* Chicago: University of Chicago Press.

Scott, J.C. 1977. 'Protest and Profanation: Agrarian Revolt and the Little Tradition, Part II', *Theory and Society*, 4(2): 211–46.

Shah, G., M. Rutten, and H. Streefkerk. 2002. *Development and Deprivation in Gujarat: Essays in Honour of Jan Breman*. New Delhi: Sage Publications.

Shani, O. 2007. *Communalism, Caste and Hindu Nationalism: The Violence in Gujarat*. Cambridge: Cambridge University Press.

Sheth, D.L. 1999. 'Secularization of Caste and the Making of New Middle Class', *Economic and Political Weekly*, 34(34/35): 2502–10.

Sud, N. 2007. 'Constructing and Contesting an Ethno-Religious Gujarati-Hindu Identity through Development Programmes in an Indian State', *Oxford Development Studies*, 35(2): 131–48.

———. 2009. 'The Indian State in a Liberalizing Landscape', *Development and Change*, 40(4): 645–65.

Yagnik, A. and S. Sheth. 2005. *The Shaping of Modern Gujarat: Plurality, Hindutva and Beyond*. Delhi: Penguin Books.

11

The State as Religious Gatekeeper

Human Rights, Resistance, and Indian Anti-Conversion Laws

Amar Khoday

Religious conversions are profound, multi-dimensional events and processes that fundamentally implicate human rights concerns. On the one hand, where an individual is forced to convert due to compulsion or threats of physical injury, such acts clearly violate her rights to liberty, the freedom to choose and practice the religion of her own selection, and the right to associate and situate herself within a particular community. A person who is compelled to convert suffers a clear harm because their individual autonomy has been curtailed. However, where an individual voluntarily converts from one religion to another, human rights are also implicated but in a different manner. Rather than violations of their human rights, individuals, acting as legal subjects, exercise and affirm the aforementioned rights. The state has a delicate role to play in deterring and punishing those who would use force or other improper means to secure an involuntary religious conversion while being careful not to create overly broad provisions which inhibit or infringe on otherwise lawful conduct. The crafting of overly broad provisions also introduces serious risks of abuse by those who would seek to otherwise prevent or deter religious conversions altogether. This chapter examines how various states in India have developed broadly worded statutes that go well beyond what is necessary to protect against involuntary conversions.

There are a number of discrete and/or intersecting reasons why individuals decide to convert to another religion, or from one particular sect within a larger religious tradition to another. It may simply arise from a lack of connection to their previous faith/sect and the values shared amongst others in that community combined with a corresponding and growing intellectual and/or spiritual nexus with the new faith or sect. Individuals do not get to choose which country, communities, or families they are born into and are accordingly subjected to a series of norms and cultural values that come with such 'membership'. Accordingly, persons may choose to be part of other communities that are more in line with their views. Furthermore, where individuals are part of oppressed sections within a particular religious community or society (for example, Dalit Hindus), their voluntary religious conversions may (also) be seen as political and social acts of resistance. The resistance may be waged against their former religious community and/or its leaders. It may also be motivated by the manner in which their original religious faith is practiced and the formulation of socio-legal and cultural norms which apply to them.[1]

Conversions for such purposes are defections, which in turn have larger cultural reverberations that touch upon the religious, social, economic, and political makeup of society. As legal scholar, Makau Mutua (2001) asserts, culture is a 'dynamic and alchemical mix of many variables, including religion, philosophy, history, mythology, politics, environmental factors, language, and economics'. (Mutua 2001: 220). To this list, I would add that law also constitutes culture. Mutua further observes that 'the interaction of these variables—both within the culture and through influence by other cultures—produces competing social visions and values in any given society'. (Mutua 2001: 220). The more publicized or well-known the defection, the more hostility it may engender for it may encourage others to follow suit. Thus there may be attempts to discourage or inhibit conversions—through force as well as threats of force, either using law as an instrumentality in this endeavour or by taking extra-judicial measures. In India, as mentioned, several states have placed limits on the ability of individuals to convert through anti-conversion laws. They place limits on the ability of persons to convert others as well as individuals converting to another religion.

I argue that such laws are framed in such a broad manner that they may deter even voluntary *bona fide* religious conversions. In so doing, such norms impact on individual autonomy and the rights guaranteed under the Indian Constitution and international human rights law. Article 25 of the Constitution of India provides that 'Subject to public order, morality, and health and to other provisions of this Part, all persons are equally entitled to freedom of conscience and the right freely to possess, practise, and propagate religion'. Article 18 of the *International Covenant on Civil and Political Rights* stipulates that 'Everyone shall have the right to freedom of thought, conscience, and religion. This right shall include freedom to have or to adopt a religion or belief of his choice, and freedom, either individually or in community with others and in public or private, to manifest his religion or belief in worship, observance, practice and teaching'.

In this chapter, I scrutinize three problematic issues respecting the various state anti-conversion statutes in India. In the first part of this chapter, I examine the content of such norms. Particularly, I analyse the wording and definitions employed and argue that they suffer from being too broadly worded and attempt to capture conduct that does not make a conversion involuntary. In addition, and drawing from a 2012 decision of the Himachal Pradesh High Court, I contend that certain procedural components mandating those intending to convert to give prior notice to a government official, the failure of which will result in penal sanctions, amounts to fundamental intrusions into the privacy of individuals. It subjects an individual's right to change their religion to an intrusive state review, a matter which is none of the state's business barring at minimum some substantially credible evidence that the conversion is a consequence of force. If an individual is being forced to convert, such a person can seek assistance from authorities as they would be expected to in any other circumstance. In the second part of this chapter, I argue that the impact of such laws has the potential to diminish the ability of Dalits and other marginalized communities in India to use religious conversions as a tool to resist socio-cultural oppression through departure from the community. Religious conversions are a potential tool for seeking emancipation from an otherwise restrictive condition. Rules that restrict such departures trap Dalit communities in what Heredia (2004) identifies as a 'no exit' situation.

I begin first with some context. The aforementioned anti-conversion laws do not operate in a socio-political vacuum. In recent decades, right-wing and far right-wing Hindu political parties and groups have sought to exploit anxieties amongst Hindus about the community becoming a minority in India and to secure a stable vote bank of those seeking to solidify Hindu interests to prevent this from happening (Narula 2003). Such attitudes are not limited to political parties such as the Bharatiya Janata Party (BJP) but can include individuals within others such as the Congress party (I), particularly at the state level where these laws have passed. Through such lenses, attention is consistently directed at the growth of the Muslim and Christian populations through mass human reproduction and/or religious conversion—all to the alleged detriment of Hindu society. What such groups find particularly troublesome are the alleged efforts made to convert those amongst the Hindu Dalit community and Adivasi populations to Islam or Christianity. As such, there is consternation that their (potential) conversions to Islam or Christianity will come at the expense of the 'Hindu' community—by depleting the number of Hindus and/or increasing the number of Muslims or Christians (Coleman 2008).

What is also striking about this concern for the well-being of Dalit and Adivasi communities (or Scheduled Castes—SCs—and Scheduled Tribes—STs—respectively) and their being forced, tricked, or induced into converting is the hypocrisy that underlies it. Specifically, mainstream Hindu communities have traditionally and still largely hold significant disdain toward these marginalized communities. This is demonstrated by the mistreatment meted out to them. With respect to Dalits, this is manifested through blatant discrimination and operationalized through exclusion and varying degrees of mistreatment (Mendelsohn and Vicziany 1998; Racine and Racine 1998). This has been consistently documented, at least in certain sections of the Indian press. In the case of Adivasis in Central India, they have been subjected to massive displacement as a consequence of massive development projects such as the Sardar Sarovar Dam project on the Narmada River (Desai *et al.* 2007; Levien 2006; Modi 2004). The poor compensation and rehabilitation that they are given, not to mention the destruction of their relatively once autonomous existence is a testament to the genuine concern many amongst mainstream Hindu society hold for these groups. In a judgement of the Supreme Court of India in 2000, the majority even spoke to the allegedly positive effects that rehabilitation would have with respect to assimilating Adivasis into Indian society.[2] Such assimilation was expressed as a positive development. This treatment is in many ways emblematic of the way Adivasis have been mistreated throughout India. As such one must approach the interpretation of such laws with a great deal of circumspection, and indeed concern that broadly worded provisions contained therein will be misused to harass minorities and deter otherwise voluntary conversions.

There is also an undertone that suggests that Dalits and Adivasis, many of whom lack the benefit of formal education, will be easy targets for the exploitation of those with money or who adopt means of artifice (Jenkins 2008). In Gujarat's *Freedom of Religion Act*, converting an individual who is an SC or ST will incur an enhanced penalty.[3] It should be remembered that a lack of education does not necessarily translate into a lack of individual autonomy, or the capacity of such individuals to choose a different world view, or to resist efforts of those seeking to convert them. As Sathianathan Clarke has observed, there is a real need to 'counter the whole idea that the Dalits are passive, dumb, and easily misled into conversion. That really disrespects their humanity. We need to see how conversion has been used by them as a powerful means of critiquing and challenging the structures of "upper" caste domination'. (Clarke and Sikand 2007). Historians have noted instances of Adivasis resisting efforts of colonial and postcolonial state regimes that impact on their independence and way of life (Baviskar 1995; Hardiman 1987; Pati 2011). To be sure, Dalits and Adivasis are vulnerable populations but they are not necessarily simple-minded or unaware. Furthermore, they are not incapable of resisting oppression. In some cases, they are as well, in their own right, participants, and accomplices in oppression (Devy 2002).

They are capable of making decisions as well as benefiting or suffering from the consequences of having made them.

Legislative Provisions

Force, Fraud, and Inducements

There are several anti-conversion laws that have been passed in India (Neufeldt 1993). Despite very minor differences between these legislative enactments, there is much that is common to all of them. All the statutes are ostensibly concerned with religious conversions that are a consequence of force, threats of force, inducements/allurements, or fraudulent means.[4] The Supreme Court of India in *Stanislaus v. Madhya Pradesh* held that such laws were constitutional.[5] They were deemed constitutional in the sense that states in India could legislate on these matters and that there was no fundamental right to convert another individual to one's own religion, even though there is a clear right to propagate within the context of the freedom of religion.

Of the three prohibited modes of converting individuals, it is perhaps outlawing the use of force which has the greatest legitimacy. Force or threats of force intended to cause physical injury render a conversion involuntary and certainly constitutes a violation of an individual's right to freedom of religion. The concept of force does not, or should not, have to be solely related to physical force or harm. As the United Nations' Human Rights Committee has determined, of similar concern are threats of penal sanctions as well as deprivation or restricted access to education, medical care, employment, or other rights protected under the *Covenant on Civil and Political Rights* (Joseph and Castan 2013: 566). Such use of force or threats can have a tangible impact on one's physical integrity and economic well-being.

However, the anti-conversion laws in question go well beyond this. Force or threats of force explicitly include 'divine displeasures' and 'social ex-communication.'[6] In the case of divine displeasures, when the type of force supposedly being imposed is supernatural, and ultimately cannot manifest itself empirically, it is difficult to take seriously how such 'displeasure' can be seen as a compelling or reasonable example of coercive force that the law should recognize as such. An individual, even one who is not formally educated, is free or capable of questioning and disbelieving the danger of divine displeasure, particularly when revelations of that displeasure come from proponents of a different faith. Furthermore, the lack of formal education does not rob someone of the ability of critical thought. Conversely, the fact that a person possesses formal education does not mean that individual will always be critical in a manner commensurate with the level of education they have achieved. But more disconcerting, if force can be represented as something as intangible and vague as divine displeasures, there is arguably little that could not qualify as force sufficient to impugn or invalidate a religious conversion, no matter how irrational or imaginary.

Unlike divine displeasures, social ex-communication can be manifested and have a tangible impact on its targets. Threats of social ex-communication can certainly be coercive, and individuals are undoubtedly impacted by the views of their peers and other actors in every day society. Presumably, the threat of social ex-communication would come from individuals who have converted, such as members of one's kin group or caste within a particular geographic space. Even if this were the case, people can be reasonably expected to stand by their faith and convictions in the face of others choosing to no longer speak to them for continuing to follow their faith. This is not to suggest that this is an easy, simple, or fair choice to make. Yet it is a choice nevertheless. The possibility of social ex-communication is the risk people may face, and the cost to be endured when engaging in a host of otherwise legal but socially 'illegitimate' activities (illegitimate from the point of views of those who do not accept them). This includes the pursuit of one's own faith. One cannot force others to speak to an individual or persons they do not care to speak to, however bigoted or pernicious the motives for such ostracism may be. I hasten to add here that I in no way mean to belittle the fact that one of the principal ways that individuals today can experience bullying or harassment in workplace, educational, or other institutional contexts is through ostracism by colleagues and peers. To the extent that social ex-communication or the threat of it serves as a basis for considering that a conversion is forced, it should be limited to when individuals are prevented from accessing public or quasi-private property normally open to the public, and/or are barred from purchasing goods and services, particularly, but not limited to those that are necessary to one's survival. This would be commensurate with the types of force recognized by the UN Human Rights Committee as noted above.

What is peculiarly ironic about the inclusion of divine displeasures and social ex-communication as examples of illegitimate 'force' is the fact that such means have been employed in other social contexts in South Asia (and indeed other parts of the world) without the need for legal regulation by the state. This is particularly so in the case of individuals seeking to marry a person from another religion, class, or caste community about whom the family or community disapproves of. Why are, or should, such means be considered socially and legally illegitimate in the case of religious conversions, but not so in other contexts where clearly individuals' choices are being undermined? The Gujarat High Court has observed that an individual who is aggrieved because they have been ostracized by being denied an invitation to some social function suffers from the loss of a social privilege, not a legal right.[7] The Court asserted that a civil court has no power in such cases to compel the members of a community to invite an individual to dinner or to any social ceremony.[8]

The various anti-conversion laws also deem conversions based on 'fraudulent statements' or 'fraud' as unlawful. These include 'misrepresentations' or some other 'fraudulent contrivance.'[9] Fraud may be understood as 'a knowing misrepresentation of the truth or concealment of a material fact to induce another to act to his or her injury' (Garner 1996: 267). In fraud cases, the material facts in question that are being misrepresented or unrevealed to those who have been defrauded are normally held in the exclusive possession of the one committing the fraud. It is certainly a legitimate role of the criminal law to deter the perpetration of fraud that deprives individuals of something which, in particular, they cannot reacquire, or easily reacquire without great expense and/or effort. This may include being defrauded of property or wealth which has been transferred to another. For instance, under Canadian criminal law, it is an offence to defraud the public or any person, whether ascertained or not, of any property, money or valuable security, or any service.[10] Legal systems also criminalize fraud in the context of sexual assault cases. For example, under Canadian law, an individual's failure to disclose their HIV-positive status to someone they are about to have sex with constitutes fraud vitiating consent (in the absence of a low viral load and use of a condom).[11] A person who acquires HIV must live with the disease (along with the stigma attached with it) for the rest of their lives, all of which impacts on them in several ways. It is an irrevocable condition.

Fraud within the context of religious conversions ought to be approached with a healthy dose of caution. As a basic idea, misrepresentations within the context of religious conversions can be situated in two broad categories—(i) statements made about the religion, belief system, and/or the practices which constitute it, that an individual is converting to ('the converted faith'); and (ii) statements made about the religion, belief system, and the practices that constitute it, that an individual is converting from ('the original faith'). Undoubtedly, communications will often involve a combination of both. I would argue that to the extent that fraud should vitiate a religious conversion, or serve as a reason to refuse to allow one to convert, it should be where fraudulent statements relate to the first category, rather than the latter. Knowledge of the original faith of the person converting is not in the monopoly or tightly held control of the individual advocating for the conversion to take place. The person converting can take reasonable steps to verify the veracity of the comments. The situation may be far different where it comes to information about the converted faith. Thus the veracity of the statements regarding the converted faith should be what is called into scrutiny.

Furthermore, in order for fraud to be a reason for invalidating a religious conversion, it should be demonstrated that it was reasonably or justifiably relied upon.[12] A number of factors should come into play. What should be considered is whether the individual converting had practical access to available and independent information or sources of information (other than the propagator and/or their agents) and chose not to avail himself/herself of these independent sources. There may be instances where the individual propagating their faith and seeking to induce a conversion is practically the only available source of information with knowledge (for example, a missionary in a remote area) and access to information through technological means is unavailable to the prospective converter or they have not been properly educated to use those means.

Furthermore, to the extent that fraudulent statements were relied upon in part to induce a conversion, it should be required that the fraudulent statements are considered a significant contributing factor for why the conversion took place. For example, where a converter indicates that they have made the decision to convert based on reasons that have little to do with the fraudulent statements, a religious conversion should not be deemed to be invalid even if there is evidence of the utterance of fraudulent statements. In other words there ought to be some strong, clear, and convincing causal connection between the fraudulent statements and the conversion.

Assuming this is an agreeable approach, one has to question what the misrepresentation relates to, even with respect to the converting faith. Specifically, to what component of the converting faith do the fraudulent statements refer? Do they include statements about the religious principles underlying the faith? As Laura Jenkins (2008) enquires rhetorically, how does one prove misrepresentation regarding metaphysical beliefs? Religious principles within a specific faith may vary and in some cases contradict one another. Does the fact that an individual seeking to persuade another to convert to his faith mentions or highlights one principle of the converting faith, but neglects to state competing or paradoxical principles, represent fraud? What if such a proponent simply does not believe that such contradictory principles should be followed and does not form part of their lived experience or series of beliefs connected to their faith? Is fraud imputed when the proponent advances ideas and principles that are held by only a minority of the converting faith, but not by a majority without indicating this disparity? I would argue that alleged misrepresentations about metaphysical beliefs and principles should not serve as a basis for invalidating or refusing a conversion, even if they are relied upon by the converter. After all, the 'alleged misrepresentations' may refer to radically different interpretations and beliefs that the majority of adherents of the converting faith may not agree with.

Perhaps the scope of the fraud should be limited to statements about religious practice and actions taken in furtherance of the beliefs. For instance, the proponent seeking to have another person convert may represent that it is the absolute practice of all persons of the converting faith within a specified area that certain actions are taken as a manifestation of that faith, for example, engaging in charitable work. The individual converts in large part because they are attracted to being part of such a community that emphasizes this as an ideal only to realize this is something that is, in fact, not practised consistently, or by many amongst the converting faith in the area. The statement was wrong and if the proponent knew this when they made the statement, they knowingly misrepresented a fact about the religious practice in question.

In addition to force or fraud, the anti-conversion laws prohibit religious conversions procured through inducements or allurements. Statutes have generally defined these as the offer of any gift or 'gratification', whether it is in the form of cash or 'in kind' or grant of any benefit that is pecuniary or otherwise.[13] First, inducements do not generally render a religious conversion involuntary. It may lead to questions about the sincerity of a putative conversion, but it is not apparent why this should be the concern of any government. Second, the inducement/allurement is given such a broad meaning that the offer of being part of a religious community that purports to treat a person from a Dalit or SC community as an equal member of the faith could be seen as an allurement/inducement. But even if inducements were limited to financial ones, how is a conversion conditioned on a grant of money or some tangible material good any more or less objectionable or involuntary than other types of private transactions in civil society that prompt a person or persons to engage in activity they might not have otherwise done? For example, businesses recruit individuals from rival businesses by offering higher salaries and bonuses. Sports teams induce free agents to leave their current employment to join theirs based on substantial financial offers and other emoluments. Politicians induce people to vote for them on the basis of some precise and/or ambiguous promises of future benefits or desired goals. Common religious practice amongst several faiths involves transactions or exchanges. Every day, devotees give offerings to a designated divine power in exchange for some requested blessing or benefit to be bestowed upon them and/or someone they care about. Some pay higher amounts of money to get ahead of the line to reach the image of God more rapidly through their 'VIP' or 'VVIP' status. Temples benefit through the patronage of wealthy devotees. Financial inducements to convert may be morally questionable depending on one's perspective, but they are certainly not involuntary or forced. What is also ironic is that Hindu groups who are strong proponents of such anti-conversion laws are active in promoting reconversion and are not above using inducements (for example, gifts to be given as part of the religious ceremony) or using or exploiting threats of force or social ostracism to push their reconversion agenda (Roy 2008).

Furthermore, individuals who convert from Hinduism, or are the offspring of those who converted from Hinduism as a result of inducements, are not precluded from 'converting back' to Hinduism or resuming their Hindu religious practice (Sikand and Katju 1994). Hindu groups going back decades have arranged for religious ceremonies welcoming back such individuals into the fold. While this may defy the common understanding that one is born a Hindu and one does not convert into Hinduism, the practice belies this belief. Furthermore, the Supreme Court of India has recognized that an individual may be born a Hindu or convert to Hinduism.[14] Some have converted to Hinduism based on the fact that as a Christian Dalit, they no longer obtain the benefits that being a member of a SC community brought them (Roy 2008).

There may certainly be exceptional and extreme circumstances where a conversion procured through inducement may give rise to an involuntary conversion. This would include, for example, where an individual must choose between accepting an inducement in exchange for converting or to refuse and suffer the probability of starving. In such cases, a person has little or no effective choice. It is in such limited circumstances where inducements would give rise to an involuntary conversion that the law should be aimed at. Of course, in such circumstances, it is striking that third parties or the state should take greater umbrage at the attempt to convert a starving individual, rather than the fact that such persons are starving and little attention is directed to assist them in such a way that it would obviate their need to accept such a questionable inducement. To the extent that the state has any legitimate interest in 'protecting' desperate individuals from religious conversion through the use of inducements, it should be limited to contexts where the person whose conversion is sought has no practical choice or option but to convert. In such circumstances, it is perhaps more appropriate to characterize it as a form of force—whereby the individual inducing the conversion exploits and effectively forces a conversion.

While it is perfectly reasonable to restrict the manner in which religious conversions may transpire, legislation should focus on preventing involuntary religious conversions. These occur due to force, threats, or coercion that renders effective 'choice' null. Although individuals who have been forced to convert may be able to convert back, the attack on their liberty should not go unpunished as it imposes a type of harm that should not be accepted, but deterred. Inducements may lead to questionable conversions, but there is little to consider these involuntary except in the narrow circumstances discussed above. Conversions procured through such means are not irrevocable and the individual who has converted may choose to convert back.

Procedural Provisions

The broad substantive provisions are not the only problematic features of these statutes. Certain anti-conversion laws contain problematic reporting and notice requirements that effectively mandate that the individual converting give prior notice and receive permission before proceeding. Such requirements are part of the *Himachal Pradesh Act* and *Madhya Pradesh Act*. In the circumstances of the *Himachal Pradesh Act*, the notice requirement is not necessary in the case of an individual converting back to his 'original religion'. The state of Gujarat has also provided that such notice may take place after the conversion takes place by the individual who has converted. Such provisions intrude into the privacy of individuals and their decision to convert without the government second-guessing their choices. The provisions of the *Himachal Pradesh Act* were challenged and the state's High Court overturned them on constitutional grounds.[15]

The *Himachal Pradesh Act* stipulated that the 'individual intending to convert from one religion to another shall give prior notice of at least thirty days to the District Magistrate of the district concerned of his intention to do so and the District Magistrate shall get the matter enquired into all by such agency as he may deem fit.'[16] Failure to give prior notice will result in the issuance of a fine of up to Rs 1,000.[17] This is an amount that many may not be able to afford, but even if they could, the mere concept is repugnant. This in effect requires that a person intending to take up a different faith, in exercising his right to practice the religion of his choice, must get prior government approval following an inquiry, and the mandate to pay money for failing to report to such an official on a matter that is none of the state's business in the first place. It is entirely one thing to allow someone to complain that they have had to undergo a conversion against their will. It is altogether a different matter and a fundamental intrusion into the personal affairs of citizens (and non-citizens) to require them to subject themselves to government bureaucracy and await permission with respect to something as closely held as their religious beliefs and identity. During oral arguments with respect to the constitutionality of the law, one justice of the Himachal Pradesh High Court sceptically asked: 'If I am dying and I want to change my religion, will I wait for some babu [official] to tell me I can do it' (Compass Direct News 2011)?

At the heart of the Himachal Pradesh High Court's holding, respecting the notice requirement is the right to privacy and its connection to individual autonomy. In an earlier decision, the Supreme Court of India stressed the importance of individual autonomy as perhaps the central concern of any system of limited government and which found protection within the Constitution.[18] Embedded within the right to life, the right to privacy is a cherished constitutional value which allows human beings to be allowed domains of freedom that are free of public scrutiny unless such persons act in an unlawful manner.[19]

An individual's belief system and religious identification is generally not the business of the state. As the High Court observed, the state has no business scrutinizing such beliefs or forcing such persons to disclose their personal beliefs.[20] Furthermore, the High Court identified an important consequence which was that by disclosing their personal beliefs individuals may leave themselves open to physical and psychological torture, and thus are prevented from carrying out their wishes.[21] The Court stated that it may lead to communal clashes and endanger the life and limb of the individual converting.[22] During the pogroms in early 2002 in Gujarat, it was documented that Hindutva activists conducted attacks on houses and businesses known or believed to be owned by Muslims (Human Rights

Watch 2002: 5, 22–3; Varadarajan 2003). In requiring individuals to identify themselves through the notice requirements, there are certainly dangers of such persons becoming identified targets in the future.

There are conceivable problems with respect to time and when an individual has to give notice. The *Himachal Pradesh Act* and others do not factor in that conversions may be long drawn out processes that do not include a religious ceremony to mark the date certain of a particular conversion. Not every religious conversion takes place through the auspices of a formal ceremony. In some, if not many cases, an individual may retain elements of their previous religious faith or culture while adopting aspects of their new one. One's identity may be in flux and indeterminate. The date for ascertaining when his/her conversion is effective may be complicated and not clear for the purposes of complying with the statute. This then poses problems for meeting the requirement to inform a District Magistrate thirty days before choosing to convert.

Lastly, the Himachal Pradesh High Court addressed the notice exception with respect to individuals converting back to their original religion. The Court deemed that this violated s.14 of the Indian Constitution, respecting equality.[23] The rationale given to the court during oral arguments was that an individual who converts back to his original religion would know or understand his religion well enough, and thus no notice should be required. There are two reasons why such an exception is questionable. First, as the court suggested, an individual who has converted from religion 'A' to religion 'B' at the age of twenty but then converts back at the age of fifty has spent more years in religion 'B' (and that too mature years), and may not know his original religion quite as well. Second, it calls into question what the purpose of the notice scheme is meant to deal with. The overall purpose of the statute is to prevent religious conversions instigated through means that are deemed improper; it is of no relevance how much the individual knows about the faith he or she is converting back to. A person may have in-depth knowledge about his/her original religion and still convert back due to force, inducements, or fraudulent means. Furthermore, arguments were made that converting back to one's original religion was in reference solely to those converting back to Hinduism. This therefore makes the specious inference that conversions from Hinduism to another religion are suspect, but those where individuals convert back to Hinduism, are free from suspicion, thus making it unnecessary to report to the district magistrate.

Conversion as Resistance

There are various reasons why people convert to another religion or sect. For many, converting has little or nothing to do with any form of intended resistance, although their decision to convert may engender feelings of anger and alienation from the individual's immediate and extended family and larger social circle. For others, particularly those amongst Dalit Hindu communities, religious conversion can entail an intentional act of resistance and an attempt at liberation (Fernandes 1999). As Sathianathan Clarke observes, 'Conversion of Dalits to religions like Sikhism, Buddhism, Islam, or Christianity has been above all a protest against Hinduism and its caste structures. So, it's more of a social issue than an individual quest for spiritual truth' (Clarke and Sikand 2007).

Resistance may be understood as individual or collective acts that challenge the dominant or hegemonic power and authority of state and/or civil society actors. As Sharp *et al.* (2000: 1–4) assert, resistance is a form of power exercised in a way that challenges those with dominant or hegemonic power. They (Sharp *et al.* 2000: 1–4) define dominating power as 'that power which attempts to control or coerce others, impose its will upon others, or manipulate the consent of others'. By contrast, resisting power is 'that power which attempts to set up situations, groupings and actions which resist the impositions of dominating power' (Sharp *et al.* 2000: 1–4). They range from subtle moments to more 'developed moments when discontent translates into a form of social organization which actively co-ordinates people, materials, and practices in pursuit of specifiable transformative goals' (Sharp *et al.* 2000: 1–4). The caste system and its impact on Dalits represent a well-known and entrenched form of social oppression that cannot just be dispensed with through a constitutional provision.[24]

The caste system is in itself, at least today, an unofficial normative system where individuals are expected to adhere to a variety of understood norms developed over generations. That such non-state normative legal structures can exist outside of the state is not surprising. Legal pluralist scholarship has long asserted the importance of recognizing that law is constituted by more than just the norms of the state. Individuals operating within any given social field are impacted by a variety of state and non-state norms. The creation, interpretation, and enforcement of legal norms are forms of power and are exercised by various sections of civil society. For instance, one jurist has observed: 'power and political influence are exercised by bodies and organizations that are not organs of government. They may exercise power and influence with the tacit consent of the government concerned. On the other hand, they may do so because the government is unable to assert its own authority.'[25] The United Nations High Commissioner for Refugees has also similarly indicated that opinions respecting any matter in which the state, government, society, or policy may be engaged in are manifestations of a political opinion.[26] Furthermore, refugee case law demonstrates that the concept of a 'political opinion' includes acts that are expressions of such opinions (Khoday 2011).[27]

Yet, as critical legal pluralists have articulated, individuals are not merely objects upon whom state or not-state legal norms are imposed. Critical legal pluralist scholarship articulates that individuals as legal subjects 'possess a transformative capacity that enables them to produce legal knowledge and to fashion the very structures of law that contribute to constituting their legal subjectivity' (Kleinhans and Macdonald 1997). For critical legal pluralists, attention must be called to the role of citizen-subjects in generating normativity (Kleinhans and Macdonald 1997). As Macdonald (1998) observes, non-compliance is not merely an act of resistance but also an alternative vision of legal normativity. In the context of religious conversions, Dalits play a role in demolishing and reshaping the normative boundaries of caste and subordination by refusing to be a part of the cultural system that keeps them subordinated.

Religious conversions, when undertaken in whole or in part as acts of resistance, are essentially defections. Defections are often perceived as acts of political resistance because they demonstrate a fundamental refusal to continue to participate within a particular system of oppression as victims, or perhaps even as silent participants, in such oppression against others. Like those who defected

Soviet or communist regimes in earlier years[28] (and who may have faced severe penalties if caught while attempting to do so), those converting religions, particularly when they hold a subordinate status within a particular religious context, are defecting from an oppressive system. As with blanket laws against emigration, broadly worded anti-conversion laws prevent or deter legitimate exit and restrict the right to liberty, cultural mobility, and the freedom to make decisions about one's life in private spheres that are amongst the most intimate. Rather than actually address and reform a cultural system that imposes oppression and prompts such conversions, advocates of anti-conversion laws would simply prefer to just stop the defections from happening altogether. As mentioned above, the *Himachal Pradesh Act* placed no barriers to converting someone back to their previous religious fold by means of force, fraud, or misrepresentation. Moreover, this is regardless of whether the original conversion was completely voluntary, without fraud, or inducement.

The process of changing entrenched oppressive beliefs and practices is often a slow and lengthy one. Resistance will not necessarily effect immediate changes and may face counter-resistance measures that significantly undermine its effectiveness. Indeed, those resisting will likely continue to face social challenges arising from their conversion (Gokhale 1986). Discrimination against Dalits, regardless of religious identity, remains prevalent—even within the communities they have converted into (Racine and Racine 1998). This does not include only counter-resistance from dominant social forces, but also political power that seeks to undermine it. Leaving aside the anti-conversion laws discussed in this chapter, the Government of India through the office of the President issued an executive order restricting those who hold SC status to those who are Hindu. In other words, those Dalits who converted to Islam or Christianity were no longer allowed to retain any eligibility to benefits that were to be issued to those holding SC status but remained Hindu (Sikand 2011). An exception was made, however, to allow Dalits who converted to Sikhism and Buddhism to retain their SC status.[29]

What seems to be most feared by upper caste Hindu political classes is the potential for Dalits to migrate in greater numbers to a Muslim or Christian identity were they to be able to retain any benefits as SCs. They fear this would result in the dilution of the demographic power of Hindu society. While it is not absolutely clear that this fear would be realized (after all what is stopping Dalits from converting to Sikhism or Buddhism in greater numbers), to the extent that Dalits can exploit this anxiety to their social and/or political benefit, why should it not be allowed, and why should the government take steps to prevent this? The answer to this rhetorical question is of course that many, if not the most, significant political parties in India are either run by, or serve the interests of, upper caste and/or middle class Indian society.

The consequence of governmental non-intervention in the resistive efforts of Dalits or Adivasis to use religious conversion may force political parties to have to address, at least in some substantial fashion, the needs and aspirations of Dalit and Adivasi communities. At the close of the 2012 United States presidential elections, it became apparent that the Republican Party, as the long-held bastion of white conservative patriarchy, could no longer rely on just this demographic to win, as it may have in the past. There have been more calls for inclusiveness and the need to address issues concerning minorities that have long been ignored in favour of retaining the loyalty of its traditional white demographic base. If Dalits were able to exercise their power in an analogous way through shifts in religious identity, upper caste Hindu and leadership in minority religious traditions may find themselves courting Dalit support in ways unfathomable previously. Such a change is by no means certain, but it should certainly be an option that Dalits should be able to explore.

* * *

Religious conversions are important ways in which oppressed sections of society can signal their dissent and engage in a form of resistance against domination by powerful forces within that same society. None of this is to suggest that resistance by itself will always effect the desired changes in the immediate future. Resistance can in many ways be a slow process creating the desired change only after a long passage of time. Yet, in the meantime, those resisting might very well (and will likely) continue to face social challenges arising from their conversion (Gokhale 1986: 278–9). After all, generations of entrenched cultural beliefs that deems certain persons as inferior do not get altered because the latter have changed religions. In fact they are likely to face some form of retaliation for resisting cultural norms that entrench their subordination (Mendelsohn and Vicziany, 1998: 44–76). Still, it should remain the choice of those seeking exit from the religious faith and community, and not be subjected to invasive interventions by the state that privileges the oppressors' interests over the oppressed.

Governments should be extremely cautious in constructing legislation that runs the risk of undermining the ability of individuals and/or communities to exercise their human rights. However, governments maintain a legitimate role in deterring religious conversions procured through force, fraud, and inducements, subject to the limitations discussed above. What is constitutionally questionable is mandating individuals to inform authorities of their decision to convert and to effectively seek permission. As the Himachal Pradesh High Court has held, such provisions violate an individual's right to privacy.

Notes

1. While it goes beyond the scope of this paper, I shall briefly describe here the caste system. As is by now well-known, Hindu society has been divided (amongst other things) along caste lines for centuries. There are two categories that are used to identify caste–*varna* and *jāti*. The broader varna category divides Hindu society into four broad occupational groups–the *Brahmins* (priestly class), the *Kshatriyas* (the warrior class), the *Vaishyas* (merchant and agriculturalist class), and the *Shudras* (menial labourers and tenant cultivators). Sitting outside this group were the so-called 'untouchables' who performed tasks that, according to upper caste society, rendered them impure and defiling (for example, touching and removal of dead bodies). Although Mohandas K. Gandhi (1869–1948) referred to such persons as *harijans*, many have come to use the term *Dalit* (lit. oppressed). Within India's Constitution, untouchability has been abolished but it makes references to certain classes as 'Scheduled Castes'. Schedule castes are used in reference to this particular group. Delving deeper into this caste stratification is a second category of caste–jāti. These might be categorized as particular sub-groups within one of the larger varna categories. There are a number of sources respecting the caste system and discrimination.

Some legal sources demonstrate that the biases against lower castes and Dalits extend as far back as the ancient period in Indian history. See Olivelle, P. 1999. *Dharmasūtras: The Law Codes of Ancient India.* New Delhi: Oxford University Press.

2. *Narmada Bachao Andolan v. Union of India and Others,* A.I.R. 2000 S.C. 3751.

3. *The Gujarat Freedom of Religion Act,* 2003, s.4, [*Gujarat Act*].

4. *Gujarat Act, s.3, supra* note 3; *The Arunachal Pradesh Freedom of Religion Act,* 1978, s.3 [*Arunachal Pradesh Act*]; *Orissa Freedom of Religion Act,* 1967, s.3 [*Orissa Act*]; *The Himachal Pradesh Freedom of Religion Bill,* 2006, s.3 [*Himachal Pradesh Act*]; *Madhya Pradesh Freedom of Religion Act,* 1968, s. 3 [*Madhya Pradesh Act*].

5. 1977 S.C.R. (2) 611.

6. *Gujarat Act, supra* note 4 at s.2(c),; *Arunachal Pradesh Act, supra* note 4 at s.2(d); *Orissa Act, supra* note 4 at s.2(b); *Himachal Pradesh Act, supra* note 4 at s.2(b); and *Madhya Pradesh Act, supra* note 4 at s.2(c).

7. *State v. Kanbi Uma Mahadeva And Ors.,* (1961) 2 G.L.R. 531 at para 7.

8. Ibid.

9. *Gujarat Act, supra* note 3 at s.2(d); *Arunachal Pradesh Act, supra* note 4 at s.2(e); *Orissa Act, supra* note 4 at s.2(c); *Himachal Pradesh Act, supra* note 4 at s.2(c); and *Madhya Pradesh Act, supra* note 4 at s.2(d).

10. *Criminal Code,* R.S.C. 1985, c. C-46, s.380.

11. *R. v. Mabior,* 2012 S.C.C. 47.

12. *Dier v. Peters,* 815 N.W.2d 1 at 7 (Iowa 2012).

13. *Gujarat Act, supra* note 3 at s.2(a); *Arunachal Pradesh Act, supra* note 4 at s.2(f); *Orissa Act, supra* note 4 at s.2(d); *Himachal Pradesh Act, supra* note 4 at s.2(d); and *Madhya Pradesh Act, supra* note 4 at s.2(a).

14. *Perumal Nadar (dead) by Legal Representative v. Ponnuswami Nadar (minor),* A.I.R. 1971 S.C. 2352.

15. *Evangelical Fellowship of India and others v. State of Himachal Pradesh,* CWP No. 438 of 2011 at para. 49 [*EFI*].

16. *Himachal Pradesh Act, supra* note 4 at s. 4(1). See also the *Madhya Pradesh Freedom of Religion (Amendment) Act of* 2006 (amending the *Madhya Pradesh Freedom of Religion Act of* 1968 to include the following provision: 'One who desires to convert his religion, he will declare such idea in front of District Magistrate or in front of the Executive Magistrate specially authorized by District Magistrate of related District, that he wishes to change his religion on his own and at his will and pleasure'.).

17. *Himachal Pradesh Act, supra* note 4 at s.4(2).

18. *Govind v. State of Madhya Pradesh and another*, A.I.R. 1975 S.C. 1378 at para. 23.
19. *Ram Jethmalani and others v. Union of India and Ors.*, (2011) 8 S.C.C. 1 at para. 83.
20. EFI, supra note 15 at para. 40.
21. Ibid.
22. Ibid., at para. 41.
23. Ibid., at para. 43.
24. Constitution of India, 1950, article 17.
25. *Minister for Immigration and Multicultural Affairs v. Singh*, 209 C.L.R. 533 (H.C.A.), 2002 WL 342793 at para. 45 (Gaudron J.).
26. United Nations High Commissioner for Refugees, *Guidelines on International Protection: Gender-Related Persecution within the context of Article 1A(2) of the 1951 Convention and/or its 1967 Protocol Relating to the Status of Refugees*, (7 May 2002) HCR/GIP/02/01.
27. For example, see *Desir v. Ilchert*, 840 F.2d 723 (9th Cir. 1988).
28. For example, see *R. v. Governor of Brixton Prison ex parte Kolczynski*, [1955] 1 Q.B. 540.
29. *The Constitution (Scheduled Castes) Order*, 1950, www.lawmin.nic.in/ld/subord/rule3a.htm

References

Baviskar, A. 1995. *In the Belly of the River: Tribal Conflicts over Development in the Narmada Valley*. New Delhi: Oxford University Press.

Clarke, S. and Y. Sikand. 7 October 2007. 'Dalit Theology.' www.counter currents.org/sikand071007.htm (accessed 26 August 2013).

Coleman, J. 2008. 'Authoring (in) Authenticity, Regulating Religious Tolerance: The Implication of Anti-Conversion Legislation for Indian Secularism', *Cultural Dynamics*, 20(3): 245–77.

Compass Direct News. 16 September 2011. 'Court in India Questions State's Anti-Conversion Law', *The Christian Post*, www.christianpost. com/news/court-in-india-questions-states-anti-conversion-law-55774/ (accessed 26 August 2013).

Desai, K., V. Jain, R. Pandev, P. Srikant, and U. Trivedi. 2007. 'Rehabilitation of the Indira Sagar Pariyojana Displaced', *Economic and Political Weekly*, 42(51): 27–36.

Devy, G.N. 2002. 'Tribal Voice and Violence', in S. Varadarajan (ed.), *Gujarat: The Making of A Tragedy*, pp. 246–66. New Delhi: Penguin.

Fernandes, W. 1999. 'Attacks on Minorities and a National Debate on Conversions', *Economic and Political Weekly*, 34(3/4): 81–4.

Garner, B.A. 1996. *Black's Law Dictionary*. Eagan, MN: The West Group.

Gokhale, J.B. 1986. 'The Sociopolitical Effects of Ideological Change: The Buddhist Conversion of Maharashtrian Untouchables', *The Journal of Asian Studies*, 45(2): 269–92.

Hardiman, D. 1987. *The Coming of the Devi: Adivasi Assertion in Western India*. New Delhi: Oxford University Press.

Heredia, R. 2004. 'No Entry, No Exit: Savarna Aversion to Dalit Conversion', *Economic and Political Weekly*, 39(41): 4543–55.

Human Rights Watch. 2002. *"We Have No Orders to Save You": State Participation and Complicity*. New York: Human Rights Watch.

Jenkins, L.D. 2008 'Legal Limits on Religious Conversions in India', *Law and Contemporary Problems*, 71(2): 109–27.

Joseph, S. and M. Castan (eds). 2013. Third ed. *The International Covenant on Civil and Political Rights: Cases, Materials and Commentary*. New York: Oxford University Press.

Khoday, A. 2011. 'Protecting Those Who Go Beyond the Law: Contemplating Refugee Status for Individuals Who Engage in Resistance to Oppression', *Georgetown Immigration Law Journal*, 25(3): 571–646.

Kleinhans, M.M. and R.A. Macdonald. 1997. 'What is a Critical Legal Pluralism?', *Canadian Journal of Law and Society*, 12(2): 25–46.

Levien, M. 2006. 'Narmada and the Myth of Rehabilitation', *Economic and Political Weekly*, 41(33): 3581–5.

Macdonald, R.A. 1998. 'Metaphors of Multiplicity: Civil Society, Regimes and Legal Pluralism', *Arizona Journal of International and Comparative Law*, 15: 69–91.

Madan, T.N. 2003. 'Freedom of Religion.' *Economic and Political Weekly* 38(11): 1034–41.

Mendelsohn, O. and M. Vicziani. 1998. *The Untouchables: Subordination, Poverty, and the State in Modern India*. New York: Cambridge University Press.

Modi, R. 2004. 'Sardar Sarovar Oustees: Coping with Displacement', *Economic and Political Weekly*, 39(11): 1123–6.

Mutua, M. 2001. 'Savages, Victims, and Saviours: The Metaphor of Human Rights', *Harvard International Law Journal*, 42(1): 201–45.

Narula, S. 2003. 'Overlooked Danger: The Security and Rights Implications of Hindu Nationalism in India', *Harvard Human Rights Journal*, 16: 41–68.

Neufeldt, R.W. 1993. 'To Convert or Not to Convert: Legal and Political Dimensions of Conversion in Independent India', in R.D. Baird (ed.),

Religion and Law in Independent India, pp. 313–31. New Delhi: Manohar Publishers.

Pati, B. (ed.). 2011. *Adivasis in Colonial India: Survival, Resistance, and Negotiation*. Delhi: Orient Longman.

Racine, J.L. and J. Racine. 1998. 'Dalit Identities and the Dialectics of Oppression and Emancipation in a Changing India: The Tamil Case and Beyond', *Comparative Studies of South Asia, Africa, and the Middle East*, 18(1): 5–19.

Roy, R.D. 4 September 2008. 'Hindus Use Christian Conversion Methods to Reconvert Villagers.' www.livemint.com/Politics/pf0JSKu9E5kM741 IX6IqNI/Hindus-use-Christian-conversion-methods-to-reconvert-village.html (accessed 26 August 2013).

Sharp, J.P., P. Routledge, C. Philo, and R. Paddison. 2000. 'Entanglements of Power: Geographies of Domination/Power', in J.P. Sharp, P. Routledge, C. Philo, and R. Paddison (eds), *Entanglements of Power: Geographies of Domination/Power*, pp. 1–42. New York: Routledge.

Sikand, Y. 2011. 'Converted Dalits Get No Justice.' *Tehelka* 8(13): Online.

Sikand, Y. and M. Katju. 1994. 'Mass Conversions to Hinduism among Indian Muslims', *Economic and Political Weekly*, 29(34): 2214–19.

Varadarajan, S. (ed). 2003. *Gujarat: The Making of a Tragedy*. Delhi: Penguin.

12

The Right to Have Rights

Taking Hannah Arendt to India

Niraja Gopal Jayal

An Arendtian Approach to Human Rights

In 1951, Hannah Arendt threw out a fundamental challenge to the discourse of universal human rights. Beginning with the late eighteenth century, the idea that all humans are 'born and remain free and equal in rights' (Declaration of the Rights of Man 1789) and that 'they are endowed by their Creator with certain unalienable Rights' (American Declaration of Independence 1776) had become hegemonic. In France, the very object of political association was declared to be 'the preservation of the natural and imprescriptible rights of man' (Declaration of the Rights of Man 1789). Only two years later, in one of the most famous pamphlet wars of all time, Thomas Paine passionately defended the rights of man as enunciated in America and France, in response to Edmund Burke's interrogation of this idea on the grounds that rights could only be historical and not natural.

The ultimate triumph of this discourse of human rights was arguably its affirmation by the Universal Declaration of Human Rights of 1948. Despite the circumstances of its enactment—the horrors of the Holocaust and the World War II—this declaration endowed the rhetoric of human rights with an unparalleled legitimacy on a global scale. Among the limitations of the discourse has been the fact that it eventually yielded two covenants, rather than one: the International Covenant on Civil and Political Rights and the International Covenant on Economic, Social, and Cultural Rights. Across the world, it has generally been easier to secure at least a formal commitment to civil and political rights as opposed to economic, social, and cultural rights. Both the notable constitutional initiatives to guarantee social and economic rights are of comparatively recent origin: the Brazilian Constitution of 1988 and the South African Constitution of 1996.

In *The Origins of Totalitarianism* (1951),[1] Arendt articulated the idea of a 'right to have rights'. Curiously, however, she made no mention here of the Universal Declaration of Human Rights of 1948. Her reflections on the question of statelessness—of the millions of people rendered homeless and stateless as a result of religious persecution and war—led her to argue that human rights, in and of themselves, are no protection of any kind.

> We became aware of the existence of a right to have rights (and that means to live in a framework where one is judged by one's actions and opinions) and a right to belong to some kind of organized community, only when millions of people emerged who had lost and could not regain these rights because of the new global situation. (Arendt 1951: 296–7).

When these millions lost their membership in the nation-state, they also lost all their rights. The loss of national rights became the loss of human rights. As such, human rights cannot be defined separately from the rights of citizens. 'To have the right to have rights is only possible if one is a citizen—and that of a polis, rather than a nation-state'. Arendt precludes, as Jean Cohen has pointed out, the possibility of a democratic nation-state in which a liberal conception of rights may be constitutionally enshrined and guaranteed for both majorities and minorities in an ethnic nation (Cohen 1996).

Arendt highlighted the irony of the fact that the very rights that had been declared as inalienable, and as originating in 'man' himself rather than in governments, appeared to be imperilled as soon as there was no authority, no institution, no government to guarantee and enforce them (Arendt 1951: 292). It is only citizenship—membership in a political community—that can provide such a guarantee, whether in one's own country or in others. The 'calamity of the rightless' (Arendt 1951: 295) is not so much that they do not have the rights of life, liberty, equality, and so on, but that they no longer belong to any political community. Refugees are people who have lost not just their right to property or life in times of war; they are people who exist in a condition of absolute and complete rightlessness. Even the Nazis, Arendt reminds us, deprived Jews of their legal status before taking them to concentration camps. So the condition of rightlessness is a condition of 'abstract nakedness' of being human and nothing but human.

> 'Man, it turns out, can lose all so-called rights of Man without losing his essential quality as man, his human dignity. Only the loss of a polity itself expels him from humanity.' (Arendt 1951: 297).

If rights were indeed natural, Arendt writes, the loss of political status should draw a human being into a regime of general universal human rights. But what ensues is actually the opposite. The loss of membership in a political community spells the end of a legal personality and juridical personhood. This loss is wide-ranging and marked by a paradox:

> The paradox involved in the loss of human rights is that such loss coincides with the instant when a person becomes a human being in general—without a profession, without a citizenship, without an opinion, without a deed by which to identify and specify himself—*and* different in general, representing nothing but his own absolutely unique individuality which, deprived of expression within and action upon a common world, loses all significance. (Arendt 1951: 302).

This, we might say, closes the circle that began with the assertion of the uniqueness of man born free and equal, and abundantly endowed with rights that have their origins in nature. Losing political status renders man once again a creature in a pre-political state of nature, ostensibly endowed with rights that can have no social or political meaning in that state. Not surprising then that Arendt should posit a civic polity (which for her stands in stark opposition to a nation-state) as the source of rights, and as the only plausible stage for any meaningful practice of these. The holding of rights is a condition that obtains only within the framework of citizenship, and citizenship in turn is something that is enriched by the practise of rights as citizens engage in public-spirited political activity.

In this sense, the 'Right To Have Rights' (RTHR) implicitly represents an inversion of T.H. Marshall's conception of citizenship rights, published only in the previous year. For Marshall, citizenship is realized in ever greater measure as rights expand from civil rights in the eighteenth century to political rights in the nineteenth century and, finally, to social and economic rights in the twentieth century. Marshall identified three elements of citizenship: (i) the civil element (the rights necessary for individual freedom); (ii) the political element (the right to participate in the exercise of political power); and (iii) the social element, encompassing rights to unemployment insurance, old-age pension, public education, and healthcare; this was defined as 'the whole range from the right to a modicum of economic welfare and security to the right to share to the full in the social heritage and to live the life of a civilized being according to the standards prevailing in the society' (Marshall and Bottomore 1992: 8).

To say, as Marshall did, that citizenship is realized through rights is very different from saying, as Arendt did, that rights are contingent on citizenship. In effect, Arendt believed that insofar as citizenship is the condition of rights, citizenship, or membership in a polity, is a precondition for the enjoyment of any rights at all. For Marshall, on the other hand, citizenship was rather more than mere legal status; it was synonymous with, and could only be properly realized through, guarantees of civic, political, and social rights. His disregard of other aspects of citizenship—especially legal citizenship and the challenges of ethnicity and feminism—has been commented upon by Marshall and Bottomore (1992).

In this paper, I explore some ways in which the RTHR may be translated into the Indian vernacular of rights discourse. What meaning does the phrase have for an understanding of the rights landscape in India? Might it help us, *pace Habermas*, to explain better the gap between the *de jure* possession of rights and their *de facto* practice? Could it perhaps help us to make sense of the gradations between rights-bearers and their rights? What can it tell us about the different sites on which rights-claims are made and the realization (or not) of those claims?

In the next section of this paper, I propose to unpack the RTHR in a way that diverges from Frank Michelman's well-known parsing of this phrase in which the first right is an 'acquisition' right, an abstract moral entitlement, while the second set of unspecified rights are object rights that are empirical and institutionally guaranteed. (Michelman 1996: 201–2). Benhabib's analysis of this phrase similarly echoes the moral/practical distinction: the first usage, she says, evokes 'a moral claim to membership' while the second speaks to the right in its more common usage, as an entitlement that places an obligation on another to perform, and the legal protection of this right by institutions like the state (Benhabib 2004: 56–7). Michelman, however, argues that Arendt's understanding of the relationship between agency and rights implies that the ideal and the moral are not differentiated from the empirical. What makes the very having of rights possible is the exercise of political agency through action that flows from political inclusion.

In the third section, I examine some examples of rights-claims and rights-recognition in India. In the final section, I conclude with some observations on what an Arendtian perspective can add to an interpretation of the rights landscape of contemporary India, and therefore to the understanding of Indian citizenship.

Unpacking the Right to Have Rights for India

What, in the Indian context, might it mean to have a right to have rights? Let me refer to the first usage as R1 and the second as R2 without, at this point, committing to the view that the first is moral and the second is empirical. I propose instead that we see the first, not so much as an abstract or moral imperative, but as antecedent as well as prior to rights as they are commonly understood. Let me explain and illustrate this through a few examples.

At some variance with the interpretations of Michelman and Benhabib, I suggest that we view R1, in Arendt's formulation of it, as something that is not so much moral as politico-juridical. For Arendt, the purely moral assertion of a right was precisely what had failed to deliver in a testing situation. The grand discourse of human rights was rendered impotent and meaningless in the absence of a juridical and civic framework of citizenship. Arendt emphasized the significance of a political community in which members/citizens have a legal standing which, articulated as R1, is institutionally guaranteed by the politico-juridical framework of the state. According to Arendt, citizens need the state; their acquisition of human rights is predicated on it. To cast R1 as moral is to fall into precisely the fallacy that Arendt warned against: the trap of believing that human rights, originating in man and nature, are adequate guarantees of anything. If it is the state that provides the essential framework within which human rights are secured to citizens, then it is not a merely moral, but a politico-juridical framework that is the primary requirement for people to have and enjoy rights. Arendt does not here distinguish between the having and enjoyment of rights in the manner in which contemporary philosophers of rights do. Through her interrogation of the idea of human rights, Arendt is questioning the usefulness of the liberal discourse of moral personhood, and suggesting that abstract moral personhood is no substitute for juridical or legal personhood.

RTHR thus conveys a lexical ordering in which R1 is both primary and prior to R2. The latter is a less easily specifiable category that may be as restrictively or expansively defined as a particular political community may determine. As such, the idea of R2 does not tell us anything at all about the substantive content of the rights that may be available to the citizens of a polity. A constitution may, for instance, provide for a robust regime of civil and political rights while denying economic rights altogether. Or, alternatively, as in the Soviet state and the present-day Constitution of Kazakhstan, it may provide for social and economic rights in abundance while denying civil and political rights. So R2 is a category that is essentially indeterminate as to content. It does not claim to offer us a substantive account of rights, and therefore does not venture to justify or defend specific rights.

In empirical terms, it is possible to envisage four (and a half) distinct ways in which R1 and R2 may be instantiated.

Neither R1 nor R2

The predicament of stateless peoples remains, notwithstanding the inauguration of a global legal regime for the protection of refugees, the best example of rightlessness. It remains entirely possible to be utterly rightless in the way Arendt described, and to enjoy neither R1 nor R2. Refugees in countries like India, which are not signatories to the Convention on Refugees, remain the best examples of people who do not enjoy either of these rights. The next section of this chapter discusses the case of refugees on the western border of India, several thousand of whom are stateless persons seeking citizenship as the only way of acquiring rights. These communities are contemporary examples of Hannah Arendt's argument that the absence of citizenship—as membership of the political community—precludes rights.

R2 without R1

It is well recognized that it is possible to have R2 without having R1. Illegal aliens in Europe, the United States, and Canada enjoy many privileges despite their undocumented status. Undocumented aliens in the US may attend public school, be entitled to the freedom of speech and association, exercise the economic freedoms of contract and property rights, and, at least formally, have the right of due process in criminal proceedings (Bosniak 2006: 117). This introduces a distinction between status citizenship (attached to legal status) and other forms of citizenship, such as economic citizenship. Many of these rights to public education, to the protection of the police, or to social safety-nets are, however, fragile for immigrants with 'precarious status'. (Bhuyan and Smith-Carrier 2012). Nevertheless, the provision of such rights to undocumented aliens is interrogated on the grounds of its manifold deleterious impact on the poor citizens of the host country. Stephen Macedo, for instance, deploys the Rawlsian

'Difference Principle' to suggest that the justifiability of policies that favour illegal immigrants must be considered from the standpoint of the least well-off American citizens (Macedo 2007: 81).

R1 without R2

It is also possible to have R1 without having R2, as the example of internally displaced people shows. The Internal Displacement Monitoring Centre (cited as authoritative by the United Nations Refugee Agency) estimates the total number of people displaced by armed conflict and violence in India as 540,000. This figure does not include the over 20 million estimated to have been displaced by development projects. Less than a quarter of those internally displaced typically get resettled; many are subject to repetitive and multiple displacements. The absence of a resettlement and reha- bilitation policy is well known; the precarious and vulnerable lives of the displaced manifest little evidence of either R1 or R2. Legally citizens of India, they may enjoy no rights at all on account of their displacement—deprived of their homes and livelihoods, they are not only deprived of access to, say, the public distribution system (for food), they are also deprived of basic political rights such as voting.

Both R1 and R2

Finally, it is of course possible to have both R1 and R2. The citizens of the advanced social-democracies of northern Europe, for instance, could be said to enjoy both. They not only have R1, but also a maxi- mally defined set of rights encompassed by R2.

Both R1 and R2 but effectively neither

An additional category that is a subset of the fourth could be of those who have both R1 and R2 while actually having neither. This provokes a shift away from the Arendtian identification of the gap between the normative assertion of a human right and its actual availability to members of a political community to another gap, that between formal (having) and substantive (enjoying) rights. Subsisting within a robust constitutional framework of rights, and despite some recent enactments of social and economic rights, India's vast population of poor citizens would appear to fall into this category.

The Arendtian conception of the right to have rights—making rights contingent upon citizenship—does not help us to comprehend this particular form of rightlessness, presumably because she assumes that citizenship—as membership in a political community—is the primary condition for it. Whether it is only a necessary condition or also a sufficient one, however, remains unclear. Only a Marshallian conception, which makes the actualization of citizenship contingent upon the realization of rights, makes this possible. For Marshall, as for many others, R1 is the threshold condition for any conversation about rights. Since only those who are members can be rights-bearers, to talk about rights is impliedly to talk about members/citizens. Beyond this threshold condition, there are various historical struggles, led by different social classes, to claim and obtain expansions of rights. This is how the trajectory of rights in Britain, on Marshall's account, has evolved from civil rights in the eighteenth century to political rights in the nineteenth to social rights in the twentieth. The future expansion of citizenship rights, and any corresponding diminution in class inequality that they effect, will necessarily be the product of further political struggle.

To return to Arendt, it would appear that her phrase can have many uses: it can serve variously as a descriptor of rights-practices, as an indicator of the gap between rights-talk and rights-practice, and as a guide to delineating gradations of rights-holders and rights-practitioners. But, in the final analysis, Arendt's pronounced emphasis on R1 to the complete neglect of R2 means that her account provides only a defence of citizenship as a status, at best of citizenship as political activity, but not a theory of the substantive content of rights. This is not surprising, for having effectively de-normativized human rights—by privileging citizenship as legal status and as political practice—Arendt could hardly offer a normatively grounded account of particular rights. Had she done so, she would have been profoundly inconsistent, for she would then have proclaimed her adherence to precisely the normative framework of human rights whose hypocrisies she had, based on the Jewish and minority experiences of the 1940s, so sharply attacked. The puzzle that remains is this: is the assertion of R1 altogether devoid of a normative basis? It is certainly possible to comprehend citizenship as legal status in non-normative terms, but not quite as easy to posit citizenship as civic engagement and political activity in a manner that is devoid of normativity. What then might be the normative basis of the citizenship ideal that Arendt advances?

It would appear that the parenthetical and secondary parts of Arendt's formulation—'the right to have rights (and that means to live in a framework where one is judged by one's actions and opinions) and 'a right to belong to some kind of organized community'—are unwisely neglected. They point to two aspects of R1 that are worthy of emphasis: (i) belonging to an organized community in which (ii) one's actions and opinions are valued. These two aspects, I would argue, qualify and give meaning to the bare statement of the right to have rights. While Arendt does not develop them here, these offer a potentially enriching way of thinking about republican citizenship.

Making Rights-Claims and Obtaining Rights-Recognition in India

Let me turn now to a contemporary Indian example that appears to be a perfect Arendtian exemplar of the denial of the right to have rights. This is the case of a population of several thousand migrants on the western border of India. These are migrants[2] from the Sindh and Punjab provinces of Pakistan who came to India with Pakistani passports and valid Indian visas, but stayed on as illegal aliens. Several waves of such migration have occurred since the Partition of 1947, and most migrants before the 1990s have become naturalized as citizens. Of the approximately 17,000 migrants who came in after 1992, some 13,000 have been given citizenship, while some 3,000 migrants remain applicants for citizenship. My field research in Jodhpur and Jaisalmer shows that the quest for citizenship among these groups is, in classic Arendtian mould, a search for the recognition of their legal and juridical personhood. However, such personhood is coveted for purely instrumental reasons, as the key to accessing welfare benefits. As such, this understanding of citizenship as R1 is significantly devoid of any moral or affective dimension let alone any connotations of political practice or civic agency.

The answer to the question of why they migrated is usually in terms of the insecurity of being a religious minority in an Islamic state, and a feeling of particular vulnerability following the demolition of the Babri Masjid in India. These communities have long-standing familial and affective ties in Rajasthan. Many of their forefathers owned land here; most have had extended families on both sides of the border. Before they migrated, they would visit for family weddings and so forth. These cross-border social ties are suggestive of the invisibility of the border as it has been experienced by these people and their families across generations. Living in a camp, subjected to the hostility of the local population and to harassment by the local police, is uncomfortable. In Pakistan, they were viewed with suspicion as Hindus; in India, they are derisively called Pakistanis. While they feel physically less insecure in India, they do speak wistfully of how, in Pakistan, they laboured in irrigated fields, while in Rajasthan they are compelled to earn a wage by breaking stones. They cannot travel anywhere in India, they are no longer Pakistani and not yet Indian, and they view citizenship as having some sort of redemptive power. As a teacher of Arabic in Jaisalmer said:

> Citizenship is a piece of paper. But for us, it is a jewel (*nagina*). We left Pakistan to come here, but now we belong neither to Pakistan nor to India, we are torn into two pieces. What is the third way before us? If we get citizenship, at least we can be called Indians, travel anywhere in India to earn a living, to meet relatives and to build a future for our children.... If we could get citizenship, the jewel of citizenship, the fields of freedom will be seen blossoming. (*azadi ke khet khilte hue nazar aayenge*). But for now, we are tied in chains. We cannot travel anywhere, we cannot do the work we want to do. We do not have domicile (*mool niwas*) so our children cannot get admission to, for instance, medical school.

Citizenship as legal status is thus coveted for the 'amenities' (*suvidhas*) it is expected to provide. These amenities are specified as land, livelihood, attendance at government schools, provision of water and electricity, as also official documentation such as certificates of caste or below-poverty-line status and, of course, the ration card that enables access to the public distribution system.

As for Arendt, the claim to juridical personhood takes precedence over that of moral personhood. The point of juridical personhood is not to exercise civic agency but to access civic amenities. It is notable that, for these migrant communities consisting mostly of poor Dalits and Adivasis, R1 is valuable chiefly for realizing R2, which they themselves specify in terms of a set of rights that can be characterized broadly, in Marshallian terms, as social and economic rights. The claims to citizenship of these groups pose a policy dilemma. As undocumented aliens, they are not entitled to any rights at all in a country that is not—like its neighbours—a signatory to the 1951 Convention on the Status of Refugees. Further, these migrants have entered a country in which there are already 250 million people living below a rather sparsely defined poverty line. It is with these people that the migrants must compete for their share of welfare benefits, be they Below Poverty Line cards, or caste certificates with which to access public education and employment opportunities. As one of my respondents said, 'Citizenship is the key to everything. Even to apply for a water or electricity connection, you need citizenship.'

However, interviews with members of these communities who have already obtained official certification of their status as citizens of India indicate that the achievement of legal status is viewed as ephemeral, even meaningless. Their citizenship certificates, carefully laminated for protection, are prized objects that decorate the walls of their homes. Nevertheless, these 'citizens' remain dissatisfied with the unfulfilled promise of citizenship. Some examples of their responses are as follows:

- We have got citizenship, but have not yet got its full fruit. We have no place to stay, no fields to till. The citizenship is lying there, but it is of no use.
- We have got citizenship, but it is just a piece of paper. We have not got one rupee of *fayeda* (gain) so far.
- We have come on to the road of citizenship, but we are still to reach our destination. Earlier, everything seemed like a maze, now citizenship shows the way out of the maze.

On the eastern border of India, the in-migration of millions of Bangladeshi nationals has given rise to a slightly different situation, in which the migrants have acquired citizenship through the acquisition of multiple, frequently counterfeit, documents that apparently validate their status as local inhabitants. Thus, as Kamal Sadiq has shown, there are millions of bogus ration cards with as many as one million being detected in West Bengal alone in the space of one month, over and above the 1.9 million detected previously. (Sadiq 2009: 120). Here, it is documents that create 'paper citizens' rather than citizenship yielding documentation. However, both 'paper citizens' and genuine citizens (with or without documentation) remain equally vulnerable in their poverty, despite their acquisition of the right to vote.

Both these cases—of the Rajasthan migrants who have acquired citizenship, as well as the paper citizens of eastern India—demonstrate that the legal status of citizenship emphasized by Arendt is a necessary, but far from sufficient condition for the enjoyment of rights. Their rights-expectations supplement Arendt's argument with an account of the specific content of R2, rights which can only be claimed through the prior recognition of R1, but at the same time cannot be accomplished exclusively through it. This specific content bears a strong resemblance to Marshall's account of social citizenship in terms of entitlements to welfare benefits. It is, however, entirely devoid of any Arendtian conception of citizenship as civic agency, or political activity in the public realm.

Civic agency or the practice of citizenship is, I suggest, a core element of Arendt's R1. Such agency requires belonging to a political community, but it mandates also that this membership is made capable of enactment within a framework in which people can hold actions and opinions on the basis of which they can participate in the public life of the community. This is clearly missing in the case of the migrants and refugees, not only for those still awaiting the grant of citizenship, but equally for those that have acquired citizenship, whether legally or through fake documentation that testifies to it. They are *not*, by any reckoning members of a political community in the rich Arendtian sense; as such, the possession of R1 in the formal sense avails them little in the matter of realizing R2.

Contrast this with another example of claims to rights-recognition, which also invokes the distinction between *de jure* and *de facto* or formal and substantive rights. *De jure* rights hold out at least the possibility of rights claims being made and citizenship struggles being mounted, and some recent examples of rights-recognition in India may be viewed as an outcome of civic agency and political action. Civil society has, in recent times, contributed to an expansion of rights through a strengthening of democracy and a heightened consciousness of rights. A Marshallian conception of social citizenship has thus begun to be mediated, even midwifed, by an Arendtian exercise of civic agency that has striven to make formal rights substantive, and also to secure the enactment of social and economic rights.

While social and economic rights were an essential part of the nationalist agenda in colonial India,[3] their inclusion in an otherwise progressive Constitution encountered formidable opposition in the Constituent Assembly's deliberations. As the country embarked on its career as a Republic in 1950, Indian citizens were furnished with a comprehensive set of civil and political as also cultural rights, while social and economic rights (henceforth SERs) remained sequestered in the non-justiciable chapter on the Directive Principles of State Policy (DPSP). The career of SERs in India has, ever since, been marked by political compromises at every turn.

The last two decades have witnessed a tectonic shift with the enactment of many positive rights. This trend arguably began when environmental public interest litigation led to the Supreme Court interpreting the right to clean air as a part of the Right to Life provisions of Article 21, which have since been expansively interpreted to encompass rights to water, healthcare, housing, and, most recently, the right to sleep.[4] In subsequent decades, a combination of public interest litigation, civil society activism, and judicial intervention has served to secure recognition for the right to education, the right to livelihood, the right of *jhuggi* dwellers against eviction, with a possibility also of an impending right to food security.

However, while many of these campaigns instantiate the role of civil society in an expansion of the landscape of rights, it can be argued that there has been slow progress in translating formal rights into substantive rights. For instance, in matters of clean air, healthcare, and water, the gap between judicial pronouncements and executive action is vast. Both the Mahatma Gandhi National Rural Employment Guarantee Scheme (MNREGS), through which a right to work is being effected, as also the right to education, are encountering immense challenges of implementation. In other words, it is clear that while more and more SERs have been legislated in recent times, their delivery has been fraught with difficulties.

This may have something to do with a qualitatively new form of statelessness that has made its appearance under conditions of globalization, making it possible for formal membership in the state to co-exist with a diminution in the actual level of protection provided by the state. Across the world, cuts in public spending have made the lives of ordinary citizens more precarious. We may characterize this as a form of quasi-statelessness, in which citizens are formally included but substantively excluded, their membership of the political community standing on a less than firm or stable footing. A diffusion of institutional responsibility is mandated by new marketized arrangements of governance such as public-private partnerships, or the outsourcing and sub-contracting of developmental activities entailed by a right to education or food security. The obligations that are generated by citizens' rights no longer fall exclusively on the state, but are dispersed across a variety of non-state institutions including markets. Private corporations, for instance, are (in however utopian an expectation) enjoined to respect people's rights by, for example, ensuring that their industries do not dispossess the poor of their lands or livelihoods. This new form of statelessness and concomitant rightlessness obviously could not have been envisaged by Hannah Arendt in pre-globalization times.

Further, the expansion of positive rights has paradoxically been accompanied by a contraction of negative rights. As SERs are (at least formally) expanding, negative rights, such as the right to freedom of speech and expression, are visibly contracting. Threats to freedom of speech and expression (for instance, the prevention of Salman Rushdie from attending the Jaipur Literary Festival in January 2012) have become disconcertingly frequent. The veteran artist M.F. Hussain was compelled to spend the last years of his life in exile abroad on account of threats from Hindu fundamentalists; and works of literary and historical scholarship, such as those by A.K. Ramanajun, Rohinton Mistry, and James Laine, have been savagely attacked. It is significant that the fundamentalist perpetrators of these attacks were indulged, and therefore indirectly supported, by those who are the very custodians of India's academic and literary cultures. What is disturbing about these recent threats to the basic freedoms is that while they do not emanate from the state, the state does nothing to protect citizens from them.

* * *

Our first example—about different categories of refugees seeking or acquiring legal citizenship—showed that citizenship can be dissociated from its performative aspect and still hold meaning, even if instrumentally rather than affectively, whether for members or aspiring members of a political community. Their actual objective is the access to welfare rights that is expected to ensue from the grant of citizenship status—not the status of citizenship *per se*, or its practice. As such, R1 is a necessary, but far from sufficient condition for the enjoyment of rights.

This is true not only of refugees (naturalized or otherwise), but also of the vast population of India's poor who live in conditions of acute rightlessness. Even as their legal and moral personhood is constitutionally guaranteed, their substantive rights-status is not very different from that of the refugees. Under such conditions of effective rightlessness, they are also not empowered to participate in the life of the polity in ways that may make their opinions and actions worthy of being judged, as Arendt said. On the other hand, the civil society-led campaigns for the realization of social and economic rights would be impossible unless these groups enjoyed R1 in the fuller sense, in which I have proposed it be interpreted, namely, as a guarantee of not only juridical personhood but also of a framework of political belonging that enables people's opinions to be voiced and heard, and that privileges civic agency. It is because effectuating R1 in this fuller Arendtian sense is necessary for the realization of R2 that some can be citizens only in the limited juridical sense while others are citizens in more substantive ways.

The empirical landscape of rights in India indicates the importance of revisiting Arendt's formulation to heed more carefully her own explication of the right to have rights, to not assume that legal membership of a political community is a sufficient condition for the enjoyment of rights, and to elucidate (as she would arguably have us do) the conditions under which our actions and opinions become worthy of the consideration of our fellow-citizens.

Notes

1. Cf. Chapter Nine: 'The Decline of the Nation-State and the End of the Rights of Man'.
2. I use the term migrants, though the official nomenclature is displaced persons, and effectively these are refugees.
3. Annie Besant's Commonwealth of India Bill (1925) supported the right to free primary education. The Motilal Nehru Committee Report (1928) enunciated a set of social and economic rights, including some relating to work, labour, living wages, old age, unemployment, and child welfare. Above all, of course, the 1931 *Resolution on Fundamental Rights and Economic Changes*, better known as the Karachi Declaration of the Indian National Congress, contained a radical and controversial list of economic rights.
4. 'Deprivation of sleep,' the court said, 'has tumultuous adverse effects. It causes a stir and disturbs the quiet and peace of an individual's physical state.... To take away the right of natural rest is also therefore violation of human rights.' Equating the right to sleep with the rights to privacy and to food, the Court brought this right within the ambit of Article 21, the Right to Life, something that is essential to maintain 'the delicate balance of health', and the violation of which amounts to torture. Such a right-claim was also advanced by the campaign against homelessness and poverty in Victoria, British Columbia. Its leader, David Arthur Johnston, took a vow of poverty proclaiming that sleep is a necessity of life, sleeping outdoors for several years, and getting repeatedly arrested for it. In 2008, in *Victoria (City) v. Adams*, the Supreme Court of British Columbia upheld his right.

References

Arendt, H. 1951. *The Origins of Totalitarianism*. Cleveland and New York: Meridian Books.

Benhabib, S. 2004. *The Rights of Others: Aliens, Residents and Citizens*. Cambridge: Cambridge University Press.

Bhuyan, R. and T. Smith-Carrier. 2012. 'Constructions of Migrant Rights in Canada: Is Subnational Citizenship Possible?', *Citizenship Studies*, 16(2): 203–21.

Bosniak, L. 2006. *The Citizen and the Alien: Dilemmas of Contemporary Membership*. Princeton: Princeton University Press.

Cohen, J. 1996. 'Rights, Citizenship, and the Modern Form of the Social: Dilemmas of Arendtian Republicanism', *Constellations*, 3(2): 164–89.

Declaration of the Rights of Man and Citizen, 26 August 1789. http://avalon.law.yale.edu/18th_century/rightsof.asp

Internal Displacement Monitoring Center. 12 March 2013. http://www.refworld.org/docid/517fb068d.html (accessed on October 29, 2014).

Macedo, Stephen. 2009. The Moral Dilemma of U.S. Immigration Policy: Open Borders versus Social Justice? In Carol Swain, ed. *Debating Immigration*. New York: Cambridge University Press.

Marshall, T.H and Tom Bottomore. 1992. *Citizenship and Social Class*. London: Pluton Press.

Michelman, F.I. 1996. 'Parsing "A Right to Have Rights.' *Constellations* 3(2): 201–8.

Sadiq, K. 2009. *Paper Citizens: How Illegal Immigrants Acquire Citizenship in Developing Countries*. New York: Oxford University Press.

Index

Editors and Contributors

Gordon Davis is Associate Professor and Chair of the Department of Philosophy at Carleton University. His research interests range from ethical theory to Indian philosophy. He is currently exploring particular ethical assumptions that underlie specific strands of Buddhist thought in Indian philosophy. His publications include *Traces of Consequentialism and Non-Consequentialism in Bodhisattva Ethics* (*Philosophy East and West*, 63(2), April 2013: 275–305) and, he co-authored with Blain Neufeld in *Political Liberalism, Civic Education, and Educational Choice* (*Social Theory and Practice*, 33(1), January 2007: 47–74).

Nigel DeSouza is Assistant Professor of Philosophy at University of Ottawa. His interests are in social and political philosophy, and ethical theory. His publications include *Language, Reason, and Sociability: Herder's Critique of Rousseau* (*Intellectual History Review*, 22(2), 2012: 221–40) and *Leibniz in the Eighteenth Century: Herder's Reading of the Principes de la Nature de la Grace* (*British Journal for the History of Philosophy*, 20(4), 2012: 773–95).

Jay Drydyk is Professor of Philosophy at Carleton University, Ottawa, and a Visiting Faculty member of the Department of Philosophy at University of Delhi (2012). His most recent book (co-authored with Peter Penz and Pablo Bose) is *Displacement by Development: Ethics, Rights, and Responsibilities* (Cambridge University Press, 2011). His journal output includes articles on development ethics, human rights, the capability approach, and other topics in social and political philosophy. He is former President of the International Development Ethics Association, and he is currently a Fellow of the

Human Development and Capabilities Association and an Associate Editor of the Journal of Human Development and Capabilities.

Niraja Gopal Jayal is Professor at the Centre for the Study of Law and Governance at Jawaharlal Nehru University, New Delhi. She served as Chair of the Centre (2002–4 and 2008–9) and as Director of the Jawaharlal Nehru Institute of Advanced Study (2004–7). She is the author of *Representing India: Ethnic Diversity and the Governance of Public Institutions* (Palgrave Macmillan, 2006) and *Democracy and the State: Welfare, Secularism and Development in Contemporary India* (Oxford University Press, 1999); and editor or co-editor of several volumes, including *The Oxford Companion to Politics in India* (Oxford University Press, 2010); *Democracy in India* (Oxford University Press, 2001); and *Local Governance in India: Decentralization and Beyond* (Oxford University Press, 2005). Her current book project is about contestations over ideas of citizenship in India across the twentieth century. As with her previous work, this is also located at the intersection of the normative and the empirical.

Amar Khoday is Assistant Professor of Law at the University of Manitoba. He received his Doctor of Civil Law at the Faculty of Law at McGill University. He is a recipient of the SSHRC Doctoral Fellowship and is an O'Brien Fellow in Human Rights and Legal Pluralism at McGill University. His research focus is in the area of legal pluralism. His publications include *Protecting Those Who Go Beyond the Law: Contemplating Refugee Status for Individuals Who Challenge Oppression through Resistance* (*Georgetown Immigration Law Journal*, 25(3), 2011) and *Uprooting the Cell Plant: Comparing United States and Canadian Constitutional Approaches to Surreptitious Interrogations in the Detention Context* (*Western New England Law Review*, 31(1), 2009).

Sumi Madhok joined London School of Economics (LSE) in 2007. Prior to this, she held the Mellon Post-Doctoral Research Fellowship at the School of Oriental and African Studies (SOAS), London. Her research interests lie in the transnational gender analyses of human rights, citizenship, post-coloniality, and developmentalism. In particular, she is interested in questions of agency and coercion, in the new citizenship movements, and in the genealogical investigations of rights discourses, cultures, and subjectivities, especially within Southern Asia. Her publications include *Gender, Agency and Coercion: Thinking Gender in Transnational Times* (co-edited with Anne Phillips and Kalpana Wilson, London: Palgrave Macmillan, 2013), *"Rights Talk"* and *the Feminist Movement in India*, in *Women's Movements in Asia: Feminisms and Transnational Activism* (Routledge, 2010), and *Autonomy and Human Right'* in *The Essential Guide to Human Rights* (Hodder Arnold, 2005).

Shashi Motilal is Associate Professor of Philosophy at the University of Delhi. Her areas of research are ethical theory, human rights, and the philosophy of language. Her publications include *Human Rights, Gender and Environment* (Allied Publishers, 2006), *Social Inequality: Concerns of Human Rights, Gender, and Environment* (Macmillan Publishing, 2010), both co-edited with Bijayalaxmi Nanda and her solo work, *Applied Ethics and Human Rights: Conceptual Analysis and Contextual Applications* (Anthem Publishers, 2010).

Ashwani Peetush is Associate Professor of Philosophy at Wilfrid Laurier University in Waterloo, Ontario. He has published papers on human rights, cultural diversity, and topics in legal and political philosophy, as well as Indian philosophy. Some of his publications include *Justice, Diversity, and Dialogue: Rawlsian Multiculturalism*, in *Multiculturalism and Religious Identity: Perspectives from Canada and India* (edited by Lori Beaman and Sonia Sikka, McGill-Queens Press), *Indigenizing Human Rights: First Nations, Self-Determination, and Cultural Identity*, in *Indigenous Identity and Activism* (Shipra Press, 2009), *Kymlicka, Multiculturalism, and Non-Western Nations*, in *Public Affairs Quarterly* (2003), and *Cultural Diversity, Non-Western Communities, and Human Rights*, in *The Philosophical Forum* (2003).

Bindu Puri is Associate Professor of Philosophy at the University of Delhi. She is interested in ethical theory and Gandhi's thought as a potential approach to issues of human rights and diversity in India. She is the author of *Gandhi and the Moral Life* (2004). She has co-edited, with Heiko Seivers, *Reason Morality and Beauty: Essays on the Philosophy of Immanuel Kant* (Oxford University Press, 2007) and *Terror, Peace, and Universalism: Essays on the Philosophy of Immanuel Kant* (Oxford University Press, 2007).

Shyam Ranganathan is Assistant Professor of Philosophy at York University. He specializes in ethical theory, philosophy of language, and Indian philosophy. Ranganathan's *Ethics and the History of Indian Philosophy* (Motilal Banarsidass, 2007) is currently one of the leading research monographs on ethics and Indian philosophy. He also recently published *Patañjali's Yoga Sūtra* (translated into English from Sanskrit, with a Commentary and an Introduction), *Black Classics Series* (Penguin, 2008).

Sonia Sikka is Associate Professor and Chair of the Department of Philosophy at the University of Ottawa. Over the last decade, she has been working on themes related to culture and pluralism in the writings of J.G. Herder, a central figure in the development of strong theories of cultural identity. More recently, Dr Sikka's research has turned towards thematic examinations of secularism and identity formation. She is currently co-editing, with Lori Beman, a volume of essays on multiculturalism and religious identity in Canada and India. Her publications include '*The Perils of Indian Secularism*' (*Constellations*, 19(2), June 2012: 288–304), '*Untouchable Cultures: Memory, Power and the Construction of Dalit Selfhood*' (*Identities*, 19(1), 2012: 43–60), *Herder on Humanity and Cultural Difference: Enlightened Relativism* (Cambridge University Press, 2011), '*Liberalism, Multiculturalism and the Case for Public Religion*' (*Politics and Religion*, 3, 2010: 580–609).

Gopika Solanki is Assistant Professor of Political Science at Carleton University. Her interests are in the area of gender equality, legal pluralism, and human rights in India. Her publications include: *Adjudication in Religious Family Laws: Cultural Accommodation, Legal Pluralism, and Gender Justice in India* (Cambridge University Press) and *Doing Caste, Making Citizens: Differing Conceptions of Religious Identities* and *Autonomy in Hindu Law, in Religion and Diversity in India and Canada* (Wilfrid Laurier University Press; Forthcoming).